RAF
WEST MALLING

RAF
WEST MALLING

THE RAF'S FIRST NIGHT FIGHTER
AIRFIELD – WWII TO THE COLD WAR

ANTHONY JOHN MOOR

AIR WORLD

AIR WORLD

RAF WEST MALLING
The RAF's First Night Fighter Airfield – WWII to the Cold War

First published in Great Britain in 2019 by
Pen & Sword Air World
An imprint of
Pen & Sword Books Ltd
Yorkshire – Philadelphia

ISBN 978 1 52675 323 6

A CIP catalogue record for this book is available from the British Library.

Printed and bound in England by TJ International, Padstow, Cornwall, PL28 8RW

Typeset by Aura Technology and Software Services, India

Pen & Sword Books Limited incorporates the imprints of Atlas, Archaeology, Aviation, Discovery, Family History, Fiction, History, Maritime, Military, Military Classics, Politics, Select, Transport, True Crime, Air World, Frontline Publishing, Leo Cooper, Remember When, Seaforth Publishing, The Praetorian Press, Wharncliffe Local History, Wharncliffe Transport, Wharncliffe True Crime and White Owl.

For a complete list of Pen & Sword titles please contact

PEN & SWORD BOOKS LIMITED
47 Church Street, Barnsley, South Yorkshire, S70 2AS, England
E-mail: enquiries@pen-and-sword.co.uk
Website: www.pen-and-sword.co.uk

Or
PEN AND SWORD BOOKS
1950 Lawrence Rd, Havertown, PA 19083, USA
E-mail: Uspen-and-sword@casematepublishers.com
Website: www.penandswordbooks.com

Contents

Introduction

This book is based on personal memories and records, including many interesting photographs, depicting events at West Malling airfield throughout its existence, and has been written as a tribute to all who served at RAF West Malling. The RAF motto on the airfield crest, *Portam Custodimus* – 'We Guard the Gate', was associated with the 'keep' at West Malling known as St Leonards Tower, which is believed to have been built in the eleventh century for the defence of West Malling. It was adopted as it symbolises the barrier formed by fighter squadrons stationed at West Malling to protect the country from enemy raids by day and night. The airfield became Britain's first RAF night fighter base.

During the 1980s I was working as a draughtsman with Metair Aircraft Equipment Ltd, which had moved to West Malling airfield after winning a contract from Saab Aircraft Co. to design and fit the interior of its SF340 aircraft, and to paint them. At the time this historic airfield was completely undeveloped, with hangars and many fine RAF buildings intact. Having served an engineering apprenticeship with Hawker Siddeley Ltd, Hatfield, into which De Havilland Aircraft Company had been absorbed, I was delighted to be working at what was RAF West Malling. My uncle, my father's brother, had served there with No. 29 Sqn at the time when Squadron Leader Guy Gibson was flying with the unit; his fame as the leader of the Dambusters was yet to come. Prior to the development of RAF West Malling, the site had been known as Maidstone Municipal Airport.

Even in the First World War, the site had been designated an emergency landing ground (ELG) and night landing ground (NLG) and was occasionally used by aircraft, although there were no RFC/RAF squadrons based there, unlike other airfields in Kent such as Detling, Biggin Hill and Manston. Civilian flying began on the site during the 1920s and it developed into a popular location for flying clubs, air displays and air races. This continued until the RAF took over the site prior to the Second World War and prepared it for wartime use. RAF West Malling played a major role in the Battle of Britain during the summer of 1940, when Lysanders of No. 26 Sqn operated from the airfield.

Many squadrons were based at West Malling during the war years and these became part of No. 11 Grp, although ultimately the airfield became a night fighter base. During the war years, squadrons took on the role of escorting bombers into Europe, and later, in 1944, they joined the battle against the V1, or buzz bomb. There were many accidents at the airfield, and numerous RAF and USAAF fighters and bombers crash-landed there. Other famous pilots based at West Malling were Squadron Leader Peter Townsend, Squadron Leader Bob Braham, Group Captain John Cunningham and Group Captain Guy Gibson, all of whom became heroes and household names.

After airfield expansion that included improved runways, night fighter operations became intense, with Nos. 85, 29 and 96 Sqn operating Beaufighters and later Mosquito aircraft in this role. There were at least forty-two RAF squadrons based at West Malling at various stages from 1940 until end of the war, not including training units and all the service echelons that supported squadrons and the RAF Regiment. Other units such as No. 41 and 91 Squadrons flew from the airfield and with other units had great success with fighter sweeps and V1 patrols. No. 500 (Kent's own) Squadron Royal Auxiliary Air Force adopted RAF West Malling as its home when it was re-formed in 1946. British prisoners of war, following repatriation, were billeted at West Malling, until they were demobbed or perhaps returned to life in the services.

There were several Battle of Britain and RAF open days at West Malling during the late 1940s and '50s, which, of course, proved ideal occasions to recruit pilots and airmen. Nos. 25, 29 and 85 Sqn served at the airfield following the war, eventually being re-equipped with the new Vampire and Meteor that were replacing Mosquitoes and other types. These played a major role during the Cold War period as night fighter squadrons, although sadly there were several accidents involving these new jet aircraft, and a visit to West Malling Church is testimony to them as it is where several young pilots and airmen are buried. During the early 1960s a United States Naval facility took over the airfield, and Short Brothers also used it. West Malling was home to gliding schools, and many ATC cadets were trained. Ugandan Asians fleeing from persecution were housed on the site until their future could be decided.

The Beatles filmed scenes for the film *Magical Mystery Tour* on the airfield, using the blast pens as a backdrop. Metair Aircraft Equipment Ltd later occupied the airfield, and during the 1980s the television series *We'll Meet Again* was partly filmed there. The story depicted the life of USAAF bomber crews in the Second World War. This led to the West Malling Warbird airshows, which continued until the airfield was to be developed as a business park in 1989. This also meant the end of the road for Metair, which moved to Biggin Hill, and the end of a famous airfield.

Today the site is covered by housing and businesses, but at least there is a permanent memorial to all those who served at RAF West Malling, and the control tower is being refurbished. Several of the original buildings are in use and there is even a public house, The Spitfire, although it does not reflect the atmosphere of The Startled Saint, the popular watering hole of many pilots and airmen during the war and after, which today is privately owned.

Acknowledgements

I would like to thank the following for their assistance during the research for this history: Alan Huggett, Tim Kimber, Norman Weller, Paul Abbott, John Chipperfield, Jim Stockley, Alan E. Wright, Edward T. Sergison, J. Roberts, B. Solly, M. Spencer, F.G. Evans, M. Edwards, Kent Aviation Historical Research Society, National Archive, R. Munday, D.G. Collyer, Aerofilms Ltd, A.J. Jackson, E.J. Riding, Peter Hall, Robin J. Brooks, G. Gilbert, J.R. Carter, P. Kennet, Peter Hobson, R. Moss, Brian Miller, Robin A. Walker, S. Glover, Air Commodore P.J. Wilkinson CVO, Imperial War Museum, RAF Museum Hendon, Kent Messenger, Aeroplane Magazine, Air Britain Publications, Metair Aircraft Equipment, Military Aircraft Photographs, Ian Allan, Polish & Sikorski Institute, After the Battle Magazine, Air Mail Magazine, The Aviation Historian, B. King, F.J. Evans, B. Solley.

Photographs AJM Collection unless shown otherwise. No. 264 Sqn photos with kind permission of Colin Gass; photos relating to Wing Commander N. Cordingly, Colin Gass.

Youth in the Skies
By H. Asquith

From: Youth in the Skies (Sidgewick & Jackson, 1940)

These who were children yesterday
Now move in lovely flight,
Swift-glancing as the shooting stars
That cleave the summer night

A moment flashed, they came and went,
Horizons rise and fall,
The speed of valour lifts them up
And strength obeys their call

ACKNOWLEDGEMENTS

The downs below are breathing peace
With thyme and butterflies,
And sheep at pasture in the shade.
And now from English skies

These who were children yesterday
Look down with other eyes,
Man's desperate folly was not theirs
But theirs the sacrifice.

Old men may wage a war of words,
Another race are these,
Who flash to glory dawn and night
Above the starry seas

'We Guard the Gate', a translation from the Latin motto of RAF West Malling airfield's crest, which refers to its association with the 'keep' at West Malling known as St Leonard's Tower, believed to have been built in the eleventh century for the defence of West Malling. (Crown copyright)

Chapter 1

Birth of an Airfield

On 1 February 1918, No. 143 Sqn was formed at Throwley airfield, near Faversham, Kent, from the nucleus of No. 112 Sqn, itself a recently formed unit based at Throwley for Home Defence duties. No. 143 Sqn was equipped with Armstrong Whitworth F.K.8s, which operated from this site. No. 143 Sqn and No. 50 Sqn, of No. 53 Wing RFC, Home Defence Group, South East Area, VI Brigade, were the first flying units to use Kings Hill, situated 1½ miles from West Malling railway station, as a second-class night landing ground for RAF Detling, previously used by the RNAS and RFC. The squadron was later re-equipped with the faster S.E.5a, for defence against the Zeppelin and later bomber raids.

On 21 May 1918, an S.E.5a that had been allotted to No. 1 Aircraft Acceptance Park at Coventry and destined for the Western Front, crashed in the vicinity of West Malling. The aircraft, C6478, was reported as burnt out.

One of the most famous First World War fighter pilots, James McCudden VC, born in Chatham, had associations with Maidstone. On 2 June, when flying a Bristol Scout from Joyce Green to Kings Hill, on a staff visit to No. 6 Wing Headquarters, Barming Place, Maidstone, he had a lucky escape after crashing. This particular Scout, which he was using while his Sopwith Pup was being overhauled, had let him down the previous day on a ferrying flight from Lympne, when engine failure forced him to land in a field near Gravesend, so he was not entirely surprised when, without warning, the engine cut dead at 1,000ft over Barming.

Too low to reach the aerodrome at Kings Hill, he saw that most of the country below was covered with hop fields, but didn't notice that the only suitable stretch for an emergency landing was a meadow of long grass growing for hay. Having little height to spare, he was already committed to a downwind landing when he saw the state of the grass, so attempted to stall the Bristol and 'pancake' on to the surface. This did not quite succeed and he hit the ground heavily, wiping off the undercarriage and damaging other

1

parts of the aircraft. Luckily the Scout remained the right way up, and for the second time in his career he walked out of a wreck unhurt. His captaincy had been gazetted the day before and, reflecting on this inauspicious beginning in the new rank, he obtained transport back to Joyce Green.

At the time of this accident McCudden had 425 hours' flying in his log book, but there was little likelihood that his nerve would be affected. It was, however, widely recommended that if possible a pilot should fly again immediately after a crash, so he climbed into his Pup, now serviceable again, and resumed the interrupted journey to Maidstone. To dispel any doubts, he performed a descending series of loops on returning to Joyce Green, landing straight after the twentieth, which he completed just above ground level.

There were several such landing grounds such as Kings Hill established in the Home Counties during the First World War, although they were used infrequently. However, on the night of 28/29 September 1917, during attempts to intercept a force of seven Gotha and three Giant bombers heading for a raid on London, a few aircraft of Home Defence units had to land at the most convenient landing ground due to the weather. Two landed at Biggin Hill and one at Staplehurst. 2nd Lieutenant N.H. Auret of No. 39 Sqn, having taken off from Biggin Hill at 2047hrs, had to make a forced landing at West Malling, the only recorded landing, and was most probably one of few pilots who used the site.

A survey of the NLG/ELG recorded that the ground was flat with no slopes and was bound by low hedges and woods and a wire fence on the south sides. The surface was smooth with a slight dip at the eastern end. Obstacles were a workhouse 500 yards north-west and oast houses 350yd south. Ground signals were placed near a guard hut, and effective landings could be made north-west and south-east by night and from all points by day. Lieutenant Auret would have been grateful that the site at Kings Hill had been selected for an NLG as he brought his B.E.2c serial A595 in to land. Officially the airfield was in existence from March 1917 until October 1919, however notification of relinquishment was posted on 13 August 1919. Following the end of the war, civilian flying was not allowed until 1 May 1919, before long many aviation companies once again began to develop new types of aircraft. However, on the back of this development, private flying became popular and many flying clubs were formed throughout Great Britain.

It is interesting to note that, in August 1928, Maidstone Town Council had scheduled Mote Park as an open space in the town planning scheme with a view to its use as an aerodrome, but this was not adopted.

The airfield established at West Malling, set in the Kent countryside, amidst the orchards and hop gardens in 1937. The clubhouse and two hangars are located in the far left corner of the airfield. (Aerofilms Ltd)

Following the First World War, the site became redundant and was not used again until April 1930, when P.H. Meadway of Kent Aircraft Services initiated flying from the landing ground. It was not long before a clubhouse and a canvas hangar were constructed. During this time the Avro 504K, the popular and reliable biplane that had been in use with the RAF as a trainer, was flown by both Kent Aeronautical Services and the West Kent Aero Club. In 1930 the airfield at Kings Hill was renamed by P.H. Meadway as West Malling and became home to Kent Aircraft Services and West Kent School of Flying. Kent Aircraft Services operated several aircraft, including Avro 504s and an S.E.5a, registration G-EBTK. This particular aircraft was later fitted with an air-cooled engine and a four-bladed propeller, and known as a Dudley Watt D.W.1. DH.60M Moth G-ABAI was owned by West Kent School of Flying and remained with it for several years. This aircraft was impressed into RAF service in February 1940 as serial number W7498.

In March 1931 British Aircraft Company (BAC) BAC Ltd, Lower Stone Street, Maidstone, was registered with a capital of £3,000 in £1 shares. The

3

The home of Maidstone Aero Club in the early 1930s, with two DH Moths parked near the recently constructed hangar and the clubhouse nearest to the camera. The second hangar/workshops is on the left. Note the vehicles parked on the outside. (Aerofilms Ltd)

company was known as a designer, constructor and operator of all kinds of land and marine aircraft, motor vehicles, motor boats and marine engines, aircraft motors, trailers, etc. The directors were C.H. Lowe-Wylde, ARAeS, of 56, Sutton Road, Maidstone; K.B. Green, Alver Cottage, Lancet Lane, Loose, Maidstone (managing director of H. Allnutt and Son, Ltd) and Sheila M. Green, Alver Cottage, Lancet Lane, Loose, Maidstone. Lowe-Wylde had been designing and building gliders since February 1930 in buildings formerly used as a brewery and BAC late set up a factory in Hanworth, Middlesex.

The first air display at West Malling took place on 12 April 1931, and Captain C.D. Barnard with his Air Pageant took part in this popular event, and despite the fact that he had only one aircraft, a Fokker F.VIIa, the day went well. Meanwhile, Edgar Percival had established his small aircraft company at Gravesend airfield in 1932, with its servicing facilities. Percival Aircraft Co. Ltd had designed the Gull G-ABUR, a three-seat, low-wing monoplane, which although built at Gravesend was later test flown from West Malling. The aircraft was a success and from its humble beginnings the Mew Gull was developed.

During this period, one of Britain's most successful aerobatic and display pilots arrived at West Malling. Geoffrey Arthur Virley Tyson was enlisted

Avro N504K G-EBSJ after coming, to grief at West Farleigh near West Malling in April 1932. Such incidents attracted souvenir hunters at the time. Note the chequered pattern on the aircraft's fin. The Avro was taking part in Sir Alan Cobham's display at Maidstone. (B. King)

into the RAF on a short service commission in 1925 and on leaving he joined Maidstone Aero Club. He flew with Sir Alan Cobham's air displays during 1933–35 and became a test pilot for A.V. Roe & Co. Ltd. In 1937 he joined Alan Cobham's Flight Refueling Ltd, and in 1940 became a test pilot with Shorts of Rochester. Tyson then moved to Saunders-Roe and flew the Princess flying boat on its maiden flight on 2 August 1952. Leaving the company in 1956, he flew with Dunlop's Aviation Division until retirement in 1958. He then settled down and lived on the Isle of Wight.

Following the formation of the National Aviation Day by Sir Alan Cobham, it was not long before his popular Flying Circus arrived at West Malling. The air display took place over two days, 21 and 22 May 1932, and was a great success. During the display, the *Golden Arrow* car once

Above: DH.60G Gipsy Moth G-AALJ was converted to a seaplane in 1929/30 and shipped to the West Indies. Returning to the UK in 1930, it reverted to a landplane and was owned by Malling Aviation Ltd, until it crashed on 8 May 1935.

Below: DH.82A Tiger Moth G-ACEZ was often flown by Geoffrey A.V. Tyson, OBE, at air displays in the 1930s. This aircraft was impressed into the RAF as BB790, restored in 1955 and written off in an accident on 23 August 1961. (F. Ramsden)

owned by Sir Henry Segrave was displayed. Sir Henry broke the world land speed Record in 1924 in this unique vehicle, but was killed on Friday, 13 June 1930, a few months after receiving his knighthood, Segrave drove his boat *Miss England II* at an average speed of 98.76mph over two runs on

Lake Windermere. However, on the third run it capsized at full speed. Chief engineer Victor Halliwell was also killed when the boat rolled over on him.

In 1932, P.H. Meadway was strapped for cash and he put the airfield up for sale. In June, West Malling airfield, together with the Maidstone Aero Club, were taken over by Land Air and Water Services Ltd, a curiously named company owned by one Count John E. Johnston-Noad. This flamboyant gentleman was known to the Metropolitan Police as a 'dodgy solicitor'. He was also a very successful motor boat racer and had a finger in many pies, many of them nefarious. He formed Maidstone Aero Club and operated two DH.60 Moths with R.F. Bulstrode as chief flying instructor.

Under the direction of Count Johnston-Noad the airfield was developed and enlarged, becoming known as Maidstone Airport. To the flying school and aero club, the company proposed to add a public restaurant and dance hall, and full facilities for aircraft overhauls, car maintenance, etc. The accommodation for the Maidstone Aero Club was redesigned to include a swimming pool, squash courts, dormitory, changing room, lounge and a large dining room with dance floor. The company had a car available should those who flew in wish to carry on to London by road, and customs facilities were also available.

It was an important day for Maidstone and its airport, when on 4 June 1932, HRH the Prince of Wales, who became Edward VIII for a brief period before abdication, flew into the airport in his own aircraft. His destination was the British Legion Factory at Preston Hall and, despite his brief time at the airport, he was nonetheless impressed by the facilities on offer. The Prince of Wales took delivery of his own aircraft, DH Gipsy Moth G-AALG, as early as 1929, although he later owned several other aircraft.

A tragic accident took place on 26 June 1932, when DH.60X Cirrus Moth II G-EBWY crashed on landing at West Malling, killing both the pilot, Reginald C. Presland, and a passenger. G-EBWY was registered on 10 March 1928 to Henry N.S. Norman of Croydon, and was the first privately owned Moth with auto-slots on the wings. It was later re-registered on 21 January 1929 to Thomas E. Rose-Richards, Stag Lane, Edgware. It was sold in July 1929 by Malcolm Campbell (London) 1927 Ltd and re-registered in August 1929 to The London Aeroplane Ltd, Stag Lane. This aircraft was one of two DH.60 Moths raffled by the London Aeroplane Club at its annual dinner on 17 February 1931, and it was won by Captain Leighton-Davies. He was an overseas visitor and did not want the Moth, so it was sold on for £250 to Reginald Clarence Presland, RAF Club, Piccadilly, London, but remained based at Stag Lane. Presland had christened the aircraft *Pamela,* and sold G-EBWY to John E. Johnston-Noad, or the Count as he was known, for Maidstone Airport Ltd, and it was flown by Maidstone Aero Club, West Malling. This aircraft also flew at Bekesbourne and at Lympne airfields prior to its crash, after which it was scrapped.

There was a steady increase in new members of Maidstone Aero Club, the membership fee being £5 5s. Those joining in August 1932 received the benefit of having to pay only a half-year's subscription. Count Johnston-Noad, now managing director of Maidstone Airport Ltd, acted as honorary organiser for the Chatham Air Display, held on 8/9 October 1932. On Sunday, 21 August, there was a grass track motor cycle meeting from 1500hrs and on the following Sunday at the same time there was a clay pigeon shooting meeting.

Maidstone Aero Club started night flying in September 1932, and a series of navigation classes commenced, continuing throughout the winter, and ground engineering and 'B' licence classes also took place. Every Sunday evening there was a dance, and everybody was cordially invited. The dancing was usually accompanied by arrangements from Hugh Wade at the piano.

Female members of the Maidstone Aero Club held the first of a series of 'at home' days on 2 October. More than 250 people accepted the hospitality

The first Percival P.1A Gull Four G-ABUR, which was constructed by BAC at Maidstone Airport during 1932. This aircraft was unfortunately damaged beyond repair on 26 August 1935. (R. Munday)

of the club, and something like twenty-five aircraft arrived during the afternoon. One particularly gratifying feature was the help given by the RAF from Manston. Captain Sidney Smith, who attended the meeting, remarked: 'A very great deal of good can be done to civil aviation by the RAF assisting the social side of the flying club's work.' He therefore gave permission for some of his officers to fly over in an Avro Lynx and two DH Tiger Moths. RAF Manston had always supported civil aviation in Kent, and the success of the recent 'Round Thanet' race was largely due to the help received from the service.

No attempt was made at putting up a flying programme as it was felt that fostering the social side of the club was better served by attending to things such as club hospitality than by laying undue stress on what often turned out to be a somewhat unduly extended display of flying.

It was unfortunate, however, that BAC's Mr Lowe-Wylde was unable to get his new aircraft design back from Hanworth in time for a demonstration, as had already been announced in *Flight* magazine, causing much interest. At the time Lowe-Wylde's machine was a standard BAC two-seater glider with a 600cc Douglas motor cycle engine above the wing as a pusher, which flew well. A more practical version was being designed, a pusher and low-wing monoplane.

Following the 'at home' day, the club held its regular Sunday evening dance, and some sixty people stayed for this. Arrangements had been made to install electric lighting on the premises at the aerodrome and advantage of this was taken to provide night flying and floodlighting facilities.

A flying meeting was held on 8 October at Starfield Aerodrome, Gillingham, in connection with the Medway Town's Civic and Empire Week. The meeting was organised with the assistance of the personnel and aircraft of Maidstone Aero Club, while Jim Mollison and his wife Amy Mollison (nee Johnson) attended, receiving a civic welcome and afterwards presenting the prizes. Included in the planned programme was a landing competition for individual owners, a landing competition for a team of three from other clubs and a Concours d'Elegance.

The weather on 8 October was wet and it poured hard. To make matters worse, there was a gale blowing. The marquee was occupied by pilots and spectators and in danger of collapse from the combined weight of wind and water, and had it not been for the heroic work of the Automobile Association (AA) Air Service, there could have been some casualties among the visiting aircraft. An arrival competition was billed for 1215hrs, but even the most optimistic hardly expected anyone to arrive, and only four pilots got through

Air Commodore J. de M. Severne took this photo during the 1930s. The notice placed on the aircraft's nose says: 'We don't know what this machine is, nor to whom it belongs!!!' The aircraft appears to be an Armstrong Whitworth Atlas army co-operation biplane, which could have come from RAF Manston, where No. 2 Sqn was based. (A.J. Jackson)

to the airfield. Almost dead on time, Flight Lieutenant J.B. Allen arrived in the Duchess of Bedford's DH.60G Moth Major G-ACUR, closely followed by W.M. Wood in an Avian III G-EBVZ, the same one that had belonged to Miss Winifred Brown when she won the King's Cup in 1930. Shortly afterwards came Mr Jackman in his Monospar S-25. Mr Bentley was next to arrive in the Shell-Mex-BP Comper Swift. A Blackburn Bluebird and DH Tiger Moth belonging to those who had hoped to do some joyriding completed the aerial visitors. Notwithstanding the unfortunate conditions, the aircraft were judged for the Concours d'Elegance, Mr Jackman, with his Monospar, gained first prize; Flight Lieutenant Allen, with the Duchess of Bedford's Moth, a second Moth secured second, and Mr Wood's Avian came third.

The catering staff engaged to provide lunch were naturally somewhat disconcerted by the combined effects of the gale and the torrential downpour, but they eventually managed to get their food laid out and the visitors were soon gratefully turning their attention to this.

Hawker Tomtit G-AEES seen at T. Campbell Black's show at Maidstone. It was impressed into RAF service as K1782, but was destroyed by fire on 2 February 1940. The aircraft in the background is Short S.16 Scion II G-ADDT, which was written off on 27 July 1936. The motorbike has not been identified. (B. King)

The rest of the meeting had to be cancelled, which was very unfortunate, particularly so as every item of the organisation seemed to have been in place. As well as the AA being present, the fire and ambulance service arrived, but naturally in the circumstances there was no hope of carrying through any flying programme. A photographer and reporters from *Flight* magazine were fortunate enough to be comfortably transported by car, from which the photographer was able to obtain one or two images. After the meeting was definitely washed out, they drove to Gravesend airfield, which had been formally opened on 25 August 1932. The farm buildings, which were already on the site at Gravesend, had been cleaned and furnished, and now formed comfortable quarters for the staff. A large barn had been extended and, when finished, was used as a hangar. The airfield itself was grass, although not yet established, while the stubble was well consolidated and firm enough for all light aircraft.

The following article appeared in an October edition of the *Kent Messenger* in 1932 regarding Maidstone Airport Ltd:

> The time when every town, and possibly every village, will have its own aviation station cannot be far distant. An enthusiastic start in that direction is being made, so far as Kent is concerned, by the Maidstone Airport Ltd., which is about to

Another aircraft at Maidstone Air Show in 1936 is this Spartan Three Seater II G-ACAD, preparing to take off with passengers. G-ACAD flew until 1 December 1946. (B. King)

be municipally confirmed and to be licensed for air liners and for the use of aviators in every direction. An ideal ground has been acquired at West Malling, and plans for this project are ambitious indeed, for here next year will be officially opened the first of a chain of airports in all fair-sized towns, which will eventually be linked up by the company. The scheme is, however, already sufficiently far advanced to attract the public, and although not started until the middle of last year the Maidstone Aero Club, instituted by the company, can boast 192 members. Comfortable club premises have already been erected, as have also a main hangar and private lock-up hangars. Attached to the airport will be the Maidstone Flying School for tuition to the general public, joy-rides, taxi work and Continental trips. It will be possible to arrange for deferred payments at the school, and to hire an aeroplane. The project is in the right hands, the managing director being Count Johnston-Noad of the British Motor-boat Club, and who was a close friend of Sir Henry Segrave.

His main aim is to gain the interest of the general public, without which flying can never come fully into its own. To this end the grounds—100 acres in extent—are being most attractively laid out. Magnificent buildings have been, and are being, erected, providing not only amenities for flying but also for social activities. At the entrance will be an up-to-date road house, where, the general public may eat, drink, dance and if they wish to fly. Noad, who was the founder of the Out-board Racing Club, is Vice-Commodore of the company, says they will have the use of a spacious and beautiful club-house, and its amenities will be available at lower rates.

A bathing pool, slipper baths, squash and tennis courts, ping-pong, private service cars to and from London, flying school lecture hall, terraces, club lounge, tearoom and dance hall, open-air wine and cocktail bar, fish pool and night floodlighting are some of the airport's attractions. There can be no doubt that a big future lies ahead for it. An 'At Home' event was held on Sunday, when the lady members invited all the guests.

Some 350 people visited the airport and there were 30 aeroplanes present. In the evening the regular Sunday evening dance was attended by about 60 people.

On Sunday, 16 October 1932, the Rochester and Chatham District Motor Club held a rally and gymkhana at the Maidstone Aero Club. The event was a great success, particularly as many of the visitors were enrolled as members of the aero club. An autumn dance was planned to be held at the clubhouse on 21 October. On Saturday, 22 October, a clay pigeon shooting sweepstake competition was held and the following Sunday a landing competition was arranged towards the winning of a challenge trophy presented by the club. Non-members were invited to compete, the entrance fee being a shilling. The winner of each competition received a silver spoon, and the holder of the most spoons at the end of the year received the trophy. On Sunday, 30 October, invited visitors from other flying clubs arrived. Many came from the Surrey Aero Club, Gatwick, and competed with the Maidstone members in a series of contests. At the time it was hoped that other clubs would co-operate in this scheme and enable it to become a monthly event.

On Sunday, 6 November the club held its monthly 'at home' day, when members were asked to come and meet the new manager, M. Spencer.

DH.60G Gipsy Moth I registration G-ABAI, of Maidstone Airport Ltd, seen here at the Folkestone Air Race in 1932 and flown by Count Johnston. It was impressed into RAF service in February 1940 as W7948. On the right is De Havilland DH.60G Gipsy Moth G-AAEW, flown by Hampshire Aeroplane Club, Eastleigh. This aircraft was impressed into the RAF on 30 May 1940. (B. Solly)

A balloon race was held on Sunday, 16 November and a balloon that went up at 1530hrs was found at 1845hrs on Monday at Lausanne, France, a distance of 450 miles. It was calculated that the balloon must have averaged 35mph. Numerous others had been sent back from the Somme and Marne, but the balloon that landed at Lausanne was declared the winner. By the end of December 1932, Maidstone Aero Club had seriously taken in hand the question of flying tuition for members and their friends, and the number being taught under the careful guidance of the chief instructor, R.F. Bulstrode, increased steadily. The New Year navigation classes commenced, and all those interested, whether members or not, were welcomed. Classes were being held for special tuition in ground engineering, cross-country and elementary and advanced navigation courses. A great number of members and their friends took advantage of the fact that the club was open throughout the whole of Christmas, and a very festive gathering was maintained throughout this period. The children's Christmas tree party was a great success, and Father Christmas arrived in the club's Moth. In the same month, 130 boys from the Maidstone Grammar School were entertained by the club.

Avro 504N registration G-AECS, which took part in T. Campbell Black's air display at Maidstone in 1936. It appears from the words 'Coop Teas' painted on the fuselage that the aircraft was used to advertise the company tea products. This Avro was impressed into RAF service as J8548 and was broken up during 1940. (B. King)

Alan Cobham's Flying Circus returned to Maidstone Airport on 17 April 1933. Hundreds of people attended the event, which always attracted crowds wherever they took place.

C.H. Lowe-Wylde's BAC company had continued to build and develop glider designs since its formation in Maidstone in 1931. These gliders were launched using auto-towing, which meant they were towed behind a car until they reached a speed where they could take off. Lowe-Wylde pioneered this technique and early trial flights may have been carried out at West Malling.

In 1932, Lowe-Wylde decided to fit a 600cc Douglas motor cycle engine into the glider version of one of these. The resulting aircraft, named Planette, proved to be a very docile and controllable aircraft with a speed range of 15–40mph. It is thought that the name Planette was not devised by Lowe-Wylde himself but came from correspondence in the 20 January 1933 edition of *Sailplane & Glider*. Author P.S. Foss, discussing powered gliders, called the motor-assisted BAC 3 Drone a Planette.

Several were built but on 13 May 1933, after the BAC 3 Drone had been flying at West Malling for around twenty minutes, it crashed, killing Lowe-Wylde. The owner was R.F. Bulstrode of Maidstone Flying School,

Several aircraft took part in the flying display to launch the opening of Maidstone Airport on 15 July 1933. Three Vickers Virginias of No. 500 (Kent's Own) Sqn fly over spectators, with a Gipsy Moth in the distance and a Hawker Audax of No. 2 Army Cooperation Sqn from RAF Manston. (F.G. Evans)

and the aircraft was being flown for demonstration purposes. During the course of the second flight that day, a turn to the left developed into an extremely rapid slide-slip at a height of about 300ft, and the machine, with the engine 'on', struck the ground, fatally injuring Lowe-Wylde. The aircraft was the fourth of the type to be completed and flown. It had met with a slight mishap at West Malling shortly after the first week of May (on its third or fourth flight there) and was returned to the works at Hanworth for the necessary repairs. The reconditioned machine was not flight-tested at Hanworth but was conveyed by road to Maidstone on 13 May 1933, and there assembled under the supervision of Lowe-Wylde, who did most of the work.

The Drone had, until the crash, been regarded as an experimental aircraft and had not been approved as a type for a certificate of airworthiness. Special permits for flights from and within a radius of certain approved aerodromes, including Maidstone Airport (West Malling), had been granted, but flights across country were prohibited. It was stated at the inquiry that Lowe-Wylde hadn't been well, as a result of lack of sleep, overwork, and irregular meals, and in fact he had not eaten on the day of the accident.

16

Above: Lowe-Wylde was killed flying at West Malling, when he crashed his light aircraft, the Planette, on 13 May 1933. This was the first fatal aircraft accident on the airfield. (Sport & General)

Below: BAC 3 Drone being flown by Lowe-Wylde on 5 May 1933 at Hanworth, prior to being transported to West Malling. and is thought to be the aircraft in which he crashed on 13 May 1933. (Sport & General)

DH.60G Gipsy Moth G-AACZ of Malling Aviation Ltd parked outside the company's hangar at the airfield on April Fool's Day 1939. This aircraft was owned by the company from 23 January 1935 and was withdrawn from use on 12 July 1939. It was flown, on occasion, by Pauline Gower. (E.J. Riding)

In 1919 the Sopwith Aviation and Engineering Company Ltd produced a two-seat version of the Sopwith Pup fighter, the company's first post-war civil aircraft. Appropriately named the Dove, the type made its debut at Hounslow in May 1919 in the hands of Major Barker, VC. Powered by an 80hp Le Rhone rotary engine, the Dove had a maximum speed of 95mph. Ten Doves appeared on the British civil register and the last, G-EBKY, was first registered on 27 March 1925 to D.L. Hollis Williams, who was employed by the Fairey Aviation Company. A certificate of airworthiness was issued on 12 April 1927, though the Dove had flown for some time previously. The first flight was made on 10 October 1926, however, on the second flight six days later the undercarriage was damaged after a forced landing. On 16 April 1927 the Dove was further damaged when the engine cowling came adrift just after take-off at the Bournemouth Easter Meeting. The wreckage was removed to the Fairey experimental shop and repaired by order of C.R. Fairey himself. A spare fuselage was obtained from Hawkers, the main planes were recovered and a Snipe-type tailplane fitted. Though the aircraft was repaired, no further flights are recorded in the logbook until the Dove was sold to C.H. Lowe-Wylde of the British Aircraft Company in 1930. The Dove was collected from Brooklands on 26 July and taken to West Malling for C of A overhaul. With a replacement engine, the Dove took to the air again on 4 September 1931. Following the death of

Lowe-Wylde, the Dove spent several years in decline. G.A. Chamberlain purchased the aircraft from C.P.B. Ogilvie of Watford High Street for £45. Although Chamberlain's name does not appear in the Dove's logbook, he made a number of flights, though neither the aircraft nor the owner's ability as a pilot were officially recognised.

In 1937 Richard Shuttleworth acquired G-EBKY and transported it to Old Warden. By removing the rear seat and mounting a machine gun on the engine cowling the aircraft was converted into a Sopwith Pup in 1938. Air tested on 26 February 1938, the Dove was given a permit to fly in time for A.H. Wheeler to fly it at the Royal Aeronautical Society's Garden Party at the Fairey Great West Aerodrome (now Heathow airport) in May. The Pup was stored for the duration of the war and in 1947 it was overhauled in time for its first post-war display, at Elstree on 27 July 1947, and given military markings with serial number N5180. The aircraft became a regular performer at airshows and during 1969/70 it was completely overhauled again. This time new fabric was applied, the Snipe-type tailplane was replaced by one constructed from original drawings and since then the Pup has appeared at many displays with the military serial number 9917.

Some aircraft from the 1930s period at West Malling survived and G-EBJO is one of these. The ANEC II was originally built for the Lympne aircraft trials in 1924, a competition to find the ideal light aircraft. It continued flying until 1937, and today can be found at the Shuttleworth Collection. (M. Edwards)

Maidstone Airport and Aero Club were officially opened on Saturday, 22 July 1933, on the occasion of a garden party at the airport. The opening ceremony was performed by Squadron Leader the Marquis of Douglas and Clydesdale, who arrived in his Gipsy Moth III and was welcomed by Sir Robert Gower. Sir Robert reminded those present of the fine work the Marquis had done for aviation, including the flight over Mount Everest and by his work in the House of Commons. The Marquis, in his opening speech, said that Great Britain must set a lead in aviation, the same as she had on the sea, and the best way to attain this end was to establish good landing grounds with petrol supplies all over the country. Maidstone had gone further than this in the equipment of its airport, and he asked for support for Maidstone Aero Club.

The deputy mayor of Rochester, after proposing a vote of thanks to the Marquis, said that Rochester intended to build an aerodrome as the firm of Short Brothers had made the town air-minded. Count Johnston-Noad seconded the vote of thanks, and called for three hearty cheers for the Marquis. Messrs Andrews and Wiltshire, whose yellow Spartan Three Seater powered by a Hermes II engine was a familiar sight at many flying meetings, set the ball rolling, offering local inhabitants a view of the neighbourhood from the air. Three Vickers Virginias of No. 500 (B) Sqn, (later No. 500 (Kent's Own) Sqn, RAuxAF, stationed at Manston, flew low over the aerodrome in close formation. Their size, and the roar of their engines obviously impressed the crowd greatly. Also from Manston came two Hawker Audax of No. 2 (A.C.) Sqn, flown by Flying Officers Murphy and Dixon-Wright.

Although No. 2 Sqn had been equipped with the Audax for only about two months, the speed and manoeuvrability of this type was well demonstrated when one of the machines flew past at about 65mph and came back at about 160mph.

Mr F. George, using a British Russell Lobe parachute, made a jump from the Club's Gipsy Moth flown by Flying Officer L.H. Snelling. He jumped over the south-west corner of the airport and landed on the north-west side. Flying Officer Snelling later gave a very neat and well-placed aerobatic display in the Moth. The same machine was later saved from serious damage by Mr Joice-Clarke, the club's ground engineer. The machine started to run forward when the engine was started, but Joice-Clarke, by hanging on to a wing, slewed the machine through two or three revolutions until it stood on its nose. The only damage was a smashed propeller. In the evening, after the visiting machines had left, a dance was held in the tastefully decorated clubhouse. Air Transport Co. Ltd took over the flying rights of the Maidstone Flying School in September 1933 and supplied three machines and a pilot, Mr Peacock. The company had no financial interest in Maidstone aerodrome other than leasing the flying rights, joyriding, taxi work, and repairs, from the present occupiers. The company began operations at Maidstone on 1 October 1933.

Unfortunately, in 1934 Count Johnston-Noad was jailed for a month for non-payment of rates. He was eventually jailed for ten years for fraud, which he served, improbably, with the atomic spy, Klaus Fuchs, later giving a newspaper interview describing his jail mate.

Gordon Weeks, a reporter in the 1930s for the *Kent Messenger*, learned to fly at Malling Aviation Ltd, and is seen here with his instructor discussing a cross-country flight by DH.60G Gipsy Moth G-ABAI. (E.J. Riding)

Meanwhile, the Count's beautiful second wife, Thelma, was known in the underworld as the 'Black Orchid' and was involved in a number of frauds and thefts, most famously an £8,000 diamond robbery in Hatton Garden in the 1950s. She committed suicide in 1955 with her lover while on the run from the police.

Johnston-Noad's short custodianship ended in January 1934 when he was declared bankrupt. Although he certainly put West Malling on the aviation map, his often-voiced claims that his was the best commercial airport in the world – a far better site than Croydon – were somewhat far-fetched! The airfield was sold for £6,000 to Malling Aviation Ltd, which quickly restored the airfield to normality under the co-owner and secretary Walter Laidlaw, and in the following year Malling Aero Club was registered.

Percival Gull 4 registration G-ACGP was owned and flown by Air-Vice Marshal A.E. 'Biffy' Borton, one of two sons whose family lived at Horton, near West Malling. He flew this aircraft in the King's Cup of 14 July 1934, reaching a speed of 157mph. G-ACGP flew until 1946, when it was scrapped at Thame airfield. A distinguished pilot in the First World War, Borton flew to Egypt on 28 May 1918 with Major A.C.S. Maclaren in Handley Page O/400 serial C9681.

Air Vice Marshall A.E. 'Biffy' Borton, son of Lieutenant Colonel A.C. Borton, who kept his Percival Gull Four G-ACGP at West Malling and often flew from the airfield. (KAHRS)

There followed several years of club and instructional flying. At this time the airfield had one steel and asbestos hangar, a smaller hangar of steel and wood and three wooden lock-ups. Full facilities were provided and landing flares could be provided with forty-eight hours' notice. The all-grass field featured four runways varying in length from 700 to 850yd, with a slight slope towards the north. For a while an area in the south-east corner was fenced off and was unusable because of water logging.

Seen at West Malling on 4 August 1936 is the single-seat Tipsy S.2 OO-TIP, which was built by Avions Fairey S.A. at Gosselies, Belgium. Flown to England in May 1935, it was demonstrated at many air displays and flown by Fairey Aircraft Ltd test pilot Chris S. Stainland. (E.J. Riding)

The main buildings were grouped together in the north-east corner of the field and the surrounding area consisted of woodland.

West Malling was frequently visited by 'Flying Circuses' and visitors included C.D. Barnard Air Tours Ltd on 11–12 April 1931, and Cobham's National Aviation Day Display on 21–22 May 1932, 17 April 1933 and 3 July 1935. On 27 June 1936, the British Empire Air Display organisation entertained the locals.

There were few accidents at the airport but on 8 December 1935, a DH Moth of Malling Aviation flown by John Sender took off a routine flight with a passenger. For unknown reasons the aircraft dived from a height of 2,500ft and crashed into hop fields that surrounded the airfield. These could have cushioned the effect of the crash as both occupants survived with minor injuries.

During 1935–36 there was an outbreak of 'fleas' at West Malling! Laidlaw embarked upon building a Mignet HM.14 Flying Flea in 1935 shortly after the craze hit Britain. His progress was reported in an article in the November 1935 issue of W.E. Johns's (author of the Biggles books) *Popular Flying* magazine and the engineless airframe had been on show at a West Malling's 'at home' day in July. It is doubtful that the aircraft received an authorisation to fly; it was never registered, although Fleas were

DH.80A Puss Moth G-ABWA, based at West Malling, was owned by Flying Officer J.K. Lawrence of Lawrence Aircraft Hire Ltd during the 1930s. It crashed into the Seine at Le Havre, France, on 30 December 1936 en route Paris–Lympne while on hire to Charles Kennett, who was uninjured. G-ABWA had been hired on 23 December 1936 to collect jewellery from Spanish Nationalist refugees. The wreckage was salvaged and believed returned to London. (E.J. Riding)

known to hop around with no kind of certification whatsoever. Meanwhile, C.E. Mercer of Lewisham built a Flea, registered G-AEFV, for Malling Aviation Ltd. The aircraft received its authorisation to fly in March 1936 and was flown successfully at West Malling and the Aero 8 Rally. However, in 1936 there were a number of unexplained fatalities involving Fleas and G-AEFV was loaned to the Air League for testing in the RAE's wind tunnel at Farnborough on 13 August 1936. There it was discovered that at certain angles of incidence, the front wing blanked off the rear 'wing', resulting in a vertical dive from which it was impossible to recover. So ended the Flea craze. G-AEFV was sold to Ray Bullock on 5 April 1937 and moved to Fraddon, Cornwall. It was again sold, this time to an owner in Somerset, and was cancelled in February 1938. By 1935 Malling Aero Club was listed in Jane's *All the World's Aircraft* as a light aeroplane club, the secretary being Walter Laidlaw. During July 1936, the club aircraft flew seventy hours and there were two first solos, one by C.E. Mercer and the other by Humphrey Dade, who was the fourth brother of John Dade, the club instructor at West Malling, to learn to fly. The large service hangar under construction was ready for use the same month.

Malling Aero Club continued to flourish and used seven DH.60G Gipsy Moths: G-AACZ, G-AAFD, G-ABYZ, G-ABAM, G-ABWN, G-ABLH

Above: DH.60G Gipsy Moth G-ABXZ inside the Maidstone Aero Club's hangar. This aircraft was painted red and grey, and was impressed into the RAF during November 1939. (E.J. Riding)

Below: DH.60G Gipsy Moth G-AFTG at West Malling on 24 June 1939. Built by students of the DH Technical School, Hatfield, during 1938, this was the final production aircraft. It was impressed into RAF service during November 1938 as X5054. (E.J. Riding)

and G-AFTG. The club had no fewer than fifty members by 1936, some of whom did not learn to fly. It was usual for budding pilots to obtain twenty-seven hours' flying time before qualifying for their 'A' licence. A silver cup was presented to the club by Mr C. McCarthy for club events and became known as the Landing Contest Cup. McCarthy was a keen member of the flying club and the cup was usually awarded to the member who could land his aircraft after flying a particular course within a specific time, landing back at West Malling. One such winner was Ken Vinson, a member with his own aircraft, which he christened *Hoof-Hearted*, his name being engraved on the cup.

Laidlaw, apart from running the club, was also a flying instructor and was joined by George Goodhew, who together trained and were responsible for qualifying pilots, Laidlaw's daughter kept the club's accounts and his wife took on office administration. Another company based at the airport was Plane Advertising Ltd, which was hired by customers to tow banners advertising an event or product. It flew several aircraft, including an ancient Avro 504N. These aircraft flew for many years in this role and many were used for joyrides and instructional flying. Many RFC and RAF pilots learned to fly on this type of aircraft. Following the First World War, they could be bought for as little as £5.

Another aircraft that is known to have flown from Maidstone Airport was DH.80A Puss Moth G-ABWA, and it was bought by Flying Officer John K. Lawrence and registered on 9 May 1936. On 30 December 1936, it crashed in the mouth of the Seine at Le Havre en route from Paris to Lympne while on hire to C. Kennett, with no casualties. It had been hired to collect jewellery from Spanish Nationalist refugees. The wreck was salvaged and believed to have been returned to London.

In 1937, the club had three DH.60 Gipsy Moths and a Spartan Three Seater. Normal flying rates were £1 15*s* an hour during weekdays but this sum was increased by a further 2*s* 6*d* at weekends. Among the club's membership, and excellent pilots, were Pauline Gower and Betty Sayers, who both became well-known figures in aviation. Sadly, Sayers was killed flying with the Air Transport Auxiliary (ATA). An even more well-known female pilot was Jean Batten, who visited the club, keeping the aircraft in which she flew to New Zealand in a hangar at West Malling.

Anec II registration G-EBJO, a single-engine monoplane, was purchased by Norman Jones in 1927 and he flew it to victory in the Air League Challenge Cup Race on 16 July 1927 from Castle Bromwich to Woodford. During the King's Cup Race two weeks later the aircraft hit a tree and was withdrawn from the race. Its next owner, A.H. Wheeler, flew G-EBJO regularly, until its Certificate of Airworthiness expired at West Malling in 1937. G-EBJO was later displayed at the Shuttleworth Trust at Old Warden.

Following a report, on 19/20 July 1937 the future of West Malling was discussed. The Air Ministry wanted to arrange for the extension of the proposed area at West Malling and then put the airfield 'in cold storage' as it required it for RAF use. In the meantime, the ministry wished the proprietors of the aerodrome to have full scope to use it or sell it as an airfield. The only way this could be achieved would be by lease and sub-lease. The ministry proposed that Laidlaw, the director of the airfield, should lease an area of the property, the lease being of a peppercorn rent. Once, achieved the company would have to spend £250 paid to it by the Air Ministry in doing certain work on the area chosen to make it fit for inclusion in the airfield. It was then proposed that the company should lease the entire airfield to the Air Ministry for a period of fourteen years.

By 1939, West Malling had been visited by the Directorate of Public Works not long before

Squadron Leader A. Bartley, DFC, was drawn by Cuthbert Julian Orde, who was best known for war art. Bartley, although not stationed at West Malling, learned to fly with the Maidstone Flying Club before the war. He married the actress Deborah Kerr. (Squadron Leader A. Bartley, DFC)

an RAF headquarters was set up, and final notice was given to the club that the airfield was to be handed over to the RAF. The Laidlow family left the area for good and emigrated to the Virgin Islands. The Landing Contest Cup was passed on to A.K. Robinson, who had flown from West Malling. Eventually he decided to place the trophy in the hands of No. 500 (Kent's Own) Sqn, RAuxAF Association. The secretary, Geoffrey Cardew, accepted the cup.

It is interesting to note that apart from the airfield development at Kings Hill and later RAF West Malling, there was an earlier plan for an airfield at Langley near Maidstone.

The Rt. Hon. Sir Philip Sassoon, Bart MP, the Secretary of State for Air, received a letter on 27 October 1934, from the Secretary of Maidstone Chamber of Commerce, Leslie Lucking FCPA, who made representation to the Borough of Maidstone Council regarding the possible acquisition of land in the vicinity of Maidstone for a municipal airfield. This was an area of 163 acres at Langley, and felt by the chamber of commerce to be too far away from the centre of Maidstone Borough to meet the future requirements of the public.

Sir Philip was asked if he would attend a chamber meeting on the subject, which was to be held at Maidstone Town Hall on 3 December 1934 at 1830hrs. Its exact location for the proposed airfield was at Furfield and Parkwoods, a 92.5-acre site together with 70.8 acres of the adjoining grassland situated within the parish of Langley that adjoined the borough boundary and ran up to the main Maidstone–Langley road, to Brishing Lane and a lane leading to Rats Castle, 2¼ miles from the town hall. The land would need levelling and earthwork removed.

The site, acceptable to the Air Ministry, had a gradual slope from south-east to north-west of approximately 1 in 80–90. In a report by the Aerodrome Special Committee, headed by the Mayor of Maidstone, H.G. Tyrwhite Drake, it was concluded that an immediate application be made to the Air Council, under Section 8 of the Air Navigation Act 1920 for consent to establish a municipal aerodrome for Maidstone Borough. Not until 1937 was a final decision was made regarding the airfield at Langley, when a report by the Director of Home Civil Aviation, Allan Attride, was received by the town clerk in Maidstone.

Since the site at Langley had originally been approved for development as an airfield, requirements affecting civil aerodromes had altered by 1934, owing to the progress made in civil aviation, and it was considered that an aerodrome intended for use by regular air services in all weather conditions would have to comply with the recommendations of a report by Sir Henry Maybury that considered the development of civil aviation in the UK. Major Mealing visited the site at Langley on 23 July 1937 for a final report. It was not until September 1939 that the idea for an airfield on the site was finally abandoned.

Despite the site originally being deemed suitable for airfield buildings beacons and VHF, eventually the Air Ministry had decided they could not foresee it being suitable for use by the RAF during the war and that it was doubtful it would be used for civil aviation.

Another pilot associated with those early days at West Malling was Pilot Officer Anthony Charles Bartley. The son of a district judge, Bartley was born in Dacca, then in Bengal, in 1919 and educated at Stowe School, Buckinghamshire. In 1938 he learned to fly with West Malling Flying Club. He entered the RAF on a short service commission, later joining No. 92 Sqn

Pauline Gower on the left, and Spartan G-ABKK christened *Helen of Troy*, one of many aircraft she flew during her civilian days before joining the ATA during the war. (D.G. Collyer)

and flying in the Battle of Britain. Bartley later met and married the film actress Deborah Kerr on 28 November 1945, and following the war joined Vickers Armstrong as a test pilot.

Pauline Mary de Peauly Gower was born on 22 July 1910 at Tonbridge, Kent, the daughter of Sir Robert Vaughn Gower and Dorothy Susie Eleanor. Sir Vaughn was a Member of Parliament. Gower was the second of two daughters. She had first flown while at school, before leaving the Sacred Heart Convent at the age of 18, and from then on she wanted to become a pilot. Her parents were opposed to her idea and refused to support the idea financially, so she earned the money for flying by giving violin lessons. After only seven hours of instruction she became the first woman to solo in such a short time. Gower received her 'A' pilot's licence after fifteen hours and fifteen minutes of flight time on 4 August 1930. However, she wanted to earn her living through flying, which would require a 'B' commercial licence, so she joined the London Aeroplane Club at Stag Lane. There she met Amy Johnson, who had just returned from her solo flight to Australia. She also met Dorothy Spicer, who would become her business partner.

On 13 July 1931 she took her night-flying test and was awarded her 'B' licence, becoming just the third woman in the world to earn a commercial pilot's licence. During August 1931 Gower and Spicer started the first all-female joyriding and air taxi service, at West Malling. A sign was erected close by, saying, 'Fly Now – First Left'. At that time, Gower was already an acclaimed aviatrix and flight instructor. This was a time when few women knew how to drive cars, let alone fly aircraft. Her log books for the period give details of various aircraft she flew. Two of these were flown by Malling Aviation Ltd from 23 January 1935; DH.60G Gipsy Moths G-AACZ and G-AAFO.

Other aircraft flown by her were Spartan G-ACEF, Hornet G-ADAK, Gipsy Moth G-AAFO and Spartan G-AAXZ, Spartan G-ABWN, Spartan G-ACCH, and Gipsy Moth G-ABAM. Gower also flew for Tom Campbell Black air displays. During 1938 Gower decided to begin a flying instructors' course at West Malling, which commenced on 26 September, her tutor being Captain W.R. Oliver. He later wrote of her: 'I put her through the course, which she passed with flying colours. I remember that spinning always nauseated her, and she would carry a little paper bag in which she would sometimes dispose of her breakfast if spinning was also on the menu.'

West Malling airfield during the 1930s with the Maidstone Aero Club hangar on the left. In the centre the airfield's landing circle is evident; these were often made using chalk. (Aerofilms)

Shortly before the course ended, Gower and the captain had a narrow escape flying a DH Gipsy Moth. Without much warning, the engine cut out and they were forced to make a hasty landing at Hale Farm, Eccles, Kent. Captain Oliver explained later: 'A connecting rod broke and pushed its way through the crankcase. We were very lucky not to have caught fire.' This incident did not stop Gower taking the final step to qualify, and on 29 November 1938, at Hanworth Airport she was examined and passed by Captain B.H. Woodhead in DH.60G Gipsy Moth G-ABFN. The same day she wrote in her log book: 'Test for Instructor's Licence OK.'

Gower's company's flights included instructors' courses, blind flying, joyrides and flying displays. Her last flight from West Malling was in July 1939. Gower also flew at Lympne, Bekesbourne and even Wye, Kent, which may have been at the location of the First World War airfield.

At the beginning of the war, there were only nine women pilots in the ATA, flying light training aircraft. However, over time and under Gower's leadership, that number grew to more than 150 women, flying all types of aircraft from light trainers to heavy, four-engine bombers. Their contribution to the war effort was recognised, and she was able to get them the same pay the men received. Gower achieved the rank of commandant, and in 1942 was appointed an MBE. Her leadership and organisational skills and her contribution to aviation were also recognised in the business world, and she was appointed a director of British Overseas Airways Corporation (BOAC). She was the first woman appointed to that position, and probably the first woman to serve on the board of an airline anywhere in the world. As busy as she was, with BOAC and the ATA, she did not neglect her personal life. In 1945, she married William Cusack Fahie. Unfortunately, her amazing life was cut short. She died of a heart attack while giving birth to her twin sons, Paul and Michael. Michael went on to write a book, *A Harvest of Memories*, published in 1995, which is a detailed account of her flying career.

Chapter 2

Action Station

The Battle of Britain and attacks by the Luftwaffe 1939–42

With war approaching, the airfield was taken over by the RAF and set up as a satellite airfield for RAF Biggin Hill and RAF Kenley. It was upgraded with a concrete runway, anti-aircraft guns and searchlights. RAF personnel were already based at West Malling, and the site covered Abbey Wood, Abbey Wood Farm including its cottages, Kate Reed Wood and the area known as Maidstone Airport. By the declaration of war on 3 September 1939, West Malling was already earmarked for requisition by the Air Ministry for use by the RAF.

On 6 June 1940, No. 51 Wing (No. 22 Group) formed its Headquarters at West Malling and No. 26 Sqn, flying Lysanders, was advised of its move to West Malling. Squadron Leader P.H.R. Saunders and Flight Lieutenant V. Mercer-Smith carried out a survey of the area to select sites for the No. 51 Wing HQ and billets. By June 1940 the grass landing strips measured 1,100yd north-east–south-west; 1,300yd south-east–north-west; 1,200yd north–south; and 1,400yd from east–west. Sommerfeld Tracking had been laid to reinforce the runway surfaces. The north–south was extended to 1,666yd and the east–west to 2,160yd later in 1940. A 'J' type hangar had been constructed and blister hangars were ready for occupation, which soon came.

On 7 June arrangements were completed for Wing HQ to be based at Addington Court and No. 26 Sqn officers billeted in two houses in West Malling village. All airmen were billeted in huts belonging to the Poor Law Institute. No. 26 Sqn HQ arrived at West Malling and both were HQs established in the airport offices. However, construction work had not been completed. On 9 June Royal Engineers and Royal Artillery AA Detachments from RAF Lympne moved with Wing Commander A.H. Flower, who was promoted to group captain.

Pilots of No. 264 Sqn enjoying a game of draughts during a quiet period at RAF West Malling in 1940. Note the tent in the background and the cribbage board on the table. (D.G. Collyer)

One company of the Royal West Kent Regiment installed on the airfield for AA defence was equipped with 2.3in guns, four Bofors plus six Lewis guns from 14 June, with Air Ministry contractors to be located on certain fields within a 5-mile radius of No. 26 Sqn.

The following day Italy declared war against France and England. The fitting of two Lewis gun tripods on the watch office roof was nearing completion and these commanded a clear field of fire over the whole airfield. Owing to a lack of fire-fighting appliances at the airfield, the local fire brigade agreed to assist if necessary.

Information was received that a searchlight would be installed for airfield defence. On 16 June the Secretary of State for Air, Sir Archibald Sinclair, visited the station and inspected aircraft and crews of No. 26 Sqn. Four days later, two armoured vehicles arrived to augment the station defences. On 17 June three photographic sorties were made of a total of three hours fifteen minutes. Two new Lysanders, R9020 and R9030, were delivered to the squadron and they came with self-sealing fuel tanks. Coastal operations commenced on 18 June at 1015hrs, extending from Skegness by North Foreland, South Foreland, and Dungeness to Newhaven, with a limit of

Above: Pilots of No. 26 Army Cooperation Sqn at 'A' Flight dispersal during Air Experience Flight training during summer 1940. The squadron's HQ was the old flying club building. (KAHRS)

Below: No. 26 Sqn pilots and ground crew of 'C' Flight pose with a Westland Lysander in the background. The squadron was based at RAF West Malling in 1940 and 1942. (P.L. Donkin)

15 miles from the coastline. Five aircraft operated sorties lasting two hours. Pilot Officer Percy and Leading Aircraftman Griffiths crashed in P1745 near the airfield on 27 June. Both crew members were unhurt but the Lysander was a write-off. On 21 June, the station commander at RAF Kenley visited West Malling and at a meeting the CO was notified that the airfield was to become a satellite airfield for Kenley.

A company of the South Staffordshire Regiment took over from the detachment of the Royal West Kent Regiment. On 1 July the squadron carried out aerial photography flights, including reconnaissance flying over advanced landing grounds (ALGs) and the following day Inspector General RAF Air Marshal Sir William Mitchell visited the airfield, during which operational flying continued.

Flight Lieutenant D.E. Mileham served with No. 26 Sqn and flew Lysanders from West Malling. He arrived on 8 June 1940, having been at RAF Lympne with No. 26 Sqn since 22 May 1940. In letters to his mother and father he wrote:

> We left Lympne yesterday, I flew and someone drove my car here. We are living in a castle owned by Colonel. He has a collection of swords and lion's heads mounted on the walls. The downside is that it's 3 miles from the airfield and I have to use my car a lot.

On 1 July he wrote:

> Last Saturday we went over to Tonbridge to a roadhouse and danced till about midnight and then all leapt in the swimming pool, with just our pants on! I went to have dinner with some Army chaps at their mess, last Friday and had quite a good time there. Next day I took the padre up for a flip. He was terribly excited about it and we went quite low over his house and all the other officers came out to watch.

In a letter received by his family on 10 July 1940 he wrote:

> I had a breathtaking moment two days ago. We were doing a spot of formation flying, the leader and myself had a slight collision. Fortunately, there was not much damage, but it was a very hair-raising moment. I went to have a look at a hun aeroplane which had been shot down near here. The fighter

boys had made a mess of it and I have one or two bits. We have a new Flight Commander starting from today. He seems quite a decent chap. Two of our pilots have been awarded DFCs, for various things done in France during the evacuation of Dunkirk. Richie and I went out for a photographic job today on the way back we landed at RAF Detling and had lunch with the boys. I also met there one or two chaps who were at Andover with me.

Flight Lieutenant D.E. Mileham RAFVR was killed on 15 April 1942. Flying Spitfire Mk.Vb AB987 with No. 234 Sqn over Cherbourg, he was shot down by Me 109s of JG26. One of No. 26 Sqn's pilots was Peter Bristow, who many years later became a High Court judge. Bristow was educated at Eton and Trinity College, Cambridge, where he read classics for the first two years and then law. Fascinated by flying since childhood, he was a member of the University Air Squadron (UAS), qualifying as a pilot at the age of 21 and joining the Royal Air Force Volunteer Reserve (RAFVR) in 1935. Around this time he also fenced for England. On the outbreak of the Second World War, Bristow was called up as a sergeant pilot. Commissioned as a pilot officer in 1940, he was sent to the School of Army Co-operation for a concentrated course, in which he came top of his class. Posted to No. 26 Army Co-operation Sqn, his first mission in 1940 was a photo reconnaissance over the Dunkirk evacuation. He later stood by at Lympne, ready for the threatened German invasion of Britain. Following the move to West Malling with No. 26 Sqn, he recalls:

> Our three flights were dispersed under canvas round the edges of the little grass club airfield, once home of the Maidstone Flying Club. Squadron HQ was in the Club buildings, with the squash court serving as one of the offices, the Officers Mess and other ranks billets were in houses well away from the airfield. At Wateringbury, a mile down the road, was the brewery which had been owned by my wife's family until taken over by Whitbreads in the 1920s. The airfield was being enlarged and turned into a fighter station. On its western boundary the buildings on a permanent camp were in the process of completion but empty. The rest of the periphery, with a minor road along the north, consisted of cherry orchards just coming into fruit. Among these were dispersed our transport and our fuel and bombs.

A tarmac perimeter track was being made, and the steam roller part of the operation had got as far as our 'A' Flight dispersal. Those of us who had not been with the squadron in France were deeply impressed by the enthusiasm with which all ranks set to digging slit trenches convenient for their pace of work. We were given some intense low-level bombing practice on the Porton Ranges. You could forget about dive-bombing with a Lysander. You reached 180mph promptly even in a shallow dive. At 200mph Westlands, who made the Lysander, expected the pilot's 'greenhouse' (cockpit) to blow out, or in. During June and early July, the Army formation, to which we were attached, had its front on the sea the whole coastline from Eastchurch, Isle of Sheppey to Thorney Island a few miles east of Portsmouth. The RDF Stations scanned high, and there was then no low-looking radar whatever. So we mounted dawn and dusk patrols to give early warning of seaborne landing attempts, with one Lysander covering the coast from Eastchurch to Rye and another from Rye to Thorney Island. It was an odd sensation flying low along the familiar Sussex coast at first light, with the towns still asleep, the piers all cut off from the shore, and wire entanglements along the beaches. If you saw anything, you were to report in Morse code. We surveyed open spaces in Kent and East Sussex on which we thought Ju52s might land, so that obstructions could be put in them to make landing difficult. After marking fields from the air we went in the CO's staff car to show the Home Guard where obstructions should be, usually meeting in a local pub. We even practised picking up messages from the Army. Two rifles were stuck in open ground by their bayonets, the message was attached to a line raised above the ground by two rifle butts, and you lowered a purpose-built hook hinge below the Lysander. We did night landing practice with a glim lamp flare-path that you could not see from above 500ft, so the Germans could not find it either. In July 1940 the CO showed me a letter from the Under Sheriff of Kent which conveyed Mr Justice Oliver's grave displeasure at the interference by aircraft noise with the proceedings of Maidstone Summer Assizes. We replied suggesting he should contact the Coastal Command Squadron based at RAF Detling. We mounted Vickers 'K' guns from the

'A' Flight aircraft which had been destroyed, in the 'A' Flight slit trenches, although no harm was caused to enemy bombers. Except when photographs were needed by the Army we were kept on the ground so as not to distract the fighter controllers. Armour was added to the Lysanders, and twin Brownings in the rear cockpit in place of the 'K' Gun, making them fly like bricks, unstable in pitch. Some aircraft had 20 mm cannon fitted to the undercarriage spats. Aircraft lost on the ground were such that on 3 September we withdrew to RAF Gatwick.

During July a detachment of No. 26 Sqn aircraft also carried out night flying operations from RAF Odiham. Sadly, Flight Lieutenant D.D. Rawlings and Pilot Officer J.P. Lees were killed in a flying accident at Odiham when their Lysander, N1292, inexplicably dived into the ground on 20 June 1940. On 1 July Wing Commander R.W.K. Stevens assumed command of RAF West Malling, and the following day Inspector General Air Marshal Sir William Mitchell visited the airfield and made a tour of defence posts and block cookhouses. A detachment of the South Staffordshire Regiment was relieved by Nos. 288 and 289 Batteries of the 67th (AT) Regiment RA. The change increased the fire power available by some four Boyes rifles, eighteen Bren guns and 100 rifles, and additional slit trenches were established near No. 26 Sqn's dispersal points.

An additional gun post was sited close to the main gate, and work commenced on a brick and concrete dugout for the defence HQ immediately outside the station HQ building. Following an inspection by Lieutenant Colonel Hill, CO of 67 (AT) Regiment RA, of all defence posts, it was decided to extend the perimeter to include a portion of the West Malling–Tonbridge road and the Kings Hill Institute, and two extra road blocks and gun posts were established.

At 1530hrs on 9 July 1940, a signal was received from HQ Fighter Command that No. 141 Sqn with Defiant aircraft would be moving from RAF Turnhouse to West Malling the following day, with RAF Hawkinge as their forward base. However, it was arranged that the Defiant crews should be billeted at West Malling, the remainder at RAF Biggin Hill. Officers, NCOs and airmen were billeted at Kings Hill Institute and messed at the airfield.

A further ninety men arrived for RAF ground defence duties. They were untrained, without arms or anti-gas equipment and one had no uniform. The station CO held a meeting with the chairman of Kent County Agricultural

Committee and obtained permission to extend the camp area and perimeter defence measures. Delayed by bad weather, the air party of No. 141 Sqn arrived on 12 July from RAF Turnhouse under the command of Squadron Leader W.A. Richardson. Despite all this activity and defence preparations, by 19 July RAF West Malling was reduced to care and maintenance status pending the completion of the buildings and its formal adoption by RAF Fighter Command. No. 141 Sqn commenced operations on 21 July 1940, but tragically six aircraft were lost while flying from Hawkinge. They had been scrambled to cover a convoy off Folkestone. Three Defiants failed to take off, the nine remaining formed three vics of three astern. Bf 109Es of III/JG51, led by Hauptman Hannes Trautloft, who were escorting Bf 110s attacking a trawler, spotted the Defiants without escort and attacked.

Two were shot down on the first pass, while another four were lost in the sea, as the Germans took advantage of the Defiant's blind spot, dead astern and below. Those shot down were Pilot Officer Kemp/Sergeant Crombie, in L6974; Pilot Officer Howley/Sergeant Curley, L6995; Pilot Officer Kidson/ Sergeant Atkins, L7015; and Pilot Officer Gardner/Pilot Officer Slatter, L7016. Another, L7009 flown by Lieutenant Donald/Pilot Officer Hamilton, crashed near Dover, while Flight Lieutenant Louden/Pilot Officer Farnes, in L7001, pulled off a forced landing at Hawkinge airfield. In addition, Pilot Officer McDougall/Sergeant Wise in L6983, despite being badly hit and the cockpit filling with smoke, managed to crash-land at Hawkinge village.

Following this disaster, No. 141 Sqn withdrew to RAF Prestwick to recover. A signal was received from No. 11 Grp that stated West Malling would revert to RAF Kenley for all purposes. On 23 July 1940, Wing Commander Stevens and Flight Lieutenant V. Mercer-Smith visited RAF Kenley to discuss RAF West Malling, and were informed by the station commander, RAF Kenley, that it was unlikely a fighter squadron would move to the Kent base for some time.

Following notification that Wing Commander T. Prickman (CO of RAF Kenley) would be taking over command of West Malling from Wing Commander R.W.K. Stevens, a message was received that the 34th LAA Battery, comprising an officer and thirty-seven men, would relieve 147 Battery LAA, whose strength was now one officer and fifty-seven men. No. 267 Battery 67th Anti-Tank Regiment moved out and was relieved by a Detachment of 2/5th Queen's Regiment – two officers and sixty other ranks. Some forty-two airmen comprised part of the newly formed ground defence crews at posts on the airfield. Owing to a shortage of NCOs, airmen were placed in charge of Army NCOs.

By 30 July 1940 the ongoing construction of a perimeter track around the airfield was causing a certain amount of inconvenience. The tarmac track had been cut about halfway round and on completion it was 50ft wide. On 3 August 1940, 'B' Flight of No. 26 Sqn, including its aircraft, were detached to Cambridge to assist No. 2 Sq. Both 'A' and C' Flights of No. 26 Sqn remained at West Malling. The same week a policy letter was received from Fighter Command and addressed to RAF Kenley confirming that it was not intended to use West Malling as a sector station, stating that it would remain a satellite airfield for Kenley and available as an advanced airfield for it and Biggin Hill.

The airfield was attacked on 10 August at 0730hrs, when a Ju 88 appeared out of cloud at 2,000ft and dropped fourteen bombs on the landing area. Seventeen workmen were injured by splinters and gun fire, and one later died. Three Royal Engineers were slightly wounded. The airmen's quarters, known as the Workhouse, was bombed and machine-gunned, with two aircraft of 'C' Flight damaged by splinters. Despite return gunfire, no enemy aircraft was hit and the Ju 88 climbed into cloud, heading off in an easterly direction. Events were recorded in the station diary:

> 10 August 1940
> Station attacked at 0730hrs. No warning of attack; aircraft emerged from thick cloud base at 800ft and did two runs entering cloud between each attack. Fourteen bombs dropped altogether on landing surface, among buildings of the new station caused superficial damage and many windows in buildings near completion were shattered. Seventeen workmen injured by splinters and machine gun fire; one of the workmen died later. One bomb fell on block of warehouse, injuring three RE sappers. Block extensively damaged by splinters and machine gun fire. Enemy aircraft attacked by Ground Defence Units Lewis Guns, 175 rounds fired from 4 posts but accuracy of fire doubtful. Bofors Guns were slow in getting into action and only fired a few rounds. Attack only lasted three minutes. Aircraft re-entered clouds after a final look round and proceeded in an easterly direction.

A further attack occurred on 15 August when thirty-eight enemy aircraft carried out a high-level bombing attack. New buildings were damaged and the airfield cratered. During the attack Corporal George Bage was reported missing and his body was found later; he had been killed in an explosion at 1900hrs. Bage was serving with No. 26 Sqn, was married and lived in Keswick in the Lake District. He was later buried at Harton Cemetery, South Tyneside, on 22 August 1940. Damage was caused to wooden buildings and an ambulance was written off. Erprobungsgruppe 210 had attacked Croydon in mistake for RAF Kenley and their Dorniers, which had also set out to bomb Biggin Hill, in fact attacked West Malling by mistake and as a new airfield it was not fully integrated as an operational part of the defences.

No. 2 Staffeln of KG 2's Dorniers crossed the coast to attack West Malling on 16 August at 1230hrs, and eighteen enemy aircraft dropped high explosives and incendiary bombs on the airfield. A workforce was still clearing rubble and filling in bomb craters when the bombers swept over the airfield from the north-east. Some eighty high-explosive and fragmentation bombs fell, and the airfield remained unserviceable for a few days. One aircraft of 'C' Flight was written off but there were no casualties. Work immediately started to repair the airfield. A further attack took place at 1325hrs the following day, when eight Ju 88s dive-bombed the airfield, releasing about thirty bombs. The attack was preceded by low-flying Me 109s. Two aircraft of 'A' Flight were destroyed by machine-gun fire, one 'C' Flight aircraft was destroyed, the airfield was cratered and a hangar roof was damaged.

The next day, 17 August, was quiet. The weather was perfect for flying, but there was no enemy activity monitored by radar or observation posts, giving RAF squadrons a day of well-needed respite. The Germans resumed their attacks on RAF airfields and radar stations in the south-east on 18 August.

The first wave of massed bombers and fighters crossed the coast at midday, coming in over Dover and going for the targets at Biggin Hill, Kenley, Croydon and later West Malling. During the attack on West Malling a Bf 109 arrived over the airfield, strafing anything that moved and damaging Lysander N1275, while another, N1306, was destroyed on the ground. There were no casualties, but further damage was done to new hangars. During the attack it was reported that at least two enemy aircraft were hit.

Enemy aircraft were heard in the vicinity of West Malling on 24 August. The airfield defences opened fire and two aircrew were seen to bail out of enemy aircraft, but no bombs were dropped. Unexploded bombs were located 400yd off the northern boundary of the airfield and quickly dealt with.

Remains of a Ju 88A of 6/KG76 possibly shot down by Sergeant P.C.P Barnes of No. 501 Sqn during a raid on West Malling on 18 August 1940. The Ju 88A crashed at Church Farm, Aylesford, at 0140hrs. (IWM HU73550)

A Spitfire pilot was reported to have bailed out at Lenham, landing safely, but he had been wounded during combat. At 1255hrs on 26 August 1940, fighters were scrambled to intercept a German bomber force bound for West Malling. Dornier Do 17Z 5K+ER of 7/KG3, was shot down and force-landed on rocks at Foreness Point, Isle of Thanet. Unteroffizier. K. Ramm was rescued from Herne Bay by a motorboat suffering from severe shock. Leutnant Karl Eggert (pilot) was mortally wounded and died two days later. Obergefreiter Knochenmuss was picked up dead. Both were buried at Margate cemetery.

On 27 August Flight Lieutenant Bryant was injured in a flying accident. Failing to pull out in time during a low-level dive bombing exercise, Lysander N1267 stalled and hit the ground at Nettleshead, near Maidstone. Despite enemy aircraft near West Malling the following day, there were no attacks and work commenced on four gun-pits for Hispano guns.

Flying Officer J.S. Bell joined the RAuxAF in early 1935 and at the time of the Battle of Britain was flying with No. 616 Sqn at Kenley. Bell destroyed a Bf 109 over Dunkirk on 1 June and was himself shot down into the sea and picked up by the Royal Navy. On 1 July 1940 he damaged an

Taken shortly after the war, this aerial view clearly shows many of the buildings still intact. Some of these were saved despite the development of the airfield. (KAHRS)

He 115 and He 111. On 30 August his luck ran out and he died after his aircraft was hit during a head-on attack on Bf 109s over West Malling. His Spitfire Mk.I, X4248, crashed on approach to the airfield.

On the morning of 2 September No. 26 Sqn received word that it was to move to RAF Gatwick, which was scheduled to take place on 3 September. Following a week of problems with telephone communications, service was eventually restored. Not long after, a surprise attack took place on 10 September, when a lone Dornier Do 17 made a run over the airfield at 1720hrs. With those on the ground caught completely unawares, the aircraft dropped six anti-personnel bombs. One of these scored a direct hit on personnel of the Queen's Regiment, killing six soldiers and wounding three, with one airman being injured after falling into a trench. Two temporary buildings were gutted by fire but any craters were quickly filled in by work parties. Throughout the next few days and nights enemy aircraft were heard and sometimes seen in the area, and airfield gun defences occasionally opened fire, but nothing was hit.

Jean Lambourne joined the WAAFs in 1940 and served for five years. She was eventually posted to RAF West Malling. She was surprised to find that she was one of five or six WAAF officers on the extremely busy base. Lambourne was responsible for the welfare and discipline of all airwomen. The officers were billeted at St Leonards, half a mile from the airfield, and used the main mess for all their meals. Despite the stress of war, the social life at West Malling was second to none. Jean was not short of escorts and on occasion brought pilots home on leave. At the time of her posting to West Malling, she remembers there was a mass of equipment and weaponry dispersed among surrounding plum and apple trees. Air Chief Marshal Sir Trafford Leigh-Mallory (C-in-C Allied Expeditionary Force) arrived to visit RAF West Malling in March.

On 11 September 1940, Pilot Officer John Mackenzie of No. 41 Sqn was involved in an attack on German bombers south of London. During the encounter he targeted an He 111 and, coming under fire from the tail gunner, he broke away, short of fuel, and at ground level headed for West Malling to refuel. Pilot Officer Eric Lock, who was also flying that day, saw the He 111 that had been hit by Mackenzie glide down and force-land at Hildenborough, 2 miles north-east of Tonbridge. By this time Lock was low on ammunition and landed at RAF West Malling to rearm.

Sgt Frank Usmar was born at West Malling on 16 September 1915, and he learned to fly at Maidstone Airport. During a patrol with No. 41 Sqn, Usmar found himself over the West Malling area on 27 September 1940, when his Spitfire, R6884, was hit during a surprise attack by an Me 109. With his aircraft on fire, and suffering a wounded leg and facial burns, he bailed out near West Malling. His parents, who lived in West Malling, later discovered they had watched their son being shot down and then bailing out from 20,000ft. Usmar's Spitfire crashed at Offham but he landed at Staplehurst, having drifted 20 miles from where he left his aircraft. Having been taken to Preston Hall Hospital, Maidstone, he was astounded to see fellow pilot Sergeant 'Birdie' Darling, who had crash-landed at West Malling in his Spitfire, X4409. Usmar did not return to flying duties until June 1941.

Following a successful combat with an Me 109 on 20 October, Flying Officer Peter Brown, flying Spitfire X4592, watched with fascination as the doomed aircraft commenced a dive. However, the German pilot had deceived his attacker and suddenly started to climb, but Brown managed to fire another burst at 100yd from astern and slightly below. The stricken Me 109 crashed near at Mereworth Wood at 1415hrs. The pilot, Feldwebel Bielmaier, bailed out and landed at Wrotham. Landing at West Malling, Brown was driven to the Bull Hotel, Wrotham. The German pilot, who had been put in the cellar, was introduced to him. Shaking hands, the pilot gave him his *schwimmweste* (Mae West) and his pilot's wings, and Brown returned later to Hornchurch with his souvenirs. In 1973, Alan Fall, of the Air Britain Excavation Committee, recovered the Daimler Benz engine and other items from the wreck site of Bf 109E-7 (5930) of 3/LG2 5/JG52, and many years later they were displayed at Lashenden Air Warfare Museum, at Headcorn airfield in Kent.

On 15 September 1940 the sky over Kent was criss-crossed with the vapour trails of hundreds of aircraft, both British and German, as Goring finally tried to neutralise the Royal Air Force. The RAF claimed 175 Germans shot down during the day, but post-war research indicated the actual figure was nearer fifty-seven. Sergeant Harry Cook of No. 66 Sqn, based at RAF Gravesend, got half a kill, although he didn't bother to put in a claim for it. Cook was on patrol over Kent when No. 66 Sqn Spitfires were fortunate enough to catch some unescorted Heinkel He 111s.

The Spitfire's normal role was to take on the Me 109s. 'One of the other pilots shot an engine out of one of the bombers and I went in and finished him off,' said Cook. 'The Heinkel crash-landed on West Malling airfield and I landed alongside, pinched the pilot's binoculars and took off again.' Trophy hunting such as this was one of the 'sports' of Fighter Command of the day, although Cook lost the binoculars at a later date.

Sub-Lieutenant Blake of No. 19 Sqn reported attacking 'a stray He 111 of II/KG53 that was being attacked by fighters'. These were Hurricanes flown by Squadron Leader Banham and Flight Lieutenant W. Smith of No. 229 Sqn. Smith reported that with his commander he went after a lone Heinkel being attacked by a Spitfire: 'From dead astern at 200 yards, closing to 150 yards. I saw bullets entering the fuselage and hitting the main plane. The port engine was smoking and brown oil from the Heinkel splashed over my windscreen.'

When Smith last saw it, the bomber was diving into cloud. During the attacks one of the Heinkel's gunners was killed and the radio operator was wounded. Oberleutnant Schirning heard the pilot shout that the port engine had also been hit and was losing power. There was a fire in the vicinity of the right engine and he was taking the bomber down for a crash-landing.

> I made my way back to my crash-landing position behind the pilot – unstrapped, the nose was no place to be for a crash landing. When I reached the position there was a bang and something behind me exploded, jarring my back.

We were under attack from fighters until the moment we touched down.

The Heinkel crash-landed near Staplehurst and slithered to a halt in a cloud of dust. When the burning plane came to a stop, the crew scrambled out and ran clear. Another Heinkel of Schirning's *geschwader*, also forced out of formation, came under attack from at least twelve Spitfires and Hurricanes from ten different squadrons.

With one crewman dead and three wounded, the German pilot attempted a wheels-down landing at West Malling at 1500hrs. Squadron Leader John Sample had a share in the demise of this bomber:

> I climbed up again to look for some more trouble and found it in the shape of a Heinkel 111 which was being attacked by three Hurricanes and a couple of Spitfires. I had a few cracks at the thing before it made a perfect landing at RAF West Malling. Then the Heinkel's undercarriage collapsed, and the pilot pulled up after skidding fifty yards in a cloud of dust.

The fighters continued their attacks on the bomber until it came to a halt, to the intense annoyance of RAF personnel on the ground. The station diarist afterwards noted: 'One enemy aircraft, an He 111, forced down on the aerodrome. Heavy firing from 8 or 9 Hurricanes and Spitfires made aerodrome unhealthy.' That particular Heinkel would be recorded at least seven times in the day's victory tally of enemy aircraft 'definitely destroyed', twice as 'probably destroyed' and twice more as enemy plane 'damaged'.

Earlier that day, Dornier bombers passed over West Malling, but despite the 3.7in anti-aircraft guns opening up on the airfield, no hits were recorded. Several pilots were involved in this combat: Flying Officer Lochnan, No. 1 Sqn RCAF; Sergeants Hunt and Parsons, No. 66 Sqn; Pilot Officers Hill and Mottram, No. 92 Sqn; Pilot Officers Bright and Simpson, No. 229 Sqn; Pilot Officer Stansfield, No. 242 Sqn; and Squadron Leader. J. Sample, No. 504 Sqn.

On the night of 17 September, Sergeant W.T. Chard (gunner) with Flight Sergeant G.L. Laurence (pilot), in Defiant L6988 of No. 141 Sqn, took off from West Malling on patrol. They were lucky that night and shot down a Ju 88A-1, which crashed at St Andrews Close, Tonbridge Road, killing all four crew and a Mrs Bridgland, the elderly occupant of house No. 1, which was gutted by fire. The Ju 88A-1 of 1/KG54, 'B3+OL', was part of a raid on

The remains of Ju 88A-1 of 1/KG54 Death's Head Geschwader shot down on 17 September 1940 by a Defiant of No. 141 Sqn flown by Sergeants Chard and Laurence. The aircraft crashed on No. 410 Tonbridge Road, Maidstone. (Kent Messenger)

London Docks, and broke up over West Malling, the main wreckage falling on Tonbridge Road at 1140hrs. The dead crew – Leutnant Rudolf Ganslmayr, Oberfeldwebel Willi Fachinger, Unteroffiziers Ernst Bauer and Karl Schlossler – were buried at Maidstone Cemetery, where they remain today. Items recovered from this aircraft such as a 7.92mm MG 15 machine gun are today on display at RAF Hawkinge Battle of Britain Museum. Photographs of Unteroffizier K. Schlossler were donated to the collection by his family.

A further attack occurred on 18 September, during which damage to buildings was sustained but no casualties were reported. Two days later, West Malling was informed by No. 11 Grp that a Spitfire squadron was likely to move into the airfield at very short notice. Billets were taken over at Mereworth Castle to accommodate 130 men to provide better dispersal and accommodation, and to relieve the situation at Kings Hill Institution huts there were used by SHQ (Station Headquarters). On 25 September, fifty men reported to form a servicing party, including NCOs, riggers, fitters and armourers. No. 99 Sportsman Cottages, just off the northern boundary of the airfield, provided billets for winter quarters for twenty of the party. Air raid alerts continued, and on 28 September several anti-personnel and

HYMN NUMBER BOARD FROM
ROYAL AIR FORCE STATION
WEST MALLING, CHAPEL

A hymn board can be found on display at Romney Marsh Wartime Museum that was once hung in the chapel at West Malling.

incendiary bombs were dropped in the vicinity of the station at 0040hrs. Three tents were destroyed in Orchard Camp site, an Army truck wrecked and two soldiers slightly injured.

As September came to an end, notification was received that No. 713 General Construction Company, Royal Engineers, would relieve No. 655 General Construction Company by 4 October 1940. October opened with several air raid alarms, and large formations of enemy fighters passed over West Malling during the day, with further enemy activity at night.

On 2 October further formations of fighters flew over the airfield during the day. One Me 109 was seen to go down about 5 miles south-west of the airfield with a Spitfire in hot pursuit. Twelve bombs were dropped short of the airfield at 1315hrs, although no damage was done. Wing Commander Prickman, RAF Kenley, and Squadron Leader Pritchard, No. 11 Grp, visited West Malling in response to complaints from night fighter pilots, who considered that the airfield was unsuitable for night flying owing to some trees on the south and east side of the airfield being a hazard. They were very soon cut down. During considerable enemy activity on Tuesday, 15 October, the Royal Oak public house at Wrotham Heath, Kent, was hit, with five civilians killed there and another four in the village.

No. 66 Sqn moved from Gravesend to West Malling on 30 October 1940. On arrival at his new home, Sergeant Jimmy Corbin tipped his Spitfire Mk.II on to its nose on landing, but he was uninjured. In his book, *Last of the Ten Fighter Boys*, Corbin recalls the incident:

> I had taken off from Gravesend in the morning to carry out a patrol and instead of returning to base I was told to continue to West Malling. Somehow I became separated from rest of the squadron and by the time I reached West Malling it was shrouded in darkness. Unbeknown to me, the airfield had been damaged in a raid with many bomb craters on the airfield. I eased the brakes of my Spitfire only for one of the Oleo legs to get stuck in a bomb hole that had been poorly filled. The leg wedged itself in the mud and acted as the axis while the rest of the Spitfire with me inside spun round it in fast tight circles. I thought having survived fierce dogfights I would die swirling round on the airfield in my Spit like a fairground attraction. I was ribbed for several weeks following the incident.

Shortly before a move to Biggin Hill, returning from a sortie over the Channel, Corbin suggested to the CO, 'Dizzy' Allen, that they could 'beat up' Maidstone. Dizzy was all for it, and the whole squadron in V formation reduced height, opened throttles and thundered over the rooftops at 300mph. As Corbin lived in Bower Street, Maidstone, he thought his family and other residents would think they were being attacked! It was unfortunate as Maidstone had recently suffered bombing, and he never admitted to his family that it was No. 66 Sqn that had flown low over the town.

The following day, Flight Lieutenant Christie's Spitfire tipped up on its nose on landing and also struck a repaired bomb crater on the airfield. In early November there was no flying owing to the waterlogged condition of the airfield. No. 66 Sqn occupied the watch office as operations room and HQ, and No. 421 Flight moved in using the HQ and civilian hangars for stores. Officers of No. 66 Sqn occupied the Hermitage, a large house at Lucks Hill, near West Malling, as their mess. By 31 October, 440 men were billeted at Kings Hill Institute, which was not very satisfactory for all concerned. Heavy rain added to problems as the airfield became almost unserviceable during the winter of 1940, however the bad weather did interfere with German raids in the area.

In early November the weather improved, although some Avro Ansons became bogged down on the south-east side of the airfield, and newly laid turf on the perimeter side was soggy. To enable aircraft to reach their pens, tracks were cut from the perimeter on harder parts of the airfield, but despite these improvements it was decided to move both Nos. 66 and 421 Flt out, and two Bofors guns also left the airfield. The CO of No. 66 Sqn reported that the landing ground was saturated and therefore unsuitable for its Spitfires. Continuous raids had meant many craters were filled in during dry weather, but these were now sinking and marked with flags. No. 66 Sqn moved to Biggin Hill on 6 November 1940, and the following day orders were received that a section from No. 421 Flt would also be moving to Biggin Hill.

Wellington N2767 of No. 99 Sqn, based at Newmarket, ditched into the sea on fire off Fairlight, Sussex, on 9 November. All six crew survived and they were brought to West Malling and soon returned to their base. Although the fuselage was recovered, the remaining wreckage was left where it crashed in 1940. Storms in January 2014 uncovered some remains, notably one of the main undercarriage tyres.

The landing area became so wet that an inspection of the airfield took place on 11 November, when it was suggested that tarmac could be laid. However, the Works Directorate insisted that the runway could be patched up and tracks laid across the boggy area. To add to the problems, communications were down due to the bombing. It was decided that a new Bitumastic preparation could be used, and it was agreed to lay two runways, each of 900 by 1,000yd. By the end of December 1940 the new runways had not been started but material was arriving and new drainage was being prepared. Drains running north-east–south-west were practically complete on the northern side of the airfield.

On 7 November 1941 representatives from the Air Ministry visited West Malling to site a Lorenz blind landing approach system. The system, developed by C. Lorenz AG Berlin, had first been installed in 1932 at Berlin-Templehof central airport, followed by Dübendorf in Switzerland in 1934 and others all over the world. Work finally commenced on the new runways on the morning of 15 January 1940, and Pickett Hamilton turrets were installed for airfield defence. Two local houses, Hamptons and Oxenhoath, were being considered for requisition for use by fighter squadrons, but both were already occupied by the Army, so negotiation took place at West Malling. On a routine cross-country flight, the Blenheim of Flight Lieutenant Henry of No. 2 SAC (School of Army Co-operation) crash-landed on the airfield in poor weather on 10 February 1941. The pilot failed to get the undercarriage down owing to failure of the lowering gear but he was not badly injured and his aircraft, L1234, was repaired to fly again.

On 20 February, Mr Herbert, the managing director of Frederick Leney & Sons Ltd, called in connection with the requisitioning of the Five Bells public house. The following day, Mr Thompson from Colonel Turner's office at the Air Ministry visited in connection with a proposed 'Q' Site (a lit dummy airfield to fool enemy bombers), the exact location to be determined. Mr Herbert was determined that permission should be given by the tenant, Mrs Baker, to vacate the property. The following day a twin-engine bomber crashed in flames at Grass Field, Paul's Farm, Leigh, and the crew were killed.

Pilot Sergeant Burtenshaw force-landed in Spitfire P7739 of No. 54 Sqn, Hornchurch, on 25 February. His aircraft had been damaged during combat.

An unusual aircraft arrived from Hawkinge on 9 March 1941, a Cierva C.30A Autogyro registration G-ACWM and with serial AP506. The Autogyro was flown by Flying Officer McLean and Pilot Officer Turner, serving with 529 Radar Calibration Flight, who were heading for RAF Detling but found themselves low on fuel. This aircraft had been pressed into service by the RAF in 1940 for radar calibration duties. Post-war, it went into storage for some twenty years in the rafters of a private garage near Tewkesbury before being rediscovered and purchased by Elfan Ap Rees. It is currently displayed in 'as found' condition alongside other C.30A memorabilia at the Helicopter Museum at Weston-super-Mare.

After a successful stay at RAF Biggin Hill, No. 264 Sqn moved to West Malling with its Bolton Paul Defiants on 14 April 1941. While on patrol that very day, Flying Officer Knocker and his gunner, Sergeant Hardie, made a successful parachute jump after RT failure.

Flight Lieutenant F.C. Sutton had served with flown with No. 111 Sqn at Gravesend and Biggin Hill between December 1940 and April 1941. He assumed the role of gunner for the CO, Squadron Leader A.T.P. Sanders, DFC, at West

Wing Commander S.C. Widdows, DFC, was the CO of No. 29 Sqn in July 1940 until he took over as CO at West Malling on 14 June 1941. (Colin Gass)

Malling, where in April 1941 he was appointed squadron gunnery officer to No. 264 Sqn, flying Defiants. In his diary he wrote:

> During the first week of April 1941, we learned to our great sorrow that we were moving a little further south to West Malling. We had had a really wonderful time at Biggin Hill and we were more upset over this move than we had been before! I had managed to arrange rooms for 'B' Flight and had even had their names neatly painted on little cards pinned to the doors. We were the only squadron on the Station for a few weeks, so there was a good room for everyone, and the boys soon settled down to the serious business of getting every ounce of enjoyment out of life. It seemed we had fallen on our feet again, for although we were further south than we had ever been before, it only took 50mins to reach West Malling from London by train.

It was not long before No. 264 Sqn was up to full strength and had a run of success, beginning in April 1941 and through to July 1941, by which time it had fourteen night-time kills. The victories then fell away as the German High Command turned its attention to Russia.

On 15 April 1941 Flying Officer W.R.A. Knocker and Flight Sergeant O.A. Hardie, flying Defiant N3369, had been hit by AA fire and their radio was put out of action. Completely lost, Knocker had flown around in circles trying to find somewhere to land, and when his fuel was getting low he headed south for the open country. He ordered Hardie, his gunner, to jump for it. Five minutes later he turned the Defiant on its back and took to the silk. Both landed without major injury and Hardie was astonished to find they were within 100yd of his uncle's home. The aircraft crashed in a coppice well away from habitation. They had abandoned their aircraft over Crowborough, East Sussex.

On 8 May alone, the squadron had two confirmed victories, He 111s for Hughes and Gash, and Squadron Leader Sanders and Pilot Officer Sutton, and three more damaged.

The following night, the top-scoring pairing of Sergeants Thorn and Barker opened their night-time account with an He 111 destroyed over Godalming. The squadron had also began flying intruder missions over northern France and on 8 May this paid off when Pilot Officers Curtice and Martin shot down one enemy aircraft and damaged another, and the following night Pilot Officer M.H. Young and Sergeant Russell shot down a Bf 110 night fighter over Merville. One of the squadron's most successful nights was 11 May as both Sanders and Sutton and Flight Lieutenant Stephenson and Pilot Officer Maggs shot down He 111 raiders, and Curtice and Martin shot down a Dornier Do 17 on another intruder mission.

On 16 May, Hughes and Gash yet again shot down a He 111, probably He 111P W/N 2801, which crashed on the South Downs near Worthing, and Flying Officer Barwell and Sergeant Martin destroyed a Ju 88 over Seaford, and then claimed a He 111 probable. On 23 May, the King awarded Squadron Leader Sanders the DFC.

On 16 June, Sanders took command of No. 264 Sqn at Hunsdon, taking over from Squadron Leader A.T.P. Sanders, DFC. The British Movietone News team visited West Malling to film, which was to be screened on 30 June 1941.

From 20 June the squadron's Defiants were deployed to Hunsdon for Turbinlite searchlight co-operation with Havoc aircraft. Lack of enemy action led to more training at the beginning of July 1941, such as air-firing practice and co-operation flights with other aircraft.

Pilots of No. 264 Sqn enjoying a break from operations at West Malling. Left to right: Sergeant W.L. 'Lou' Butler, DFC (RNZAF) with the squadron's mascot, unknown, and Sergeant F.J. 'Freddie' Barker, DFM and Bar (RAFVR). (Colin Gass)

The camaraderie in RAF squadrons was important, as this group of airmen of No. 264 Sqn testifies. Pilots and aircrew depended the hard work of ground crew in all weather conditions to keep the Defiants airworthy. (Colin Gass)

Gunners/navigators of No. 264 Sqn at West Malling. Note the gun turret of the Defiant, which is being worked on by one of the squadron's mechanics. (Colin Gass)

August was a quiet month, due again to poor weather, but on 31 August, Flying Officer Knocker and Flight Sergeant Hardie bailed out from Defiant T4049 at approximately 0130hrs. Both suffered leg fractures, although their condition was not serious. Flight Sergeant Hardy was particularly lucky as he bailed out, very low, at 800ft. At the beginning of September the squadron had to contend with 'teething' problems with the Defiant Mk.II, which were quickly sorted out. On 27 September the Secretary of State for Air, Sir Archibald Sinclair, visited the squadron. Following a visit to Boulton Paul, the manufacturers of the Defiant, Flight Lieutenant Scott, Engineer Officer, returned to base with representatives of the company, to smooth out problems with the Mk.IIs.

On 12 October, Pilot Officer Gray chased a Do 217, which later crash-landed, but it had not been fired at. The following day Flying Officer Martin was posted 'missing' while on leave during an unscheduled flight in a bomber. On 19 December several members of the squadron attended the presentation at Wolverhampton of a silver salver from Boulton Paul Aircraft Ltd, which Flight Lieutenant Thomas received on behalf of the squadron.

During the week of 25 April 1941, Wing Commander Charles Widdows, CO of No. 29 Sqn, and others visited West Malling in connection with

An unidentified pilot of No. 29 Sqn returns from another patrol during April 1941. The aircraft is a Beaufighter Mk.IF and is most probably coded RO-F. (Squadron Leader A. Moor)

the squadron's move to the airfield. On 27 April an advance party of the squadron arrived. No. 29 Sqn, equipped with Bristol Beaufighter Mk.IFs, had been based at RAF Wellingore, and 'A' Flight arrived on 30 April 1941. His Royal Highness the Duke of Kent arrived on 1 May 1941 to inspect the airfield and talk to officers and airmen. His visit was well received by all who had the opportunity to meet him.

Somewhere in woods at Tovil, Maidstone, is hidden a chapel, once covered in undergrowth until restored to commemorate the death of Wing Commander Guy P. Gibson VC, DSO and Bar, DFC and Bar. The chapel was constructed in 1935 by cutting into the rockface, and services including weddings were held there. On Gibson's death the 1st Tovil Scout troop lit candles at the site, a tradition that continued until the end of the war. A scout hut stood near the site in which could be found photos of Gibson, and a memorial cross stood at the front of the chapel entrance. Its restoration and that of the cross during the summer of 2004 was largely due to the efforts of local stone mason Gordon Newton and aviation historian Robin Brooks. Gibson was killed on 19 September 1944 flying Mosquito B.XX KB627 of No. 627 Sqn.

Gibson was ordered to report to No. 29 Sqn as the commander of 'A' Flight on 13 November 1940. The squadron was stationed at RAF Digby, but flew from a small satellite field at RAF Wellingore about 6 miles away. The officers' mess was nearby in The Grange. When he arrived the CO, Squadron Leader S.C. Widdows, later Wing Commander, was in the process of rebuilding the squadron following an outbreak of indiscipline that nearly led to its disbandment during July 1940. He was weeding out under-performing pilots and replacing his flight commanders.

Widdows had been educated at St Bartholomew's School, Newbury. He joined the RAF in 1925 as an aircraft apprentice, joining No. 1 School of Technical Training at RAF Halton. He was awarded a cadetship to the RAF College, which he represented at shooting, and attained the rank of flight cadet corporal. During his time at A & AEE in September 1937 he test flew the prototypes of the Hurricane and Spitfire.

Gibson attracted some hostility from some longer-standing members of the squadron because, as one of these new flight commanders, he was seen as part of Widdows's reforms and he had been chosen over an existing member of the squadron. He had also come from a bomber squadron. The root cause of the low morale was a lack of combat success. The Bristol Blenheim was not designed as a night fighter and the airborne interception (AI) radar was still in its very early days of development. Also, Widdows was required to split the squadron up with a few pilots each at Ternhill, Kirton and Wittering, and with no more than half at Digby at any one time. Gibson flew six operations in Blenheims.

The squadron started to convert to the Bristol Beaufighter Mk.IF and Widdows personally supervised his pilots during the process. Gibson's first flight in a Beaufighter was on 1 December 1940. He then undertook some intensive training on AI procedure. He found the night fighter culture very different from bombers as the two-man crew had to work as a team, with the pilot relying on the guidance of the AI operator to find their targets. Gibson made his first operational flight in a Beaufighter on 10 December with Sergeant Taylor as his AI operator. That winter saw bad weather and he flew only three operations in the whole of January. He claimed a kill on 12 March, but it was not confirmed. However, his kill on 14 March was confirmed as an He 111. He went to Skegness to collect the tail assembly as a trophy for the squadron and the crew's dinghy for himself. He was attacked by an intruder when landing at Wellingore on 8 April. Gibson was unharmed, but his AI operator, Sergeant Bell, was injured in the leg.

Donald Wiseman had been promoted to flight lieutenant and posted to Gravesend, where the Air Ministry had decided to form the first night fighter wing and base. The Blenheim had not yet been replaced by the Bristol Beaufighter and had a primitive AI radar set held in place with straps and string! Following a brief spell as intelligence officer at Biggin Hill, he was posted as senior intelligence officer at West Malling 1941, which was being developed as the first night fighter airfield under Wing Commander Widdows. In his book, *Life Above and Below*, he wrote:

> I took over the first floor of the Control Tower as my office. To furnish it I took a 15cwt truck with a note from Wing Commander McNeil to the Stationary Office in Kingsway and came back loaded with furniture and supplies which were to last a few years. Life was busy and we were a happy team with three Officers, P/O Hackett of 29 Squadron and P/O John Stevens of 264 Squadron and P/O John Walford waiting for a replacement. John was restless as he was scheduled to go on a flying course. Not long afterwards he was killed in action. From the word go our lives were hectic. West Malling served as an emergency landing ground for damaged bombers landing back from Europe.
>
> All crews had to be debriefed, often late at night, and we received aircraft of every kind since this forward base

served for many emergency landings over a 24hr period. We had to climb some twenty feet up to rescue the crew of our 29 Squadron's Beaufighter which had undershot coming to rest amid the tangled branches of the trees which lined the periphery of our airfield. Another had landed too heavily, damaging its undercarriage and blocking the runway. Soon after dawn one day, three Spitfires landed, one of which, grazed by the wing-tip of another, came to a sudden halt, the pilot dead. Then not long after a badly shot up Spitfire taxied up to the Control Tower and I went to investigate as we had to make an intelligence report of any such incident. The furious Polish Sergeant pilot of 303 Polish Squadron based at RAF Northolt complained that his glycol tank had been pierced and demanded an on the spot repair, so he could take off again. With the danger of fire I tried to pull rank and ordered him to abandon the aircraft. However, when I turned my back he made a swift take off, saying he was going to get his own back on the 'damned Germans'.

One evening we were visited by the BBC and questioned by Alan Whitaker. He was intrigued by the Defiant sorties on the newly planned Intruder sorties during which they had attacked German airfields in the Pas de Calais. They had caused a German bomber to crash on the runway, thus putting an end to flying for the night. Another Defiant had switched its lights on and flown in the circuit with the homecoming foe at another airfield. With its versatile turret it had shot down another aircraft and all the Luftwaffe bombers attacked as they were not experienced night flyers, and were then diverted to another zone, some crashing low on fuel.

The BBC put out a vivid account the next evening and our activities became a morale booster for the nation. Once with F/O Miles of 29 Squadron we fired at a suspected Ju 88 but were then nearly shot down by our own AA barrage at Dover. Hoping to land at West Malling, we were delayed as Control were trying to bring in a damaged Wellington. As we circled in the gathering poor visibility we unknowingly drifted north-west. Radar plots showed that we had passed through or over the balloon barrage which shielded the capital. Low on fuel, we asked for the flare-path lights to be switched on as soon as we flashed our landing lamps.

As we did this I could not recognise the characteristics of the Malling approaches, so on landing told the pilot to keep his engines running and turn into the wind while I investigated. I saw what I thought was an Me 109, I sheltered behind it until a fire tender roared up. In the light of its searchlight I saw that the aircraft was in fact a Hurricane! We had landed at RAF Debden. 'Why it's dear old Wisecrack', the nickname often used of me, said an approaching officer. I had been recognised by a fellow Intelligence Officer.

Colonel and Mrs Sterndale Bennett allowed us the use of their swimming pool not far from the perimeter of the airfield at West Malling and we often went down the hill to the Vicarage at West Malling where the Rev. Jim Walkey lived. He had the pre-war RAF Chaplain-in-Chief and knew my father. I occasionally played the organ at the Sunday Service with the help of the Vicar's two daughters pumping the bellows. With many hours of night flying and experiences behind me including details of enemy beacons, and of successful night intruder operations, I thought it time to write another Intelligence Report. This was sent to 11 Group Fighter Command, and I was summoned to a meeting and quizzed about my source for my observations. Some details in my report mirrored the information otherwise only known from Ultra Secret Enigma. I was immediately posted to HQ Fighter Command, Bentley Priory.

RAF personnel often adopted a particular public house not far from their airfield. In the case of Biggin Hill, for instance, it was the White Hart; Hawkinge, the Cat and Mustard Pot. Both these pubs survived and are still popular today. Sadly, at West Malling, St Leonards Cross, the Startled Saint, the most popular location for a social evening and a few drinks, is today a private house. In *Enemy Coast Ahead*, first published in 1946, Guy Gibson recalls his time in Kent:

> Then there were the trees, green, impassive and tall, miles of them. It takes more than a bomb to shift trees, and these had been here for hundreds of years and meant to stay. Green trees, fields of green, green England. A lovely sight. We were glad, as we roared over the 'drome' in a tight box formation, pleased to be at West Malling. That night we stood by, but the

weather was bad and Group released the squadron at about 2100hrs. Down to 'The Startled Saint' we went, complete with our groundcrews, to sample the beer, it was good and everyone was happy.

The pub was named after St Leonard, who, legend has it, slayed a dragon at Horsham Wood. Work started on its construction in January 1940, being completed by September that year. The artist Violet Rutter designed and painted the unusual pub sign. Another pub was built at Wateringbury, this being the Duke Without a Head, and both were licensed to Whitbread and designed by the same architect. A naming ceremony took place at the Startled Saint on 16 December 1940, and was opened a few months before the 'Duke'. It is said that the entertainer Max Bygraves, who served in the RAF, cut his teeth at the Startled Saint and was based at West Malling. He also served at RAF Lympne, near Hythe. The original design for the sign depicted in the bottom right-hand corner was a hooded and startled saint facing a Spitfire diving down towards him from the top left-hand corner, but was not adopted. During the war the landlord, Mr Baker, was killed in action and his wife, Alice, took over the tenancy and carried on for many years. RAF police dog handlers were frequent visitors and if a dog was retired he was first offered to Alice as a pet. As this is still quite a remote spot, a

The much loved Startled Saint, sadly no longer a pub, was a place where men and women of the RAF and other services spent many happy hours during the war.

Designed by Violet Rutter for Whitbread, the Startled Saint pub sign cannot be seen today, but for those who collect the miniature Whitbread signs, is still sought after. Today another pub can be found on the Kings Hill Business Park, and this was opened by Air Chief Marshal Sir Christopher Foxley Norris in 2001, himself a decorated pilot and one-time CO of RAF West Malling.

THE STARTLED SAINT
West Malling

steady stream of ex-police dogs would be quite a comfort. The pub closed in 1993 and was sold by Whitbread. The 'Duke' did not survive and was demolished.

In April 1941, Widdows obtained a transfer of the squadron from No. 12 to 11 Grp and a move to West Malling. Gibson flew down with him on 25 April to inspect the facilities and the full squadron flew down on 29 April. Gibson was promoted to acting squadron leader towards the end of June 1941 and started to deputise for the commander in his absence. Widdows took over command of RAF West Malling from Wing Commander A.M. Wilkinson DSO on 14 June 1941. He was replaced by Wing Commander Edward Colbeck-Welch.

The London Gazette wrote of him on 4 April 1941:

> This officer has commanded the squadron since July, 1940, and under difficult circumstances, has maintained a high morale among the personnel. Wing Commander Widdows has carried out a large number of difficult patrols in bad weather and has shown extreme keenness to engage the enemy. He has flown a considerable number of hours of operational flying at night, and succeeded in destroying a Junkers 88 one night in March, 1941.

Sergeant E.R. Thorn. DFC and Bar, DFM and Bar and Sergeant F. Barker, DFM and Bar, with their Defiant. Together they destroyed twelve enemy aircraft. Thorn, who later became a squadron leader, was killed on 15 February 1946. (Colin Gass)

Flying Officer J.R.A. Bailey No. 264 Sqn, about to climb into his Defiant Mk.II, while a member of his groundcrew stand by to assist. Bailey, with his gunner, Sergeant O.A. Hardie, earned the distinction of shooting down a He 111 on his first operation with No. 264 Sqn. Bailey was posted to the squadron from the Havoc flight at West Malling on 21 July 1941. (Colin Gass)

Gibson claimed two more kills, which were confirmed. Another unidentified bomber, possibly a Heinkel, was claimed to have been in flames on 3/4 May. On 6 July he downed a Heinkel He 111H-5 of 8/KG4 near Sheerness. His AI operator on all his successful claims was Sergeant R.H. James, who was awarded a DFC. However, the Luftwaffe's bombing offensive was tailing off and Gibson started to get bored by the relative safety, beginning to describe missions as 'stooge patrols' in his log book. He made some further interceptions but on each occasion his guns or cannons failed. He was also concerned by his relative lack of success compared with his fellow flight commander, Bob Braham. Gibson seems to have been happy at West Malling and said: 'Of all the airfields in Great Britain, here, many say, including myself, we have the most pleasant.' His final patrols with the squadron were flown on 15 December and he left with both flying and gunnery ratings of above average. He was awarded a Bar to his DFC.

On a bright moonlit night on 6 May 1941, seven patrols were flown by No. 29 Sqn, three operating for the first time with control at RAF Kenley. Pilot Officer Freer, with the aid of AI and GCI in RAF Biggin Hill sector, saw and fired at a Ju 88 off North Foreland, but was unsuccessful. Wing Commander Widdows, in Beaufighter Mk.IF R2260, made contact with a Ju 88 off Beachy Head. He fired and saw the starboard engine was burning. Return fire from the Ju 88 damaged his aircraft and Widdows was hit in the leg. The navigator, Sergeant Ryall, bailed out and was killed.

Remains of a Heinkel 111 of 2/KG27 shot down by Flying Officer Braham and Sergeant Ross of No. 29 Sqn. The aircraft crashed at Wimbledon Common on 9 May 1941; the crew were killed. (IWM HU73231)

Civilian contractors load the remains of a Heinkel 111 of 2/KG27 on to a truck to be taken to a salvage unit and scrap yard, a frequent occurrence in Kent and Sussex during the war years. (IWM HU73232)

On 9 May, Pilot Officer Braham intercepted an He 111, which he shot down and it crashed near Richmond, London. Pilot Officer Lovell also successfully shot down a Ju 88 into the sea off Ramsgate the same day.

Several patrols were flown on 10 May, during which Pilot Officer Grout shot down a Ju 88 off Beachy Head. He was vectored on to another Ju 88 and attacked, badly damaging it.

Sadly, Beaufighter Mk.IF R2245 crashed on landing, killing Pilot Officer P.F. Freer and Sergeant V.J. Wingfield. Such crashes were often caused by bad weather, although it is thought that R2245 had been damaged by return fire from a German bomber. Widdows could not risk sending the fire and rescue vehicles to such incidents, leaving the airfield unattended, as the crew had obviously died. Despite this, he personally visited the crash of R2245, and it was particularly sad for him as he remembered training the young pilot lying badly burnt in the wreckage.

The day after a visit to the airfield by No. 513 Sqn ATC on 18 June 1941, a Beaufighter Mk.IF of No. 29 Sqn, serial R2262, crashed while carrying out a forced landing at Champions Orchard, Mereworth, not far from the airfield at 1730hrs. Flying Officer Lovell was injured and Flight Sergeant Lilley seriously injured.

Pilot Officer French and Sergeant Hogg were lining up to land on 22 June 1941 when they suffered an engine failure. Beaufighter Mk.IF R2245 cartwheeled in the forced landing and crashed, bursting into flames at Dickens Street, East Farleigh. Despite fire crews efforts' they could not save those onboard.

Two other squadron members, Pilot Officer Parrott and his AI operator, Sergeant Booth, were killed on 22 June when they crashed just short of the airfield. They had taken off from West Malling at 2345hrs on night patrol. One of the engines had cut out and their Beaufighter, R2240, cartwheeled on landing, crashing at Dickens Street, East Farleigh. It would appear that the aircraft had banked steeply to avoid an oast house and the wing dropped.

Despite several successful interceptions during May and June, everyone was feeling the loss of two exceptional crews. June continued with many night operations and Squadron Leader G. Gibson and Flight Lieutenant Braham both destroyed an He 111 and Ju 88.

Yet another accident occurred on the night of 21 July when Pilot Officer Grout and Sergeant Patterson were killed when their Beaufighter, R2141, crashed in woods near Marden, Kent, twenty minutes after take-off. It was believed that Grout had mistaken nearby railway lights for those of West Malling. The aircraft burst into flames and burnt out.

Night patrols continued at a pace throughout June, July and August, and several practice flights were undertaken with ground-controlled interception (GCI) in Willesborough, Ashford, but few contacts were made. Occasionally, contacts turned out to be friendly aircraft and these usually fired a flare to ensure they were not fired on, but in reality there were occasions when pilots were trigger happy. On one occasion in 1941, Flight Lieutenant Bob

Wing Commander G. Gibson DFC, and Bar, VC, who served with No. 29 Sqn at West Malling during 1941. His final patrols with No. 29 Sqn were flown on 15 December 1941, and he then joined No. 51 OTU at Cranfield.

Braham, Flying Officer Miles and Sergeant Hall, flying Beaufighter Mk.IF R3355, had established contact with an enemy aircraft and opened fire. The aircraft returned fire and the aircraft turned away. At this point Braham was horrified to see he had fired at a Wellington, and immediately broke off combat, a near miss.

Flight Sergeant C. Webb and Sergeant J. Mathers of No. 29 Sqn, flying Beaufighter Mk.I X7564 in July, were practising slowing the speed of their aircraft by lowering the undercarriage, an approved method. Webb inadvertently caused the flaps to be lowered at a speed of 20 miles in excess of that permitted by Bristol Aircraft Company, and failure occurred. As a result, the aircraft flicked over onto its back, stalled and subsequently spun in. From a height of 10,000ft, the Beaufighter crashed near RAF Detling. Selecting 'flaps recorded down' instead of 'undercarriage down', Webb later stated that he was thrown violently forward and the aircraft flicked over on its back, rolling to the left. The crew, had bailed out and survived to tell their story in the mess at West Malling that night.

Flying Officer Miles and Sergeant Hall lost their lives when Beaufighter Mk.IF T3355, on patrol over Sussex on 7 October 1941, flew into high

No. 29 Sqn at RAF West Malling during December 1941. The author's uncle, Flight Sergeant A. Moor, or 'Dinty', as he was known, is standing, middle row sixth from left. Wing Commander Colbeck-Welch, CO, Squadron Leader G. Gibson and Flight Lieutenant J.R.D. Braham are seated front row centre. Flight Sergeant A. Moor served an apprenticeship at RAF Halton, later joining No. 25 Sqn at RAF Hawkinge in the 1930s. (P. Hall)

A Beaufighter Mk.IF of No. 29 Sqn, with which the unit was equipped on arrival at West Malling on 21 April 1941. It had been based at Wellingore since 27 July 1940. Note the open cockpit.

ground at Westfield Sole. They had left formation and dived steeply. The crew were reported as saying they were over an airfield and were going to land.

Pilot Officer R.M. Carr and Sergeant Whitby in Beaufighter Mk.IF X2196 had a lucky escape on 1 November. Carr had taken off on a routine air test but on coming into land the starboard wheel would not come down, and every attempt to release it had no effect. He made an excellent belly landing, only damaging the Beaufighter slightly. There were only two patrols flown on 21 November, during which the weather deteriorated and became very foggy. Sergeant Wilson and Sergeant Miller were killed when Beaufighter Mk.IF R2183 flew into high ground at Boxley Grange, Kent.

No. 4 Works Sqn was formed at West Drayton on 24 March 1941 under the command of Squadron Leader E.J. Fawdry. During April, ten works flights, which made up the squadron, began to form on various RAF airfields in Kent, Surrey and Sussex. The flights were all well trained in

YEAR 1941		AIRCRAFT		PILOT, OR	2ND PILOT, PUPIL	DUTY
MONTH	DATE	Type	No.	1ST PILOT	OR PASSENGER	(INCLUDING RESULTS AND REMARKS)
—	—	—	—	—	—	— Totals Brought Forward
May.	19	BEAU	2250	SELF	SGT MOSS	N/F TEST.
..	20	..	..	..	..	WEATHER TEST.
..	21	..	..	..	F/SGT LAMEY.	To BOXOMBE/RETURN SAW THE NEW MO - 0. LOOKS GOOD.
..	22	..	..	..	SGT FREEMAN.	AI PRACTICE.
..	23	..	..	..	SGT FREEMAN.	G.C.I. WITH SOME CONMOTION
..	23	..	..	..		ON GUARD. BMO.
..	23	..	..	..	P/O WILLIS	X RAID. RETURNED.
..	24	..	..	..	L.A.C CORREL.	AIR FIRING INTO SEA. OK.
..	25	..	..	..	L.AC KEENAN.	To SUTTON B. (WITH HANGOVER)
..	25	..	..	..	..	AIR FIRING ON CONE.
..	25	..	..	..	..	FROM SUTTON B.
..	27	MAG.	8239	..	SOLO	To DETLING TO SEE DENTIST AND RETURN.
..	28	BEAU	2250	..	SGT SAMES.	G.C.I. AI.
..	28	..	..	..	..	N/F TEST.
..	29	..	..	..	..	AI HOMINGS.
..	31	MAG.	8279	..	SGT. MOOR.	COBWEBS FLYING!

On 31 May 1941, Sergeant A. Moor, later a squadron leader, took off in Beaufighter Mk.IF R8279 with Wing Commander G.P Gibson, who flew with No. 29 Sqn during this period. Gibson's log book was produced as a facsimile by *After the Battle Magazine* in 1976.

a special 'blitz drill' and were organised for the rapid repair of damaged airfields, in particular damage to runways, perimeter tracks and drainage. Repairs were carried out using material that had been stockpiled around the airfield for the purpose. In the early days there was a shortage of plant and plant operators, but in spite of this many rapid repairs were carried out. In some cases the repair personnel came under machine-gun fire from German bombers.

In quiet periods the flights were employed on other tasks such as digging slit trenches, building shelters, various sand bag protective tasks and so on. In September and October the squadron laid areas of Sommerfeld track as landing mats at West Malling, Manston and elsewhere. Other work was undertaken, including the construction of aircraft pens.

No. 74 (Trinidad) 'Tiger' Sqn had been based at Gravesend from 30 April 1941. On 11 May, some of its aircraft were operating from West Malling. Flying Officer Roger Boulding was one of the pilots on detachment flying Spitfire IIA P8380 'ZP-Q' *Black Velvet*, a presentation Spitfire. He was in the company of Squadron Leader Mungo-Park DFC, Flight Lieutenant John Freeborn DFC, Pilot Officer Bob Poulton and Sergeant Tony Mould. Flying in the vicinity of London at night, he attacked a Heinkel He 111H-5.

The Heinkel He 111 of 5/KG53 A1+JN at Kennington, Ashford, which Flying Officer Roger Boulding, No. 74 Sqn, shot down flying Spitfire Mk.IIa P8380 'ZP-Q' *Black Velvet* on 11 May 1941. Avoiding the houses in Kennington, Hauptmann. A. Hufenreuter, brought the bomber to rest behind houses in Church Road. The area looks much the same as it did in 1941. (D.G. Collyer)

Intelligence officers and a salvage team inspect the Heinkel He 111 at Kennington, prior to it being loaded onto a vehicle and transported to RAE Farnborough. (A.E. Wright)

Night fighting was still in its infancy, and the Spitfire was not suited to this new role as the glow from the two rows of exhausts of the Merlin impaired the pilot's vision. On the Hurricane night fighters a horizontal metal plate had been fitted just in front and below the cockpit to obscure the glow but it would appear this modification was not carried out on the Spitfire. The narrow undercarriage of the Spitfire also caused problems for the pilot landing at night. The Heinkel of 5/KG53, A1+JN, was flown by Hauptmann A. Hufenreuter, Feldwebel R. Futhrthmann, Unteroffizier K. Gerhardt, Unteroffizier J. Berbach and Gefreiter E. Weber. It was purely by chance that Flying Officer Boulding intercepted the German intruder as 'Knockout 17', as he was known to the controller that night, had experienced air screw pitch control and turned for home.

Descending to 17,000ft on an easterly direction, he noticed a twin-engine bomber at the same height, 200yd to his starboard side. Approaching from behind and below, he was now sure of the aircraft's identity. With the target in his gunsight, he opened fire at close range. Caught in a hail of bullets, the pilot, Hufenreuter, decided to fly nearer the ground. Flying Officer Boulding recalls the chase:

We carried on like this until he was indulging in some quite fancy low flying across Kent. I don't think that I hit him again. Eventually I lost sight of him so I circled the area and obtained a radio fix from base, which established where I was, and I returned to West Malling. There we found signs of minor damage to my Spitfire, such as to the oil cooler debris guard, indicating that I had flown into small pieces of wreckage. When the position of the radio fix coincided with the discovery of the Heinkel on the ground, it was credited to me. The rest of the squadron had droned around all night and seen absolutely nothing!

The bomber crash-landed at Kennington, Ashford, Kent, in a recreation field close to houses and near to what is today the Collingbrook Hotel. The crew were all taken as prisoners of war. In 1978, Hufenreuter, by then a retired teacher, returned to Kennington to find the sight of the crash. During the visit he met several eye witnesses to the event, one of whom was a Mr Field. The Heinkel had belly-landed behind his house, at the rear of Church Road, which still stands today. Boulding was himself shot down on 17 June 1941 by Me 109s while flying Spitfire Mk.II W3251. He became a PoW. It is interesting to note that the radio mast from the He 111 is displayed at the Kent Battle of Britain Museum at Hawkinge, near Folkestone, and certain other items are in private collections.

Joyce Ethel Granger (nee Wycherley) joined the WAAF in 1941 and was posted to RAF West Malling, having been trained as a telephonist:

> Like any of life's journeys we take, we start at the beginning and try to remember as much as possible, sometimes our memories play tricks on us. Anyway here I am, I'm 17½ years of age, a hairdresser's apprentice. The war is on and not going very well for us. My then boyfriend was in the RAF and I thought I wanted to become a WAAF. My parents were very much against it and my boyfriend also, but at 17½ years of age that was what I wanted to do. We had no fears and really thought we would change the world. I was very spoilt as a child and no one would change me. However came the day in 1941, I arrived at Innsworth Lane, RAF; it was such a shock! But the next day there I was resplendent in my WAAF uniform, so proud! ACW2, the lowest of the low, I remember the first time

I put my uniform on and polished the buttons, they did shine! Our issue was two uniforms, shoes, Lyle stockings, gas mask, our irons (knife, fork, spoon), beaker, ground sheet, overcoat (mac), gloves and hat (which blew up when it was windy!).

Six weeks on, square bashing began, how to fold your bed and make it 'service style'. I was always worried that my feet would hurt with the heavy shoes, but surprise, surprise, they were comfortable. Came the day of posting then to our various stations, I decided I would like to be in signals, my boyfriend was, and he must have thought I'd be OK and so, up to London first, and then they sent me to be taught how to be a telephonist by the GPO. I was then posted to West Malling in Kent, No. 11 Group under the umbrella of RAF Biggin Hill, it was a night fighter station. The Battle of Britain had just finished but the station was a considerable mess. Life began to settle down, on duty, coming off, sleeping. They said the only time we service personnel had any free time was from 2359 hours to 0001hrs, but life was how you made it, I still have a WAAF friend from West Malling days, and that friendship will continue till one of us dies.

The cinema and tea dances were the thing to do in off-duty periods, so into Maidstone we would go, but there was one night a week, if you weren't on duty, you had to clean your bed space and do your chores. Coming home on leave for the first time was so memorable, feeling so important in my uniform and I know my parents were proud of me. My boyfriend was in India by then. But going back was an ordeal, I had two miles to walk from the station to the camp and mustn't be late, otherwise you were on a charge. I was only in trouble once and that was for wearing my stockings inside out. The military police stopped me and I had to go before the CO, who was Peter Townsend. Unfortunately I was caught again and for my pains, I had to do 7 days CB. I had the cooks' toilets to clean when I was off duty – silly girl! I just thought they looked finer inside out! In 1944 I was posted to Bushey Park for 6 weeks with the Americans. We were so envious of the American girls in their uniforms, which were just like our officers; silk stockings, silk underwear. We shared the telephone switchboard with them and shared their food, no shortage there I can tell you.

General Eisenhower was the overall CO and I can honestly say I spoke to him (Just to say 'number please'). Back to West Malling for a time and lots happening. I also remember we had to 'man' a single position in flying control and could have lots of dog fights over the channel. Quietness was when it was foggy (no flying). Another famous flyer at West Malling was 'Cats eye' Cunningham. The Allies by now were getting the better of the Germans, but of course on came the 'Buzz Bombs'. I was posted again for the last time, to Stanmore Fighter Command Headquarters.

No. 19 Sqn arrived at West Malling on 21 May 1941, joining Nos. 310 and 266 Sqn to take part in a large offensive operation by Bomber Command. Several other fighter squadrons were involved. The role of the squadron was to patrol with Nos. 310 and 266 Sqn over the south-east area of England, at 20,000ft, to protect the bomber squadrons, which raided two areas in enemy-occupied France, from German fighters, should they pursue the Blenheims as far as the English coast and beyond. However, the Luftwaffe was not so ambitious. The operation as a whole was a success.

At 1955 hours on 17 June 1941, the squadron took off from West Malling to patrol the Manston–Dover–Hawkinge area in support of No. 11 Grp, which was co-operating with Bomber Command in an offensive operation over enemy-occupied France. Although bandits were reported in the area, none were seen and the squadron landed back at Fowlmere two hours later.

No. 19 Sqn took off from West Malling at 1150 hours on 21 June 1941, while squadrons of No. 11 Grp acted as close escort to a small force of bombers on an offensive operation against an objective near Saint-Omer. The squadron, together with Nos. 266 and 65 Sqn, patrolled just out to sea off Mardyck to cover the bombers' retreat. They patrolled at 15,000 to 18,000ft and the Blenheims returned unmolested, and although a message was received of enemy aircraft approaching, none were seen. However, as the squadron approached the east coast coming back, there were numerous reports of enemy aircraft near Deal. They were down to 6,000 to 8,000ft but no enemy aircraft were sighted. After about fifty minutes the squadron was ordered to return, although some aircraft had landed at other airfields when they became low on fuel.

Two days later, eleven aircraft took off from West Malling at 1305hrs to patrol Le Touquet–Boulogne at 18,000ft. Squadron Leader Dutton took off late owing to starter trouble and joined up with the squadron at 1345hrs. At 1355hrs, 5 miles west of Le Touquet at 17,000ft, two Me 109s dived down through the squadron formation, fired at them and dived away. Squadron Leader Dutton managed to fire at one Me 109 and claimed it as damaged.

Pilot Officer G.W. Scott did not see the Me 109s until he was hit on his starboard aileron by a shell. He broke away sharply to the left and as he did so was hit by a second burst on the tail unit. He went into a partial spin and the enemy aircraft passed underneath him. Scott gave him a five-second burst from dead astern but the enemy aircraft was travelling very fast and was soon out of range.

During the evening of 23 June 1941, Nos. 19, 65 and 222 Sqn arrived to refuel, prior to operations over France. This was followed by further sweeps by them, including No. 65 Sqn. Sadly, Sergeant R.G. Howe was killed when two Spitfires of No. 65 Sqn collided on 26 June. Howe was flying P8065, but the squadron records do not record the other aircraft's details, and other reports state he collided with an Me 109F during combat and was killed while crash-landing at West Malling.

On the next day twelve Spitfires of No. 19 Sqn took off from West Malling at 1612hrs with No. 266 and 65 Sqn. They were to patrol the Hardelot–Saint-Omer–Gravelines area at 20,000ft. A formation of twelve Me 109s was encountered. Several of these enemy aircraft dived on Pilot Officer Tucker (Yellow 2). Sergeant Kosina (White 2) turned towards the twelve Me 109s above him when he saw two below him. He dived, firing at the leading Me 109 from astern and slightly above, closing to 200yd with two short bursts. He saw his bullets hitting the fuselage and cockpit. The enemy aircraft turned on its back and spiralled slowly down. He followed it down to 7,000ft, where he left it still diving steeply and spiralling slowly. Pilot Officers Scott (Green 1) and Andrews (Green 2) became separated from the squadron. Pilot Officer Scott saw a Spitfire diving in flames and the pilot bailing out. He engaged three Me 109s but without any visible results. He attacked another three, one of which dived away after being hit by a short burst at 250yd and was not seen again. He evaded the other two, which had chased him to the French coast. Pilot Officer Andrews (P7379) was shot down by an Me 109.

In the late evening a patrol of ten Spitfires was over the same area flown by the same squadrons, Nos. 19, 266 and 65. The enemy were encountered at 2140hrs. Heavy and accurate flak was experienced and the red bursts attracted five or six Me 109s in line astern. No. 19 Sqn was led by Flight Lieutenant Lawson in loose formation. He did a climbing quarter attack at the rear enemy aircraft, which pulled up and stalled. Glycol vapour poured from under its wings and the enemy aircraft went into a spiral dive. After 1,000ft smoke and flames spurted from the fuselage and the dive became steeper. The aircraft disappeared into the haze, diving vertically and on fire. Flight Lieutenant Lawson found himself alone after the combat but not for long – six Me 109Fs were climbing very fast in his direction. He turned towards them, delivering a diving attack at the rear machine and opening fire from slightly above at 200yd. The Me 109F fell over onto its starboard wing and went into a dive with glycol vapour streaming from its right wing root. Lawson did not observe anything else as he was attacked by the remaining five Me 109s. He thought discretion the better part of valour and took no action, returning to West Malling.

Pilot Officer Vokes (Yellow 1) was climbing to 24,000ft when he saw an Me 109F attacking a Spitfire. The enemy aircraft saw him, dived and attacked. Three times the enemy managed to attack him but the German was not allowing for deflection. The Me 109F pilot made a third attack, slower this time, and this allowed Vokes to turn on him. Vokes, his trail of bullets converging on the enemy aircraft, followed him down to 12,000ft, where he was lost in a vertical dive in haze.

Sergeant Plzak (White 1) delivered a stern attack on an Me 109, firing two short and long bursts. He saw his bullets hitting the enemy aircraft on the engine and fuselage. Smoke came from the engine and the enemy aircraft turned on its back and dived slowly into haze. Sergeant Cox (Green 2) got behind four Me 109s and attacked the rear one, giving two second bursts as he closed to 150yd. Flames came from below and behind the pilot of the enemy aircraft, which turned over and went down vertically in flames. He was about to turn away, when he saw what he thought were eight Spitfires. He was surprised to see four streams of tracers pass him on his left and his Spitfire, P8460, was then hit in the glycol tank and wing. Cox's engine failed and he glided home and crash-landed 2 miles south-west of Lydd. Pilot Officer Cowley in Spitfire P7813, reported missing, was later confirmed as killed in action.

Early experiments were made on searchlights in aircraft in the First World War using a filament lamp rated at 3kW. In 1940 a further investigation was made on the possible use of high-power airborne searchlights but the matter was apparently dropped. In October 1940 the Research Laboratories of the General Electric Company of England were approached by the late Air Commodore W. Helmore of the Ministry of Aircraft Production and asked to co-operate in a new development, which included the concept of an illuminating aircraft operating with separate fighters.

This was the birth of the Turbinlite, although it was originally called Air Target Illumination (ATI). Its main function was to help night interceptions using the primitive air interception (AI) radar of the day, which had a minimum range well in excess of normal night-time visibility. The late L.E.W. Jolley, who was the boss at the Laboratories, had been concerned with both the previous projects. He was also closely concerned with turbines, hence the code name Turbinlite, usually referred to as the Helmore Turbinlite. At this time, Wing Commander F.S. Cotton was concerned jointly with Helmore in the direction of the project. However, for practical purposes Helmore was regarded as the originator, with electrical design, development and co-ordination by GEC to his overall requirements.

All aircraft modifications and design were under L.E. Baynes, chief designer of Alan Muntz Ltd, also to Helmore's requirements. The Douglas DB-7 Havoc was chosen for the role because it was readily available, it could carry a bulky power source and equipment weighing 2,000–3,000lb and could be modified to carry a large mirror in the nose. It also had the necessary speed and manoeuvrability to deal with the enemy bomber targets of the time. Most of the flight development was done by a special experimental night fighter equipment flight of the Ministry of Aircraft Production (MAP), No. 1422 Flt at Heston, under the command of Wing Commander A.E. Clouston, later Air Commander CB, DSO, DFC, AFC and Bar. The first sixteen aircraft, either Havoc Mk.Is or IIs, were fitted out at Hunsdon. These aircraft were completed by the end of July 1941, just nine months from the start of the lamp development. Three similar Boston Mk.IIIs were fitted at Heston shortly afterwards. The remainder of all types were fitted and modified at the Burtonwood Repair Depot. The total number of aircraft including those from Heston was about 100. These aircraft were deployed to some six airfields throughout England. According to Clouston, the handling of the aircraft was virtually unaltered and the extra drag and speed reduction due to the flat nose were very small due to the use of the Townend Ring, as suggested by Baynes. The fact that the handling was still very good appears confirmed by the way Clouston and other pilots threw the aircraft around. The light in the nose was powered by four banks of twelve 12V 35A/hr lead acid accumulators, two banks in each half of the bomb bay. These were charged externally, which provided ventilation to prevent build-up of hydrogen. Each battery weighed approximately 1,920lb. Turbinlite aircraft flew in company with two Hawker Hurricane Mk.IIc aircraft, one flying off each wing.

The Turbinlite pilot was supposed to get the target in azimuth – the vector from an observer to a point of interest is projected perpendicularly onto

A Havoc Mk.I, which was adapted for use with Turbinlite squadrons such as No. 531 Sqn, formed from No. 1452 Flt on 8 September 1942 at West Malling. These aircraft were painted matt black, as were the Hurricane Mk.IIcs that flew with them.

a reference plane; the angle between the projected vector and a reference vector on the reference plane is called the azimuth – near either edge of the beam, so that return fire aimed at the light source should pass behind his aircraft. He would see no direct light from the Turbinlite and at altitude back-scatter, the reflection of light waves from the direction they came, should not be serious in the absence of cloud or high-altitude haze. The outer fighter pilot was in a much better position to see the target because of his large offset from the beam and he could on occasion see a target in or against the beam even when the Turbinlite pilot could not. Station keeping was achieved by the use of special illuminated strips on the upper and lower wing surfaces of the Havoc, the former for the fighter above and the latter for the pilot below.

A white strip with special characteristics was provided on each wing surface and illuminated by small projectors mounted high in the fuselage for the upper surfaces and in the engine nacelles for the lower. The optics were such that the light could pass out through a small hole in the aircraft skin and almost no light could be seen outside other than off the white strips. The light intensity was under the control of the Havoc pilot.

To get into formation, maximum light intensity was used, sometimes assisted initially by the navigation lights or radar. When the fighter was in position above or below the Turbinlite and 200 to 300yd behind, the Havoc pilot would reduce the light intensity to the minimum required by the fighter to maintain station. There were obvious problems in the presence of cloud or poor visibility. The problem of cloud was overcome by sending the fighter ahead, with the Turbinlite aircraft following by means of its own radar. One of those pilots who knew the frustration of Turbinlite missions was Flight Lieutenant L.G. Holland, who found himself assigned to No. 534 Sqn based at Tangmere during the summer 1942. Turbinlite units were based at Predannack, Cornwall, Drem, Turnhouse, Tangmere, Hunsdon, Acklington and West Malling. No. 534 Sqn had a mixture of Havoc and Boston Mk.I, 11 and IIIs. Holland recalled:

> They all carried the same equipment – a searchlight in the nose behind a flat glass disc and a pair of doors and a belly full of very heavy batteries, though I only recall one case of them falling out due to abnormal loading. The nose was surrounded by a Townend Ring. The aircraft were also equipped with AI Mk.IV but carried no armament.

One or two Hurricane Mk.IIcs (with four 20mm cannons) flew formation on a pair of diminutive station-keeping lights. Most of the Hurricane pilots preferred to rely on the Havoc exhaust. It was incredible how they kept station in the filthiest weather at night and it is surprising there were no collisions despite the abrupt manoeuvre demanded by the radar operators. The function of this 'weapons system' was, of course, to track and close on a target using ground control and AI or the searchlight 'box'. Having closed to about 400yd, the searchlight arc was struck but the doors kept closed and the attendant Hurricane given a code word – 'Boiling' or some such – drew ahead. After a few seconds, the light was exposed, supposedly pinning the victim in the beam light right in front of the fighters. It was a very bright light and most embarrassing for anyone caught in it, especially if they were unwise enough to look towards it. The 'searchlight box' depended on ground searchlights only being exposed within a map reference square over which the target was passing, attempting at the same time to illuminate it and indicate its direction. In this latter they were rarely successful but the general indication was as good as ground control except for altitude information. The 'box' was, of course, used with all forms of night fighter and probably contributed to many successful interceptions. In the latter half of 1942 enemy targets were few and far between and were called 'straight' targets. Night fighters using AI Mk.IV, V, and VII were always given the 'scramble' targets. No enemy aircraft were destroyed by Turbinlite flights and at the end of 1942 when all units were disbanded, the lights were fitted on Wellingtons, Warwicks, Catalinas and, perhaps, Liberators for anti-submarine patrols over the Bay of Biscay.

The Havoc was a popular aircraft despite its permanent deadweight of a Turbinlite. While the 'straight' night fighter squadrons and intruder squadrons enjoyed a good measure of success in the Havoc and Boston, Turbinlite squadrons could claim that they formed a few bricks in the defensive wall and that they learned much through flying in all weathers at night. However, by the time the aircraft were deployed, the blitz against England had reduced, the minimum range of the AI radar that it was intended to assist had improved and the speed and altitude of the enemy bombers had increased. If sufficient number of Turbinlite aircraft had been available during the blitz of 1940–41 it might have been a different story.

Two Turbinlite Havocs, serials AW411 and HJ897, arrived at West Malling on 2 July 1941 and No. 1452 (Fighter) Flt was formed on 7 July 1941 in No. 11 Grp with eight Turbinlite-equipped Havoc aircraft to test the practical application of searchlight aircraft fitted with AI radar. Squadron Leader J.E. Marshall DFC, who was serving with No. 85 Sqn at Hunsdon, was given command of No. 1452 Flt. Acting Flight Lieutenant J.A. Hemingway, DFC, was posted with his observer (radio) from No. 85 Sqn. Flying Officer J. Sinclair was posted with his observer (radio) from No. 249 Sqn at Tangmere but attached to No. 1451 Flt, Hunsdon, for training. Two more Havocs, AW409 and BJ486, joined the flight on 21 July 1941.

The object of the formation of No. 1452 Flt was to test the application and to fully develop the technique of a searchlight aircraft fitted with AI operating at night, with one or two parasite fighters in formation. Various difficulties were encountered at the outset, but with constant day and night practice the following techniques were evolved, using one aircraft, a Defiant. This aircraft took off first, orbiting roughly in the position of the 'leading in' lights.

The Turbinlite aircraft then took off with all lights on, and the Defiant joined up, the Turbinlite then using the minimum amount of light required by the Defiant.

When contact was made on the AI, the range was decreased and held at 3,000ft, the fighter being told in code to prepare for attack. The fighter climbed 500ft above the Havoc to gain its initial speed of dive. On being informed that the Turbinlite would be exposed, the 'parasite' started creeping forward. The light was then put on and the attack delivered.

Sergeant 'Butch' Marfell, RCAF, and Flight Sergeant 'Jonnie' Horan, RNZAF, served with No. 264 Sqn. When later a rear gunner of a Supermarine Sea Otter in Burma, Horan had a hand shot off during an attack by Japanese aircraft. Hit again in the head, he continued to fire. The pilot managed to beach the aircraft but Horan died of his injuries. (Colin Gass)

On 20 August the flight received Havoc BJ471. BB897 took off to join No. 43 Grp but it crashed on landing and Havoc BD110 then joined the flight. The heavy landing was directly attributable to the windscreen icing up and attempts were made to fit an electrical windscreen heater similar to the hot air sandwich used in some cars of the period.

The success of the flight was heavily reliant on the services of a competent AI specialist, and it was necessary to maintain a high standard of co-operation between the fighter aircraft and the Turbinlite. In order to reach maximum efficiency it appeared to be necessary to incorporate the fighter aircraft in the flight. It was suggested on 31 August 1941 that, owing to No. 264 Sqn being equipped with Defiant Mk.IIs, the ideal arrangement was thought to be to transfer at least six of the surplus Defiant Mk.Is and four fighter crews to No. 1452 Flt, which was finally equipped with eight Havocs and eight fighters, complete with crews. In the event of the flight being re-equipped with Boston Mk.IIIs it was suggested that Defiant Mk.IIs fitted with Mk.VI 'AI' could render valuable assistance in picking up the target.

As it attempted to land at 2310hrs on 11 September 1941, Havoc BJ486 overshot the runway and crashed, killing the crew, Flying Officer B.G. Curtis and Sergeant Smalley, his observer (radio). The wreckage was later collected by No. 86 MU, part of No. 40 Grp based at Sundridge, Kent. Over the next few days four Havoc aircraft joined No. 1452 Flt, serial Nos. BB907, AW418, AW909, BB909 and BB116. Also joining the flight at the beginning of October was Tiger Moth T7466, used for communication flights.

On 20 October 1941 Havoc NB907 was damaged internally when a Very pistol was accidentally discharged, following which the aircraft was transferred to No. 43 Deposit Account. Fortunately, no one was injured in the incident. At the end the month, Flight Sergeant Hopewell attended an investiture held by the King at Buckingham Palace for the presentation of his Distinguished Flying Medal.

Havoc AW409 crash-landed at 2315hrs on 17 November following the collapse of the port main landing gear, but it was later repaired. On inspection it was found that the aircraft's hydraulic selector box was faulty owing to incorrect positioning of ports in the adaptors during assembly. The jack of one of the main wheels was starved, the leg failing to lock. The same Havoc crashed on farmland in Suffolk during August 1942.

Bubbles, Jock, Freddie and Denny, who served with No. 264 Sqn flying Defiants at West Malling during 1941 and 1942. (Colin Gass)

An unusual visitor to West Malling is this Handley Page Hampden P1220, serving with No. 25 OTU, here in the markings of No. 106 Sqn, code 'ZN-L', based at Coningsby. The photograph is dated 28 October 1941, West Malling Intelligence, and the bomber could have landed after returning from a raid on Mannheim, which took place on this date. (KAHRS)

From 1 January 1942 Bostons began to replace the Havocs and from May No. 32 Sqn provided four Hurricanes for co-operation in addition to four Defiants of No. 264 Sqn. By 15 February the flight had collected nine Boston Mk.IIIs over a period of fourteen days. Various minor difficulties of a technical nature had to be overcome with these aircraft. There was a particularly bad blow out of the oxygen high-pressure line between the bottles and valve in the front cockpit of aircraft W8265. The pipeline was punctured in no fewer than twenty places and was, apparently, not of sufficiently stout gauge. There were also problems with spares during this period and poor weather conditions did little for morale.

On 21 January, Havoc BD116 of No. 1452 Flt crashed near West Malling, killing the pilot, Warrant Officer J. Hopewell, DFM, and injuring Sergeant Craig. Their aircraft had hit trees at Mereworth Road on its return from an operation.

Hopewell had flown in the Battle of Britain, destroying five enemy aircraft with No. 616 Sqn. Earlier that day, a Hampden of No. 408 (RCAF)

Defiants of No. 264 Sqn flying low over Maidstone in close formation during the 'Wings for Victory' week on 15 March 1942. (Colin Gass)

Sqn from Balderton crash-landed at West Malling returning from a raid over enemy territory. Sergeant Farrow, the pilot, was not seriously injured but other crew members were. The Hampden slid across the airfield on its belly before coming to halt. The gunner was not seen, but luckily he was found sitting in the snow with wreckage from his gun turret. Flight Sergeant May died on 22 January and Sergeant Baker the following day.

On 27 January, Turbinlite Havoc BJ497 of No. 1452 Flt was coming into land when the nose oleo leg collapsed. Fortunately there was little damage and the aircraft was sent to No. 43 Grp.

Following a visit to Hunsdon on 18 April, a Havoc taxied out to return to West Malling. Just after take-off at 2022hrs, the aircraft crashed at Widford, 2 miles from Hunsdon, killing Squadron Leader J.E. Marshall, OC No. 1452 Flt, Pilot Officer R.J. Beard and Sergeant C.W. Allen. The aircraft, W8276, caught fire and burnt out, with the crew not surviving the inferno. Another Havoc of No. 1452 Flt crashed on take-off on 3 May but both Sergeant Hillman and his navigator were uninjured.

On 2 June, Boston Mk.III W8257 was involved in a mid-air collision with Hurricane Mk.IIc Z3842 of No. 32 Sqn. Both Pilot Officer A.F. McManemy and Sergeant G.R. Fennel, in the Boston, were killed. The wreckage was found at Fant Farm, Farleigh, not far from West Malling. Flight Sergeant Josef Vejlupek, a Czech pilot who was flying the Hurricane, managed to fly back to the airfield, landing safely. He was taken to hospital, and following his recovery was posted to Medicine Hat, Canada, as a flying instructor, later returning to England for further RAF service. He was later transferred to the Czech Air Force in August 1945, escaping the Communist coup and returning to the RAF as a 'ferryman', flying the last Spitfires and Meteors to Penang and Singapore. Vejlupek died in his home country in 1997. Flying Officer McManemy was buried at Sevenoaks, his home town, while Sergeant Fenel was buried at Maidstone cemetery.

On 8 September 1942 the unit was renamed No. 531 Sqn. During November, Havocs BD110, AW411 and BB909 were flown to Heston, where modifications to add AI aerials were undertaken. Havocs AW411 and BD110 were also fitted with a new nose.

At 1955hrs on 21 July 1941, twelve Spitfires of Nos. 19, 65 and 266 Sqn took off from West Malling. Their instructions were to cover the retreat of bombers from the French coast. They were informed that there were enemy aircraft in the Saint-Omer area. The squadrons were flying in loose four formation when they were attacked from behind and above by Me 109s. Flight Lieutenant Cunningham (Blue 1) followed one pair of Me 109s with Pilot Officer Stuart (Blue 2), and although not able to get within effective range, fired one burst in their direction. Pilot Officer Stuart was then attacked by another pair of Me 109s but was able to evade them. Flight Lieutenant Cunningham found himself orbiting above the squadron and sighted six Me 109s coming from the north-west. He climbed to engage and as the enemy aircraft attacked the Spitfires below he followed, firing at the last enemy aircraft from 300yd. He saw his tracers enter the fuselage and although no apparent damage was observed the enemy aircraft broke away and dived steeply.

Sergeant Charnock (Green 1) of No. 19 Sqn saw tracer going past him on his port side. He throttled back and skidded violently to starboard. He was overshot by the Me 109 slightly to port and below. He turned after the enemy aircraft, fired two short bursts from 250yd and started to climb. White glycol smoke appeared from the enemy aircraft and it went into a gentle spiral, Charnock then closed and fired three more bursts, which caused black smoke to pour out followed by a sheet of flame. He fired one more burst, followed the enemy aircraft down and saw it crash 5 miles north of Montreuil. The pilot did not bail out.

Sergeant Brown (Green 2), also No. 19 Sqn, turned to attack an Me 109 as it went by and got in a short burst as the enemy aircraft out-climbed him. He was then attacked by other Me 109 and had to take evasive action.

Sergeant Brooker (Yellow 2) was with Flying Officer Oxlin (Yellow 1), both No. 19 Sqn, when he saw two Me 109s coming from below and behind just in range. One attacked Oxlin and the other himself. Cannon shells were passing to his right, so he turned violently left. Bullets came through the hood and various parts of the aircraft, injuring him about the right eye. As he turned back, he saw three Me 109s and sprayed them with a short burst in a beam attack. The hood and another piece came off the second machine but Brooker was going too fast to see what happened to it. He landed at Manston slightly wounded and was detained in sick the bay. Pilot Officers Oxlin (P7547) and Tucker (P7860) of No. 19 Sqn were both missing. At the end of July, Squadron Leader W.J. Lawson, DFC, took over command of No. 19 Sqn from Squadron Leader R.G. Dutton, DFC, Bar.

Twelve Spitfires of No.19 Sqn took off on 7 August 1941 to join Nos 257 and 401 Sqn at 1730 hours. Their duty was to patrol the Mardyck–Saint-Omer area to cover the withdrawal of bombers from the Lille area. The squadron, flying at 24,000ft, sighted several formations of Me 109 as they crossed the French coast. The enemy adopted its usual nibbling tactics, one or two aircraft at a time diving on a section, and a general 'melee' ensued. Sergeant Charnock (Green 1) became separated from the squadron during one of his turns and joined another Spitfire squadron at 25,000–26,000ft. He saw eleven Me 109Es and Fs ahead, some 1,500ft below. He dived out of the sun on the last Me 109E, opening fire at 350yd. His burst hit the tail of the enemy aircraft and it turned to the right. His second burst resulted in a large piece of the enemy aircraft somewhere in the region of the cockpit flying off, followed by the whole hood, which just missed Charnock's starboard wing. The Me 109E turned on its back, dived vertically from 17,000ft and disappeared in cloud at 3,000ft still diving vertically and clearly out of control. Flight Lieutenant Vokes (Yellow 1) saw an Me 109E attacking a Spitfire and climbed to attack. He got in several short bursts as they dived down to 8,000ft, observed one spark in the fuselage but otherwise saw no result.

Sergeant Brooker (Yellow 2), having become separated from the squadron, was pursued by two Me 109Fs across the Channel. He turned away and as they passed him fired a full deflection shot of two seconds at 150yd. One of the enemy aircraft flew straight through his line of fire, but he then lost sight of it. Brooker was able to turn inside the Me 109F, which supports the view that a Spitfire can turn quicker.

Pilot Officer Scott was also returning over the Channel but saw that he was being followed by an aircraft he thought to be a Spitfire. This aircraft was actually an Me 109F, which was making no attempt to overtake or attack him; it seems that the identification mistake was mutual. Scott noticed, however, that the Me 109 had a dark brown spinner, which put him on his guard. He turned round to have a closer look and the Me 109F dived steeply away. Scott managed a quick burst from 250yd but observed no results. Flight Sergeant Plzak (P7771) was believed shot down by flak and was missing. Pilot Officer Milman (P7924) crashed at Charing Hill on returning home and died later in hospital.

Twelve Spitfires of No.19 Sqn took off from Ipswich at 1130hrs on 12 August 1941 as part of Group Wing on Operation Circus 77. The function of the wing was to act as high cover for Blenheims, which were attacking a target in the Ruhr. The wing patrolled in the Schouwen–Walcheren area at 1,500ft. Some twelve to sixteen Me 109Es were engaged in a dogfight but due to the amount of cloud no decisive results could be claimed. Pilot Officer Cox (White 1) saw two Me 109Es appear from behind cloud. One aircraft dived on him, followed by a second, and he skidded aside from both, turning sharply after the second aircraft and giving it two bursts. Immediately there was glycol and grey smoke from the German's engine and he went from a hand turn into a vertical dive, disappearing into cloud. Cox went into cloud after him but could not find him as he came out on the other side. Squadron Leader Lawson also got in a squirt at an Me 109E. He chased it through two banks of cloud and got in three bursts at 300yd. Pilot Officer Calvert (P7693) was missing. No. 19 Sqn moved to RAF Matlaske on 16 August 1941.

In accordance with a signal received by No. 255 Sqn at Coltishall from No. 11 Grp HQ, 'A' Flight had equipped with Beaufighter Mk.IIFs in May 1941, replacing its Hurricane Mk.Is. Changing from a single-engine fighter to a twin-engine fighter bomber, much faster than the Hurricane, was the cause of mixed feelings. Five Merlin-powered Beaufighter Mk.IIFs moved to West Malling on 3 January 1942 to assist No. 29 Sqn. Pilots Squadron Leader Clennell, Flying Officer Wright, Pilot Officer Humes, Pilot Officer Cox and Pilot Officer Clarke were joined by radio operators Flying Officer Wynar, Pilot Officer McChesnney, Sergeant Sayer, Sergeant Croft and Sergeant Biggs.

No. 29 Sqn lost another crew on the day of the move, Pilot Officer Prior and Sergeant Pengally died when the aircraft, Beaufighter Mk.IF X7563, exploded on impact at West Farleigh near West Malling. Later investigations revealed that the aircraft's flap synchronising gear had failed.

An air transport party consisting of Flight Sergeant Milliner, Sergeant Rudd and thirty-three other ranks completed the move, arriving by road at 0300hrs on 4 January. A flight of six Beaufighter Mk.IFs of No. 29 Sqn moved to No. 255 Sqn at RAF Coltishall, arriving at 1100hrs on 4 January, and consisted of Squadron Leader Moon, Flight Lieutenant Hawkes, Flying Officer Robinson, Pilot Officer Pepper, Flying Officer Davison, Pilot Officer Martle, and radio observers Sergeant Read, Flight Sergeant Gregory, Pilot Officer Crowther, Sergeant Mosley, Sergeant James and Sergeant Longhorn.

Also joining the flight on attachment at West Malling was scientific advisor E.J. Smith of Fighter Command Research Operations. The following day, 5 January, Beaufighter Mk.IIF R2430, flown by Pilot Officer Hawkes, collided with Mk.IF serial R2267 when its starboard engine failed immediately on take-off. The pilot, who had never flown this type of aircraft before, managed to avoid a number of Beaufighter aircraft at dispersal points. The crews survived, and both aircraft were repaired and flew again. However, R2267 spun into the ground at Tangmere in 1942. On 23 January two flights of Nos. 29 and 255 Sqn changed places between Coltishall and West Malling and No. 255 Sqn moved on to High Ercall on 2 March. Despite being scrambled to intercept enemy aircraft, No. 255 Sqn did not destroy any during its short time at West Malling.

In February 1942, the *Scharnhorst* and *Gneisenau* made a dash for freedom. The two German cruisers had been hunted by the Royal Navy and RAF for some time and Operation Fuller was implemented to locate them. One of the units involved was No. 207 Sqn based at Botsford, and on 11 February it was laying mines off the Frisian Islands. The weather was so bad that the squadron's Manchester bombers were diverted to Boscombe Down, Manston and Horsham St Faith, and one of these, L7486, landed at West Malling. The following day, L7486 was airborne in the search for the two German cruisers, but only one of the squadron's aircraft located any ships, dropping twelve 500lb GP bombs on the *Prinz Eugen* from 800ft without success. Returning home, L7486 piloted by Flight Sergeant 'Ginger' Hathesich, had to land following the failed attack on *Scharnhorst* and *Gneisenau*, and again put down at West Malling to refuel, later returning to Botsford. In March 1942 the squadron converted to Lancaster Mk.Is and IIIs.

Pilot Officer John Murray Pope had recently joined No. 29 Sqn and was preparing to land at West Malling on 8 March, having taken off in Beaufighter Mk.IF X7622 on a routine flight. Returning to base, he came into land and overshot the runway, bounced and opened up to go round again. Using too much throttle on final approach, the aircraft flipped over

Manchester L7486 of No. 207 Sqn, which had to land at West Malling returning from a raid on the German battleship *Prinz Eugen* on 11 February 1942. (Air Britain)

onto its back, crashing onto the carpenters' workshop, behind the station HQ. Gas bottles exploded, creating an inferno. The young pilot died, he had been flying alone, and ten people were injured.

On 3 May, at 1925hrs, a Boston Mk.III of No. 418 (Canadian) Sqn based at Bradwell Bay crashed on take-off from West Malling and all the crew were killed. The accident was caused by the starboard undercarriage leg fracturing. The aircraft crashed into an orchard 300yd from No. 264 Sqn's dispersal. The crew, who were all serving with the RCAF, were Pilot Officer H.H. Whitfield, Sergeant G.E. Pallis and Sergeant R.E. Williams. The station engineer officer, Flight Lieutenant H.W. Biggs, and medical officer, Flying Officer J.A. Elliott, were running over to the crash site when 250lb bombs on the aircraft exploded, killing them both.

This incident was recorded in *The London Gazette*, as Elliott, MRCS, LRCP, Royal Air Force Volunteer Reserve, was awarded the George Cross:

> In May 1942, a Boston aircraft crashed shortly after taking off and burst into flames. An airman who was on duty nearby hastened to the scene, where he was joined by 5 soldiers. Although the fire was intense and ammunition was exploding in all directions one member of the crew (the Air Gunner, who was seen to be hanging out of the turret) was dragged from the wreckage by one of the soldiers and then, with the assistance of the remainder of the party, carried on a stretcher to an ambulance which had arrived.

The party, was returning to the aircraft, which was then being approached by the Station Engineer Officer and F/O J.A. Elliot, Medical Officer, when a bomb exploded. The engineer officer was thrown to the ground bleeding from the chest. F/O Elliott, although also knocked down, was uninjured and immediately went to the aid of the engineer officer. He gave him morphine and was aware that other bombs were in the aircraft only 8 yards away. A second bomb exploded which wounded F/O Elliott but he valiantly attempted to remove his injured comrade. Eventually F/O Elliott was assisted away by one of the soldiers, whilst the remaining men of the party removed the engineer officer, who was found to be dead. Throughout F/O Elliott displayed great determination and complete disregard for his own safety.

At 2030hrs on the same day, Defiant N3366 flown by Sergeant A.D. Lofting of No. 264 Sqn also crashed on the airfield. Both crew members were uninjured.

Formed at Drem on 22 November 1941, No. 1528 Beam Approach/Radio Aids Training Flight was located at West Malling on 24 April 1942. It was equipped with Miles Masters to instruct fighter pilots in VHF (fighter) beam approach. An advance party moved from Drem on 20 April, the main party with Flight Lieutenant G. Dyke in charge, proceeding by train on 21 April.

Defiant Mk.I of No. 264 (Madras Presidency) Sqn, a presentation aircraft christened *Nellore II*, parked on the unit's dispersal in 1942. (Colin Gass)

An unnamed Australian pilot of No. 264 Sqn enjoying a spell on a swing, which appears to be hanging from a maintenance crew's engine hoist. (Colin Gass)

Over the next three days, eight Masters arrived at the airfield. Following aircraft test flying, four pilots of Nos. 219, 23 and 29 Sqn commenced No. 6 Beam Approach Course. While taxiing out for take-off on 11 June, Miles Master II AZ538, pilot Flight Lieutenant M.C. Kinder, collided with a DH Dominie. Although some damage was sustained to the aircrafts' wings, neither pilots were injured.

Pilot Officer G.C. Smythe, who was on the Beam Approach course, was killed on 17 June 1942 in a road accident close to the village of Hadlow, near Tonbridge, not far from West Malling. Throughout June, courses continued, and as well as flying instruction, pilots spent many hours training on the Link trainer, a flight simulator with which many pilots and airmen had become familiar. It was decreed that fighter pilots should do four hours' Link training, which caused some overcrowding, and a second Link trainer was ordered.

On 20 July Master Mk.II AZ559 was involved in a taxiing accident. The pilot, Flight Sergeant MacPherson, collided with an Air Ministry Works Department (AMWD) tractor and injured the driver. Flight Sergeant MacPherson sustained injuries to his left eye, while the aircraft suffered damage to its propeller and centre section front main spar and bulkhead. This was followed by another taxiing incident on 16 August, when Master II AZ540 caught fire during start-up, causing some excitement, and practice for the RAF Fire Service. Fortunately, the pilot, Pilot Officer Gill, exited the aircraft rather urgently, fortunately uninjured.

The aircraft was later dispatched to No. 71 Maintenance Unit based at Slough. Gill's bad luck continued when the engine of Master Mk.II

An aerial view of West Malling taken during the war. Note the camouflage of the central hangar, in front of which the control tower can be seen. (KAHRS)

The southern end of the airfield. Aircraft dispersals are evident, as are blister hangars and craters that were repaired following the airfield being bombed. (KAHRS)

AZ553 cut out during beam approach training on 22 October, and crashed. He was not injured. The aircraft was taken to Sundridge, Kent, where No. 86 MU repaired the damage. As with many of these instructional units, No. 1528 Beam Approach was finally disbanded on 7 November 1942, its Miles Master aircraft and staff dispersed to other units.

Chapter 3

Night and Day

Squadrons over Europe 1942–43

No. 12 Grp Wing was comprised of Nos. 133 and 412 Sqn, based at Kirkton-Lindsey in May 1942. On 16 May, led by Wing Commander Walker DFC, the group was detached to West Malling, arriving at the airfield at 1445hrs. They were joined by No. 19 Sqn and flew convoy patrols. On 27 May, No. 133 Sqn, together with Nos. 616 and 412 Sqn, left West Malling to rendezvous at Southend with the North Weald Wing. On reaching Ostend, about thirty Fw 190s were seen above 21,000ft and Blue section of No. 133 Sqn engaged them. Pilot Officer Pewitt claimed one destroyed and Pilot Officer Baker of White section, No. 133 Sqn, fired at another, which he claimed probably destroyed. Shortly after, the wing turned for home and Flight Sergeant W.C. Wicker, No. 133 Sqn, flying Spitfire VB BM264, was heard on the RT to say he had been hit. No more was seen of him until his body was washed up at Dover two days later. No. 133 Sqn returned to Kirkton-Lindsey on 29 May 1942.

Biggin Hill had been the home of No. 32 Sqn as far back as September 1932, although when war began it had been based at Gravesend and Manston during the hectic days of the Battle of Britain. In May 1942 it was operating from Manston, moving to West Malling on 5 May 1942 for night fighter training and intruder operations. Initially, it commenced searchlight co-operation and some firing practice, including dusk patrols. During November the squadron also operated from RAF Manston for Army co-operation flights, but was pleased to return to West Malling following seventeen hours of intense exercises. All aircraft and ground crew had returned to the airfield by 27 May.

The following morning the squadron was again flying these operations in the local area. That evening, several pilots decided to drive to Maidstone to enjoy a night out at a dance. The event was spoilt when they realised the bar closed at 2230hrs, and the CO was put out as he had just bought a round of drinks.

Army co-operation flights were delayed as a telegram was received stating that an Army vehicle column, used in such exercises, would be disrupted by fighter attacks by the Luftwaffe. That evening, 29 May, Sergeant Thomas crashed at Westfield Wood, Boxley Gill, near Maidstone. Although the pilot was not injured, his Hurricane Mk.I, V7644, was considered a write-off. Flight Lieutenant Endersby, the engineer officer, and adjutant went to fetch Sergeant Thomas and found him, rather shaken, in a local farmhouse. A guard was mounted on the remains of the Hurricane, although Thomas did not return to the sergeants' mess until evening.

On 31 May four Hurricanes took part in a convoy patrol but no enemy aircraft were seen. On return, three aircraft landed at Gravesend and the fourth at Biggin Hill. The first day of June started with aircraft scrambled to intercept enemy aircraft raiding Canterbury. Flight Sergeant Vejlupek and Sergeant Tickner both got two bursts at two enemy aircraft but lost them in cloud. Flight Sergeant Merrithow was involved in a mid-air collision and was killed. The following day, he was buried at Maidstone War Graves Cemetery, and his funeral was attended by the CO, flight commander, adjutant and fellow sergeant pilots. It was believed he collided with both a Havoc and Vejlupek's Hurricane.

On 4 June, Pilot Officer Merehof was involved when gunfire was exchanged between German E-boats and British light naval forces, during which he extinguished a searchlight that had exposed one of the British ships.

During a patrol between Hardelot and Le Touquet, searchlights were very active and there was much light flak. Pilot Officer R.D. Schuman, an American with the RCAF, flying Hurricane Mk.IIC Z3681, fell victim to the gunfire. He crashed near Le Touquet and was taken prisoner of war.

The remainder of the patrol, seven Hurricanes, landed at Manston. Patrols and Army co-operation flights continued and on 13 June the squadron was ordered to proceed to Friston, an advanced landing ground in Sussex, for an indefinite period. In the morning crews were flown to Friston in a DH Dragon and a period of intense training began. Billeted in tents, it was dusty and hot, and for the next few days the squadron flew mock attacks on RAF Ford and Friston ALG, and practised formation flying.

There was a fatal accident on 20 June when, during a practice attack on Ford, Sergeant Murphy, flying Hurricane Mk.IIC Z3518, touched the ground with his wing-tip, crashed and was killed in the ensuing fire. On 21 June, three airmen, Leading Aircraftmen Strachan, Pillow and Dorey, like many other airmen, took the opportunity after bathing to go for a stroll, according to No. 32 Sqn records. They wandered into a minefield and Dorey and Strachan were both killed when a mine exploded. Dorey's funeral took place the following day at Ford, and the adjutant represented the squadron. On 26 June, four Hurricanes took off to attack enemy shipping. Flight Lieutenant O. Posluzny, in Z3088, bailed out over the sea and his body was washed up at Stella Plage on 4 July. Sergeant H.E. Love, flying HL655, was also hit but returned to base.

In the first two days of June 1942, two crews and three aircraft of No. 1452 Flt had been lost, one through colliding, leaving the flight non-operational. The squadron had also taken on charge Boston Mk.III (Turbinlite) W8392 from No. 1422 Flt, Heston, and Havoc Mk.I PF501 (fighter) from No. 605 Sqn, Ford, for operational use. Nine operations were flown between 11 and 13 August, when PF501 was returned to Ford.

Boston Mk.III W8296 of No. 1452 Flt crashed-landed on 21 June. Sergeant J.L. Thompson, the pilot, was slightly injured and his observer, Sergeant L.W. Waters, was uninjured but severely shaken. Later that day, Sergeant V.G. Lambert, pilot, and Sergeant E.A. Brace, observer, were killed when Havoc BJ470 spun into the ground on take-off at West Malling.

During the period 29 June 1942 to 18 July 1942, day and night practices totalled ninety-two and six respectively, eighty-six of the day practices and all the night practices being successful. Bad weather prevailed over the period, and attention was drawn to the fact that, of 34.35 hours flown by night, only 9.35 hours were devoted to Turbinlite practice, the bulk of the hours remaining being taken up with searchlight co-operation. The solution to this problem was that searchlight co-operation and night training could be carried out by non-operational crews reaching a semi-operational stage, with operational crews remaining from Turbinlite readiness and training.

Between 1 and 21 August the training of new crews had been much slower than was previously anticipated, firstly because of the unserviceability of the only Havoc Mk.I, PF501, that had returned from Ford, and secondly because it was not fitted with AI. Havoc Mk.I AW405, Boston Mk.II W8257, Hurricane Mk.IIc HL604 and Tiger Moth T7466 were used as support aircraft.

On 8 September, No. 1452 Flt was redesignated No. 531 Sqn with orders to move from West Malling to Debden on 2 October. On 10 September, Hurricane Mk.IIcs were allotted to No. 531 Sqn, specifically HL605, HN373, HL859, HL658, HL861, HL660 and HL604 from No. 32 Sqn, and operations continued. During this period eighty-six day practices and twenty night practices were flown successfully.

New pilots arrived from 56 Operational Training Unit (OTU), to fly the Hurricane Mk.IIcs, which had already arrived. Pilots from No. 43 Sqn, also recruited for No. 32 Sqn, were not particularly keen on their new posting to West Malling, and it was felt by the squadron that pilots fresh from the OTU would be more suitable.

The squadron remained at Deben for just seven days, returning to West Malling on 9 October. On 22 November Boston Mk.III W8279 crashed on landing a West Malling with its nose wheel retracted, but there were no casualties. The decision to disband the Turbinlite units in January 1943 came after a period of some nineteen months of hard work and endeavour on the part of the personnel of the squadron.

Summoned to assist No.11 Grp was No. 616 (South Yorkshire) Sqn, which arrived from RAF Kings Cliffe on 3 July 1942. Pilots anticipated some real action at last. At the time of their arrival there was a glut of strawberries in the West Malling countryside, which were devoured with much enthusiasm by all concerned. It was indeed a brief stay and they only took part in sector reconnaissance, cannon tests and formation practice and Balbo sorties before they were on the move again, to Kenley to replace No. 485 (NZ) Sqn.

No. 32 Sqn returned to West Malling on 8 July, its Hurricanes landing at the airfield at 1600hrs. Other ranks returned later that evening by train and a small group arrived the following day. At 1555hrs, Pilot Officer G.W. Gomm took off in Hurricane Mk.IIC Z5256 assigned to No. 1452 Flt for one of the day's last exercises. Unfortunately, he crashed into the sea off Dungeness and was picked up by a trawler. Although still alive, he died a short time afterwards of shock and exposure. In the accident report there are statements from several witnesses, one of whom was Flying Officer Stuart Law:

> On the 8th July 1942 I was flying No 3 to Upton 37 at 8,000 ft when I noticed P/O Gomm lagging behind. Telling 'Upton 37' flying control I would go investigate, I proceeded after him at about 360 mph and noticed he was diving straight for the sea. I then lost sight of him and patrolled the area for about half an hour but saw no further trace.

Another pilot of No. 32 Sqn who had flown Hurricane Z5256 on two previous occasions stated that it handled perfectly and all ancillary controls were in perfect condition. The skipper of the trawler that located Gomm floating in the water stated he was returning to Dover from patrol when at 1715hrs one of his men spotted the aircraft coming down. The location of crash was given as '5 miles NNE Dungeness'. When the trawler arrived at the scene Gomm was observed floating with his head under water. His Mae West was damaged and he was knocked out and had head injuries. The trawlermen stated that they saw the Hurricane enter the water at 40–45 degrees, with no engine running, and it sank immediately. They went on to say that it appeared the Hurricane was making its way towards the coast when it crashed.

Other findings concluded that no parachute or dinghy were used, and there was no indication of engine or R/T failure. The point was made that weather conditions were good, so even if there had been R/T failure Gomm could have found his way home. If there had been engine failure the pilot was at a safe height (8,000ft) to bail out or pancake land near a ship.

Practice firing continued at Shoreham and Army co-operation became a regular occurrence. The occasional intruder patrols took place but nothing was intercepted by the keen pilots of No. 32 Sqn.

On 26 July, Pilot Officer R.S. Davidson took off for patrol near Ypres and Lille. The pilot spotted a train, which he attacked twice, derailing and damaging the engine. Flight Sergeant D.R. Higgin was also on patrol but, thinking that his aircraft was hit, he returned to West Malling, although little damage had been sustained. Intruder patrols continued throughout July, but with nothing to report.

Sergeant Norman Poole had joined No. 29 Sqn at West Malling at the end of May 1942; he had just completed a navigator course and was pleased at last to be posted to an operational squadron. He was billeted with other sergeant navigators in the village at the Abbey of St Benedictine. It was occupied by a lone monk, who was always cheerful and willing to talk with the airmen based there. They slept in during the morning, rousing themselves in the evening for air tests, testing their equipment and returning in the evening and remaining on readiness until day squadrons took over.

Poole recalls:

> No meals were available at Quest House, we ate on the Station and this is where we developed a taste for night flying suppers, a welcome joy to be served real eggs, sausage with bacon and sometimes fried potatoes. We started flying our Beaufighters straight away and had to get used to the powerful aircraft which was more difficult to fly than the Blenheim as it had two Hercules engines which had to be balanced in output as you opened up for take-off. It was easy to give more boost to one and start a swing in the opposite direction before you

had enough airspeed to control direction with your rudder. For the next six weeks we flew only by day directed by ground control, who used their radar to bring us into contact with the target within the radar of our airborne sets. We flew in pairs and took turns as fighter and target. We spent a good deal of time preparing for our secondary role of all-weather fighters for our day partners had no navigation aids other than their voice transmissions which could be picked up by two more ground stations to establish their position. Ground radar helped considerably if it had an established plot on the fighter but it was limited in its coverage at lower levels when the fighter most required help.

Sergeant Poole and other pilots and navigators new to No. 29 Sqn did not have their first night flight until the middle of July 1942, six weeks after they joined the squadron. Their task was searchlight co-operation exercises, and they also carried out air firing during this period, when they attacked a canvas drogue towed over the sea in areas away from shipping. Attacks were usually made some 1,000yd, which gave a wide spread of bullets, often giving warning of approach.

On the afternoon of 28 July, Flight Lieutenant H.K.I. Kaston (NZ) of No. 32 Sqn, flying Hurricane Mk.IIC HL655, was killed when engaged on ground firing practice at Shoreham. While turning to make an attack, his aircraft plunged into the sea. Pilot Officer R.S. Davidson succeeded in destroying a train near Lille the following day. Watching as it blew up, he then high-tailed it back to base. Flight Sergeant D.R. Higgin took off to attack other trains but flying over Gravelines he observed a trawler, which he attacked with some success. Sergeants R. Thomas and R. Tickner succeeded in causing damage to three trains and disabling two others. Pilot Officer C. Merehof blew up a train near Gravelines, damaging another before landing back at base.

In August, No. 32 Sqn flew many patrols and took part in several exercises, including patrols with Havoc aircraft on Turbinlite operations.

One of the most celebrated Royal New Zealand Air Force squadrons was No. 485. It was based at RAF Kings Cliffe shortly before Operation Jubilee (Dieppe). On 16 August, eighteen pilots landed at West Malling at 1425hrs to participate in the Dieppe operation. They were joined by the remainder of the squadron, which travelled by road later that day. On 17 August, the squadron took part in wing formation practice. During the afternoon they took off on a fighter sweep to Abbeville with Wing

Commander Jamison leading, but apart from seeing some Fw 190s flying in the opposite direction, there was no contact made with the enemy. The following day the squadron took part in Rodeo (low fighter sweeps over enemy territory) operations in the Nieuport–Dunkirk area, and convoy patrols, with nothing to report.

A plan to raid the coastal town of Dieppe had been conceived in April 1942 at Combined Operations Headquarters. The idea was to land troops at the French port, supporting Commandos attacking gun positions overlooking the beaches. Originally codenamed Operation Rutter, it was to be launched at the end of June 1942.

However, a new plan was agreed on 27 July, this being Operation Jubilee, and was to take place between 18 and 23 August, when the weather was considered more favourable.

No. 485 Sqn was briefed on 18 August to take part in the assault. Its role was to act as cover for ground forces. Taking off 0445hrs, the Hurricanes set off over Beachy Head and were confronted with a convoy of barrage balloons. Although having to split up to avoid them, they managed to re-form and continue without incident. Attacks were made on the gun positions on the cliff tops, and despite some damage, no aircraft was shot down. After returning to Friston ALG to refuel and rearm, they continued their patrols over Dieppe. On the return flight

Hawker Hurricane Mk.IIB Z3263 of No. 402 Sqn at West Malling during 1942, flown by Sergeant E.W. Rolfe. This aircraft was gifted by the native chiefs of various tribes in Kenya and christened *Mau Molo Ruri*. It later went to Russia. (IWM CH 7676)

they were intercepted by Me 110s, but suffered no casualties and landed safely at Friston. A section was scrambled to attack gun positions on the high ground in the Dieppe area and during this sortie Flight Lieutenant H. Connolly, leading the section flying Hurricane Mk.IIc HL860, collided with Sergeant H. Stanage in Hurricane Mk.IIc HL605 while avoiding flak. Connolly's aircraft crashed in flames and he was killed but Stanage, despite losing a 3ft section of his starboard wing, managed to land safely at Friston at 1230hrs. His aircraft was repaired to fly again. No. 32 Sqn remained at West Malling until 10 September, when it moved to RAF Honiley.

On 19 August No. 485 Sqn was airborne at 0745hrs, arriving over Dieppe at 4,000ft. Fw 190s attacked by diving out of the sun and combat was intense. There were no losses but one Fw 190 was hit. All the aircraft returned to West Malling at 0945hrs. Later in the day, Flight Lieutenant Baker caught a Dornier 217 as it flew out of cloud. He opened fire and strikes were seen on the fuselage and main plane. Baker followed the aircraft as it dived but it broke away and did not crash. On the morning of 22 August, following further sweeps, No. 485 Sqn returned to Kings Cliffe.

For No. 609 Sqn at Duxford, the alarms and the feeling that things were brewing on the eve of 18 August, and the intense air of secrecy, had formed the impression in the minds of the pilots that they would be called upon to assist or repel an invasion. This impression was confirmed when, at 0000hrs on 19 August, a briefing was held and the CO, Squadron Leader P.H.M. Richey, DFC, referred to the news on the radio at 0800hrs mentioning combined operations. Still without knowing anything about the operation as a whole (except that it was called Jubilee), twelve Typhoons led by Wing Commander D. Gillam set out at 1053hrs as leading squadron of the Typhoon wing to rendezvous at Orford coastline and fly from Mardyck to Ostend to distract attention from Dieppe. Landing at West Malling at 1215hrs, except for the CO, who had to return to Duxford to change his aircraft, they took off again at 1400hrs with orders to sweep from Le Touquet to Le Tréport. They saw bombers and chased some Fw 190s, during which some pilots managed to open fire, but there were no kills. Flying Officer Wilmot managed to lose contact with the rest of the squadron, only to be fired at by a Spitfire Mk.II near Dungeness, fortunately without serious damage. The Typhoons returned to West Malling, except Pilot Officer Dopere, who returned to RAF Duxford. Feeling that the squadron had at last been involved in the war, No. 609 along with Nos. 266 and 56 Sqns, then returned to their base.

Spitfire Mk.Vbs of No. 411 Sqn (RCAF) prepare for a sweep in August 1942. They were deployed to West Malling from Digby from 16 until 20 August 1942. (Colin Gass)

In August, No. 411 Sqn (RCAF) was based at Digby, but was using West Malling as an advanced landing ground. A detachment was assigned to fighter sweeps and bomber escort duties over France and the Low Countries. Their CO, Squadron Leader R.B. Newton, DFC, had joined the unit in February. The squadron was equipped with the Spitfire Mk.Vb, which it would continue to fly until November 1943. By 16 August the squadron was en route to West Malling by road, in fact it was escorted through London by two Scotland Yard dispatch riders, which turned out to be a great help, as they made their way through the war-torn city. Meanwhile, No. 411 Sqn's Spitfires arrived at 1430hrs, and the road party arrived at 2100hrs. The men were billeted in tents but made the best of the situation, as did others on the airfield. The following morning the squadron carried out a practice wing formation, followed by a fighter sweep during the afternoon, and flew no fewer than thirty-three hours.

The pilots of No. 411 Sqn were briefed on the evening of 18 August for Dieppe operations, relieving the RAF Hornchurch Wing. Dieppe turned out to be costly for No. 411 Sqn. Pilot Officer P.R. Eakins, flying Spitfire Mk.Vb BM406, was shot down and killed during an engagement with an enemy aircraft. His aircraft had been hit in the radiator, as was Spitfire Mk.Vb

BL542 of Pilot Officer D. Linton, who was also killed. Flight Sergeant S.A. Mills was luckier when his Spitfire Mk.Vb AD263 was damaged in combat by an Fw 190 and he was slightly wounded, he but managed to return to West Malling and landed safely.

Pilot Officer Reid was hit by cannon and machine-gun fire but returned safely to West Malling. Despite being outnumbered, the pilots fought bravely. Squadron Leader Newton damaged an Fw 190 and destroyed another. Later that day they acted as escort to three Blenheim aircraft assigned to lay a smokescreen and they also escorted two Boston aircraft. Operations continued with the Kenley Wing, during which a Do 217 was damaged by Squadron Leader Newton and Flight Sergeant Matheson. On 20 August, No. 411 Sqn flew twenty hours from West Malling, attacking marshalling yards and fighting off Fw 190s. Fortunately, no other pilots were lost. The Canadians returned to their home base at Digby on the morning of 21 August; it had been a hectic two days.

Eighteen Spitfire Mk.Vbs of No. 610 (County of Chester) Sqn, RAuxAF, arrived at West Malling from Ludham, Norfolk, on 16 August, their role being to act as 'temporary reinforcement' of No. 11 Grp for Operation Jubilee. The morning of 19 August saw an early start for the pilots. Ground crews had been busy during the night, fitting long-range 90 gallon fuel tanks to the Spitfires, which gave pilots an increased ability to act as top cover. Four times during the day the squadron took off on patrol, returning in time for lunch at midday. Having just sat down for a meal, they were immediately put on readiness again.

Sergeant Hamish Brown, serving with No. 485 (NZ) Sqn, remembers flying to West Malling from Kings Cliffe, on 16 August, just prior to the Dieppe raid:

> Next day, Sunday, we flew down to West Malling, not far from our old base in 11 Group. On Monday, we did a bit of a sweep over France and a rather funny incident occurred. After the briefing we only had five minutes to get everything ready, so we all piled into the two small transports we had and away down the perimeter track we went. We had not gone far when a back wheel flew off the first car and she did a couple of rolls – what a panic! Three of the boys were temporarily off sick and most of them had bumps and bruises. Our force of fit pilots was somewhat reduced so the rest of us flew most of the remaining Dieppe trips.

On Tuesday the 18 August there was another piddly sweep which I did not go on but flew up to Kings Cliffe in a Tiger Moth taking Sergeant Metcalfe with me to bring it back while I returned with the Magister. It seemed odd back in the Moth doing about 75 mph and getting very fed up and tired with the length of the journey. However, we made it with my expert navigation – following all the railway lines! That night we were all to be in the wing's pilot room and we were given the dope on the Dieppe show, which was to come off next morning at dawn.

We were at readiness at 0340hrs and though we expected to get off early we missed out on the early action. We got off at about 0800hrs as 'cover' and ran into a bit of a hornets' nest, which comprised Fw 190s. There were four squadrons of us that day. I do not know the losses of one of the squadrons with us. The other two squadrons included in our wing lost two and three pilots respectively as well as a couple damaged. Our squadron was lucky in that we had all experienced fellows with us and I must say they flew well and kept their eyes open. My No. 2 got a bullet hole in his tail. I had yelled out a warning on the R/T and he just managed to save himself from serious mishap. We spent half an hour dodging the cows. Jamie Jamieson, the NZ Winco leading us, destroyed one, as did Mick Maskill and Lindsay Black, and Reg Baker got a damaged. I didn't fire my guns. I only had one chance of doing so and thought better of it as my foe had a friend!

The next show our squadron did I was not on. It was the withdrawal which was carried out according to schedule and the boys only saw four Hun bombers which were pounced on by a couple of squadrons of Spits and were blown to bits, poor beggars. The next one was carried out soon after the return and I missed it as I thought I would sneak in a lunch and a bath at the mess. I went on the last one and there was a bit of excitement as a few Dorniers were trying to squeeze through and drop a bomb or two and then buzz smartly off. Our section saw one and I opened out in full pursuit but he got into the cloud and there were a few Spits in a better position than me. The poor fellow was in for a reception when he got to the other end of the cloud as I should say there were 16 Spits in pursuit, some on top of the cloud, some underneath and some in the middle. Reg Baker, leading yellow section, was first there and used all his ammunition and claimed one damaged. He won't have got far as Reg said there was a queue of Spits waiting for a shot! So much for Dieppe.

The peace was shattered as three Spitfire squadrons, accompanied by three Typhoon squadrons, took off on further operations over Dieppe. As the aircraft returned, airmen watched in amazement when Pilot Officer L.E. Hoken safely landed his Spitfire Mk.Vb serial EP238 with the tail almost shot away. It was with great relief that evening when the squadron was notified that Flight Sergeant S.C. Creagh, who had bailed out of his Spitfire Mk.Vb, EP198, during the first patrol, had been picked up from the sea uninjured. He had been shot down by an Fw 190 and rescued by a RN motor gun boat. Sadly, the relief was short-lived when it became known that two other pilots of No. 610 Sqn, Flight Lieutenant P.D. Poole, flying EP235, and Sergeant J.G. Leech, in EP342, had been shot down and killed by Fw 190s. No. 610 Sqn's last patrol was on the afternoon of 20 August, and it returned to RAF Ludham the following day. However, the squadron would return to West Malling in June 1944.

Following a raid on Düsseldorf on 10/11 September, a Stirling bomber, BF347, of No. 15 Sqn, then based at Bourne, Cambridgeshire, was damaged in an attack by night fighters. It was soon clear that the crew would have to put it down a soon as possible, so they headed for West Malling. The pilot, Flight Sergeant Harry Bannister RAFVR, tried an emergency landing, however, the aircraft hit trees and crashed. All seven of the crew were killed. They had taken off from their base at 2105hrs and were part of a huge force of 479 aircraft. Three of the crew – Flight Sergeant H.E. Bannister, Pilot Officer Clarence William Higgins and Sergeant Henry Allan Prime – were buried at Maidstone Cemetery and given service funerals.

Sergeant Henry Eric Williams was buried at his home town of Faversham, Sergeant Wilfred Ernest Pittendrigh at Little Stanmore, Sergeant Henry Howard Maginn at Segoe, Ireland, and Sergeant Sidney Charles Mansfield at Cannock. Wing Commander Young from Bomber Command arrived the following day to make a report on the accident.

During the night of 19/20 September, two Wellingtons of No. 150 Sqn, and two others of Nos. 419 and 156 Sqns, all made landings at West Malling while low on fuel. They were joined by two Stirlings of Nos. 301 and 218 Sqns, which were also running low. One Wellington, taxiing fast to clear the

P-38 Lightning 41-7631 of the 1st Fighter Group, 94th FS, 1st FG, 8th USAAF. The fighter group arrived at West Malling for fighter sweep operations in early October 1942. (American Air Museum)

runway for another, crossed the perimeter track and ran into some barbed wire. None of the crew were injured but the aircraft was slightly damaged. One of the Wellington's pilots had lost his crew, who had bailed out over Germany when the aircraft caught fire. Fortunately, this turned out to be just a flare that had gone off. Despite this, the pilot landed on the airfield by himself without further incident. Later, the AOC No. 11 Grp congratulated 'Control' at West Malling for its excellent work in landing these aircraft without injury or loss of life.

There was much interest on 2 October when several P-38F twin-engine fighters of Nos. 27, 71 and 94 FS, 1st FG, 8th USAAF, descended on West Malling. They were based at Ibsley and flew from West Malling on one of the first daylight sweeps over northern France by American aircraft. Following the operation, they returned to their home base. The following day, advance parties of Nos. 310, 312 and 313 (Czech) Sqn arrived at 1700hrs for operational patrols.

At 2321hrs on 5 October a Lancaster of No. 50 Sqn, based at Swinderby and piloted by Squadron Leader G.H. Everitt, DSO, crash-landed on the runway in fog and heavy rain. The crew were uninjured. Other aircraft were in the vicinity of West Malling, but despite illumination on the airfield and rockets and a Very pistol being fired at intervals, they were unable to get in. Approaching its target at Aachen, the Lancaster had been hit and seriously damaged by anti-aircraft fire. In spite of this, Everitt continued to drop his bombs and even secured a photograph to prove the accuracy of his attack. The aircraft's fuel system was damaged and the two starboard engines failed on the return flight. Despite losing height, Everitt managed to reach West Malling. In deteriorating weather, he lowered the undercarriage and flaps in preparation for landing, but was twice thwarted by low cloud. He then retracted the undercarriage and made a successful belly landing, later describing the flight as 'a shaky do'!

A Halifax of No. 405 Sqn crashed near Wrotham, 5 miles east-north-east of Sevenoaks, Kent, on the night of 5/6 October. Five of the crew of seven died, with the victims all Canadians of the RCAF. They were Pilot Officer R.S. Erickson, Sergeant J.E. Park, Sergeant M. Hudema, Sergeant N. Gislason, and Sergeant J.F.P. Behn – all died. Sergeant R.M. Reilly and Flight Sergeant F.R. O'Neill survived. The Halifax, W7703 'LQ-Q' based at Topcliffe, was returning from an operation over Aachen. Though short of fuel, the pilot, Hudema, made it as far as the south coast of England and he decided to land at West Malling. His first attempt failed and while making a second the aircraft stalled after running out of fuel and crashed at 0034hrs. Reilly and O'Neill (RAF) had parachuted to safety.

Seventeen other aircraft and crews were lost that night, among them Wellington BJ829 'JN-G' of No. 150 Sqn., based at Snaith, Yorkshire, which crashed at Bodiam. Four of the crew survived and were brought to West Malling.

A Stirling of No. 149 Sqn crashed near Faversham the same night, killing all the crew. The crash was attended by RAF Detling. Canadians in the crew were buried at Brookwood, while the fifth victim was buried at his home town. The Stirling, N3755 'OJ-S' flown by Pilot Officer Ralph Lonsdale, RNZAF, ran out of fuel on return to England. Lonsdale ordered the crew to bail out, staying at the controls until all had left the aircraft. He was unable to make good his escape and died in the crash at Arnold's Oak Farm, Eastling. Other crew members who perished were, Sergeant P.A. Radomaki, observer; Sergeant G.S. Reynolds, air gunner; Sergeant J. Brigden, air gunner flying as mid-upper gunner; Sergeant C. Hill, flight engineer; Sergeant V.W. Tulley, observer/bomb aimer flying as front gunner; and Sergeant W.A. Summerson, air gunner flying as rear gunner.

On 10 October, No. 486 (New Zealand) Sqn arrived from North Weald to carry out operations with its Typhoons.

Joe Davis, the world snooker champion, arrived on 15 October to give demonstrations of both snooker and billiards. The event took place in

Wing Commander J.R.D. 'Bob' Braham, DSO, DFC, AFC, CD, with radar operator Sergeant 'Sticks' Gregory, both of No. 29 Sqn, were one of the most successful night fighter crews of the war. This photo was taken in 1944 when Braham flew Mosquitoes with Nos. 613, 305, 21 and 107 Sqn.

the NAAFI and money raised went to the RAF Benevolent fund. Sadly, Sergeant D.B. Clark of 486 (NZ) Sqn was killed flying Typhoon Mk.Ib R8698 when it crashed near Battle, Sussex. 'Nobby', as he was known, was returning from an evening coastal patrol. The Typhoon, coded 'SA-Q', had been pronounced unserviceable by Flying Officer Don MacAlister with a leaking radiator the previous week but was certified as OK. The engine caught fire and 'Nobby' tried to make an emergency landing in a field. He reported on the R/T that he was on fire and moments later his No. 1, 'Wally' Tyerman, saw the whole plane, now a mass of flames, crash-land. The exact reason for the fire could not be established; Clark was buried at Maidstone Cemetery.

Following a successful interception on 19 October by Squadron Leader Braham and Pilot Officer Pepper, No. 29 Sqn's celebration was overshadowed by the death of Sergeants Wright and Akeston on 21 October, when their Beaufighter, V8229, was shot down by home anti-aircraft fire a mile north-west of Winchelsea, Sussex. On 23 October, Typhoon R8812 of No. 609 Sqn, Biggin Hill, flown by Pilot Officer R. Dopere, was killed during a patrol in bad weather. The aircraft crashed at Battle, and the pilot was brought to West Malling. Two bombers, a Stirling of No. 149 Sqn and a Wellington of No. 115 Sqn, made successful emergency landings after returning from raids.

Flight Sergeant J. Pearse or 'Shorty' as he was fondly known by other members of No. 486 Sqn, was killed flying Typhoon R8814 on 25 October 1942. Returning from a patrol, his aircraft suffered engine failure and

Flight Sergeant J. Pearse, or 'Shorty', of No. 486 Sqn, was killed flying Typhoon R8814 on 25 October 1942. Here 'Shorty' is seen on the wing of the squadron's previous aircraft, a Hurricane Mk.IIB. (No. 486 (NZ) Squadron Archive)

he attempted to bail out. Pearse lost what chance of survival he had in steering his aircraft, which was at 1,000ft, away from houses and went down at Willesborough, Ashford. He was buried three days later in the War Graves Cemetery at Maidstone, Plot: C.C. 1.Grave 137, alongside that of 'Nobby' Clark. Wreaths were laid on his grave by residents. Flight Sergeant J. Pearse was the son of George and Isabella Pearse of Whakatane, New Zealand, and he attended Hamilton High School in 1934–35. He had been selected to represent the squadron as half-back in a rugby match that was scheduled in London in November 1942. He wrote from Scotland on 22 December 1941:

> Dear Mum and Dad,
> I am getting the boys to forward this letter in the event of my death owing to enemy action or such circumstances, and sincerely hope you may never open it. My life has been very short but very sweet, never knowing sickness, poverty or unhappiness and this is entirely up or due to your efforts and

cannot possibly write my feelings towards you both. All I say is please do not grieve as life is so short for all of us and sorrow should not enter into it, although in many parts of the world, especially now, peoples are suffering from this malady. You in NZ, are indeed extremely fortunate to have such fine conditions and one does not realise until seeing other parts. I thank you for giving me this knowledge. My savings I leave in your custody for 'young Johnnie's' education, it is a small amount but will give him 3 years secondary education. That is a sound base, even if he prefers the land it is essential that he obtains this standard. I can't stress this too much and only wish he could carry on further for a profession. While in Canada I met a very nice girl, and unashamedly I can say love her very much. We did not talk of these things as I thought under the conditions of war time it is hardly fair to both parties, especially when one is a pilot. However it was my intention to bring her home, and hope that someday Pauline will stay with you awhile. The address is 233 Scotia St, Winnipeg, Canada. I am sure she would appreciate an invitation.

Flying has been a wonderful experience and all through it has been one happy holiday, so you can be assured I have gone down with a smile. My religious life has not been a full one but was always aware at all times of distinguishing between right and wrong and that again reflects on your teachings. Yes Dad and Mum, you have done your duty well and only wish I could have had children to love and teach God will forgive and you will find comfort there. It is wonderful to know I have fine brothers in John, Dick and Sam and hope you are always near them. I have never forgotten our farewell scene, so with so much love I say simply thank you. God bless you. Jesse.

He was only 23 years old when he was killed and almost all those attending his funeral were New Zealanders from his own squadron. A New Zealand flag draped his coffin. His roommate. Pilot Officer Frank Murphy, another pilot of No. 486 Sqn, wrote to his family and also sent photographs.

October ended well for No. 29 Sqn, which had destroyed four Do 217s on the night of the 31st, their most successful period since May 1941.

November began with a visit to the airfield by Sir Garrard Tyrwhitt, the Mayor of Maidstone. Flying Officer Pepper DFC was presented to him and the mayor thanked him for all his and No. 29 Sqn's efforts on behalf of the people of Maidstone.

On 7 November, a Lancaster of No. 106 Sqn landed at 0145hrs, and later a Halifax of No. 10 Sqn and a Stirling of No. 218 Sqn landed after returning from a raid on Genoa, Italy. Much to everyone's surprise, the pilot of the Lancaster was Wing Commander Guy Gibson, DFC and Bar, recently awarded a DSO.

He had been a flight commander with No. 29 Sqn, and was awarded his DFC while at West Malling. The AOC No. 11 Grp, Air Vice Marshal T.L. Leigh-Mallory, CB, DSO, visited the airfield on his farewell tour, and a mess dinner was held in his honour.

Lieutenant J.G. Straus was posted to No. 29 Sqn and moved to West Malling in November 1942:

> Most of our flying was done at night – patrolling over South East England and doing practice interceptions. But we also regularly flew in daylight in order to test our Beaufighter, and Air Interception equipment. As winter gave way to spring in 1943, I indulged in my love of the English countryside, flying over the Kentish orchards when they were in full bloom and circling around stately homes like Leeds Castle near Maidstone. It was during one of our daytime flights that our starboard propeller malfunctioned, with the result that as we landed the aircraft became uncontrollable. I saw the starboard wing-tip touch the ground and fold up like cardboard and the next moment the aircraft turned like a cartwheel but not catch fire and we both climbed out uninjured. The following night we flew again, without incident.

On 17 November Detling reported that a Beaufighter had crashed, and it was revealed to be V8320, flown by Flying Officer G. Pepper, DFC, and Pilot Officer Toone, of No. 29 Sqn. The aircraft had got into a spiral dive from 1,500ft and hit the ground at Halsted. This was a tragic loss for No. 29 Sqn as both crew members were very popular on the squadron and were missed by aircrew and ground crew alike. A Havoc, AW412, also suffered an undercarriage collapse while landing on 14 January 1943.

On the night of 17 January 1943, Pilot Officer A.Q.H. Davidson, No. 531 Sqn, was engaged on a searchlight co-operation flight in the Romney Marsh area and had been recalled to West Malling due to enemy activity. After several attempts to land, and running short of fuel, he bailed out and landed near Lydd without serious injury. His Hurricane Mk.IIc, HL604, crashed near cottages close to the Lydd–Rye road. A witness, Bud Abott recalled the event:

> I was on leave from RAF Lossiemouth (Scotland) and staying for a few days, at a three-storey house at Hammonds Corner, New Romney, (opposite the Lydd road). As I was walking back to the house from New Romney between 2100-2200hrs, the sky in the direction of Lydd/Dungeness suddenly lit up with a string of explosions, and the ground under my feet trembled from the shock waves. I was rather puzzled as no air raid siren had sounded and I had not heard any aircraft, but when 1 got to the house all was revealed. Sitting on the ground with his back against the wall, was an RAF pilot. He explained that he was P/O Davidson and that he had been on patrol in the area for his allotted time and was about to return to his base at West Malling when he received orders by radio asking him to stay on in the area until he was relieved, as enemy activity was expected. Sometime later his radio went U/S (unserviceable) and he later found that he was getting low on fuel and would not have enough to return to base, so he had no alternative but to bail out. He went on to say that he pointed his Hurricane towards the sea, turned it over and dropped out, but as he did so he injured his leg or hip. As he floated down he saw what he assumed was his aircraft crashing into a minefield! He then landed in a ditch, it was obviously not his night! But he managed to drag himself across the road and bang on the door, where he was found by the occupant, Fred Pettit who I was staying with. The pilot was later taken by ambulance to hospital, presumably the Royal Victoria at Folkestone.

During the 1970s, Brenzett Aeronautical Museum, Romney Marsh, Kent, had tried to recover this aircraft. However, it met with limited success, locating only a few items such as part of the tail wheel. Since then the newly formed trust became keen to have another attempt as it was felt that the recovery of a Hurricane Mk.IIc was rather unusual on Romney Marsh, particularly as the fighter was based at West Malling in 1943. In the late 1980s, with the sad news about the future of the airfield, it was a good time to recover the aircraft. Fortunately, the landowners were extremely keen to help. HL604 flew with No. 32 Sqn prior to its detachment to No. 531 Sqn and was engaged in the Turbinlite flights. Most of the remains were found embedded deep in the soft mud, but the items recovered were in incredibly good condition and can be found on display at the newly formed Romney Marsh Wartime Collection, at the village of Brenzett, Romney Marsh, an area that yielded many such crash sites, particularly from the Battle of Britain period.

On 25 January a decision was made to disband No. 531 Sqn after thirteen months of hard work and endeavour on the part of the personnel of the unit. At the time it became clear that unless opportunities for operational flying presented themselves, interest in the Turbinlite would wane and it therefore was not unduly surprising when the decision to disband all Turbinlite squadrons was announced.

Wing Commander C.M. Wight-Boycott, DSO, of No. 29 Sqn had the distinction of destroying three aircraft on the same night, that of 17/18 January. He and Flying Officer E.A. Sanders, DFC, were flying Beaufighter Mk.IF X8270.

The first aircraft, a Ju 88A of 1/KG6 codded '3E+CH', crashed at 0825hrs at King Street railway crossing, Brenzett, Romney Marsh, Kent. The aircraft disintegrated, killing all the crew members: Unteroffizier K. Sailer, Obergefreiter P. Funk, Unteroffizier J. Fleischmann and Unteroffizier J. Binder. In 1982, Brenzett Aeronautical Museum recovered some remains of the Ju 88 and the tail fin is today on display at Lashenden Air Warfare Museum, Headcorn Airfield.

A second aircraft was shot down at 0430hrs, at Pilgrims House, Westerham, Kent. The Dornier Do 217E-4 of 7/KG2 crashed into a chalk pit and disintegrated. The crew of Unteroffizier J. Schnabel, Gefreiter W. Schafer, Gefreiter E. Raab and Unteroffizier R. Hartenberger were all killed.

The third aircraft to fall to Wight-Boycott and Sanders was a Junkers Ju 88A-14 of Stab 1/KG6. The wreckage fell at the Town End Recreation Ground, Caterham, Surrey, at 0530hrs. Three of the German crew, Obersleutnant R. Bernd, Obergefreiter. M. Schiewick and Gefreiter K.H. Prophet, were killed, while Feldwebel K.H. Schulz bailed out and was taken prisoner.

The last raider allegedly shot down by Wing Commander C.M. Wight-Boycott that night, was, eventually credited to another crew of No. 29 Sqn, Squadron Leader I.G. Esplin and Flying Officer A.H.J. Palmer. Ju 88A-14 '3E+GK' of 2/KG6 was abandoned by the crew and crashed at 0550hrs at Lovelace Place Farm, Bethersden, a village not far from Ashford.

Oberfeldwebel K. Dieke was injured, while Unteroffizier K. Fenger and Unteroffizier K. Losch bailed out. They were all taken prisoner. Feldwebel E. Muller's parachute failed to open and he fell struggling to his death.

Wight-Boycott was awarded the DSO for his 'hat-trick'. He and Sanders later received a congratulatory telegram from the Secretary of Air and were awarded the DSO and a DFC respectively. Two weeks later they were both rested, going to the staff of No. 81 Grp at RAF Aston Down, a night fighter training group. Later they joined No. 25 Sqn.

On 29 September 1942, RAF Nos. 71, 121 and 133 Sqn had been activated and re-designated as the 334th, 335th and 336th FS, 4th FG, 8th USAAF, operating from Debden. They had been flying Spitfire Vbs, and were now re-equipped with P-47 Thunderbolts. In March 1943, P-47s of the 335th and 336th FS used West Malling for operations during daylight in an effort to protect USAAF aircraft bombing targets in Europe. The first mission from West Malling was on 8 March, when Major D. Blakeslee led the 335th and 336th FS on a Ramrod and fighter sweep to St Valery, France. Lieutenant Colonel Peterson, who was to have led the group, experienced engine trouble and returned to base, so Blakeslee took over command.

Further escort missions took place on 12 and 13 March 1943 from West Malling but despite seeing Fw 190s and Me 109s, all were uneventful. However, on 12 March, the 336th FS was jumped by Fw 190s

Sergeant L.F. Williamson managed to land Wellington Mk.X HE239 of No. 428 Sqn RCAF at West Malling, despite the death of a gunner and the obvious damage to the aircraft. His heroic flying and determination without a doubt saved the lives of his crew. (IWM 9867)

and Lieutenant Hazen Anderson was hit off Saint-Omer, bailed out and taken prisoner of war.

A damaged Vickers Wellington Mk.X, HE239 'NA-Y', of No. 428 Sqn RCAF landed at West Malling in April. The aircraft, based at Dalton, Yorkshire, received a direct hit from anti-aircraft fire while approaching Duisburg, Germany, on the night of 8/9 April. Despite the loss of the rear turret and its gunner, Sergeant Lorenzo Bertrand, as well as other extensive damage, the pilot, Sergeant L.F. Williamson, continued to bomb the target, following which it was found that the bomb doors could not be closed because of a complete loss of hydraulic power.

Williamson nevertheless brought HE239 and the remainder of his crew back for a safe landing at West Malling. They were: Flight Sergeant W. Watkins, navigator; Flight Sergeant H. Parker, bomb aimer; and Sergeant J. Powley, wireless operator. Bertrand's body was found near Holtwick/Haltern-am-See, Germany, and he was buried in a cemetery near Sythen, Ehrenfriedhof, on 9 April and later exhumed to Reichswald Forest War Cemetery.

The capture of Fw 190s on the night of 16/17 April must surely rank as one of the most bizarre incidents involving West Malling, and it was a Beaverette armoured car of No. 2769 (AA) Sqn, RAF Regiment, that was instrumental in this achievement. That night, a single-engine aircraft orbited the airfield and came into land at 0110hrs. The aircraft was thought to be a Defiant. The fire tender led it in to be parked by the side of the watch tower. One of the crew of the tender jumped out and informed the pilot where he was, upon which the pilot replied in German. At that moment the fireman saw the German cross on the side of his aircraft and immediately ran off to the watch tower for a rifle.

The aircraft, a Fw 190, commenced to turn towards the runway with its engine running, but as he was covered by guns of the Beaverette and obstructed by it from taking off, the pilot surrendered to Lieutenant Barry of the 4th Ulster LAA Regiment, who was unarmed but had dashed out from the watch office.

Feldwebel Otto Bechtold, who had landed in Yellow H of 7/SKG10, was taken away for questioning but while this was going on a second Fw 190 landed. This belonged to 5/SKG10 and was being flown by Leutnant Fritz Sezter.

When Setzer realised he had landed on an enemy airfield and attempted to take off, his aircraft was destroyed by the Beaverette, which dashed around the perimeter to head him off. Leading Aircraftman Sharlock, the gunner in the armoured car, gave the aircraft a long burst from his twin

An Fw 190A-4/U8 that landed in error at West Malling on 17 April 1943, flown by Feldwebel Otto Bechtold, 7/SKG10 based at Amiens. Evaluated by the Royal Aeronautical Establishment, Farnborough, and given the serial PE882, it was flown by No. 1426 Enemy Aircraft Flight (EAF) and crashed on 13 October 1943, killing Lieutenant R.E. Lewendon, the commanding officer.

Vickers machine guns from 15–20yd range and a small fire was seen in the rear of the cockpit. The aircraft was still moving away, so he gave it another long burst and the Fw 190 was immediately enveloped in flames. Setzer more or less fell out of the cockpit with some of his clothing alight, and walked towards the Beaverette.

Setzer surrendered to Wing Commander Peter Townsend and Leading Aircraftman Sharlock. In the meantime, the oxygen bottles in the aircraft had exploded and immediately afterwards the whole of the machine was blown to bits by a large explosion. Parts of the aircraft were picked up as much as 300yd away. Setzer was found to be wounded in the shoulder and one leg, and suffering from burns on both hands.

A third Fw 190 undershot the runway and was also destroyed, the pilot escaping with concussion. A fourth Fw 190 crashed at Staplehurst, killing the pilot. All had been attempting to attack London but had become lost over Kent.

Both Aircraftman No. 1 Class K.J. Williams, driver of the Beaverette, and Leading Aircraftman F. Sharlock, the gunner, both of No. 2769 (AA) Sqn, RAF Regiment, were congratulated for their bravery and quick thinking.

Bechtold's Fw 190 was later evaluated by the Royal Aircraft Establishment at Farnborough.

Wing Commander Peter Townsend recalls the incident in his book, *Duel of Eagles:*

> A special van operated by two WAAF girls went to guide the aircraft in, believing it was a returning RAF aircraft. The girl driver turned her van and switched on the lighted panel 'FOLLOW ME', which the German pilot did, until he reached the tarmac, where he switched off. At that moment he felt something sticking into his back, it was a pencil, held by an officer who had left his revolver behind in his room. The German immediately surrendered. During his interrogation, which I attended, he answered every question with 'Ich bin ein Deutsch soldat' (I am a German soldier). This frustrating interview was interrupted when an officer rushed in and shouted: 'Quick sir, there's another one landing'. The armoured car had already started after it, so I yelled to the crew: 'Don't shoot!' But they did, the idiots, setting fire to the Fw 190, whose pilot, also on fire, jumped down to the ground. We leapt on him, smothering the flames, as the German kept shouting and struggling like a madman, we pinned him down. Meanwhile his aircraft was blazing some fifty yards away. Suddenly it exploded – at which the German, just as suddenly, stopped his raving. I got off his chest and went to help two of our firemen, badly hit. One had a chestful of splinters (which we, who were kneeling on the German, had escaped), the other a hole in his neck from which blood was spurting. The German pilot, asked what he was shouting about, replied: 'I was trying to tell that idiot (me) that there was still a bomb on my aircraft! Questioned, the German pilots explained their nocturnal escapade. Lost in the haze, they had spotted our flare-path, and landed, believing they were in France. The most deeply mortified of them was the one we had sat on, he thought we were French!

Squadron Leader W.A.K. Igoe, the senior controller at RAF Biggin Hill on the night of 16/17 April, recorded his own recollections of the event:

> RAF West Malling was at the time the main night fighter station for the Biggin Hill centre, of which I was the Senior

Controller. The Sector Commander from Biggin was Group Captain A.G. 'Sailor' Malan. There had been about a week of casual activities, nothing much, and the weather was bad. I was sitting watching the table one night which showed about six raids, three or four marked friendly and the others were marked 'X', three of them were in a triangle area comprising Ipswich, Cambridge and Southend. I had assumed they were Intruders going home and the 'X' probably malfunctioning IFF (Identification Friend or Foe). We had nothing flying because the forecast was bad. To our astonishment, bombs were dropped in the Colchester area, whereupon Group turned every raid 'X' and I was asked if I could put some night fighters up to investigate.

The interesting part of the story, to the best of my memory, I think the squadron commander was (Wing Commander C.M. Miller DFC, I told him I did not like the weather but the situation was so unusual I suggested I put a vertical searchlight just south of the Isle of Sheppey and told the pilot to patrol around the searchlight, thereby relieving him of any navigational problems and making it a simple matter of returning to West Malling if the weather clamped down. Meanwhile, the raids north of the Thames had turned south but the plotting was bad and the whole situation mystifying. One more lot of bombs was dropped again, roughly in the same area and time went by. I must have had my sole night fighter orbiting in the vicinity of the searchlight for about half an hour when I got a call from the Observer Corps near the searchlight complaining that I had advised him there was one aircraft, a twin, round the light which they had heard clearly to begin with, but now there were two. You can imagine the reaction.

We had no plots showing an aircraft approaching the line. Next thing I called up the pilot to tell him there was another aircraft on the landlight, could he see anything? He answered something like 'Rubbish, but I'll have a look.' In the meantime I was checking a list of missing aircraft, single-seaters, and the only one that had been missing, a Defiant, since mid-day could obviously not have been that as petrol would have long since been exhausted. To my astonishment, a little later, the pilot said, 'Yes there is something beneath me. I have just seen a shadow twice.' Still thinking it was one of our own I said to him, 'Right, stay where you are, I shall deflect the searchlight down on West Malling,' which I did. 'I have forgotten why, and I think now it was a Saturday night, but it was certainly a night where there was a certain amount of celebration going on because Sailor had gone to London to attend a party.

There was a dance that evening at West Malling. We were approaching midnight and of course, a Controller in charge of a Sector was in charge of all operations subject only to Group control who rarely intervened. I advised the duty pilot at West Malling that I thought a strange aircraft was orbiting my light and I would attempt to land him, would he switch on the flare path, which he did. The aircraft came into the circuit and I switched the beam back to the vertical, and the aircraft finished up at the end of the runway.

No. 85 Sqn, equipped with the Mosquito Mk.XV until March 1943 at Hunsdon, converted to the Mk.XII the same month, and moved to West Malling for the first time on 13 May. All aircraft arrived at the airfield safely, and took over the dispersals vacated by No. 29 Sqn when it moved to Bradwell Bay. They were not considered as good as the dispersals at Hunsdon. The main party of No. 85 Sqn arrived at West Malling station at 1530hrs in a special train, and were met by the station commander, Wing Commander P.W. Townsend, DSO, DFC. He had been CO of the squadron from May 1940 until June 1941, when it flew Hurricanes and Defiants.

The airmen of 'A' Flight were delighted with their new accommodation at the Retreat and Quest House in Malling. Those of 'B' Flight were billeted in a large mansion in the park called Hamptons, a few miles away near Hadlow. Despite having to cycle to and from the airfield, most men thought this a minor inconvenience compared with the pleasure of living at the park and cycling everyday through the Kent countryside. NCOs were billeted at the sergeants' mess and officers at March House, while some officers had a mess at the Old Parsonage. The squadron's orderly room was tucked away just behind 'A' Flight dispersal.

Squadron CO Wing Commander John Cunningham's thoughts turned to coming operations. On the night of 16/17 May, the squadron destroyed four Fw 190s with one probable. There had been some doubt as to whether the Mosquito was a good match for the Fw 190, this success surely proved the case.

Prior to Cunningham joining No. 85 Sqn as CO, both he and Flight Lieutenant C.F. Rawnsley were sent to Westland Aircraft Co. at Yeovil to see the new twin-engine Westland Welkin. Later, on hearing how the keen pilots of No. 85 Sqn had beat up the airfield at Hunsdon before flying on to West Malling, he was not pleased. It was a miracle that none of the Mosquitoes had hit the control tower, but one had managed to cut a swathe in the grass. Meanwhile, Cunningham had dropped off Rawnsley at Ford, where he was to attend a navigator leaders' course before joining the squadron at West Malling. In his book, *Night Fighter*, he recalls his first impressions of his new base:

> The airfield at West Malling, a few miles west of Maidstone, was deep in the midst of the orchards and hop fields of Kent. When I arrived from Ford, the Garden of England was at its best, the whole countryside alive and aglow with fruit blossom and spring flowers. The airfield itself was a grass one with a strip of Sommerfeld track—wire mesh pinned down over the turf—to form the main runway for take-off and landing, with a concrete perimeter track surrounding it. Brick crew-rooms and offices for the squadrons were dispersed around the fringe, hidden among the plum trees of a half-cleared orchard. The overall effect was more that of a garden city than an RAF base. The surrounding countryside, whichever way one looked, was thick with woods and orchards, and to the north the long, clean line of the Downs swept across the skyline until it broke where the valley of the Medway wound through the hills. Of the grim battles which had been fought in the skies over this part of England in the difficult days of 1940 there remained little sign. Here and there one occasionally found a few grass-covered craters where a bomb load had been jettisoned or a scar on a hillside which marked the grave of some stricken aircraft.
>
> West Malling was just off the main London to Maidstone road, a fortunate state of affairs because it had enabled the village to retain its old world charm and local character rather than becoming nothing more than an untidy prolongation of the dreary south London suburbs. At the western end of the village there was an attractive old church, and just beyond that stood the Manor House, which became our squadron Mess. It was a mellow, creeper-covered, Georgian house, with a

beautifully kept walled garden at the back. The garden in front of the house was terraced, with a drive leading to a sunken road, across the other side of which there was a long, reed-banked lake, the home of ducks, swans and moorhens. Over dinner the night of my arrival at West Malling I heard exciting news about the fighter-bombers the Germans had started using. During the time I had been away there had occurred what could only be described as a red letter night in the history of the squadron, they had destroyed their first Fw 190. We had all known from the beginning that we were going to be up against something that would be pretty hard to catch. The Fw 190 was one of the Luftwaffe's latest single-seater fighters. Once it had got rid of its wing drop tanks and the two thousand pound bomb that it carried externally under its belly it was quite a fair match even for a Spitfire. It could easily run away from us if it chose to do so, or make rings around us if we caught it.

Those fortunate to be billeted at the Manor House had settled in and, compared with other RAF bases, members of No. 85 Sqn felt comfortable. The day-to-day management of the manor was in the capable hands of the WAAF, and apart from meals taken when on duty, crews rarely visited the station mess. This was not surprising as the assistant catering officer was Warrant Officer Helen Tyson, who, having finished her usual daily duties, would turn up at the Manor House to supervise the evening meal. Considering the rationing, these were considered to be excellent.

The WAAF who served behind the bar took no nonsense from exuberant airmen, as drinking sessions would often continue late at night. 'Nina', as she was known, often read palms as a game, but on two occasions she had refused to look at certain airmen's palms. In each case the pilot had been killed on operations, and palm reading was dropped.

Another activity in the mess was using the plasterboard on the walls for cartoons. These were often drawn by Squadron Leader David Langdon, who had once been the station's intelligence officer and was visiting West Malling for a few days. One of these was a depiction of Bill Maquire, a pilot of No. 85 Sqn, who appeared to have a bird flying out of a nest in his handlebar moustache. Flight Lieutenant Arthur Woods, a film director before the war, also contributed to the artwork by adding frames around each portrait. Following the war, the owners cut out the panels and hung them in the station mess.

No. 85 Sqn had only been at West Malling for three days when, on the night of 16 May, the sirens began to wail as Fw 190s came streaking across the narrow Straits of Dover. That day 'B' Flight were on duty. The phone rang and pilots jumped to their feet, expecting some action, but were ordered not to scramble. Much to their annoyance, No. 3 Sqn, based at Manston with Typhoons, took off to intercept the raiders. Unlike the Mosquitoes of No. 85 Sqn, the Typhoons were not equipped with AI, and raced blindly around the dark sky. Fortunately, the controller understood the decision was a mistake and after an hour the Mosquitoes were scrambled.

That night, Squadron Leader W.P. Green and Flight Sergeant A. 'Grimmy' Grimstone became the first night fighter crew to destroy an enemy aircraft over England at night, an Fw 190A-4/U8 of I/SKG10 near Dover. They were rewarded with a bottle of gin and champagne. A silver model of a Mosquito was presented to the squadron by Squadron Leader Brainshaw-Jones, the senior control officer at RAF Hendon. Another was destroyed by Flight Lieutenant G. Howitt DFC and Flying Officer G. 'Red' Irving. Three others were shot down on that same night, 16/17 May, and the party at West Malling went on until the 'wee' hours of the morning.

The role of the night fighters was to protect London, guarding the area from the Foreland to Beachy Head. Intruders would fly through the area, across the Estuary, to the east of London, and changes in the tactics used against this threat were essential. It was of great importance that the controller had aircraft in position, at high altitude, to give a distinct advantage over the German aircraft. Two night fighters were on standing patrols and had access to two ground control interception (GCI) stations, Skyblue and Recess, each of these controlling one of these aircraft.

Flight Lieutenant J.P.M. Lintott and Flying Officer G.C. Gilling-Lax, No. 85 Sqn, were scrambled on 9 July, taking off in Mosquito Mk.XII HK172 at 1700hrs, but never returned to West Malling. They were vectored onto a target and Wartling Control watched as the two aircraft faded together. Soon after 1730hrs it was reported that the two aircraft had crashed near Detling. It transpired that the Mosquito had crashed at Boxley near Maidstone, and both crew members were killed, and that a Do 217 had crashed at Bicknor about 5½ miles away, to the east of Boxley, the crew and aircraft being blown to smithereens. Reports received indicated cannon fire was heard just before the impact and AA guns were also in action. It appears that Flight

Lieutenant Lintott shot down the Do 217 and that either debris flew off the enemy aircraft and hit the Mosquito, causing it to crash, or more likely still, after shooting down the aircraft, the Mosquito suffered structural failure. Both crew members were very popular and their loss was a severe blow to the squadron.

The Mosquito crashed within half a mile of the south escarpment of the North Downs. It was later claimed that the ack-ack guns had shot down the Dornier, but equally they may have hit the Mosquito, although the German was credited to No. 85 Sqn. The accident report remarked that Flight Lieutenant Lintott was prone to be heavy on the controls of the aircraft he flew, and that on 22 May he found himself overshooting the target and attempted to slow down by violent use of the rudder and ailerons. A shudder was felt throughout the aircraft and on landing it was discovered that No. 7 bulkhead and fuselage shell forward of it had failed. He and Gillling-Lax had already shot down three aircraft and both had been recommended for the DFC. Gilling-Lax had been a headmaster at Stowe School before the war and had a brilliant career previously at Marlborough and Cambridge.

Ground crews of No. 130 Sqn moved from Honiley to West Malling on 5 August, where they had been kept waiting not knowing where they were to move, or when. The squadron, along with No. 234 Sqn, was destined for an overseas posting, but this was cancelled. Instead the squadron was to re-form with No. 234 Sqn, also based at Honiley, and pilots and officers arrived by train. There were no aircraft and very little equipment when they arrived, and it was thought that both squadrons would remain at the airfield for six weeks. There were also few people in RAF blue, and many had to wear tropical khaki. No. 130 Sqn was allotted a dispersal among the trees, and while pilots lounged about in the sunshine, some of them went to work to try and find out what was happening to the aircraft they had been allocated. It was discovered that they were Spitfire Mk.Vbs, awaiting collection at Detling. As it turned out, they had been flown by No. 65 Sqn, and No. 234 Sqn collected those of No. 122 Sqn, who were being re-equipped with Spitfire Mk.IXs. This was not popular and pilots were briefed that their role at West Malling was close support work with medium bombers. Work commenced on bringing the aircraft up to standard. On the plus side, the squadron was part of No. 11 Grp, and there should be some action. This was reinforced by a rumour that all leave was to be cancelled. Meanwhile, there were parties on the camp and the cinema at the airfield became a popular venue, while attractive local towns and London were not far. Most importantly, the local pub, the Startled Saint, known by most as the *Strangled Virgin,* was within walking distance. The local girls were popular, as was the free supply of local fruit, mostly apples and plums. Flying Officer Hugh Palmer was the first to fetch his car, which encouraged others to purchase cars and bikes. Another, Flying Officer T. Saunders, paid £10 for a wreck in Maidstone and Flying Officer R.J. 'Drone' Kenyon paid £50 for a Norton motorbike. Flying Officer J.J. Parker celebrated his commission by buying a baby Morris, as did Flying Officer Jock Wilson, who recruited the help of several pilots and ground crew to get the car moving. Despite restrictions and rationing, petrol for all these vehicles was not much of a problem!

Their first operation took place on 18 August, being recalled when in sight of Flushing, the target for the bombers being escorted. The following morning they took off for Amiens-Glisy, being joined by Flying Officers Dave Glaser and Con Conway of No. 234 Sqn. Twenty-four Spitfires took part in this operation. They both claimed an Fw 190 damaged, but Conway's aircraft was hit by flak. He was badly shot up but he struggled home, escorted by Flight Lieutenant Wedd, and completed a successful crash-landing at the airfield.

During an operation on 5 September, Spitfire Mk.V AD329, flown by Flight Sergeant G. Jones, was hit but stayed with the formation. Flying Officer Joe Hill's aircraft was badly hit in the rear of the fuselage but his controls were not damaged and he got home, where he received a warm welcome. Flight Sergeant D. Jones was not so fortunate when he was pounced on by two Fw 190s, which shot away his Spitfire's ailerons. He entered an uncontrollable spin and went down. Jones released his harness and was about to put the stick over to bail out when the aircraft began to judder and straighten out. He took control again and eventually pulled out. His German appointment was not finished as he was attacked again, upon which Jones dashed for home. He landed at Manston, where his damaged Spitfire was repaired by the station engineer while he went to the doctor. He had been wounded in the head and his aircraft was declared a write-off.

In January 1943, it was decided at the Casablanca Conference by the Allies that the threat of a cross-Channel invasion by the Germans must be deterred and that large-scale operations to be planned give relief to Allied operations in Italy and the Russian front, by keeping a large-scale German force in Europe for as long as possible.

In the spring of 1943, Lieutenant General F. Morgan, Chief of Staff to the Supreme Allied Commander, and his team planned a deception programme aimed at Norway and Brittany and another to pretend a threatened amphibious landing in the Pas-de-Calais codenamed Operation Starkey.

Spitfires taxi out in preparation for take-off; an interesting view taken from the balcony of the control tower at West Malling. It is thought this photo was taken by staff on duty at the time; the exact identity of the Spitfires' squadron is unknown.

On the morning of 9 September, pilots of No. 130 Sqn assembled, with those of other squadrons, at dispersal in the cold light of dawn. Their Spitfires had been painted overnight. The wings of all participating fighters now featured black and white stripes to make the aircraft easily distinguishable, and the operation took place on 9 September. Aircraft from Nos. 64 and 410 Sqn also took part in Operation Starkey, but with little success.

Although a ruse, the plan was devised so that it could become a real landing if conditions became favourable. Boulogne, having beaches, would be an ideal point to break through to take Calais and Antwerp. A large-scale force was assembled at embarkation areas along the south coast between 25 August and 7 September. It was expected to draw the Luftwaffe into battle. As part of this operation, Nos. 10, 12 and 13 Grp had reinforced No. 11 Grp with a few of their squadrons; this inevitably included those mentioned operating from West Malling in the Pas-de-Calais between 25 August and 7 September.

There were night bombing attacks on 6/7 and 7/8 September, attacks on enemy airfields and communications on 8 September by heavy and medium bombers, and fighter bombers, and a finally an umbrella over the naval assault force and escorts for the bombers. Nos. 130 and 234 Sqn acted as close escort to bombers attacking the airfield at Lille. However, there was no real activity by the Luftwaffe, which demoralised the squadrons involved. Some 3,000 missions were flown by fighter and bomber squadrons. It was also a great disappointment for them to only find out the operation was deemed a success by listening to BBC broadcasts.

Following Starkey there was not much happening and this gave rise to speculation that Nos. 130 and 234 Sqn would soon be moving again. Meanwhile, a party was held at the Startled Saint whereby several WAAFs joined pilots and ground crew and a dance was arranged. On 16 September both squadrons were notified that they were to move again, this time to Catterick, Yorkshire. Both had hoped they would remain in Kent, or hoped perhaps to move to another airfield with No. 10 or 11 Grp.

Shortly after 0700hrs, they were informed they would soon be taking off. Leaving at 0720hrs, the CO led twelve aircraft, however Flight Lieutenant Joe Hill had to return because of trouble with his cockpit hood. There was no enemy activity, possibly due to heavy fog. Later, No. 130 Sqn was again airborne, returning somewhat disappointed from Catterick due to fog.

Flying Officer Hedgecoe, pilot, and Pilot Officer Whitham, of No. 85 Sqn, took off from West Malling in Mosquito Mk.XII HK123 on 15 September at about 2200hrs. They were vectored onto a Ju 88 reported at 22,000ft. Climbing rapidly, Hedgecoe caught up with his prey, and at 60–70yd behind the target it was apparent that the German crew had seen the Mosquito. It peeled off very hard and strikes were seen on the port wing of the German bomber, outboard of the engine. It continued in a steep dive to port. Hedgecoe fired again but immediately there was a loud roaring noise as if air were rushing into the fuselage of the Mosquito, and a jolt shook the whole aircraft. It was later described by both crew members as being like the aircraft's windscreen blowing in. The Mosquito went into a violent spin and both crew members blacked out temporarily. On recovering, the aircraft was rolling to the left.

Pushing the control column forward as far as it would go and giving full right rudder and full right aileron, Hedgecoe had to use considerable force to get the stick over but once there it was easy to hold. The rudder appeared to be operating well. Expecting not to be able to control the aircraft, Hedgecoe ordered Whitham to bail out, following close behind. Both landed successfully but Whitham had lost both boots. They both heard the Mosquito screaming into the ground and saw and heard the explosion

The original dart board that gave many pilots and aircrew a chance to have a go at Hitler. This artefact from wartime West Malling is on display at Romney Marsh Wartime Collection, Kent.

on impact. They had landed at Woodchurch, about 1½ miles from the crash site, and one of the missing boots was found 2 miles from the crash. The Mosquito had crashed at extremely high speed in a vertical dive with engines full on. Fire broke out on impact, and owing to the depth of the depth of the crater it could not be easily dealt with. The wreckage was still smouldering two days later and ammunition was still exploding. The aircraft made a crater 17ft deep. A report concluded there had been no structural failure but that the port undercarriage door had come off and that the nose perspex had disintegrated, which had happened before when cannons were fired.

Night fighter crews were informed that they would be training on the new Mark X AI system, and on 1 October a Wellington bomber fitted with it arrived at West Malling. The navigators' compartment had been darkened with blackout curtains to enable crews to see the cathode ray tubes in daylight. Under instruction this was watched by two, three and sometimes four pupils sitting in a row with an instructor on what was called 'the mourners' bench'.

At the same time, crews continued flying, operating with the Mark VIII AI. On the night of 7/8 October, Wing Commander J. Cunningham and Flight Lieutenant Rawnsley took off at 2030hrs. Shortly afterwards, they developed technical problems and were heading back to West Malling when suddenly they obtained a chance visual on an enemy aircraft and Cunningham immediately gave chase. Closing on the target, it was identified as a Ju 188 with its distinctive long, pointed wings. Having decided it was a Ju 188, Cunningham closed in to attack and was just about to open fire when the rear gunner, opened up and smashed the wing commander's windscreen. Shaken but determined to press home an attack, he fired a burst but was unable to observe the results.

Despite the damage, Cunningham and Rawnsley nursed their damaged Mosquito Mk.XII, DZ302 'VY-R', back to West Malling, landing at 2125hrs. Removing themselves from their aircraft, they strolled over to the squadron's crew room. As they entered everyone looked up and could see the CO's face was cut and bleeding. He was at once taken off to the sick quarters by the medical officer, Flight Lieutenant Mortimer, who removed several tiny splinters from his left eye, forehead and head. It was a narrow escape.

On 15 October, Flying Officer H.B. Thomas and Warrant Officer C.B. Hamilton in a Mosquito Mk.XII of No. 85 Sqn intercepted and shot down Junkers Ju 188E-1 3E+HH of 1/KG6, which crashed and burnt out at Brooks End Farm, St Nicholas at Wade, at 1115hrs. Leutnant K. Geyer was captured after bailing out of the stricken aircraft, but Feldwebel Walter Flessner, Obergefreiter Dietram Kretzschmar and Obergefreiter Otto Schmidt were killed.

Predannack in Cornwall had been the temporary home for No. 410 Sqn (RCAF), on detachment from Coleby Grange, since 21 February 1943. The squadron's Mosquito Mk.IIs had been fitted with AI Mk.IV or V units and they were brought south-east to increase the strength of the defenders. On 22 October it was decided to allow searchlight-aided night fighters over London, provided they kept above 20,000ft, so leaving the guns to fire in a zone up to 18,000ft. The main move south-east was delayed until 22 October. During a twenty-four-hour period from 22 October, four aircraft from West Malling were ordered off on patrol on three night Rangers a night during the moon period.

Flight Lieutenant R.H.B. Jackson and his navigator, Flying Officer M.C. Murray, were airborne at 1845hrs. At 1957hrs contact with enemy aircraft was made but failed at 0545hrs. Nothing further was heard from Murray and his Mosquito Mk.II, HJ927, was reported missing, Flight Lieutenant Jackson was deputy commander and the crew's loss was felt deeply.

Better news was announced on 26 October when both Flying Officer H.H. Ladbrook and Flight Lieutenant M.A. Cybulski (Polish) were awarded the DFC for an earlier mission. They were the first crew to fly an RAF Fighter Command Mosquito on daytime operations over west Germany and flew many offensive patrols. They had taken off from Coleby Grange, where they were based before moving to Predannack and West Malling, shortly after 2000hrs, to make a Mahmoud (a sortie flown by Mosquitoes equipped with rear-facing radar) patrol between the Zuiderzee and Meppen. Except for some heavy flak, a concentration of searchlights and jamming of the AI set, the ninety-minute patrol was uneventful. Homeward-bound, Ladbrook got a radar contact and despite jamming he held it until he and his pilot caught sight of a Do 217 flying east. As the enemy pilot went into a steep climb, the night fighter closed rapidly to deliver a three-second burst. The Dornier immediately exploded with a terrific flash and descended, enveloped in flames. Burning petrol and oil flew back onto the Mosquito, scorching the fuselage from nose to tail, the port wing inboard of the engine, the bottom of the starboard wing, the port tailplane and the rudder, from which the fabric was torn away. Pieces of the aircraft struck the port oil cooler, resulting in the loss of oil and making it necessary to shut down the engine. The pilot was completely blinded by the explosion and it was necessary for the navigator to take control of the aircraft for approximately five minutes until Cybulski regained normal vision. A course was set for base and after a remarkable 250-mile flight on one engine with the aircraft seriously damaged the Mosquito got home safely. 'Cy' and 'Laddie' had more than once distinguished themselves on operations and the squadron was delighted when they received the DFC to climax the long period of splendid work.

On several other nights there were chases after 'bogeys', but the crews were unable to close. Once Squadron Leader March and Flying Officer K.M. Eyolfson followed a bandit, a Ju 188, to near the French coast, but it flew into a heavy cloud bank just as March was about to open fire. When the Mosquito followed, electrical disturbances caused the AI set to blow up and the hunt had to be abandoned.

Finally, on 5 November, the luck changed and No. 410 Sqn, nicknamed the Cougars, made the first of their long series of kills after the move to No. 11 Grp. While on patrol over the Channel off Dungeness Flying Officer C.F. Green and Pilot Officer E.G. White (RAF) were vectored after a bandit flying north at 23,000ft. White picked up the raider on his AI and Green closed in below, identifying it as an Me 410. The first cannon burst high around the port engine, whereupon the enemy went into a tight diving turn with the Mosquito in close pursuit. After further strikes, the Me 410 exploded with a brilliant white flash, breaking into burning fragments that caused another explosion when they struck the water.

Although only at West Malling for a few weeks, No. 410 Sqn had certainly been busy, but it was moved on to Hunsdon on 8 November.

During the evening of 30 October, Flying Officers R.L.T. Robb and R.C.J. Bray, in a Mosquito Mk.XII of No. 85 Sqn, were on patrol near Rye,

The Manor House accommodated many RAF officers and pilots during the war. It looks much the same today, and can be found on the right as you drive out of West Malling village. (KAHRS)

Sussex. They were vectored onto a target, which turned out to be a Ju 88S-1, '3E+AS' of 8/KG6. Closing in, they opened fire, striking the bomber. It immediately dived into the sea some 20 miles south-south-east of Rye at 2215hrs. Unteroffizier Freiberger was killed, his body being recovered and later buried at Hawkinge Cemetery on 2 November. Two others, Obersleutnant K. Selck and Unteroffizier H. Keppler, were reported missing. Their fate was unknown but they were thought to have perished, trapped in their sinking aircraft.

On a lighter note, the Air Officer Commander (AOC) Sports Cup was played at West Malling on 11 November, against Detling. The rugby and hockey teams lost their games but the football team won with a decisive 4-2 victory. Even in wartime there was still time to indulge in sporting activities, which no doubt was good for morale. A station dance was held in the officers' mess and many guests arrived including Group Captain Miller, Group Captain Malan (AEAF), Wing Commander P. Townsend (once the CO of RAF West Malling), Wing Commander Raphael (CO, RAF Manston), Wing Commander Hawkins (CO, RAF Detling) and Sir Albert Stern, who had much to do with the development of Army tanks.

The day 14 November was cold and wet, and a lone Spitfire Mk.VII of No. 124 Sqn, piloted by Pilot Officer Nowell, had taken off at 1310hrs to locate B-17 Flying Fortress *Del Cheyenne*, serial 42-30837, of the 385th BG, 8th USAAF, piloted by Lieutenant Hoder and based at Great Ashfield. Lost in poor weather, Nowell was vectored on to the bomber over Tonbridge and shepherded it back to West Malling. Flight Lieutenant C.F. Rawnsley wandered over to the B-17 as one of the gunners crawled out of the aircraft and started to dismantle his guns. Rawnsley asked the American if they had had much trouble with German fighters. 'Sure, dey keep comin' on in,' he said. 'But we got plenty o' dis stuff, see,' waving a gun barrel over his shoulder towards the ammunition trays. When asked where they had been, the American replied: 'We don't get paid nothin' for takin' it back, so I just keeps givin' it away. De ole one-two, see. We been around – we bin a ways. Say, what's dat lil country … next to France?'

When the weather cleared and the crew had rested they flew back to their base.

The following day, teams took on those of RAF Lympne and managed to win both the football and hockey but were thrashed at rugby, losing 25-3.

On 15 November, the CO of No. 85 Sqn, Wing Commander J. Cunningham, received documents from No. 11 Grp HQ. The document was an investigation of engagements of friendly fighters by searchlights and AA Gun batteries in England, which were becoming a problem for night fighter crews as they hindered promising interceptions. With such incidents it highlighted the breakdown in the control organisation of fighters, searchlights and AA units, all of which were under the operational control of either a group controller or a sector controller. Responsibility for this failure was blamed on RAF controllers, the assistants or the AA command control. Generally speaking, the system worked but unless these incidents, usually caused by negligence or even deliberate disobedience of rules, were investigated they were likely to increase. To improve the situation, meetings were held between the sector commander, squadron commanders, controllers and AA regimental commanders.

The following procedure was agreed by Cunningham and other commanders. In the event of a crash of a friendly fighter due to the engagement of AA gunfire or searchlights, a normal court of enquiry would be held by the air officer commanding (AOC) of No. 11 Grp if in the south-east. If a fighter was engaged or hit by AA fire, or engaged by searchlights, resulting in an interception being lost, an investigation would take place by all units involved. Pilots were encouraged to report such incidents, which would then be logged and investigated. Squadrons provided eight aircraft and eight crews each night operating in both moon and dark periods.

Group Captain Roderic Chisholm, CBE, DSO, DFC, who flew with No. 604 Sqn, RAuxAF, and was later CO of the Fighter Interception Unit (FIU) in 1942–43. Here he is pictured with groundcrew, and behind is a Beaufighter in night fighter matt black. He destroyed several German aircraft and later wrote of his experiences in his book, *Cover of Darkness*, published in 1953. (E.T. Sergison)

In addition, two fighters and two crews per squadron were held at one-hour notice, to be deployed in the event of heightened enemy activity. Crews were on duty from sunset to sunrise, a long stretch, but were not allowed to exceed their period of duty.

On a joint operation with No. 85 Sqn during early November 1943, Group Captain Rory Chisholm CO and Flight Lieutenant George Cook in a Mosquito of the Fighter Interception Unit (FIU) at Ford, were aided by Wing Commander J. Cunningham and C.F. Rawnsley in their Mosquito. Chisholm had served with Cunningham on No. 604 Sqn, RAuxAF, earlier in the war flying Blenheim Mk.IFs. The two aircraft took off from West Malling to patrol above the Inner Artillery Zone, in which guns were limited to 18,000ft and the fighters flew above 20,000ft. It was felt that the guns were not effective at higher altitude, and that fighters could fly over them to reach German aircraft. More of an exercise in propaganda, the patrol was not fruitful, and both aircraft failed to make contact. In addition to routine patrols, the sector controller maintained the remainder of the aircraft and crews at readiness on the ground. Crews detailed next to take off would be deployed at the first sign of enemy activity.

Another improvement was the instruction that all fighters manning searchlight orbit beacons were to test their AI in conjunction with searchlights before action began. There was little activity in the area, but during a night patrol by Mosquito Mk.XIIs of No. 85 Sqn on 16/17 November, one aircraft crash-landed at 2200hrs. Piloted by Flying Officer R.L.T. Robb and Flying Officer R.C.J. Bray, the observer, Mosquito HK173 was flying at 20,000ft when the port engine spluttered and coughed, due to icing in the carburettor, and lost power. Dropping down to 15,000ft, the engine appeared fine but again lost power. The pilot made for home and prepared to crash-land. He fired off the colours of the day and, lowering the flaps, he crash-landed at Nettleshead Green, 4 miles south of West Malling. Fortunately, although shaken, both crew members were uninjured. Ten bombers landed at West Malling on 18 November, one of these, Lancaster 'QR-Z' of No. 61 Sqn, RAF Skellenthorpe, had suffered damage during a raid on Berlin and the undercarriage collapsed on landing. The Lancaster had been hit on the port side and sustained damage to the tailplane. It was also damaged internally.

A Stirling of No. 214 Sqn landed with strikes to the starboard wing and upper and tail gun turret. The fuselage and starboard tanks were also damaged. It had been attacked by Fw 190s, but the rear gunner managed to hit the first, which blew up. On 26 November, a Mosquito of No. 96 Sqn, flown by Lieutenant Pritchard, collided with another Mosquito when taxiing out and, in another incident, Flight Lieutenant Kennedy swung to port on take-off, damaging the undercarriage, and carving up a section of runway.

Lieutenant G.M. Walker, pilot, and Lieutenant Commander P.N. Humphreys, navigator, of No. 96 Sqn took off from West Malling in Mosquito HK407 and crashed 3 miles west of the airfield near Swanton Valley Lake, killing both crew. The same day a Halifax of No. 77 Sqn landed at West Malling, during which a 1,000lb bomb dropped through the bomb doors but no casualties were reported.

In December, No. 554 Sqn was based at Benson, a photo reconnaissance unit that had been equipped with the Mosquito Mk.IX since September that year. On 2 December, Flight Lieutenant A.S. Pilcher and his navigator, Flying Officer D.F. Robins, had taken off in Mosquito Mk.IX LR419. The flight was their first high-altitude operational sortie, and they had been briefed to climb to 15,000ft over Benson and then to set course for Beachy Head. They had taken off at 1035hrs and no subsequent radio communication was received from them. At about 1113hrs, personnel at West Malling heard an aircraft diving in cloud at very high speed. Experienced Mosquito pilots described the sound it made as the 'bluest note' (RAF jargon) they had ever heard and estimated the speed as well above 450mph. The Mosquito descended to an estimated 5,000ft, when there was a terrific explosion and the aircraft crashed at Yalding. The Royal Observer Corps post nearest to the crash site had logged the altitude as 3,000ft when it exploded directly overhead, about 1½ miles from the actual position of the main wreckage. Pieces of the aircraft were then scattered for a distance of 4 miles downwind of the main crash site. On approach to the area, Robins was found dead some 60yd from the main wreckage. He had died on impact and his parachute was found 8 miles away; it had floated down fully deployed. The ROC had picked up the flight of the aircraft at Tring, and it was discovered that several Mosquitoes from Hatfield were in the area, confusing reports of its course. Both wings, the tail and fuselage had disintegrated in the air, and the starboard engine had become detached. The pilot's body was found strapped to his armour plate close to the remains of the cockpit. The last stage of the Mosquito's flight was an uncontrolled dive through cloud at very high speed and the significance of the setting of the pilot's oxygen register could not be ignored. It was likely that the pilot had passed out due to lack of oxygen and that cloud was entered before control of the aircraft was registered.

The month ended with another incident. During a patrol, Flight Lieutenant Pritchard crashed his Beaufighter, EL182 of No. 96 Sqn, at 1200hrs near Wateringbury, near West Malling. The crew were injured and taken to Preston Hall Hospital. No. 544 PR Sqn suffered a loss when Mosquito LR419 from Benson crashed from a great height at Reeves Farm, Yalding, about 4 miles from the airfield, killing both crew members, Flight Lieutenant A.S. Pilcher RCAF, pilot, and Flying Officer Robins, navigator. Their bodies were brought to West Malling.

No. 515 Sqn was formed at Northolt on 1 October 1942 from a unit known as a Defiant Flight. It had been secretly working on a system to jam enemy radar. During October, operations were flown on four nights. The Defiants flew over the Channel ahead of Bomber Command's raids to jam enemy radar, preventing the Germans from knowing the bombers' destination and where they were coming from. No. 515 Sqn was based at Heston and 'Moonshine' operations, as these flights were known, were flown by aircraft detached to Coltishall, Tangmere, Exeter and West Malling, eventually basing their ground crews on these forward bases.

The squadron's first operation from West Malling took place on 6 December 1942. The flight comprised of eight Defiant Mk.IIs, three of which took off from West Malling on night patrol, led by Squadron Leader S.D. Thomas, accompanied by Flying Officer B. Simmonds, in Defiant Mk.II AA438. These flights were carried out under No. 11 Grp's instructions. The other five aircraft took off from Tangmere and Coltishall; Such flights continued throughout December and January.

A night operation was ordered for 23 January and Defiant AA420, accompanied by AA430 and AA570, took off from West Malling at 1515hrs. Owing to poor conditions at West Malling, the Defiants' radiators became choked with mud. All three developed high radiator temperatures and had to return there at 1835hrs. The weather was bad and all aircraft remained at their various bases, with the exception of AA570, which flew from West Malling to Ford, arriving there at 1440hrs, and AA420, which flew from West Malling to Bradwell Bay, arriving at 1440hrs.

On 3 April a programme of air-to-air firing took place at Southend range and six aircraft of No. 515 Sqn took part with various crews. Warrant Officer S. Lewis and Flight Sergeant G.H. Korn, in Defiant AA435, upon landing at Southend at 1500hrs were unable to pull up by braking as the landing was downhill. The Defiant finally came to rest in a nose-down position. It was later found that the landing toe indicator was downwind, and after the accident it was turned around by the control officer. Both crew members were uninjured but AA435 was damaged.

In May, the squadron began converting to Beaufighter Mk.II aircraft, later flying collaboration flights and searchlight co-operation flights. On 8 June, all eight Defiants of No. 515 Sqn based on the forward bases headed for Hunsdon during the morning. All aircraft arrived safely, except for Flight Sergeant F.C.A. Steel and Flying Officer A.E. Gray, in Defiant AA535, who had left Tangmere. They crashed into a hill near Beachy Head and both were killed. They had been returning from patrol in thick fog. The last Defiant remained with No. 515 Sqn until December.

An unusual sight appeared in the sky over West Malling on 2 October 1943 when a DC-3 of BOAC, with mail and passengers bound for Lisbon, had to land due to poor weather. Later the same day, a B-17 Flying Fortress of No. 220 Sqn, RAF Coastal Command, landed completely lost in the foul weather. At the time it based at Thorney Island on anti-submarine patrols. Unfortunately, the B-17 swung to port on landing and disappeared over the bank at the southern end of the runway. Luckily, the crew climbed out, dazed and lost but uninjured.

On 21 December 1943 there was intense enemy activity in the area, more than experienced in 1940–41. Incendiaries were dropped on the airfield, in fact the first since 29 December 1940. Later that day, two Wellingtons of No. 30 OTU, Leighford, landed. The port engine of the first was unserviceable and the second landed with its escape hatch open, and spun badly on landing. Meanwhile, German incendiaries were dropped on the Bofors gun site on the south-east corner of airfield, destroying a generator hut and contents. At 2142hrs the power failed but was quickly restored at 2201hrs using the standby supply.

That night there was widespread enemy activity over London and south-east England, and both Nos. 85 and 96 Sqn were kept busy, destroying two Ju 88s. During these raids, bombs were dropped on a 'Q' Site located about 2 miles from the airfield. There were, in fact, two sites, one at Collier Street and the other at Hammer Dyke. As midnight approached incendiaries fell on the west end of the airfield and a hut was burnt out. One went through a blister hangar and was quickly extinguished.

Chapter 4

Airfield Expansion

Operations in 1944

The new year of 1944 started on a high note for No. 96 Sqn as it was granted a squadron crest and motto, *Nocturni Obambulamus*, (We prowl by night). The crest featured a lion passant facing to the sinister charged with ten stars representing the constellation of Leo.

The following day, 2 January, Wing Commander John Cunningham DSO, DFC and Flight Lieutenant Rawnsley, of No. 85 Sqn, destroyed an Me 410, which crashed on the French coast, and Flight Lieutenant Head and Flying Officer Andrews, No. 96 Sqn, brought down an Fw 190, which was later found at Rye, Sussex.

On 21 January, the day ended badly when West Malling was notified of a Mustang crash at Snodland, Kent. The aircraft, Mk.III FZ146, dived into the ground, killing Flying Officer Page, a pilot of No. 19 Sqn of No. 122 Wing, Gravesend, which comprised two other units, Nos. 65 and 122 Sqn, which had recently been re-equipped with the Merlin-powered Mustang Mk.III. Page's body was brought to West Malling prior to burial. It was later discovered that the Mustang had lost its tailplane.

An attack took place on the airfield on 21/22 January, which was recorded by Flying Officer Cook, the deputy defence officer of No. 2769 Sqn, RAF Regiment:

> 2003hrs. Red Warning. 2130hrs Incendiaries were seen to fall SSW corner of aerodrome outside perimeter track, and on 'D' Group Bofors site. Fire started in generator shed, also incendiaries fell in the surrounding woods. Fire extinguished at 2150hrs. Generator set damaged, a stretcher (First Aid), 7 gallons of petrol, ½ pint oil, Galvanised Shed, all destroyed. Damage to roof of shed, flying operations not affected.

The Royal Observer Corps reported that:

> An aircraft was alight on the ground at 0435hrs SSE of site. Another explosion was heard, and smoke seen due East. The all clear began to sound owing to the siren being hit on the fire station, and all through the remainder of the raid the siren sounded intermittently, due to a faulty electric short. Approximately 20 to 30 hostile aircraft height 15,000ft were heard in the vicinity, approaching from South, South West, travelling North. On several occasions aerial combats were heard to take place, or evasive action being taken North in an arc. Time unknown. A local inhabitant living near Mr Pierce's farm heard a falling missile at 0520hrs on 22 January 1944 near Comp Lane, Offham, which later turned out to be a container of bombs. Guns heard firing towards the Thames, a few searchlights seen in the distance for a short while.

Following the raid a bomb was dug out of a hedgerow on the road leading to Comp Lane, on the north side of the road from Offham to Paddock Wood. Another five bombs were found in ploughed fields along Comp Lane. The blast from one bomb caused damage to windows and the roof of farmhouses. The bomb exploded on a hill and the houses were below the level of impact, which accounted for the slight damage. Other bombs caused damage to Wateringbury Manor Farm and Latters Buildings and Hermitage Farm, Wateringbury, setting light to straw stacks. Unexploded bombs were located at Swan Wood and Pierces Farm.

On 23 January, a German pilot was reported to have been seen in the neighbourhood and search parties were sent out to find him, while precautions were taken at West Malling.

A Ju 88A, A4 of 6/KG30 '4D+EP', was shot down on 22 January by Sub Lieutenants J.A. Lawley-Wakelin and H. Williams in a Mosquito Mk.VII of No. 96 Sqn. It crashed on the railway embankment opposite the Hop Pocket public house, Paddock Wood Station, at 0432hrs. The crew, Leutnant H.J. Petzina, Gefreiter G. Lotz, and Obergefreiter O. Schweigel, were killed. Feldwebel K. Scherger bailed out but was injured and taken prisoner. The remains of the crew were brought to the mortuary at the airfield and later buried at Maidstone Cemetery. In 1973 the Ashford and Tenterden Aircraft Recovery Group recovered a Jumo 211J engine and bombs were also located.

The following day, a Spitfire Mk.VII of No.124 Sqn, West Malling, escorted a B-17 Fortress to RAF Eastchurch, Isle of Sheppey, Kent, where many B-17 Fortresses and Thunderbolts often landed. The squadron had been operating from the airfield and twelve Spitfire Mk.VIIs had taken off. On return, one burst a tyre and blocked the runway, although the pilot was uninjured.

Mosquito Mk.VII HK122 of No. 85 Sqn was reported missing on 28 January. Squadron Leader T.H. Blundell, RNVR pilot, and Squadron Leader J.A.T. Parker sent a Mayday call to Wartling control, 'Starboard engine on fire having to bail out.' The aircraft was thought to have crashed into the sea and an Albacore from Manston was sent out to search for the crew. An ASR launch from Dover joined in the efforts to locate the men and coastal lights were illuminated. Sadly, both had been killed when the aircraft crashed in the sea off Dungeness.

There was considerable enemy activity during the evening of 29 January, during which a parachute mine was dropped 200yd to the east of Cannon Court at the end of the south extension runway, just outside the perimeter wire. It damaged the roof and windows. Slight damage was also caused to a searchlight unit, and a hut was moved off its footings, but there were no casualties. Fortunately, ground crew of No. 85 Sqn 'B' Flight occupying a dispersal billet were uninjured. The Germans had targeted the bases at West Malling, Detling and Snodland.

No. 36 Maintenance Unit (MU) was based at the disused lime works with a small dock south of the works on the bend of the River Medway, with marshland to the south of the works. On the opposite side of the river, ¼ mile south of Woudham Hall, another lime and cement works had been taken over by the Admiralty. During the raid, fifty cordite rocket motors caught fire, a blaze that lasted for thirty-five minutes, and was dealt with by the fire service. It is difficult to say if any of these locations was the target due to bombing taking place above cloud, but West Malling and Detling operations were continued. At Detling, the RAF camp on a footpath north-east of Binbury Cottages was burnt out. Other damage was caused to Reservoir Cottage and Burham cement works. However, in retaliation, Flying Officers Hibbert and Moody of No. 96 Sqn destroyed a Ju 88, adding another German aircraft to West Malling's growing list of victims.

On 6 February, a play was presented in the NAAFI by H.M. Tennant Ltd with the help of Flying Officer Constance, the adjutant of No. 85 Sqn. The production, *Private Lives* by Noel Coward, was very popular and money collected for the station commander's benevolent fund amounted to £15. Well-known Fay Hammond, John Clements, Nicholas Phipps and Peggy Simpson made personal appearances.

The following day a loose barrage balloon drifted north of the airfield. Permission was granted from Biggin Hill sector to shoot it down but before this could happen it came down between Birling and the Wheatsheaf Inn on the Wrotham–Maidstone Road.

Aircraft from bomber operational training units (OTUs) took part in 'Bullseye' operations assisted by aircraft from West Malling. The bombers were engaged by searchlights and dummy attacks took place by night fighters from the airfield. To simulate an attack, the fighter flashed its navigational lights from the gunner's turret. During a Bullseye operation on 8 February, contact was lost with Flight Lieutenant Arthur Woods, AFC, and 2nd Lieutenant Jan Otto Richard Bugge, a Norwegian, of No. 85 Sqn. A message was received that their Mosquito NF.XIII, HK374 'R', had crashed into the sea off Emsworth following a collision with Wellington LN185 of 18 OTU over Southbourne, Sussex. It was reported that six members of the Wellington crew were also dead. The crew, all newly qualified, had flown from Finningley, then out over the Channel and turned back in towards Portsmouth to simulate the bombing run.

Woods was an experienced pilot. Aged 39, he was considered to be too old for combat and his experience was being used to train younger pilots and navigators. His navigator on this occasion was a member of the Royal Norwegian Air Force. The Mosquito had been fitted with an upgraded radar and this was Bugge's second flight with the squadron and with this equipment. A memorial plaque can be found in the area.

The crew of the Wellington were all buried at their home towns. They were Sergeant Ronald Henry Ramsey, pilot; Sergeant Reginald Graves, bomb aimer; Sergeant John Lomax Harrison, wireless operator/air gunner; Sergeant Alfred Cecil Jones, navigator, Sergeant William Varley, air gunner; and Sergeant Stanley Gordon Johnson, air gunner. A court of enquiry took place presided over by Wing Commander Lasbury during the week regarding the accident.

Another raid took place on 13/14 February 1944. Two RAF fighters had landed at West Malling, one at 2045hrs and one at 2052hrs, on the east to west runway, with Drem lights (airfield lighting) in operation. At 2045hrs and 2100hrs hostile aircraft were heard over the airfield, although the decoy airfield was in operation from 2040hrs. A further aircraft landed at 2140hrs and it was thought that the operation of the Drem lights had aided the attacking aircraft. Bombs fell in orchards at Swanton, south of Fish Pond and

Wing Commander E.P. 'Hawkeye' Wells, DFC and bar, a New Zealander, took over command of the Tangmere wing on 20 March 1944. This included Detling and West Malling wings. He is seated in his Spitfire Mk.Vb W3645 'OU-S', a presentation aircraft named *Waikato*. (IWM CH5061)

north-north-east of Worlds End Wood, damage being caused to fruit trees and cottages. Other damage was caused to Yotes Court near Paddock Wood, allotments north of Mereworth School and cottages at Smartwell Shaw.

A party was held in the officers' mess on 16 February to celebrate the award of a Second Bar to the DSO of Wing Commander J. Cunningham DSO, DFC. At the same time, No. 85 Sqn celebrated its 200th victory of the war. The 200th victors were Flying Officer C.F. Nowell and Flight Sergeant F. Randall. Among those present were the AOC, Air Vice Marshal H.W.L. Saunders, CB, CBE, MC, DFC, MM; Group Captain D.G. Morris; Group Captain Maxwell (Sector Commander); Group Captain Clark; Group Captain C.E. Moore; Wing Commander Grice; Wing Commander P.W. Townsend; Wing Commander B.R. Hoare; Wing Commander Hartley; Wing Commander D.J. Scott; and Wing Commander C.M. Miller, late CO of No. 29 Sqn at West Malling.

Snow fell on the morning of 19 February, at 1510hrs Flying Officers Hibbert and Morely, of No. 96 Sqn, crashed Mosquito Mk.XII HK297 in an orchard near the airfield at Mereworth; neither were seriously injured. An engine had failed on approach and the other cut out. Reacting quickly, Hibbert put down among the trees.

A narrow escape and cause for a small celebration as the same day England beat Scotland 6-2 at football! At 2215hrs on the night of 27 February, two airmen, S.N.N. Reid and J.B. McPherson, were involved in a car accident in which Reid was killed. Both served at West Malling with No. 2752 Sqn, RAF Regiment. The driver, Flight Lieutenant P. Hayward of No. 124 Sqn, was also killed. In a court of inquiry held at the airfield, the cause of death was decided to be accidental.

Following an air raid message at 0240hrs on 1 March, bombs were dropped near the airfield but apart from damaged windows there were no injuries or destruction.

Wing Commander J. Cunningham, DSO, DFC, was posted to No. 11 Grp from No. 85 Sqn and his place was taken by Wing Commander C.M. Miller. DFC, who was once CO of No. 29 Sqn.

Cunningham had been awarded the Russian Order of the Patriotic War, after being recommended for the decoration by West Malling. He had already destroyed sixteen enemy aircraft by the time he took over command of No. 85 Sqn and in 1943 and early 1944 he added a further four victories, one probable and one damaged. Cunningham's combat career ended with twenty victories, three probable and six damaged. He spent the remainder of the conflict in various staff officer positions. By the end of the war in Europe in May 1945 he had attained the rank of group captain.

Cunningham was made a CBE, and by the time he finished flying for the RAF had received a DSO and two Bars, and a DFC and Bar, also an AEM. He was not very keen on the nickname he was given, 'Cats Eyes'. On a personal note, when the author was an apprentice at De Havilland at Hatfield in the early 1960s, shortly after the company had been taken over by Hawker Siddeley Aviation, he was the chief test pilot. He was once said to have become most put out when some students removed a windsock. He was also known for giving advice to long-haired apprentices about getting a haircut!

Due to poor visibility over Sussex, aircraft based at Tangmere were diverted to West Malling. Between 1815 and 1830hrs on 6 March 1944, the following aircraft landed without incident: ten Spitfires from No. 44 Sqn, four Typhoons of No. 183 Sqn and six of No. 197 Sqn. However, Typhoon MN137 'TP-X', flown by Flight Lieutenant P.D.L. Roper of No. 198 Sqn, Manston, crash-landed 200yd short of the west–east runway, sliding along the runway with the undercarriage up. The pilot climbed out uninjured.

Overcrowding was becoming a problem at West Malling, which was not helped when, on 8 March, a Liberator, a B-17 Fortress and six Marauders landed between 1628 and 1835hrs from operations owing to their own base closing due to fog. The following day, three Mustangs returning from operations landed at 1225hrs and returned to their base at Leiston at 1430hrs. At midday on 11 March, the C-in-C of Allied Expeditionary Air Force, Air Chief Marshal Sir Trafford Leigh-Mallory, KCB, DSO, arrived by air, and No. 2769 Sqn, RAFR, provided a guard of honour. He spoke to all aircrews and later to squadron and flight commanders, lunching in the mess before leaving for RAF Gravesend shortly afterwards.

His visit was followed by that of Air Commodore C.C. Darley, chairman of the Aerodrome Committee, Air Ministry, who attended a meeting concerning the development of West Malling. Shortly after the meeting, everyone watched as Defiants of No. 264 Sqn, the first night fighter squadron at West Malling in April 1941, landed to take up residence for twelve months.

Returning from operations on 15 March, six Halifax aircraft of No. 432 Sqn arrived short of fuel, but two remained with mechanical faults, later taking off for their base at East Moor.

No. 124 Sqn left the same week for Church Fenton after being based at West Malling for nearly six months. They were replaced by sixteen

Flight Sergeant Chambers of No. 124 Sqn standing by his Spitfire Mk.VII during February 1944. The squadron had been based at West Malling in September 1943. Chambers was the first person to fly as a passenger in a Gloster Meteor; he was seated on the lap of the pilot, Flight Sergeant Ned Kelly, on an unauthorised flight. (W. Fricker/T. Neilson)

Spitfire Mk.VIIs of No. 616 Sqn, and No. 186 Sqn sent six Spitfires from Lympne for night flying practice.

A crash report was received by West Malling on 18 March when a B-24 Liberator crashed at Goudhurst, killing four crew members. The surviving six airmen were all injured. The aircraft, 42-52218 of the 733rd BS, 453rd BG, was based at Old Buckenham and had been bombing Friedrichshafen. The exact location of the crash was Tillinghurst, between Goudhurst and Kilndown.

Flying Officer E.R. Hedgecoe, pilot, and his navigator, Flying Officer N.E. Bamford, flying Mosquito NF.XVII HK823 of No. 85 Sqn, were on patrol on 24 March during an evening of high enemy activity over London and south-east England. They intercepted a Ju 188, one of seven to ten aircraft crossing the coast, none of which flew very far inland. At 21,000ft, they closed to 1,000ft, obtained a visual and opened fire. The first burst missed and, closing to 300ft to fire again, the Ju 188 exploded and disintegrated, covering the Mosquito with burning petrol and oil. Rudder fabric burned away and Hedgecoe ordered Bamford to bail out, but he cancelled the order when the flames went out and the Mosquito appeared

On 24 March 1944, Flying Officers E.R. Hedgecoe, DFC, and N.L. Bamford, of No. 85 Sqn, intercepted and destroyed a Ju 188 off Hastings. In the ensuing explosion their Mosquito Mk.XII, coded 'VY-O', was severely damaged but the pilot, despite being temporarily blinded, managed to return to West Malling, landing safely.

Flying Officers N.L. Bamford and E.R. Hedgecoe, DFC (on right), of No. 85 Sqn, one of the most successful night fighter crews of the war.

stable. With great skill, Hedgecoe managed to bring the damaged aircraft back to West Malling, where he landed safely. Sadly, both Hedgecoe and Bamford were killed on 1 January 1945 while serving with No. 151 Sqn at Hunsdon. They were awarded the DFC and Bar.

At 1400hrs on 1 April, Flight Sergeant D.E. Johnston, Royal Australian Air Force (RAAF), was on patrol during Operation Flash with two other Spitfire Mk.VIIs of No. 616 Sqn when he crashed near Tangmere, Sussex. His body was found with the wreckage of Spitfire MD116 'K', and he was later buried at Brookwood Cemetery. He had taken off from West Malling with Flying Officer Clegg and had flown into heavy cloud. That was the last Clegg saw of Johnston.

On 7 April, Flight Sergeant Roeson and Sergeant Piggott of No. 96 Sqn took off in Mosquito Mk.XIII HK405 at 2135hrs for circuits and bumps. Their first attempt to land resulted in an enormous bounce, on the top of which Roeson opened up and went round again. On the second attempt, in floodlights, they managed a three-point landing but the undercarriage

Flying Officers E.R. Hedgecoe and N.L. Bamford, looking unperturbed following their close call, inspect damage to their Mosquito. (KAHRS)

Another view of the damaged Mosquito. In the background stands a Mosquito NF of No. 29 Sqn. (KAHRS)

Flight Lieutenant John Cunningham, DFC, perhaps one of the most famous night fighter pilots of the war, who later became CO of No. 85 Sqn. Cunningham went on to be a successful test pilot with De Havilland Hatfield, flying the world's first jet airliner, the Comet. (Colin Gass)

Pilot Officer J. Allen, on the right, and Flight Sergeant J.M. Patterson of No. 29 Sqn, inspect the wreckage of the Ju 88 that they shot down on the night of 18/19 April 1944. Note the local people peering over the hedge. (IWM CH12786)

collapsed and caught fire. The wooden aircraft burnt out but miraculously both crew members staggered from their aircraft not badly injured. They had crashed on the interception of the east–west runway.

On 19 April, Wing Commander C.M. Miller, DFC, and Captain L. Lovested, flying a Mosquito of No. 85 Sqn, shot down a Ju 188E-1, which crashed at Golding Farm, Ivychurch, Kent, at 2330hrs. Feldwebel H. Richter, Obersleutnant. A. Hein and Unteroffizier J. Kohler were all killed but Unteroffizier H. Harbauer bailed out of his aircraft, '3E+BP', and was taken prisoner. The crew, like many others, were buried at Hawkinge Cemetery.

No. 616 Sqn continued operations and during one such, on 22 April, Warrant Officer D. Kelly, RAAF, was hit by flak over the Cherbourg peninsula. The perspex hood was splintered and he received a serious injury to his left eye, causing a loss of sight. Although in severe pain, he showed great determination and brought his Spitfire Mk.VII, MB767 'F', back to a forward base where, after two attempts, he made a normal landing without causing further damage to his aircraft. He was later put in for immediate award of the DFC, but most importantly the loss of sight was temporary.

The same day, No. 2769 Sqn, RAFR, and the WAAF supplied two parties of about fifty each to take part in a 'Salute the Soldier' parade at Southborough, Kent. Squadron Leader Sweeting and Flight Lieutenant Burrus were in command of each section. Salute the Soldier week was a fund-raising scheme to encourage civilians to save their money in government accounts, such as war bonds, savings bonds, defence bonds and savings certificates. Cash would be paid into post offices or banks. In much the same way as War Weapons Week, Salute the Soldier would coincide with a week of parades and exhibitions. In 1944 it was decided the national scheme would be themed around raising funds to equip an Army that would be good enough to take on the German Army on its own ground.

No. 91 Sqn, then part of No. 148 Wing, 2nd Tactical Air Force, arrived at West Malling from Drem early on the evening of 23 April with its Spitfire Mk.XIVs to take the place of No. 616 Sqn, which was moving to Fairwood Common with No. 6616 Service Echelon.

During these preparations, some fifteen enemy aircraft were reported south of the Isle of Weight moving in a south-westerly direction. Ten Spitfires were scrambled but a raid did not develop and they returned to West Malling just in time to witness a Mustang of the 9th USAAF based at Staplehurst advanced landing ground gliding into the airfield with engine trouble. Not long after, a Halifax of No. 76 Sqn arrived following an operation over Germany, followed by a Lancaster of No. 83 Sqn, No. 83 Grp, short of fuel.

Flight Lieutenant 'Johnny' Johnson flew Spitfire Mk.XIV RB188 while with No. 91 (Nigeria) Sqn during the busy month of July 1944. This aircraft was christened *Brumhilde,* and the nose art was one of the few photographically documented examples. 'Johnny' claimed thirteen V1s destroyed and one shared; five of these were shot down in RB188. (Squadron Leader J. Johnson)

Groundcrew swarm over Spitfire Mk.XIV of No. 91 Sqn during 1944. The aircraft is painted with the black and white stripes of D-Day. Note the RAF fuel tanker in the background, beyond a blister hangar.

Pilots of No. 91 Sqn enjoy a break from operations. The squadron had arrived from Drem on 23 April 1944 and had been based previously at Lympne, Hawkinge, Manston and Biggin Hill. The squadron returned to West Malling on 3 June 1946. (P. Hall/M. Llewellyn)

Jean Lambourne, a WAAF officer who arrived in 1940, also remembers 23 April. In her diary she wrote: 'I was in the entrance hall of the Officer's Mess and I saw them tumbling out of the back of their transport … the Station Commander, later Wing Commander J.A. O'Neill DFC, greeting them with drinks.'

It was the same evening that Jean met Capitaine Jean Maridor, a lively pilot. 'Mari' as he was known, was once asked why he did not wear the French badge on his uniform and remarked: 'Why should I? Everyone knows I am French!' No. 91 Sqn had many pilots of many nationalities: Canadian, New Zealanders, Australian, Belgian and two French, Mari being one and the other, Henri de Bordas. They were soon joined by another, Jacques (Jaco) Andrieux.

The squadron was commanded by Squadron Leader N.A. Kynaston, DFC. Jean remembers Jacques proudly showing her his Spitfire, and she was even allowed to sit in the cockpit. That evening, the 'Gang Show' gave a memorable performance, not to be forgotten. Romance blossomed between Jean and Mari, and when he asked to marry her she accepted. Their marriage was arranged for 10 August but fate stepped in, as described later in this chapter.

Air Vice Marshal J.B. Cole Hamilton, AOC No. 85 Grp, presents Flying Officer Jacques 'Jaco' Andrieux of No. 91 Sqn with the DFC on 9 May 1944. Andrieux had several victories flying Spitfire Mk.XII MB839. Note the Spitfire Mk.XIV in the background. (KAHRS)

A farewell party was given by No. 85 Sqn at Manor House Mess on 27 April. It had been based at West Malling for almost a year and was being moved to join No. 100 Grp at RAF Swannington on 1 May, but it would return in July. The party was well attended and both Wing Commander Cunningham and Flight Lieutenant Rawnsley joined in the festivities, along with Flying Officer E.R. Hedgecoe, who had been awarded the DFC.

The month did not close well, as Flying Officer J.A. Collis of No. 91 Sqn, flying Spitfire Mk.XIV RB187, was killed on a defensive patrol over the Thames Estuary on 29 April. The Spitfires they flew were considered very successful in their role at West Malling, and No. 91 Sqn's total score for the year was forty-seven and a half destroyed, twelve probables and fourteen damaged. The squadron was visited on 30 April by Air Vice Marshal J.B. Cole-Hamilton, CB, CBE, AOC No. 85 Grp, and Air Marshal Sir R.M. Hill KCB, MC, AFC, commanding Air Defence of Great Britain (ADGB). They were particularly interested in seeing the squadron's new Spitfire Mk.XIVs, lined up for inspection with pilots and ground crew. While they were at the squadron's dispersal, a scramble took place at the precise moment when the CO, Squadron Leader N.A. Kynaston, was telling the AOC how good was No. 91 Sqn. Flying Officer Johnny Johnson nipped off smartly but forgot to raise his undercarriage and was last seen disappearing over the horizon with it still down. He further aggravated matters when returning to base by doing a slow roll over the airfield. Not surprisingly, everyone, including the CO, rushed out of the mess thinking he had destroyed an enemy aircraft. Whether or not the display impressed the AOC is not recorded, but he most probably enjoyed the spectacle as Johnson performed his aerobatics.

At the beginning of May, 'A' Flt of No. 85 Sqn took off for its new base at Swannington. It was later followed by 'B' Flt and No. 6085 Service Echelon set off to join them. At 1000hrs, eight Mosquitoes of No. 29 Sqn landed from Drew. A further nine arrived at 1055hrs. Having been absent for a year, the squadron was surprised to find a number of its old personnel still at West Malling. Shortly after they taxied away to dispersal, a B-17 from the 305th BG at Chelveston, piloted by Lieutenant Martin, landed short of fuel. He was returning from operations, but landed without incident.

Air Vice Marshal A.E. Borton, CB, DSO, AFC, Regional Air Liaison Officer to No. 12 Region, brought Lord Monsell, the Regional Commissioner, HQ Tunbridge Wells, to visit the airfield on 2 May. They were given the grand tour of West Malling. The following day, Brigadier Learmouth and staff officers of (Searchlights) 2nd AA Grp arrived to be shown the workings of AI Mk.VIII and given a demonstration flight in a Beaufighter. That evening, Wing Commander P.W. Townsend, DSO, DFC, an ex-station commander and previous CO of No. 85 Sqn, arranged for officers of No. 85 Sqn to attend a dance at Windsor Castle.

For No. 91 Sqn, May began with shipping patrols at dawn and later at dusk. Most were uneventful, although they were hindered by poor weather. Many pilots suffered from the severe cold experienced on such flights, and were pleased when they were able to return to West Malling and warmth. Most of these patrols were flown by 'B' Flight and totalled thirty hours' flying time.

On 9 May, Flight Sergeant Geoff Kay narrowly avoided an accident when taking off on patrol. He headed straight for a Spitfire parked on the airfield and, despite being able to pull up, knocked the tip off one of the propeller blades with his starboard wing. Damage was caused to his starboard aileron but he nearly hit several airmen who were at work on the Spitfire he had hit. They only saved their skins as they saw him heading their way and ran like hell, scattering in all directions.

RAF West Malling as it looked during the war. The 'J' type hangar is situated top left with the control tower directly opposite. The runways are also visible, as are blister hangars out of the way in the trees in the lower area of this photograph. (KAHRS)

The weather on 9 May was fine and warm with no low cloud. This was ideal for No. 91 Sqn, which flew no fewer than ten defensive patrols. It turned into a busy day at West Malling, as a Marauder of the 323rd BG (USAAF) from Earls Colne flown by Lieutenant Parkinson landed with wounded crew, who were quickly removed from the damaged aircraft and taken to the station sick quarters. Onlookers were surprised to see another Marauder in the circuit, which landed safely on one engine without incident. The aircraft, of the 386th BG, was based at Great Dunmow.

A further four Mosquitoes of No. 409 Sqn from Hunsdon arrived on the 9th to reinforce No. 29 Sqn. The day ended with a visit by Air Vice Marshal Cole-Hamilton CB, CBE, AOC No. 85 Grp, who presented Flying Officer Andrieux of No. 91 Sqn with his DFC. A parade was organised outside and many photographs taken. Jaco, as he liked to be called, showed that he could be just as good on parade as he was flying. The parade ended with a march past by airmen that, considering they had not been on a parade ground since joining up, was performed well.

The following day, No. 91 Sqn flew its first fighter sweep in its Spitfire Mk.XIVs over France led by Wing Commander Oxspring, during which they escorted B-17s over eastern Germany. Their aircraft were fitted with 90 gallon drop tanks and the squadron flew 460 miles on this mission. Returning from a mission on 15 May, the CO, accompanied by Flying Officer Georg Balcombe, Flying Officer Jaco Andrieux and Flight Lieutenant Ray Nash, spotted a German staff car near Fécamp. They attacked and eliminated the vehicle and its three occupants.

That evening a party was held at the George, West Malling, by pilots of 'A' Flight and ground crew, and the following morning some were suffering the effects of a boisterous night! During the same week, the squadron was asked to perform a mock attack on the AA gun posts positioned around the airfield at West Malling so those manning them could get some practice at firing on attacking aircraft. The CO, with Flight Lieutenant Ray Nash, beat up the gun positions as requested, and the exercise lasted for twenty minutes with good results.

During a thunderstorm on 13 May, at about 1245hrs, Marauder '9F-Y' of the 597th BG crashed, piloted by Lieutenant Colonel Wood USAAF, after it had been hit by flak. Unable to lower its undercarriage and flaps owing to damage, the result was inevitable and the Marauder landed on its belly. Sadly, the bomb aimer, Lieutenant Frank K. Evans, was killed. Captain T. Nestlerode, 2nd Lieutenant I. Sanow and Staff Sergeant William Clifford were injured in the crash and taken to Preston Hall. The same day, the Secretary of State for Air, Sir Archibald Sinclair, Bt. KT, CMG, MP, visited West Malling by air. He was accompanied by Group Captain Louis Greig, who inspected the squadrons at dispersal.

During the afternoon of 15 May, Mosquito Mk.XIII MM575 of No. 96 Sqn crashed in a field at Cherry Orchard, Curtisden Green, near Staplehurst, Kent, following a reported mid-air explosion. Both crew members, Flying Officer R.D. Warren and Flight Sergeant D. Motherwell (Canadian), were killed. The crew had been detailed to carry out a night flying test and took off at 1435hrs. There was also an arrangement made for another Mosquito to join up with MM575 to carry out an air speed indicator comparison on completion of the flying test.

At 1512hrs, Flight Sergeant Motherwell radioed to the effect that he had been unable to contact the other aircraft. He was then at 2,000ft and intended climbing to 6,000ft before returning to base. Witnesses who saw the aircraft at about 1510hrs stated that it had dived out of the cloud and was flying level when there was a noise like an explosion and fragments were seen to fly off. After this the aircraft continued on its course for a short distance and then turned back through 180 degrees and crashed into the ground at a very flat angle.

The main wreckage, with the exception of the engines, was completely destroyed by impact and fire. Subsequent examination showed that the bodies of both members of the crew were still in their seats. It was concluded that the crash was caused by structural failure of the wings under pull-out conditions. The evidence indicated that the aircraft dived out of cloud and it is probable that loss of control led to a high-speed descent and a too rapid attempt to regain level flight. Splitting of the front spar lower booms was evident and may well have contributed to the collapse of the wing structure.

The same day, a lone enemy aircraft crossed the coast during the night and dropped a bomb on the headquarters. Some fourteen airmen were killed and fifteen seriously injured.

West Malling administered the advanced landing ground at Great Chart, Ashford, in 1944. There were twelve ALGs in Kent during 1943–44. It was at Great Chart that No. 5003 Airfield Construction Unit was based during May.

No. 2814 Anti-Aircraft Regiment moved to West Malling on 22 May, having just returned from Nyetimber RAF Regiment Camp, No. 83 Grp, near Chillington, where it was based. It was billeted under canvas and was due to move to Hunsdon. It came as a surprise when on 22 May, all available airmen were asked to help Kent Police to search and apprehend four boys who had escaped from a remand home at Hastings. Having stolen uniforms rifles and ammunition at the airfield, they were captured in woods nearby by Flight Sergeant Corr and two other airmen. The boys, following the theft, were cold and hungry and were found in a barn. Fortunately no shots were fired and there were no injuries.

Sir Bernard Montgomery landed at RAF West Malling at 1100hrs on 25 May, in his Dakota, which had taken off from Thorney Island on the way to Tunbridge Wells. It was not his first visit to the airfield, as he had previously arrived in March 1942 before he went to Egypt. During his visit he talked to many pilots and airmen, and inspected aircraft. Following lunch, he and his entourage boarded their aircraft and it took off for Hawkinge at 1347hrs.

During the afternoon of 29 May, Flight Sergeants McLardy and Devine of No. 96 Sqn were coming into land when a wheel came off their aircraft, Mosquito HK426. The undercarriage gave way and the aircraft caught fire and burnt out. Fortunately, both crew members escaped with minor injuries. However, one of the National Fire Service (NFS) firemen was injured by exploding ammunition, and the east–west runway was put out of action for six hours.

Field Marshal Montgomery, KG, GCB, DSO, PC, DL, visited the airfield on 25 May 1944. He was accompanied by General Crear, seen standing behind Montgomery. On the right, closest to the camera, is the CO of RAF West Malling, Wing Commander J.A. O'Neill, DFC. Note the control tower in the background.

Field Marshal Montgomery climbs into his Dakota following his visit, which came only two weeks before D-Day.

On 1 June, a Halifax of No. 77 Sqn based at Sutton landed badly damaged by flak on the way home from a mission. Flying Officer Dye was hit in the leg and arm and taken to Preston Hall EMS Hospital. He was later placed on the dangerously ill list and died of his injuries at 2035hrs.

Throughout May, No. 91 Sqn had continued with shipping and patrols over the French coast, during which many vessels were seen to be concentrating in the Solent, which indicated to all that an invasion was soon to be a reality.

On 5 June there seemed to be little doubt that this was indeed the case, and this was confirmed when No. 91 Sqn was confined to camp. That evening all pilots were rounded up and the wing commander briefed them on what was about to take place. That night everyone, somewhat apprehensive, but excited at the prospect of encountering the Luftwaffe, slept fitfully. Everyone at West Malling was up early on 6 June and watched as all the aircraft had the fuselage and wings painted with broad black and white stripes, for easy recognition by all services.

On D-Day, an announcement by General Dwight Eisenhower, Supreme Commander Allied Expeditionary Force, was heard over the tannoy system at West Malling as the BBC broadcast his message to all Allied Services.

No. 91 Sqn carried out a sweep over Saint-Omer, taking off at 0835hrs, but did not meet any German fighters, and it was a disappointing day for the eager pilots. Patrols continued over the French coast and, on returning from a sweep on 8 June, the squadron was delighted to find Warrant Officer 'Red' Blumer, who had returned to No. 91 Sqn after a somewhat prolonged absence. He had been shot down by flak during Rhubarb (fighters flying low attacking targets such as railways, airfields and army units) operations over Grémonville, France, crashing in Spitfire Mk.XII EN626 'DL-E'.

With a name like 'Red' it was obvious he had had to dye his hair black to pass off as a Frenchman! He escaped to Switzerland and then Spain, where he was interned, but eventually arrived in England via Gibraltar. His aircraft was captured by the Germans and was the first Griffon-engined Spitfire they recovered intact. Following scrutiny by the Luftwaffe, EN626 was flown at the Rechlin test centre, before joining 2 Staffel Versuchsverband Oberkommando der Luftwaffe (2nd Flight of the Luftwaffe HQ Trials Unit), but the aircraft's final fate is unknown.

The previous few days had been hectic as everyone had been extremely busy preparing for these operations. Mosquitoes of No. 96, 29 and 409 Sqn were on night patrols, in total thirty patrols were flown on the night of

6/7 June. The station commander, Wing Commander J.A. O'Neill, DFC, joined Squadron Leader Bond of No. 91 Sqn and took off in Spitfire Mk.XIVs on convoy patrol, on 6 June, the CO wanting to play his part. On return to base, they heard that Flying Officer J.C.O. Allen and Sergeant W.M. Paterson had both been killed when their Mosquito NF.XIII, MM451, crashed into the sea off Ramsgate. Despite ASR launches searching the area their bodies were not recovered.

During a routine patrol on the night of 7/8 June Mosquito Mk.XIII HK413 'RO-O' was reported missing while on patrol off Beachy Head. The aircraft crashed into the sea and both crew members, Flight Lieutenant Densham and Flying Officer Ellis, navigator, were killed. Their bodies were later recovered and both were buried at Bayeux Cemetery. However, fellow crews of No. 29 Sqn had some success that night when three German aircraft were destroyed, one being confirmed as a Ju 188.

After D-Day the role of No. 409 (Night Hawk) RCAF Sqn changed. Prior to D-Day, night patrols were on the defensive, now they were offensive and operations were flown at night over the beachhead. Crews ranged deep into hostile territory attacking and breaking up enemy formations of bombers and strafing aircraft on the ground, and 'kills' became a common occurrence. Flying Officer 'Red' Pearce, one of the most colourful pilots of No. 409 Sqn, had the distinction of being the first West Malling pilot to attack enemy aircraft on 5/6 June.

Pearce, with his navigator, Flying Officer Don Moores, were scrambled and on reaching 23,000ft made contact with a Ju 188. They were seen by the German crew, and violently peeled off, but Pearce managed to reduce the distance to 2,000ft, confirming it was indeed a Ju 188. At 400yd he fired a short burst, but saw no strikes. Closing in to 250yd, he fired again and this time numerous strikes were observed on the fuselage and cockpit area. The Ju 188 went into a steep dive but, owing to cloud, Pearce was unable to following it all the way down and they were only given a 'probable' destroyed.

It is well known that during flying operations aircraft sometimes came under fire from the same squadron or another unit in the area. Once such incident occurred on 12 June when Flying Officer A.B. 'Scotty' Sisson, pilot, and Flying Officer Nick Nicholson of No. 409 (Night Hawk) Sqn RCAF were on a routine night patrol over France flying Mosquito NF.XIII HK576. Sisson usually flew with Flying Officer Tom Lennie of Calgary as his navigator, but he was sick at the time of this operation.

'It's one of ours, Nick. He's opening fire!' Sisson saw tracer bullets arc towards them and he threw the Mosquito's wing up as though to ward off the blow. It worked. The machine-gun fire hit the wing and penetrated the starboard engine, while some entered the bottom of the cockpit. One bullet hit Sisson's foot, taking off the heel of his flying boot. The hydraulics were ruptured and everything was a mess; they knew the Mosquito was finished! 'Let's get the hell out of here, Nick,' urged Sisson. They were both wearing their parachutes and jumped out the navigator's side door, landing safely a few minutes later. They had attempted to fly home, but after a few minutes realised the Mossie wouldn't make it.

Sisson was from Elm Creek, Manitoba, and Nicholson was from Cloverdale, British Columbia, and had tried to join up in 1939 but was still waiting for a reply when he applied again in autumn 1941. He went to Manning Depot at Edmonton, Initial Training School (ITS) at Saskatoon, Elementary Flying Training School (EFTS) at Prince Albert and Service Flying Training School (SFTS) at Carberry. He graduated as a pilot officer pilot in autumn 1942 and went overseas in December.

In Bournemouth, at the RAF Personnel Reception Centre, there were nearly 10,000 Canadian aircrew and a surplus of pilots. Many pilots were being asked to remuster to other aircrew trades and even some to non-flying capacities. Sisson had always wanted to be a night fighter pilot so he refused the frequent urgings. He began to work on the Link trainer daily to improve his flying abilities and was judged to have good eyes for night flying. Finally, a posting came for advanced flying at an OTU at Grantham, near Nottingham, and Charter Hall, just over the border into Scotland. In late 1943 he was in No. 409 Sqn flying the Beaufighter Mk.II, then Beaufighter Mk.VIFs and finally in March 1944 they got Mosquitoes. Sisson recalls: 'They were a delight to fly and what speed, we began doing practice flying late in the afternoons before going on ops at night.'

Sisson and Nicholson parachuted down in the vicinity of Rouen and, after laying low for a while, managed to buy some civilian clothes and a couple of French passports. They hoped to be rescued by the advancing Allied armies but at this stage didn't even know if the invasion was successful. After a couple of days they were picked up by the German army, handed over to the Gestapo and spent six weeks being interrogated in Fresnes prison in Paris. Having been captured in civilian clothes, they were suspected of being spies because they happened to be near the V1 launching sights. There was a strong possibility of their being shot, but they were lucky in being sent to Stalag Luft III for the duration. By March 1945 the POW camp was breaking up and they began their march west, to keep ahead of the Russians. During the march, there were many tense moments from the enemy and also from strafing Allied aircraft. However, they finally made their destination north of Hamburg, and they were flown back to England next day in a Lancaster. No. 409 Sqn lost more than forty aircrew killed in the war, but only had two POWs.

The following day, two Halifaxes of No. 78 Sqn, based at Linton-on-Ouse, made emergency landings at West Malling, during which damage was caused to the runway and as a result a number of based aircraft were diverted to Ford until it was repaired. One of the crew, the rear gunner, Sergeant Lillies, who had been injured, died later, having been taken to Preston Hall. Shortly after, a Liberator of the 861st BS, 493rd BG, Debach, landed on three engines and low on fuel. At about 1730hrs on 10 June, the first V1 or Buzz Bomb/ Doodlebug, was heard to circle the airfield, but at the time no one at West Malling was officially aware of it.

It was reported by flying control on 11 June that:

> Enemy appeared to use a new weapon against this area on three occasions during the early morning. Radio Controlled pilot-less planes or glider bombs may be the answer. Several passed over or in close proximity to the airfield. One exploded approximately 1 mile West of airfield and possibly another NE. Beacon crew reported bomb in Chatham during first alert. Great difficulty in plotting this new weapon. Squadron Leader Mackinson and Flight Lieutenant Pilcher searched area where enemy projectile was thought to have exploded west of airfield. Projectiles found to have exploded in a field at Crouch.

A new 'Q' site decoy airfield at Lenham and Hammerdyke was activated at 0355hrs on 12/13 June. As some decoys covered a considerable area, their existence during the war was well known to the farmers on whose land they were often situated, and to others who lived or worked in the countryside. In keeping with the wartime code of secrecy, however, no one talked about them. Nevertheless, an article, 'Red Herrings for Luftwaffe', appeared in *Flight* magazine as early as November 1945. The author wrote of the decoy lighting, decoy fires and dummy production plants complete with parks of derelict cars, dummy roads, real smoke from dummy chimneys, and all the other necessary trimmings, including dummy aircraft on the alleged tarmac. Decoys had first been used during the First World War on the Western Front by the Royal Flying Corps, which constructed fake airfields consisting of tents, huts and a few unserviceable aircraft 3 miles from real airfields and in the likely line of the flight of bombers. Paraffin flares were added at night.

Chapter 5

The V1 Campaign

On the front line in 1944–45

The first report of V1s by aircraft from West Malling took place on the night of 12/13 June 1944. A Mosquito of No. 96 Squadron flown by Flight Lieutenant Frank 'Togs' Mellersh, DFC, was approaching to land when a V1 crossed the airfield at 1,500ft travelling slowly and trailing a yellow flame. Another crossed over the airfield at about the same height, crashing 5 miles due south.

At 0515hrs on 15/16 June, the CO of No. 96 Sqn, Wing Commander E. Crew, DFC, had taken off in an effort to intercept a V1. The squadron diary records: 'The robot bombers (V1s) started to come in strength tonight and continued in a steady stream into the morning. The ack-ack was terrific and fighters couldn't get anywhere near them, though the CO went up to find one and was hit by flak himself.'

It was not until the night of 16/17 June that No. 96 Sqn opened the score, when Flight Lieutenant D.L. Ward in Mosquito Mk.XIII HK415 'ZJ-R' intercepted a V1 between Dungeness and Boulogne, and it exploded over the sea at 2302hrs. This was followed by an attack on another at 2330hrs by Squadron Leader A. Parker-Ress in Mosquito Mk.XIII HK248, which exploded in the air off Dover. During a defensive patrol on 16 June, flying Mosquito Mk.XIII HK370, Flying Officer I.S. Girvan and Lieutenant Caldwell shot down a Ju 88 but was hit by flak over Velognes. Despite the damage, they nursed their aircraft over the Channel and crash-landed at RAF Ford. Both crew members were uninjured.

An unidentified aircraft was heard in the vicinity of West Malling at 0330hrs, thought to be a V1 reported by Biggin Hill, which exploded near the airfield. Flare path lights were put out pending identification. The aircraft crashed beyond the west extension about half a mile from the airfield and it turned out to be a Mosquito of No. 141 Sqn flown by Flying Officers

Lagouge and Van den Berghe, both Dutch. They sustained shock and minor injuries. The Mosquito was badly shot up and was flying on one engine.

During a barrage against V1s on 18 June, personnel of No. 2814 Regiment had a narrow escape when debris and shrapnel fell onto tents used as an orderly room and officers' mess. Although they were occupied at the time there were no injuries. Later, on 22 June, the unit moved by road to Hunsdon to join 148 Airfield.

The advanced landing ground at High Halden, near Tenterden, was home to the 358th FG, 9th USAAF, comprising three squadrons. One of these, the 367th FS, was equipped with the P-47-15-RE Thunderbolt. On 21 June, a mass formation of forty-six aircraft took off from High Halden, tasked with giving withdrawal support to B-17s attacking targets in the Berlin area. Gradually the group formed up, entering dense overcast cloud at 1,500ft, and it was during this manoeuvre that Lieutenant George T. Malone of Blue Flight, flying P-47 42-76278, lost sight of the other aircraft. At 0855hrs he collided with P-47 42-76577, flown by Captain Edward H. Sprietsma. In the ensuing crash 2 miles south-west of West Malling, both died instantly and when personnel from the airfield and High Halden arrived they found wreckage strewn over a large area of countryside.

No. 41 Sqn was stood down following two days of unsuccessful V1 patrols and poor weather in June. Pilots had a chance to relax and a good session was held at the officers' mess, where Flight Lieutenant 'Tommy' Burne hosted the evening as undisputed chairman and 'noggin master'. Burne could have sat out the war as he was disabled. In 1942 he had been serving as a Hudson pilot in Singapore and was severely wounded, after which his leg was amputated. Determined to return to flying, he volunteered to fly fighters and was eventually posted to No. 41 Sqn and flew his share of V1 patrols and operational sorties.

During the evening of 25 June, Lieutenant Henri de Bordas, flying Spitfire NH654, and Warrant Officer R.A.B. 'Red' Blumer (Australian), in RM617, took off from West Malling at 2230hrs on Diver (the code name for V1 operations) patrol. They headed south over the Weald of Kent on a patrol line from Ashford to Tenterden, where the Frenchman destroyed a V1 over Woodchurch. The two Spitfires then turned for home. Blumer landed at the advanced landing ground at Staplehurst to refuel. By then the weather had deteriorated as he took off for the short flight to West Malling. As 'Red' approached West Malling, he inexplicably dived into the ground. It was not until the morning that the crash site was located and his body recovered. His death was felt deeply as he had just returned to the squadron on 8 June, having been shot down over France on 6 November 1943 and had evaded capture for six months.

In late 1943, a small order was placed for Miles M.38 aircraft for use in a VIP transport role with the name Messenger, and eventually a total of twenty-one were built. Among the VIPs allocated personal Messengers were Field Marshal Sir Bernard Montgomery, Marshal of the RAF Lord Tedder and the Under Secretary of State for Air, Harold Balfour. Having flown with No. 43 Sqn during the First World War, Balfour often took the opportunity to indulge his passion for flying. The M.38 he flew was looked after by No. 24 (Communications) Sqn, then based at Hendon, from where he would take off, mostly at weekends.

In his book, *Wings over Westminster,* he recalls one of these flights:

> Each weekend I flew off, sometimes alone and sometimes with a Parliamentary colleague as passenger, to visit fighter and bomber training stations. When the boys saw my little M-38 almost standing still in the air, flutter down like a leaf and touch down on the concrete apron—all strictly out of order—they were quite amused. The more so when I lent them the M.38 to try out for themselves. One morning I was at Biggin Hill going on to West Malling, near Maidstone. Wing Commander Peter Townsend of Battle of Britain fame also wanted to get to West Malling so he came along in my passenger seat. The weather was overcast and misty with a ceiling of about 300ft. I was quite happy with this for the trip was only a few minutes and there was no high ground to cross. We started off and then ran into fog rolling in from the Channel spreading over Kent. The ceiling went down to 100ft. I put flaps half down, throttled back and stayed on course very comfortably at about 45 m.p.h. forward speed. As we came to the edge of West Malling village we were getting pretty low over the chimney tops. I asked Peter if he recognised exactly where we were. Peter's reply was what is to me an all-time classic flying instruction. 'Go straight up the main street and turn left at the traffic lights.' This I did and sure enough a moment later the end of the runway loomed out of the fog below us.

June ended with a visit by Duncan Sandys MP, who was touring various airfields to inspect anti-Diver measures. A total of 128⅓ V1s were

Stories of fighter pilots tipping over V1s during the hectic summer of 1944 were indeed true. Here one such pilot, of No. 316 Sqn, proudly displays the damaged wing tip from his Mustang Mk.III, during early July 1944.

destroyed by squadrons at West Malling from 13 to 30 June 1944, and No. 91 Sqn topped the scoreboard with 57⅓. No. 322 Sqn brought down 31½; No. 41 Sqn, 11½; No. 610 Sqn, 12; No. 96 Sqn, 9; No. 409 Sqn, 1; and last but not least, the RAF Regiment shot down another 6.

To assist with the overwhelming number of V1s launched towards England, No. 316 (Warsaw) Polish Sqn arrived from Coltishall. It had been equipped with the Mustang Mk.III adapted for the RAF and powered by Merlin engines. The squadron's engineer officer recalled that the Mustang Mk.III could be given 'extra speed' to catch up with the V1 by increasing the boost of the engine, though only for five minutes as any longer would cause damage. Senior Rolls-Royce representatives arrived at Coltishall with the necessary parts for modifying the Mustang's engines, after which they were flown to West Malling to take on the V1s. Another feature much appreciated by the Mustang pilots was the Malcolm hood, which gave the pilot all-round vision.

Polish pilot Warrant Officer Aleksander Pietrzak of No. 316 Sqn posing for a photo during the squadron's few days at West Malling in July 1944. He claimed four V1s and one shared, plus three German fighters, one shared. Note the 500lb bomb; the squadron was also flying ground attack sorties as well as V1 operations. (Sikorski & Polish Institute)

No. 316 Sqn's diary gives an insight into its involvement in operations against the V1:

> From the first days of July 1944, we were engaged in shooting down flying bombs. Our daily patrols, each section at a time, two aircraft to each section and one section must be airborne always. We were doing our duty in rotation, one section from 'A' Flight then one section from 'B' Flight but spasmodic change takes place sometimes owing to the shortage of aircraft. Modified Mustang IIIs giving 25 Boost and 420 mph at 2,000ft, not always gave the results which we expected. Overworked engines began giving trouble, which could be felt by sudden kick and vibration. New 150 octane petrol, which was supposed to eliminate that, caused reduction of speed, engine became sluggish, kicks and vibration continued and four aircraft had 'air intake' blown out. New petrol increased

the kicks, and vibration during the use of boost, which also caused build-up of lead deposit on the sparking plugs. We were advised to burn up that deposit by running to 22 pounds per square inch, alas without noticeable results. There were days when the squadron only had 5 or 6 aircraft suitable for flying. Constant delivery of new aircraft saved the situation and kept the intensity for the patrol. Allocation of a specific district for our squadron to patrol was frequently changed by the AOC Air Defence of Great Britain (ADGB), so there was a possibility of co-ordination for the use of every branch of defence. Air Force, anti-aircraft guns and balloons. Equally individual types of aircraft could perform its task according to its capability. In the beginning of disorganised defence quite often six aircraft were firing at one flying bomb, then each section was allocated a specific time for patrol. A section was not allowed to leave their time, except on the order of the control tower and shoot down only the flying bombs in reply to the German tactics, who started sending bombs in waves, sometimes only one minute apart. Before all aircraft were pursuing one bomb letting the next wave fly undisturbed, now these kind of incidents didn't take place. Our squadron (316 Squadron) in the beginning was patrolling over land, then next time was near the Channel and finally, when near Friston we were allocated on two occasions to the French coast. First time near Boulogne and then Le Havre. Spitfires were patrolling in the middle of the Channel. Tempests, being the fastest aircraft, were patrolling over land between anti-aircraft defences and balloons.

Of course, being furthest from London, we had less chance of shooting down flying bombs, as they were sent from many places on the French coast forming a radius on London, which means they were more crowded near the target but only few at our allocated time and it was difficult to spot them. It was understandable that our patrols returning to the base quite often not encounter any, although London received its portion and Tempests pilots did not have reason to complain that their endeavour was unproductive. Culmination point of our harvest of flying bombs was the first two weeks at West Malling when nearly every pilot reported success not only over the bombs but over the Tempests, which considering their speed, did not beat our Mustangs. Day after Day the number of bombs shot down by our pilots was growing with encouraging speed and quite often a pilot would shoot down two or three. Soon when a pilot returned reporting he had shot down only one he was sarcastically asked if his guns had jammed. During four incidents when aircraft after inspection were test flown, four bombs were shot down. Once when a patrol was taking off, a pilot was blinded by the sun and was separated from his leader. He noticed a flying bomb in front of him, he fired and the bomb exploded. Fortunately he did not sustain any damage.

The technique to combat the latest German invention was to increase speed difference, which was the main factor in spite of the fact that the flying bomb's speed was less than 400mph. Our superior speed was not sufficient, therefore we later adapted a technique when we were positioning our aircraft in line with the bomb in front and above. As it passed under the aircraft we pushed the control column slightly down and fired from a distance of 300yds. Guns were synchronised accurately for that distance because any closer range would be dangerous if the bomb exploded. The squadron did not perform any test training flights. The squadron did not perform any test training flights. 'A' Flight flew to West Malling, from RAF Coltishall, where 'B' Flight remained until all aircraft modifications are finished. Later 'B' Flight re-joined No. 316 Squadron at West Malling, a very pleasant airfield, despite being situated right in line of flying bombs.

We now have the opportunity to watch these monstrous machines from the ground anytime, day or night. Because of overcrowding in the mess, our quarters are in the big house four miles away from the airfield, very comfortable. This house with a very interesting history was built by the Freemasons, later sold to the Spiritual Society. The house was given to the RAF during the war for its use, completely furnished, without charm, but comfortable.

The large garden was planted with trees and magnificent rose beds, each rose represented a member of the society, everything appeared like a place you dream about.

The Great Hall had no electric lights. One day we had a ceremony for receiving the Polish Air Force banner, as each squadron had a privilege of having it for three months, the banner was made by ladies of Wilna, Poland during the war and smuggled to England in 1941. We received the banner from 315 Squadron, it was a solemn occasion, our thoughts and hearts were in Poland, together with those brave people, who believed in us, in victory, and told us to carry this banner high as other free countries. F/O Karkowski, trying to tilt a flying bomb with the wing of his aircraft had bad luck, damaging the wing and flap but was lucky enough to land safely. The squadron was moved to Friston near Eastbourne.

No. 316 Sqn was led by the newly appointed and legendary Polish ace Squadron Leader Bohdan Arct, Polish Air Force, who wrote at the time:

On 1 July we received posting to West Malling airfield, right on the route of the Flying Bombs and for this reason we anticipated to be in the midst of fighting and chasing the infernal projectiles. I took one flight only to West Malling, as the other had not yet finished modifications. Flying in close formation we beat up the airfield to show how the Poles fly, then formed an echelon to land with perfect precision. I taxied to dispersal point, switched off the engine, jumped out and reported to the station commander, who was already waiting outside the barrack. 'You certainly know a lot about formation flying,' he said in a friendly manner. 'Well, let's see if your aiming is as good. There is plenty of good shooting around here, Look there.' I glanced in the indicated direction and saw the well-known silhouette whizzing past the airfield with lightning speed. Guns roared, the bomb cackled overhead and disappeared in the direction of the capital. 'How many of them pass over here, Sir? I asked. 'Too many! Swarms of them every day. Some blow up around West Malling, most get to town (London). Serious damage is being done. Well, Squadron Leader Arct, you'll find yourselves bloody busy, mark my word. The bomb chase has high priority. Good hunting!' The station commander warmly shook my hand and departed. This way I became the leader of the first Polish squadron assigned to combat the flying bomb.

Several Mustang IIIs became unserviceable due to engine failure, with some pilots having exceeded the advice on boosting the power of the engines.

The 'chuck wagon' was always a welcome sight on any airfield, and here airmen que for their morning tea and a bun at West Malling during July 1944. (Sikorski & Polish Institute)

At least four Rolls-Royce fitters were billeted at West Malling to assist with modifications. It was not long before the Poles settled down at West Malling and indeed also the two ALGs at Friston, Sussex, and Brenzett, located on Romney Marsh, where they were to become successful in destroying the V1s.

Arct recalled: 'There was no time for any leave or days off, although our unit contained thirty pilots and twenty Mustang IIIs. We talked exclusively of "flying bombs", discussing and arguing the best methods of shooting them down.' The Poles boasted that they would not press the firing button until they could see the red-hot ring of the engine's exhaust nozzle.

Polish airmen normally refereed to the V1 as the 'witch', while other terms such as Buzz Bomb, Doodlebug, Flying Bomb and Diver were the most commonly used. The Germans christened them, *Vergeltungswaffe*, Vengeance weapon, while they were also known as *Kirschkern* (Cherrystone) or *Maikäfer* (Maybug). The V1 was an early pulse jet-powered cruise missile, the first production aircraft of any type to use this type of propulsion.

It was not long before Polish pilots added to the scoreboard, Flight Sergeant Toni Murkowski, flying Mustang FB352 'SZ-C', was the first pilot

Warrant Officer Aleksander Pietrzak of No. 316 (Warsaw) Polish Sqn, destroyed four V1s with one shared, two of these while at West Malling. He received the Virtuti Militari 5th Class and the Cross of Valour and two Bars. Pietrzak died in a flying accident on 2 August 1945 in Mustang FX876 at Oaks Field, Goulds Farm, Braintree, Essex. (Aircrew Remembrance Society)

of No. 316 Sqn to attack a V1. Monday, 3 July was a foggy day at West Malling and many of the Polish officers had strolled over to the officers' mess for lunch. The tannoy sounded and he scrambled to intercept a V1 over Rye. Murkowski was in for a shock as he kept the over-boost revs up for no more than ten minutes so as not to ruin the engine. He opened fire at 250yd and the V1 exploded with such violence that pieces flew over his Mustang. On landing, the wing-tips of the aircraft had to be changed! A large chart was hung in the squadron's dispersal and Murkowski's name with a miniature V1 at the side was written honourably at the top.

Flight Sergeant H.C. Cramm, a Dutch pilot of No. 322 Sqn, destroyed a V1 off Dungeness at 1700hrs. During the ensuing explosion his Spitfire, NH699 'VL-R', was caught in the explosion, but it was able to landed safely at West Malling. He recalled: 'Patrolling 10–15 miles south of Dungeness when vectored on to Diver. Attacked line astern range

Operations against the V1 could be extremely hazardous. During one such interception, Spitfire Mk.XIV NH699 '3W-P' of No. 322 (Dutch) Sqn, flown by Flight Sergeant H.C. Cramm, was damaged as it flew through the fireball created by an exploding V1. Fortunately the pilot, who was not injured, managed to return to West Malling and land.

250 yards, and saw strikes in starboard wing. Diver slowed down and I closed in to 100 yards and attacked again. Diver exploded and my Spitfire was scorched by the explosion.'

No. 6 Works Flights arrived at the airfield on 4 July and were quickly settled in as they were to erect balloon sites to the north and west. These formed additional V1 defences. As this work progressed, Nos. 80 and 274 Sqn arrived from Gatwick, accompanied by No. 6080 and 6274 Service Echelons attached to the fighter units. The new arrivals soon joined Nos. 91, 322 and 316 Sqn on anti-Diver patrols.

At 1845hrs on 6 July, Flight Lieutenant Snic, of No. 316 Sqn, crashed Mustang Mk.III FB373 at West Malling. During the landing the undercarriage collapsed but the pilot was uninjured. On the same day, another No. 316 Sqn pilot, Flying Officer K. Cynkier, in Mustang Mk.III FB352 also crash-landed with engine trouble. The fighter was badly damaged but the pilot was not seriously injured. Later that day, Flying Officer Hanney, in Spitfire Mk.V JL227 of No. 80 Sqn, crashed at Penshurst but escaped from his aircraft uninjured.

On 8 July, West Malling earned the distinction of destroying 210 V1s, of which No. 2769 Sqn, RAF Regiment, shot down nine. Sadly these celebrations were marred on 9 July, when Pilot Officer N.J. Purce of No. 274 Sqn, in Spitfire Mk.IX MH826, flew into a balloon cable near Wrotham Heath in bad weather and was killed. The aircraft came down west of Fern Pond Road, Ightham. The accident was investigated by Wing Commander Lasbrey, Air Defence of Great Britain, who reported to West Malling on 11 July.

At approximately 1745 hrs on 11 July a V1 was shot down by Flight Lieutenant T.H. Hoare, RCAF, in Tempest JN869 'US-D' of No. 56 Sqn based at Newchurch ALG, Romney Marsh. The V1 crashed into a quarry at Offham and shattered the windows of Offham House, occupied by no less than the station commander of West Malling. His comments are not recorded, but would have left little to the imagination!

On 9 July, personnel on the ground at West Malling were alarmed to see Canadian Flight Lieutenant J.W. Draper, DFC, who had joined No. 91 Sqn on 14 June having claimed four and one V1 shared, flying over the airfield in Spitfire Mk.XIV RM620, firing at a V1 from a distance of 100yd behind his target.

Polish pilots of No. 316 (Warsaw) Sqn line up for an inspection and award ceremony during July 1944. Behind them is the main 'J' type hangar at West Malling. Just visible to the left is the control tower. (Sikorski & Polish Institute)

At 2206hrs the same day, Flying Officer Bill Marshall, flying NH701, destroyed a V1 north of Dungeness that had been heading straight for Lydd. He closed in to 50yd and fired. The V1 exploded in mid-air, a close call for the townsfolk. Bill was lucky to escape with his life as he flew thorough the explosion. The Mayor of Lydd, Gordon Paine, tracked down Bill, congratulating the pilot on his victory and expressing the town's gratitude for saving many lives. In June 2006, a plaque was unveiled on the wall of the Royal Mail public house, Lydd, by Bill Marshall's widow, who had travelled all the way from Barbados. In an interview she said: 'He just knew it was going to blow up a town unless he destroyed it and his job was to destroy all enemy aircraft. Obviously he pulled that one off and I think he pulled off a few others too. I am sure other people would have done the same thing.'

Marshall was born in Newcastle upon Tyne. A father of seven, he died in Barbados aged 87. Visitors to Lydd who call in for a drink at the pub will learn of the pilot's bravery.

On 13 July, No. 2769 Sqn, RAF Regiment 'B' Site, based at West Malling, fired on a V1 and it exploded in mid-air. By 14 July no fewer than 259½ V1s were destroyed by units of West Malling, of which No. 2769 Sqn had destroyed twelve. On one memorable occasion on 15 July, West Malling was visited by Captain the Rt. Hon. H.H. Balfour MC, MP Parliamentary Under Secretary of State for Air, who often visited the airfield. He had been with the station commander and was about to take off when a V1 was destroyed by the Bofors gun of No. 2769 Sqn, its thirteenth. He went over to the gun site to congratulate them and later flew over the site and waved to the airmen below. This incident was mentioned by the BBC midnight broadcast without giving away the unit's identity.

Beaufighter R2080 of 51 Operational Training Unit (OTU), Cranfield, struck a balloon barrage on 17 July. The navigator, Warrant Officer W. Addison, bailed out and landed unhurt, but the pilot, Flight Lieutenant G.L. Barker, was killed. The aircraft came down at Werke Farm near Kingsdown, Kent.

On the night of 18/19 July, a Halifax B.III, MZ788 'EY-F' of No. 78 Sqn, No. 4 Grp, based at Breighton, landed at 0123hrs. The aircraft had no brakes so overshot and crashed into trees at the end of the east extension runway.

The aircraft had taken off on a mission to attack the V1 sites at Acquet as part of a force of sixty-two aircraft. It was hit by flak or a night fighter on the starboard side of the fuselage and an explosion took place within the flight engineer's area during its return from the target.

When fire broke out, Flying Officer D.F. Rayment, navigator; Flight Sergeant A.L. MacKenzie, air bomb aimer; and Pilot Officer J.R. Harmer, air gunner; bailed out but were lost, drowning in the North Sea.

The remainder of the crew managed to bring the Halifax back. The pilot, Flying Officer M.S. Buchanon (Australia), survived injured and Sergeant W.J. Bailey, flight engineer, was badly injured in both legs. Sergeants J.H. Rice and J. McCannon, both air gunners, survived.

On the morning of 19 July, a Halifax of No. 78 Sqn arrived to collect the surviving crew members and return them to Breighton.

The pilot was awarded the DFC and Sergeant Bailey the CGM. Sadly, Buchanon and others who survived this crash were later killed in November 1944 in Halifax MZ810 'EY-F'.

No. 91 Sqn was detached to Deanland, an ALG not far from Lewes and the Sussex coast, later moving on to Biggin Hill on 7 October, having converted to the Spitfire Mk.IXB.

On 22 July, No. 157 Sqn was the first unit to use the searchlight system of beacons. The defences were distributed as follows: Aircraft on patrols over the Channel, a gun belt along the coast from Dover to Brighton, and aircraft confined to their own patrol; their area stretched only from the gun belt to the balloon barrage. This was of great density, and once to within 3 miles of West Malling, thus making diversion inevitable in anything but good weather.

On 24/25 July, Warrant Officer McLeod of No. 157 Sqn crashed his Mosquito Mk.XIX, MM654, when the undercarriage collapsed. Both crew members were uninjured, although the aircraft was a write-off. While on patrol in Mosquito Mk.XIX MM681 'RS-K' was reported missing. This was later confirmed and both crew members, Flight Lieutenant J.W. Caddie and Flying Officer G.F. Larcy, were killed. It was thought an explosion of a V1 brought down the Mosquito off North Foreland.

On the night of 25/26 July, Flight Sergeant T. Bryan, pilot, and Sergeant B. Jaeger, navigator, flying Mosquito Mk.XIII MM468 of No. 157 Sqn, had taken off from West Malling on V1 patrol but failed to return. They had intercepted a V1 over the Channel at 0045hrs, and it is believed they fell victim to friendly AA fire from the coastal guns. Aircraft searched the area for the crew or wreckage but the only item found was an empty Mae West.

During the search, Mosquito Mk.XIII MM494, flown by Lieutenant Frank Richards, RNVR, and Lieutenant M.J. Baring, RNVR, was also fired on by coastal guns. The aircraft was hit in the port engine and this stopped, but Richards managed to make an emergency landing at Friston

Sergeant Bernard Jaeger was a school master at Cranbrook School, not far from West Malling, Jaeger joined the RAF Volunteer Reserve and flew with No. 96 Sqn at West Malling in 1944. Jaeger, in the scrum cap second from the left in the middle row, played for Cranbrook Rugby Club. (Cranbrook Rugby Club)

ALG. He overshot and collided with Mustang HB882 of No. 316 (Polish) Sqn, parked on the airfield. Both burst into flames and were destroyed but fortunately the pilot and navigator managed to escape uninjured.

No. 96 Sqn shot down six V1s before daybreak. Flight Lieutenant Togs Mellersh destroyed two, the second causing damage to his Mosquito Mk.XIII, MM577, but he returned to West Malling safely.

Sergeant Jaeger was a school master before the war, at Cranbrook School not far from West Malling, Bill, as he was known, was a language teacher until the outbreak of war, and a respected figure in the community. Jaeger had German ancestry and before the war had arranged school trips to Germany. He lived in a Victorian stable block close to Cranbrook School. which was also occupied by a disobedient horse named Horace. Bill, a keen rugby supporter, devoted much of his time to coaching rugby and co-founded Cranbrook Rugby Club, which is still active today. He had purchased a field to grow oats and hay for the horse, developing part of the field as a rugby pitch for the town. Not long before he joined the RAF, he left instructions stating that in the event of his death, the field should be gifted to the town of Cranbrook.

After the war, and following his mother's death, the field passed to Kent County Council, which in turn gave the site to Cranbrook School and it became known as Jaeger's Field. In 2004, locals were concerned about preserving Jaeger's legacy, as the field was under threat of development. A commemorative event was organised for 14 November 2004 to mark the sixtieth anniversary of Jaeger's death. Derek Smith, a retired history teacher, who lived close to the rugby pitch, tried to get an information board placed near the site but the proposal was turned down, although a plaque now resides at the school listing Bill as one of the school's benefactors.

Mosquito Mk.VI NT130 of No. 151 Sqn was reported missing on 28 July on Ranger (freelance flights over enemy territory) patrol during the afternoon. Flying Officers W.A. Lindsay and A. Brodie were hit by flak over Niort, but later landed on one engine at Predannack. News was received on 1 August that Wing Commander J.R.D. Braham, DSO, DFC, who was CO of No. 29 Sqn at West Malling in 1941, had been shot down on 24 June and taken prisoner with his navigator, Flight Lieutenant Walsh. They returned to the UK on 6 May 1945. Returning from an anti-Diver patrol on 6 August, Lieutenant P.F. Pryor, RNVR, and 2nd Lieutenant D. Mackenzie, FAA, crashed Mosquito Mk.XIX MM649 at Finningham Manor near Detling. Both crew members died of their injuries. Other aircraft returning were diverted to Ford due to heavy fog.

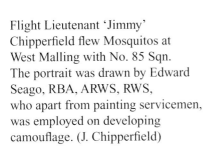

Flight Lieutenant 'Jimmy' Chipperfield flew Mosquitos at West Malling with No. 85 Sqn. The portrait was drawn by Edward Seago, RBA, ARWS, RWS, who apart from painting servicemen, was employed on developing camouflage. (J. Chipperfield)

Mention performing circuses and the name Chipperfield springs to mind. Perhaps not so well known is that Jimmy Chipperfield joined the RAF during the war and flew with No. 85 Sqn at West Malling. At the beginning of 1944, Chipperfield had expected to be posted to Burma, until he received a telegram while on leave instructing him to go to West Malling, where he was to join No. 85 Sqn and fly Mosquitoes. By coincidence, a friend and son of the owner of a local cycle and petrol station near to Chipperfield's home at Stockbridge, Hampshire, Sub Lieutenant Jack A.T. Parker, a navigator in the Fleet Air Arm, had been posted to West Malling on attachment to the squadron. Jimmy and Jack were pleased to meet up again. Chipperfield wrote:

> I have always remembered how he sat on standby in the Operations Room that evening, scribbling away at a letter and looking slightly out of place in his RNVR uniform, with his cap on the table in front of him. He was a big man, good looking, pleasant, generous and keen, at one point he said: 'I'd give my eyes to get a Hun tonight'.

With his RNVR pilot, Sub Lieutenant T.H. Blundell, Parker took off from West Malling on 28 January and not long after a garbled radio message was received saying that one of engines of their Mosquito Mk.XVII was

Flying Officer J. Chipperfield, who with his friend and navigator, Flight Sergeant J. Stockley, DFM, hit a V1 on 23/24 July 1944 and it exploded over the Thames Estuary. (J. Chipperfield)

running hot. Nothing more was heard from HK122. The starboard engine had caught fire and both pilot and navigator bailed out over the sea. Both were killed and the aircraft crashed in the sea off Dungeness.

It was a bitter blow to Flying Officer Jimmy Chipperfield, who was asked by Wing Commander J. Cunningham, who knew they were good friends, to tell Jack's parents the tragic news. Jack's father said: 'Don't let it affect you or get you down, go back and carry on flying.'

Chipperfield's first few weeks at West Malling were uncomfortable, and he found it difficult to find anyone who would show him over a Mosquito, which he desperately wanted to fly. Novice crews were not very popular, in fact on one occasion Cunningham was so disgusted with one crew he posted them off the station at once and more experienced crews felt that these new crews had been dumped on them! Chipperfield finally arranged for Flight Lieutenant Geoff Houghton to take him up in a dual-control Mosquito T.Mk.III, but this aircraft was so special he would not let him fly it. Eventually, a clapped out Mosquito was found and Chipperfield was told to fly it without a navigator! Taking off, he soon found himself in cloud, so headed south, avoiding the barrage balloons, only to find himself among American bombers staggering home from bombing operations. Not allowed to use his radio, he decided to land on an airfield and as he came in he saw sheep! Taxiing, Chipperfield saw an Army Jeep racing towards the Mosquito. 'This is the first twin engined aircraft we've had land here,' the excited driver announced. He had landed at an ALG at Great Chart, Ashford, on an experimental runway made of felt, not designed for the size of Mosquitoes. The runway was not long enough to take off, so he phoned West Malling. Cunningham was furious. 'Have you bent the bloody aircraft?' he shouted. He was told to stay there overnight and an experienced pilot would be sent down. On arrival, he removed any unwanted weight, then took the Mosquito to the far end of the runway and just managed to take off.

Chipperfield and his navigator, Flight Sergeant J. Stockley, intercepted a V1 at 0018hrs on 23/24 July in Mosquito Mk.XVII 'VY-W'. Firing at close range, it crashed in the Thames Estuary. This was the partnership's only V1 claimed, and they returned to intruder operations as the campaign against them was coming to an end. Sadly, Chipperfield's eyesight was causing problems and he only completed one tour of flying before becoming a freight officer, his RAF career ending in May 1945. Chipperfield returned to West Malling on 10 July 1953 and presented a silver model Mosquito to No. 85 Sqn. The squadron was invited to attend his circus, which everyone enjoyed.

George E. Roper, a Canadian from Ottawa, Ontario, had enlisted into the RCAF and eventually joined No. 85 Sqn at West Malling following training as a radar mechanic. He remembered the period when the V1s first appeared over Kent:

> I joined 85 Squadron at RAF Swannington when the Doodlebugs attacks began we returned to RAF West Malling to help intercept them. I was responsible for moving the squadron's Radar Beacon by road; it was mounted on a trailer, and the low power of the lorry resulted in us having to drive in extra low gear to climb any hill. I recall having to stop often to cool the engine during the final run from London to West Malling. On one such stop we saw the balloon barrage for the first time – most impressive. There was little traffic and the countryside was otherwise peaceful. I can recall little about the sequence of events, but do remember the high level of activity on the airfield, involving extra squadrons, including one Tempest/Typhoon Squadron. We would bet on the outcome of the interceptions, when we were on duty on dispersal for long hours and had a good view of the activities. I suspect that the two doodlebugs which landed near our billets were shot down and exploded upon impact. I recall that it was life as usual in the West Malling area. We continued to visit 'The George' and 'The Startled Saint' and to go to the dances in Snodland at every opportunity.

Squadron Leader Bob Spurdle, DFC and Bar, took command of No. 80 Sqn following a summons to RAF Uxbridge, while based at West Malling, where the squadron had moved to from Gatwick on 5 July 1944. Flying in the circuit one day at West Malling while test flying a Spitfire following repairs, he spotted a house close to the airfield – it had its own swimming pool. Landing at the airfield, he found the adjutant and requisitioned the house, called Springfield. This caused a bit of a fuss as the owner, a naval officer, happened to be at sea at the time, and apparently no sooner had the officer's wife moved out than officers of No. 80 Sqn moved in. Their joy was short-lived when they were themselves evicted from their dispersal to make way for one of the newly arrived Mosquito squadrons, especially when they were moved into converted airmen's lavatories!

Spurdle's wife sometimes stayed at Springhill and one night they heard what sounded like a motorbike. Looking out the window, a V1 appeared to be approaching the house. Spurdle tried to assure his wife that they were safe, when the sound stopped abruptly, and they could hear the V1 diving towards them. He quickly grabbed his wife, dived under the bed and yelled at others in the house to take cover. There was a terrific explosion and glass from the French windows were blown apart. They were all surrounded by timber, glass and debris.

Returning from an uneventful operation on 10 July, acting as cover with No. 274 Sqn protecting Mosquitoes bombing targets near Paris, Flying Officer Friend of No. 80 Sqn crashed on approach to West Malling. His engine cut out and Spitfire Mk.IX MA806 smashed through trees into a wood about a mile away from the airfield. The aircraft finished upside down and was completely written off, however the pilot suffered only minor scratches and bruises.

Owing to Nos. 29 and 85 Sqn arriving at West Malling, both Nos. 80 and 274 Sqn members had to move from Addington Hall to Springhill and move to smaller dispersals on the other side of the airfield. Returning from close escort to Halifaxes and Lancasters on 6 July, Flying Officer Hanney, in Spitfire JL227, and Lieutenant Gilhuus, flying BS400, both had to land at Penshurst airfield due to the weather. Flying Officer Hanney overshot the runway but was unhurt.

No. 80 Sqn, which operated Spitfire Mk.IXs during July and August 1944. The squadron's CO, Squadron Leader 'Bob' Spurdle, DFC and Bar, stands in the cockpit of his Spitfire.

The 24th July proved more fruitful when both Nos. 80 and 274 Sqn, led by Wing Commander Wells, took off on Rodeo 378, an offensive sweep in the Domfront–Laval area of France. They bagged four military trucks destroyed and blew up a storage facility, while Lieutenant Gilhuus (Norway) shared a damaged staff car. Warrant Officer Lang, however, was hit in the port wing from ground fire and 80mm shells, leaving a large aperture two foot square in the trailing edge, but he managed to return home and land safely at 2020hrs.

The weather was not the only problem in July, as returning from Ramrod operations on 31 July, the squadrons had to land at Detling due to two stray barrage balloons. At 2225hrs the same day, Flight Lieutenant Milne was scrambled to shoot them down and both caught fire. The inferno could be seen from West Malling and Detling.

On 29 July, at 0600hrs, No. 2852 (Ack Ack) RAF Regiment Squadron's convoy of vehicles with all its equipment headed from Chivenor to West Malling. Squadron Leader Ganter, CO of the unit, travelled with the remaining personnel by train. Immediately on arrival, they were detached to All Hallows. Their mission was to defend the South-East against the V1. By 1500hrs the following day, the regiment's guns were ready for action, and at 2350hrs they engaged incoming V1s, firing at a rate of fifty-seven rounds of 40mm and forty-one rounds of 20mm per minute, but without success. The unit was billeted in tents, and had already lost one of these, which was acquired by Wing HQ, so accommodation was somewhat cramped. In between warnings, the airmen dug slit trenches and dug in the tents, which were inspected by Lieutenant Colonel Goldsworthy, MC.

The guns opened fire on several occasions but without shooting down any flying bombs. In fact, the only major incident during the first week of August was when a cow wandered into a nearby minefield and was blown up. The unit's butcher was very pleased and set about preparing the unfortunate remains of the beast for consumption by everyone, which was well received. It was not until 17 August that No. 2852 AA Regiment hit a V1, which was not brought down, and news that their leave was cancelled did little to boost morale. On 22 August, some airmen were talking to locals living in the area and were told that during the winter months their camp would become marshland. Shortly after this conversation, a V1 flew directly over them and was hit by another AA unit, which was followed by the sound of a large explosion.

One noticeable effect of the warm weather was the appearance of several ant hills. Unfortunately, some ant colonies took a shine to the tents, making life somewhat unbearable, but heavy rain later flooded some of the tents, and the ant population was drastically reduced. On 25 August, Leading Aircraftman Hagen, who had set off in a Bedford van, hit a telegraph pole and this broke. He finished up in hospital, but was not seriously injured.

A working party was formed to build a better road into the site, which was bit of a bugbear for all concerned. No. 2852's stay at West Malling, on detachment to All Hallows, passed without scoring any direct hits and they moved yet again to Fairwood Green. News of the move was well received.

On 3 August, Jean Marie Maridor was killed when his Spitfire Mk.XIV, RM656, was caught in the explosion from a V1, which he had destroyed. It was a great shock to members of No. 91 Sqn, who were fond of this cheerful Frenchman. His close friend, Henri de Bordas, had to go to Benenden to identify the body. In his logbook, Bordas wrote: 'I never thought it would be the last time I should see him.' Distraught by her fiancé's death, Jean Lambourne, a WAAF officer who was due to marry 'Mari', was sent home on seven days' leave. Jean later collected the wedding cake and, on a visit to Wingfield Hospital near her home town of Oxford, gave it to wounded soldiers injured during the D-Day landings. Maridor was buried at Brookwood Cemetery, a funeral that was attended by many people, including General Valin, who made the French airman a Chevalier of the Legion of Honour (posthumous). One of the many wreaths laid by those attending read: 'To Jean Maridor, with grateful thanks from the people of Folkestone.' Jean Sharp, a resident of Benenden, Kent, witnessed the loss of the French pilot:

> My mother and I were in the grounds of Benenden School (which had been used as a hospital) when the V1 approached. This was not a unique occasion at the time. We sped back to Meadway House to take shelter. Suddenly we heard cannon fire. Almost immediately afterwards we saw the flying bomb, which was losing speed rapidly and gliding down on a path which would inevitably have meant it landing on either Meadway House or on the main building of Benenden School. I don't think the pilot knew about the children, but knew of the hospital. Firing again, he did not fully destroy the bomb, and it then became quite clear that the hospital was going to be hit. At point that I believe that he flew his wing under that of the V1. He succeeded; the bomb veered, just before exploding. In the explosion Jean Maridor's plane was also blown up. But the hospital was saved.

Jean Lambourne remained at West Malling until March 1945, moving to the HQ No. 11 Grp, No. 5351 Wing, St Albans and Binbrook, remaining in the WAAFs until 1954.

There was an air of excitement on 9 August as this was the day when No. 274 Sqn took delivery of its new Hawker Tempests. Pilots of No. 80 Sqn were able to borrow four of these formidable fighters. Everybody seemed very keen on these new aircraft, although their loyalty to their Spitfires was very strong. There being no operational flying on 10 August, many pilots of No. 80 Sqn completed short flights in the gleaming new machines, gaining useful experience. The last time Nos. 80 and 274 Sqn flew together as a wing was on 11 August. An unfortunate incident took place on the same day when two Spitfires of No. 274 Sqn ran into each other on landing at West Malling. No. 80 Sqn was released from operational duties and preparations were made for a move to Manston.

At the unearthly hour of 0500hrs on 20 June, all personnel of No. 322 (Dutch) Sqn, based at Hartfordbridge, were busily engaged in striking their tents and loading them in lorries together with their kit. At 0730hrs a road convoy moved off the airfield according to plan. At 0845hrs, eighteen Spitfire Mk.XIVs left the airfield in three flights and headed for their new home at West Malling. Several hours later the convoy arrived, only to find that the squadron was already operating. Everybody set to at once to get the ground organisation working and by the evening things were fairly straight. From what they had seen so far, life at West Malling looked promising and there was every indication that they would have plenty of opportunity to shoot down a few V1s. No. 322 Sqn was itching to get to grips with the V1s as its aircraft arrived at West Malling. It was not long before the squadron opened its score, when at 1835hrs, Flight Lieutenant L.C.M. van Eendenburg, flying Spitfire Mk.XIV RB184 'VL-B', destroyed its first V1. He recalled:

> Patrolling Beachy Head at 5,000ft when a Diver crossed the coast at 2,000ft. Chased Diver and it changed course to go through a gap in the Balloon Barrage. I followed and caught up, giving a long burst at 600yds. Pieces flew off including half the starboard wing. Diver fell to the ground and exploded three quarters of a mile NE of Swanley Junction.

By 26 June the squadron had already destroyed seven V1s and flown no fewer than sixty sorties.

On Monday, 9 July 1944 a V1 dived on to a house at Northumberland Avenue, Welling, Kent but did not explode. A bomb disposal unit later discovered that the detonator had been placed in the fuse pocket by either sabotage or a production line fault. (KAHRS)

It was not only pilots who got excited when chasing the V1s as whenever one crossed the airfield, the ground crew kept shouting advice and encouragement to the pilot, and should one get away the ground crews were every bit as disappointed as the pilot. Occasionally, the Spitfire would run out of ammunition and, refusing to accept defeat, the pilot would try and bring down the V1 by flipping the target over with the aircraft's wing-tip. Many did so, bending the tip of the wing, which invariably meant it needed to be hastily replaced on return to West Malling.

On 28 June, Flight Sergeant W. De Vries, while destroying a V1, got mixed up with some flak with the result that he lost the starboard aileron and had bullet holes in his starboard wing, engine cowling and fuselage, making it necessary for him to land at Kingsnorth ALG near Ashford. Fortunately, he was not injured and landed without further damage to his Spitfire.

The squadron suffered a sad loss early on the morning of 12 July. At 0620hrs, Warrant Officer J. Maier took off on anti-Diver patrol and saw a V1 being attacked by a P-51. The Diver exploded, knocking off the Mustang's wing and turning over, but the pilot bailed out. Maier's Spitfire, RM678 'VL-Q' was also turned over but he was unable to bail out and he was killed. Warrant Officer Maier proved himself to be a very able pilot and at the time of his death had destroyed 3½ V1s. The P-51 was most probably of the 8th USAAF. Maier was buried on 18 July at Charing. The CO, Major K.C. Kuhlmann, DFC, attended and several pilots were also present. Maier is remembered on the Maidenhead Register. On 21 July, No. 322 Sqn left West Malling for Deanland ALG.

At 2305hrs on 11 August, a V1 was brought down by a Tempest Mk.V of No. 501 Sqn based at Manston, close to the DFI station about 250yd east of the north runway extension and just off the airfield at West Malling. There were no injuries but the DFI station was damaged, although it continued to operate as usual. The pilot who shot down the V1 later had a call put through apologising and hoping there were no injuries. He and two other Tempests had been firing at the V1. Before they came to the airfield ring lights, the V1 caught fire and flew on a considerable distance before crashing. The pilot concerned was most probably Flight Lieutenant C.B. Thornton, who had been on patrol with Flight Lieutenant E.L. Williams and Flying Officers R.G. Lucas and B.F. Miller.

Patrolling on 12 August, Wing Commander H. de C.A. Woodhouse, DFC, AFC, and Flight Lieutenant W. Weir of No. 85 Sqn, flying Mosquito Mk.XIX MM632 'VY-E', were lost and later confirmed killed. Woodhouse had borrowed the Mosquito from No. 85 Sqn to carry out a patrol. No. 274 Sqn also lost a pilot, Flight Sergeant R.W. Ryman, flying Tempest Mk.V EJ637. He lost control of his aircraft and crashed at Ealham during bad weather. Flying was temporarily suspended in the area during the early hours of 14/15 August due to twenty-five drifting balloons. They were detected in a position east of West Malling at 6,000ft, drifting south-west at 0140hrs. Sometime elapsed before the identity of the balloons could be established but later West Malling was informed, eventually, that they were part of Operation Outward, of which more later. Those responsible appeared to have failed to check the wind direction before releasing them.

Chasing the V1 was a dangerous occupation, and despite the pilots' best efforts to bring down these highly successful 'flying bombs', there were several tragedies. One in particular involved Flight Lieutenant John Alfred Malloy, RCAF, based with No. 274 Sqn at West Malling during the V1 campaign.

Wednesday, 16 August was a busy day for No. 274 Sqn, which opened the score early that day when Flight Lieutenant O.E. Willis destroyed a V1 in the Sittingbourne area at 0705hrs in Tempest Mk.V EJ640. Airborne during the afternoon, Flight Lieutenant J.A. Malloy attacked another at 1615hrs.

An Army officer, possibly of a bomb disposal unit, inspects the wreckage of a V1 in the Maidstone area. The flying bomb had exploded, possibly shot down by pilots at West Malling. (KAHRS)

He recalled: 'I sighted a Diver just inland of Dover at 2,000ft. I chased it to Rainham, opening fire from 800 yards but saw no strikes. I closed in and tipped it with my wingtip, it crashed on the railway line near Rainham.'

In fact it was Oak Lane railway bridge, near Upchurch in Kent. The blast destroyed the bridge just before the 1535 Victoria to Ramsgate train carrying 400 passengers was due. The train was unable to stop, despite efforts by the driver and fireman. The engine tender and the first three coaches hit the gap where the bridge had stood. The fourth coach hung across the track but did not fall. Train driver Charles Bennett and his fireman David Humphreys from Balham survived.

The driver, who came from Worcester Park, said in his report:

> My hat was blown from my head … I saw a cloud of smoke in front and made an emergency application of the brake. I felt the engine turn over and hung on to the reversing wheel and it was then that the injury to my right shoulder occurred. My fireman helped me from the cab, then went forward to protect the up-road. My injury was causing me great pain.

The train fireman, David Humphreys, ran back along the track to the Newington signal box to alert it of the crash and was met by Home Guard officer Captain Edward Marsh. Marsh, from the Rochester Home Guard based at Fort Clarence, was one of the first on the scene and helped with early rescues. He later wrote to Sir Eustace Missenden, Southern Railway's general manager to praise the fireman's 'extreme devotion to duty'.

Seven people were killed in the first three coaches and Arthur Edward Naylor, a railwayman from Tufton Road, Rainham, who was picking blackberries at the trackside, also died. Among those who died were George Skinner of Upper Brents, Faversham; Ethel Emily Beadle of Pemdevon Road, Croydon; Ivy Maud Smith, ATS Biggin Hill, of Herne Bay Road, Swalecliffe; Frank Arthur Snazell of Lennard Road, Beckenham; Private Geoffrey Herbert Gallop, Queens Royal Regiment, Faversham; Albert Edward Eley, Steam Ship Queen, Faversham; and Charles Williams Cummins, RN Chatham.

The official toll was eight dead, thirty-three seriously injured and twenty-five slightly hurt. Brunt & Ayletts in the High Street, Newington, was used

The aftermath of the V1 brought down by Flight Lieutenant J.A. Malloy No. 274 Sqn on 16 August 1944. Railway workers and engineers preparing to raise the train caught in the blast at Oak Lane railway bridge at Upchurch, Kent. (KAHRS)

The engine No. 30806 *Sir Galleron*, a Southern Railway class N15 4-6-0, being salvaged at Oak Lane railway bridge. The 3.35 p.m. Victoria to Ramsgate train was carrying 400 passengers at the time; mercifully many were spared. (KAHRS)

as a mortuary and Rainham School was used as a first aid post. A transport cafe nearby was used as a hospital. Local people from the village of Upchurch helped with the rescue and care of the passengers.

The V1 was heading for central London and would have caused much greater loss of life and damage to property had it got through the defences. The young Canadian pilot was mortified on finding out what followed. 'Jock' Malloy was from Ottawa, Ontario, where he had lived with his parents. However, Malloy was again airborne during the evening and at 2050hrs destroyed another V1 in Tempest EJ633, of which he recorded:

> I picked up a Diver (V1) near Dover at 2,000ft, at 350mph. I chased it to the Isle of Sheppey area but failed to score strikes, so I closed in and tipped it over. It exploded on the ground. A Meteor pilot [probably of No. 616 Squadron, the first squadron to be equipped with the new jets] confirmed my claim.

Malloy was only 23 years old at the time and he was killed on 13 January 1945, still with No. 274 Sqn and based at Volkel, Holland, when he failed to pull out of a dive in Tempest Mk.V EJ639. It crashed near Euskirchin, near Munster.

The victims of the tragic incident have not been forgotten as local historian Richard Emmett gave a presentation to Upchurch Parish Council, asking for a plaque to be installed on the bridge to remember all the dead, as yet not undertaken. Many in the village of Upchurch still remember the train crash, and some recall bringing water and fresh bandages to help with the recovery. After the wreckage had been cleared, a new bridge was constructed in November 1944 at a cost of £3,800 and it still exists today. The disaster turned out to be the most serious and tragic incident to hit the area during the Second World War.

Operation Outward was the name given to the Second World War programme to attack Germany by means of free-flying balloons. It made use of cheap balloons, filled with hydrogen. They carried either a trailing steel wire intended to damage high voltage power lines by producing short circuit or incendiary devices that were intended to start fires in fields, forests and heathland. A total of 99,142 Outward balloons were launched; about half carried incendiaries and half carried trailing wires. Compared to Japan's better-known fire balloons, Outward balloons were crude. They had to travel a much shorter distance so they flew at a lower altitude – 16,000ft (4,900m), compared with 38,000ft (12,000m) – and had only a simple mechanism to regulate altitude by means of dropping ballast or venting lifting gas. This meant the balloons were simple to mass produce and only cost 35 shillings each, approximately equivalent to £86 in 2016. The free-flying balloon attacks were highly successful. Although difficult to assess exactly, they had an economic impact on Germany far in excess of the cost to the British government.

The following day, at 0905hrs, Tempest Mk.V EJ590 'SD-L', flown by the V1 ace Joe Berry from Newchurch's No. 150 Wing, shot down a V1, which fell on West Malling about 30yd west of No. 34 barrack block in woods. One airman was slightly injured by glass. The gymnasium and chapel, located 75yd away, suffered some structural damage but the barrack block did not suffer much in the blast. Windows and doors were damaged in the officers' mess and windows in the sick quarters were broken. The V1 was seen cartwheeling out of control in the sky by astonished airmen at the airfield, and many dived under tables and into ditches.

Apart from V1s launched from ramps located in Europe, the Germans also developed other platforms to launch the flying bomb, in particular by air. The main units involved were III/KG3, I, II and III/KG53, flying He 111s,

Following examination by engineers, remains of unexploded V1s were reconstructed and put on display at many locations. Here such an example is on display at Maidstone in 1944, giving the public, pilots and ground crews a chance to see the weapon intact. (KAHRS)

based at Varrelbusch, Ahlhorn, Vechta and Bad Zwischenahn. No. 157 Sqn, then based at West Malling, was the only unit on the airfield to be involved in operations against the launch aircraft.

These operations began on 16 September and ended in March 1945. Squadron Leader Benson and Flight Lieutenant Brandon were scrambled on the night of 18/19 August on anti-Heinkel patrol:

> We were sent on a low-level patrol just off the Dutch Islands. The idea was to try to intercept the launching aircraft, which were mostly Heinkels. If we could shoot the Heinkel down before it launched its toy, so much the better. Almost from the moment we arrived on patrol we began a series of chases that got us nowhere. We spotted some lights on one of the islands, but they went out as we approached and we could see nothing when we got there. Then we had two long and difficult chases on aircraft, both of which turned out to be Mosquitoes. We then saw what we thought must be a launching some way off.

No AI contact appeared however. Again we saw a launching some distance from us but had no joy when we investigated it. Finally we returned to West Malling tired and dejected.

No. 80 Sqn was released from operational duties on 27 August and preparations were made for a move to Manston. Pilots took the further opportunity to fly their Tempests, and, along with No. 274 Sqn, they were now busy converting to the new aircraft. Everything was in readiness for their 'farewell' to West Malling. Six Tempests were flown during the morning, the rest arrived in the afternoon. Flying Officer Adams had a passenger with him in his new Tempest – the squadron mascot, a kitten, which had previously been flown from France. All but one of the squadron's old Spitfires were flown from West Malling by pilots of No. 310 (Czech) Sqn, who were to take them back to their base at North Weald. However, one of them did not take off as planned and ran into a signal post near the perimeter track. At Manston, it was not long before pilots of No. 80 Sqn flew their new Tempests in action against the V1.

On 5 September, B-24 44-40264 *Kiss Me Baby* of the 753rd BS, 458th BG, based at Horsham St Faith, returning from a raid on Karlsruhe, Germany, with one engine out of action and another very nearly so, decided to put down at

B-24 44-40264 *Kiss Me Baby* of the 753rd BS, 458th BG, following its successful crash-landing. Fortunately none of the crew were injured. (American Air Museum)

West Malling. Captain Gerald W. Matze, the pilot, managed to land the B-24 on its belly and there were no injuries. They were lucky as the airfield was undergoing considerable work by the airfield construction flight. The American crew were taken to Detling, where they were to be picked up by another B-24 from the 458th BG, and were soon back on operations over Europe.

On 10 September, the sound of distant explosions were heard throughout the day and buildings were shaken on the airfield. The cause was later to be discovered to be the bombardment of Le Havre by the RAF and Royal Navy, and a cross-Channel gun duel. Airfield construction continued during September and officers from the School of Airfield Construction arrived to inspect the work being carried out.

A B-17 Fortress of the 487th BG of the 8th USAAF crashed at Wrotham, Kent, at 1330hrs on the afternoon of 10 October. The aircraft was returning from Brussels, became lost and flew into the ground. The crew of four were injured, one seriously, and were attended at the scene by the station medical officer Squadron Leader Elliott. They were later removed to Preston Hall Emergency Hospital. That afternoon, two Norsemen aircraft from Heston arrived to collect the crew and return them to their unit. On 26 October, Nos. 4832 and 4854 Flt arrived to assist in the construction of the runways at West Malling and the Air Disarmament Maintenance Detachment (ADMD) units were moved on to Kenley. In addition, No. 5011 Works Flight commenced work during the black-out period by installing floodlights.

An advance party of airmen of No. 30 Air Disarmament Area HQ (ADAH), Kenley, consisting of Squadron Leader Coatley and Squadron Leader Baird, left Kenley by road bound for West Malling on 1 October to make preparations for the reception of No. 30 ADAH and the five mobile detachments due to leave their practice camp at the end of their exercise. The convoy containing No. 30 ADAH personnel and equipment left Kenley en route for West Malling, arriving at 1145 on 2 October, and were parked on The Square, senior officers were accommodated in HQ Mess, junior officers in The Parsonage, an outside billet about a mile from the airfield, and airmen in No. 1 Billet, referred to as The Workhouse. On arrival convoys were parked by detachments on the dispersal sites near flight offices on the perimeter of the airfield.

No. 30 ADAH comprised Nos. 300, 301, 311 and 312 ADMD and were detached from their base at Cardington to take part in a practice night road convoy exercise, Operation Cardgame, from West Malling. These units were responsible for the disarmament of Luftwaffe units in Europe. Their total strength consisted of 118 officers and 350 airmen. They were soon joined by the advance party of Nos. 2707 and 2797 Sqn RAF Regiment from Hawkinge. The plan was to remain at West Malling and undertake security lectures and training of personnel, prior to their move to Meerbeke in Belgium. No. 312 ADMD would be detached to Grammont and Nos. 300 and 301 ADMD were to move to Terlanen, Belgium. Officers of Nos. 301, 300, 310, 311 and 312 ADMD were billeted at Addington House. Group Captain A. Leach, MC, the CO of No. 30 ADAH, returned from leave and other ranks who had not had leave in the past three months were given seven days.

Daily routine duties continued, with all units standing by to receive orders to proceed overseas. Lectures were given to officers of No. 30 ADAH and mobile detachments on 'Land Mines and Booby Traps', followed by films on the same subject. Orders arrived on 25 October for advance parties to proceed by road to Tilbury on 26 October. No. 310 ADMD moved to Avington Park near Winchester on an exercise designed to last until Monday, 30 October, to accustom 'B' class drivers in convoy driving and to acquaint all personnel with the domestic arrangements of a mobile detachment in the field. Instruction in mines and booby traps was attended by all personnel of No. 30 ADAH and Nos. 300, 301 and 312 ADMD. All personnel were lectured relating to the background of the Nazi Party and the causes of the deterioration in European relations leading to the outbreak of the war, in order to give them a grounding of the subjects in which they would be concerned.

Early in December all ranks were issued with pistols and giving instructions on firing care and maintenance. The MT section was on the move to Detling, providing experience for personnel and in spite of certain difficulties all equipment was transferred by the due date. The final convoys, comprising Maintenance Sub Units (MSUs) Nos. 312 ADMD and No. 32 ADAH vehicles, moved during the afternoon of 11 January and arrived at Detling on time and without mishap. No. 32 ADAH, No. 312 ADMD, No. 5472 'D' MSU, No. 5475 'C' MSU and No. 5476 'D' MSU, proceeded by road from West Malling to Detling and on the same date three RAF Regiment squadrons, Nos. 2479, 2814 and 2878, arrived at Detling by road from Hawthorn, Wiltshire. Advance parties were sent by each unit the previous week.

One of many WAAFs who passed through West Malling was Phyllis Quest, who had joined earlier in the war and was posted to the airfield in the summer of 1944, following the V1 campaign:

> It was decided that by the hospital authorities to send wounded pilots there to convalescence. That's when our trouble began.

Can you imagine it? The pilots with too much time on their hands and an RAF station with many WAAFs. At night I would have to go around with an airman NCO shouting at them to get back to their quarters at once, then placing them on a charge if they were late in. The job was made most difficult, as we had to be careful not to fall over the couples on the ground! One of the saddest things I had to deal with at West Malling was to discharge girls who got pregnant, it happened quite often and can you wonder?

On 17 November, the chief engineer, Fighter Command, received information regarding the construction of a new runway at West Malling, and the question of demolishing and re-providing various buildings as a result. Although five blister hangars were to be demolished, which would be reduced to four if the extension to the perimeter track was not approved, it was decided that all the huts to be demolished should be re-sited to provide dispersal accommodation in the south-west corner for the large number of aircraft that West Malling was bound to receive when the new runway was completed, and for ground crews to service them. The accommodation provided for this purpose was to be drawn entirely from existing huts to be demolished, and no additional huts would be required. The existing radar workshop would have to be demolished, and an improvised radar workshop provided on the north-east side of the airfield. Priority was given to these changes.

For several days in December 1944, the airfield had been fog-bound and when the sky cleared on the afternoon of 21 December, Squadron Leader Fulton, 'B' Flight commander, No. 410 Sqn, took off for England from Lille–Vendeville, France, in the squadron's Airspeed Oxford, R6329. With him were three officers and two airmen, all going on leave. Near Wrotham, the aircraft crashed and only one of its occupants survived. Killed with Fulton were his navigator, Flying Officer A.R. Ayton (RAF), who had accompanied him on posting to the Cougars in October, Flight Lieutenant F.G. Thomson, DFC (RAF), who had arrived late in November to begin a second tour, and Leading Aircraftmen E. Wahlers and R. Seefried.

Flying Officer W. Rumbold, another RAF navigator, was seriously injured. He had been with the squadron for two months. The injured were taken to Preston Hall Hospital for treatment.

The last V1 destroyed by units based at West Malling was credited to Squadron Leader J.H.M. Chisholm in Mosquito Mk.XIX MM674 'RS-T' of No. 157 Sqn in August. For West Malling, 1944 had been a particularly exciting and busy year.

Chapter 6

The Cold War 1945–50

The jet age arrives

The new year of 1945 began with No. 2797 Sqn, RAF Regiment, being moved to Selby, Yorkshire, and No. 2847 Sqn moving to Lympne, near the Kent coast. Work continued at a pace on the runway, uninterrupted due to the good weather for the time of year and despite the sudden arrival of various aircraft such as a B-17 of the 525th BS piloted by Lieutenant Merton that was, like so many returning bombers, short of fuel.

Returning from a bombing raid on 12 January, B-24H-10-CF serial 41-29276 'J4', christened *Rotten Sock*, of the 458th BG, force-landed at West Malling following severe damage to its tailplane. The crew remained at the airfield until their aircraft was repaired, returning to their base at Horsham St Faith, Norfolk.

On 19 January, Warrant Officer R.J. Cowan of No. 287 Sqn had a lucky escape when he force-landed Tempest Mk.V JN796 at Culdrun Farm, Trotters Cliff, near Wrotham. He was uninjured. Even as late as March 1945 the occasional V1s were still flying over the area.

On 26 March Tonbridge police reported a crashed aircraft at Cranbrook, which was attended by No. 2769 Sqn, RAF Regiment. The aircraft, a B-17 of the 545th BS, 8th USAAF, was piloted by Lieutenant Gordan, who was killed. Two other crew members were injured and all were brought back to West Malling for the night.

To everyone's relief the work on the runway was completed on 20 April, except for clearing up. Following the end of the war on 8 May, a VE Day party was arranged and took place in the main hangar. All personnel were free to attend and all ranks' dance was held that evening.

West Malling closed temporarily, on 19 May until Tuesday, 23 May. The Air Ministry had decided that the airfield should be expanded and plans were implemented to have two regular RAF squadrons and a Royal Auxiliary

The crew of *The Rotten Sock,* B-24H 41-29276 of the 753rd BS, 458th BG, were lucky to make it safely to West Malling on 8 September 1944. Despite the damage, they limped back over Europe, landing without loss or injury to crew. This aircraft was also known as *Urgin' Virgin.* (American Air Museum)

Air Force squadron based permanently at the airfield. These would later be Nos. 25, 85 and 500 (Kent's Own) RAuxAF Sqn, and Nos. 29 and 153 Sqn would also be based at West Malling.

In early February, the superintendent engineer of No. 13 Works Area informed West Malling Council that, while it was not the intention of the Air Ministry to proceed in the immediate future with any work on the extension of the airfield at West Malling, it was possible such development would be carried out at a later stage and no guarantee could be given. It was pointed out that under the present scheme for the airfield extension, both Kings Hill Cottages and Kingshill Farm would obstruct flying and would have to be demolished if the development went ahead. Both properties had been damaged by enemy action.

However, it was not RAF squadrons that were accommodated at the airfield in the summer of 1945, as West Malling took on the role of a rehabilitation centre for British and Commonwealth servicemen returning

Mosquito NF.36 RL179 in No. 25 Sqn markings. The NF.36s were replaced in July 1951 by the new Vampire NF.10. This aircraft also served with Nos. 29 and 85 Sqn. (G. Gilbert)

from prisoner of war camps. Transport aircraft arrived with the ex POWs and work began processing the unfortunate servicemen, who despite being somewhat confused were happy to be on English soil again.

Flight Lieutenant D.A. Codd, DFC, had joined No. 10 Sqn as a navigator and was shot down by enemy fire on his forty-second operation and taken prisoner. He was later liberated from Stalag Luft IIIA at Luckenwalde, where he had been imprisoned from February 1945 until April, and sent on the RAF rehabilitation course at West Malling. He wrote:

> It may have been helpful to some of those who had been incarcerated for a long time. To me it seemed like a holiday at the expense of the RAF. We were pampered and 'mollycoddled' on the Station and taken on several outings in coaches, visiting such places as the Sharps Toffee Factory in Maidstone. At the end of the course I was sent home on leave, which was broken only when I had to return to West Malling briefly for a new 1250 (RAF Identity Card) following the theft of my wallet.

Codd later, retrained and continued his career as a navigator until an accident in a Jeep ended his RAF service.

Sergeant M.A. Clarke, a flight engineer, also had the misfortune of being shot down and taken POW while serving with No. 102 (Ceylon) Sqn based at Pocklington. He also was sent to Malling in 1945 and remembers a visit to Chatham Dockyard and many other places. Many ex-prisoners attended

An excellent view of post-war RAF West Malling, showing most of the buildings and hangars constructed on the site, including some married quarters and blast pens. (Skyfotos Ltd)

receptions given at Dover, Margate and Folkestone. Like Codd, he returned to RAF service, joining No. 46 Maintenance Unit in January 1946.

Squadron Leader H. Baxter had taken over as CO, RAF West Malling, from Squadron Leader G.T. Block on 9 March. The new CO was tasked with the expansion of the airfield. No. 5011 Airfield Construction Squadron had been tasked with developing the airfield, and the target date for completion of this work had been 31 March. This involved the construction of 2,000 × 50yd of concrete runway involving all earthworks, drainage, airfield lighting, concrete PSP perimeter tracks and the provision of some additional lighting. A further twenty-two working days were allowed for final completion. Nos. 4741, 4742, 4744. 4745, 4746, 4748, 4745, 4750, 4751, 4823, 5532 and 5533 Flt were employed to carry out additional works to reinstate 1,000yd of perimeter tracks in concrete, and corresponding excavation. The amount of development was extensive, and a Nissen hut and dispersal were built at the south-west end of the runway, and drains reinstated round the perimeter on both sides. A radar workshop was built with an approach road and paths added. There were two blister hangars constructed with the approaches resurfaced. In addition, the barrack blocks were painted and considerable repairs were made to hardstandings.

Many of these construction units were later disbanded and by the end of June, West Malling was declared operational again. The airfield was keen to take part in the nationwide Victory in Europe celebrations. An open day was held at the airfield for the benefit of the people of Maidstone and the county of Kent. An impressive flying display took place, involving Mustangs, Spitfires, Tempests and Mosquitoes, and included the new Meteors, which had not long been in service. The finale was a mass formation that flew over Maidstone.

During June it was decided by the Air Ministry that, of the three blister hangars on the north side of the west end of the new east–west runway, only one should be demolished. The superintendent engineer subsequently reported to HQ Air Ministry that a second blister hangar, namely the most westerly one, had already been demolished, without permission. It had been taken down in the early days of the runway construction by airfield construction units, who acted on the mistaken assumption that it would form an obstruction to the margin of the new perimeter track. However, the hangar was never replaced.

It was not until 10 September, when all prisoners had finally left the airfield, that the first RAF unit, No. 287 Sqn, arrived from Bradwell Bay, having been based there since 15 June. Spitfire Mk.XVIs landed and were to take part in co-operation flights with both ack-ack and Royal Navy units. The main task was towing targets for gun practice and there were often remains of these targets to be found hanging from surrounding trees. Joining them to maintain the Spitfires of No. 287 Sqn was No. 1003 Servicing Sqn.

No. 287 Sqn's stay at the airfield passed fairly peacefully until 9 November, when operations were restricted due to shortage of aircraft caused by an accident when Sergeant Kent crashed in Spitfire Mk.IX NH578. Operations were again restricted on 15 November when Warrant Officer R.B. Farmiloe was killed when he crashed in Tempest Mk.V JN763 at Harlow, Essex. Such crashes, apart from the tragic loss of life, created a shortage of aircraft. The accident was investigated by Wing Commander Larking, No. 11 Grp, at a court of enquiry held at the airfield.

Many bombers had landed in Switzerland during the latter part of the war and were usually interned, the country being neutral. So it was with great surprise that, on 1 October, a Liberator from Switzerland landed at the airfield and taxied to the control tower, which had been recently restored. The crew was met by Air Ministry officials, who arrived especially for the occasion.

Mosquito NF.30 NT582 'RO-B' of No. 29 Sqn. The squadron returned to West Malling in October 1945. (D.G. Collyer)

No. 29 Squadron returned to West Malling, equipped with Mosquito Mk.30s, on 29 October having been based at Manston, its association with West Malling going back to April 1941. The squadron's new role was as part of the post-war fighter defence programme, and personnel were pleased to be back. They were also delighted with the new dispersal areas and hangars. There was, however, a certain buzz in the air as the squadron was due to re-equip with the Meteor, but the changeover to the NF.11 variant did not occur until July 1951. At least they were not alone, sharing the airfield with No. 287 Sqn, and both squadrons worked well together during the remainder of 1945.

On 1 December, Wing Commander J.W. Allan DSO, DFC, of No. 29 Sqn, inspected aircrews and aircraft during the morning, and the squadron then dispersed for the rest of the weekend.

On Monday, 3 December, pilots of No. 29 Sqn were detailed to visit the firing range at Leysdown on the Isle of Sheppey, and in the afternoon night flying training was carried out in good weather. The night flying programme consisted of a 'Calf's Eye' exercise with four bombers and two fighters. The bombers arrived in time over the target area after carrying out cross-country flights, but three of them were considered as being knocked down before reaching base. Sodium flares considerably improved the airfield lighting.

Following the end of the war, life at West Malling was somewhat subdued and, apart from flying training, lectures, films and the occasional air-sea rescue flights, December passed without incident for the squadron.

While waiting to take off from West Malling on 4 January 1946, Tempest Mk.V JN797 was being taxied out by Sergeant S. Brooks of No. 287 Sqn. However, he was shocked to see Oxford NM361, also of No. 287 Sqn, heading towards him. The Oxford collided with the Tempest, causing some damage to both aircraft, but fortunately Brooks and the crew on the Oxford were not seriously injured.

On 11 February, fourteen Mosquitoes of No. 29 Sqn took off for RAF Spilsby for firing practice, near Boston and the Wash. Unfortunately, the accommodation left a lot to be desired as they were living under canvas. They remained at Spilsby until 21 March, when they returned to West Malling.

The squadron had the honour of being the highest-scoring unit based at No. 2 Air Firing School, Spilsby, to date. This included No. 3 Sqn with its Tempest Mk.Vs. On 5 April, preparations were started for a squadron detachment to Lubeck and all crews concerned attended a briefing during the afternoon. In the morning, six Mosquitoes and an Oxford were airborne and set course for Germany, all arriving safely later the same day.

During a busy day on 11 April, Air Commodore Russell came into the airfield's circuit but was unable to let his undercarriage down. Flight Lieutenant Foster took off to give him any assistance possible, although his wheels remained only partially lowered. Russell came in and made a very nice belly landing, fortunately uninjured. The first detachment returned from Lubeck, where the weather had been very poor and had interrupted training.

The month ended with four aircraft airborne on an air-to-ground firing exercise at Nordheim in Germany. Four sorties were made; two night flights and two ferrying.

VE Day celebrations continued and on 9 May six Mosquitoes flew to the Channel Islands, where four took part in a fly past and the remaining two carried out interception exercises. On 17 May, five aircraft were airborne doing test runs over the course of the VE Day fly past, due to take place in June. On 15 June, No. 287 Sqn was disbanded at West Malling. Its target towing was no longer a requirement and, like many RAF squadrons and units, it was axed in the post-war economy drive.

During April, West Malling hosted German prisoners of war. A conference was arranged to discuss their future, chaired by Wing Commander A. Ingle, DFC, AFC, who was station commander at the time. By 10 April there were fifty POWs and they were set to work on the airfield, under guard. The last had left by October.

Operation Bulldog, a massive joint RAF exercise, took place during May and this kept everyone at West Malling extremely busy. In early July, a Wellington bomber was engaged on aircraft interception exercises with several Mosquitoes. On 12 July five aircraft were airborne, one giving dual instruction, two on cross-country flights, one on AI practice and another doing an air test. Warrant Officer Dall, on an air test in Mosquito NT290, had to come in with a damaged undercarriage, and on landing the starboard leg collapsed. This was the first accident for several months. On 21 July, Flight Lieutenant Brian Foster was married and a few pilots were able to attend and well and truly launch him into his married life. There was another mishap when Warrant Officer Sewell swung his Mosquito taking off. The undercarriage collapsed but neither crew members were injured. On 12 August, three aircraft were airborne and flew to Tangmere. These aircraft and the crews were attached to the High Speed Flight based there, which was attempting to break the world air speed record.

No. 500 (Kent's Own) Sqn, RAuxAF, was re-forming at West Malling on 10 May. By 13 June, the squadron was re-formed as a night fighter unit

Many National Service airmen passed through the gates of West Malling. It was an opportunity for those keen enough to learn a skill. Here, Peter Kennet, second left back row, is photographed with other NS recruits. (P. Kennett)

and equipped with the Mosquito NF.30, under the leadership of Squadron Leader Patrick Green, OBE, AFC, who had served with No. 500 Sqn in 1936–40. His new posting was Air Staff Instruction No. 1, issued by Reserve Command on 21 August. He had flown with Nos. 221 and 621 Sqn, and as an instructor with No. 7 OTU. During July and August, NCOs and other ranks were posted to the squadron, and it was visited frequently by officers of the Air Ministry. Reserve Command and No. 61 Grp HQ proved very helpful. On 26 August the squadron moved into its own HQ and began to work as a separate unit. The training flight dispersal was taken over on 28 August and also accommodation for one operational flight.

On 2 September preparations began for a visit and inspection by AOC No. 11 Grp, and a parade took place. On 7 September, Group Captain E.M. 'Teddy' Donaldson set a new world record of 615.78mph flying Meteor F.4 EE549 off the Sussex coast at Rustington. During the flight, Donaldson recalls seeing a Mosquito of No. 29 Sqn flying out to sea off the Sussex coast, the pilot tasked with checking the height of the Meteor as it built up speed.

On 13 September, the adjutant interviewed Flight Lieutenant Newport, Mr Clarke and Mr Mitchell of Maidstone, who were keen to join the

Flight Sergeant 'Dick' Moss, of No. 500 Sqn, instructing Air Training Corps cadets on the belt-feed mechanism of the Mosquito NF.30's 20mm cannon. In the background is NF.30 NT256. (R. Moss)

No. 500 (Kent's Own) Sqn, RAuxAF, also flew Harvard Mk.IIB FX432, seen here in the distinctive markings of this squadron. (Airfix Magazine)

RAuxAF. Many local men joined No. 500 Sqn during the squadron's residence.

On 14 September, both pilots of Nos. 29 and No. 500 Sqn were briefed to take part in the Battle of Britain fly past, but it was cancelled due to poor weather. However, the following day a march past was headed by Flight Lieutenant Leggett and another officer led the RAF contingent of No. 500 Sqn personnel. After the parade a service was held to commemorate the Battle of Britain. An inspection of a blister hangars and dispersal buildings was arranged for 4 October, as the squadron was due to receive its first aircraft. A few days later an Oxford aircraft was flown and serviced by the squadron personnel. This aircraft belonged to SHQ. The idea of having an aircraft in No. 500 Sqn's own hangar was keenly received and a boost to morale.

A representative from the Air Ministry Works Department arrived at West Malling on 9 September with information regarding the building of a T2 type hangar for specific use by No. 500 Sqn. Meanwhile, some flying experience took place locally using the Oxford for instructional duties.

Geoffrey De Havilland took off from the DH factory at Hatfield on 27 September, flying the high-speed DH.108 Swallow, TG306. Having reached an altitude of 10,000ft and getting into a dive, the aircraft was seen to break up and crash into Egypt Bay, north-east of Gravesend in the Thames Estuary. Seven Mosquitoes of No. 29 Sqn took off on a routine flight and one of these was diverted to search for remains. The search continued the following day and the body of De Havilland was later recovered. It was indeed a tragic loss for his family, the company and the country.

In October, No. 29 Sqn was involved on night flying training and cross-country flying, often between West Malling and Lubeck and also flying over France. Operations continued throughout November and December with many lectures and bomber interception flights.

On 13 December, a lecture on accident prevention and films on the subject was attended by aircrew. Following this aircraft carried out night flying exercises. Unfortunately, Flight Lieutenant Crone belly landed Mosquito RL127 after unintentionally feathering both engines and, having little time to use flaps, the aircraft caught fire and burnt out. However, both crew members escaped uninjured.

On 5 October, at night, three Mosquito crews of No. 25 Sqn were briefed for the interception of a B-29 Superfortress *Pacusan Dreamboat* over London, flown by Lieutenant General C.S. Irvine, US Air Force. Irvine was Deputy Chief of Staff, Pacific Air Command, 1944–47. He flew the B-29 on several record-setting flights, including Guam to Washington, DC, and Honolulu, Hawaii, to Cairo, Egypt. He eventually served as Deputy Chief of Staff for Materiel. Only one of the three Mosquitos took off, NF30 NT434, flown by Warrant Officer A. Riley and Flight Sergeant H.K. Sellers, but they were unable to catch up with the B-29 as it was ahead of its schedule. The Mosquito, being 10 miles behind it over the French coast, was recalled to West Malling, mission aborted.

Mosquitoes of No. 25 Sqn were briefed to the intercept B-29 Superfortress *Pacusan Dreamboat* over London, flown by Lieutenant General C.S. Irvine of the US Air Force, on 5 October 1946.

On 17 October, No. 500 Sqn took charge of its first aircraft, Mosquito T.Mk.III VA882, a dual-control aircraft. It was immediately air tested, found serviceable and accepted. On 21 October, VA832 was again flown and tested for any tail fin adjustment. Further recruitment commenced on 1 November, the squadron strength increased and comprised four regular officers and thirty-four other ranks. Oxford HN164 was transferred from No. 287 Sqn (now disbanded) through Fighter and Reserve Command to No. 500 Sqn, and was given a thorough air test and found to be in excellent condition. Meanwhile, improvements were being made for the squadron, and arrangements made for installation of telephones at Astley House, Maidstone, the squadron's HQ. Flight Lieutenant Rogers inspected the house and arranged for the CO and adjutant's offices to be furnished, together with a 'waiting room'. At the end of October, the adjutant attended a conference at Maidstone Territorial HQ with Air Force inspectors and Rolls-Royce Engine representatives to initiate modifications to the engines of all Mosquito aircraft arriving at West Malling for No. 500 Sqn.

It was not until after the war that No. 25 Sqn was to serve at West Malling. It had arrived from Boxted on 5 September 1946 with Mosquito Mk.VIs, which the unit had been flying since February 1945. At West

Mosquito NF.36 MT487 'ZK-Y' of No. 25 Sqn, gets a major service. Note the flame-damping exhaust on the engine and the Mk. X Air Interception (AI) radar in the transparent nose.

Malling the squadron was re-equipped with Mosquito NF.36s, which it operated throughout its stay at the airfield. They arrived just in time to take part in the Battle of Britain fly past and five aircraft were allocated for the event. The squadron was split into 'A' and 'B' Flights and each aircraft was given the identification of 'Workman', followed by a number. Workman 42 of 'A' Flight returned from an operational flight on 10 September with mechanical trouble, landing on one engine. Throughout September the squadron operated sector experience flights, night fighter training and practice interceptions, and crew attended many lectures and periods of training on Link trainers. The whole programme was a welcome interlude from flying. On 26 September, aircraft of 'A' Flight were tasked to search for a crashed Lancaster, although shortly after take-off they were informed that wreckage of the aircraft had been found. At the beginning of October, the squadron took part in dinghy drill at Maidstone swimming baths and visits to Short Brothers at Rochester.

On 9 October, eleven aircrew visited the Fremlins Brewery at Maidstone. Needless to say, it was very informative and everyone made the most of sampling the local brew, which was much appreciated. Wing Commander

Members of No. 25 Sqn football team with their much-cherished Trophy Cup, which they won when based at West Malling 1947–49. (J.R. Carter)

Campbell visited West Malling from HQ, No. 11 Grp on 28 October, the same day Captain Staugenberg of the Swedish Defence Staff arrived.

During October, members of No. 25 Sqn visited Farnborough. They watched film of ditching aircraft and were invited to view the high speed and vertical wind tunnels, the structural mechanical engineering department and various aircraft in the hangars.

Three Mosquitoes had the pleasant task of performing a fly past over a church in Canterbury for the wedding of Flying Officer Hallet, MT officer. Wing Commander Sing and Squadron Leader Peddington from No. 61 Grp visited No.25 Sqn on 1 November.

Air Marshal J. Robb visited West Malling during the afternoon of 15 December 1946, landing at the airfield in a Meteor, not long after the CO of No. 500 Sqn, Wing Commander M.G.F. Pedley, DSO, had returned from flight training with engine trouble. By 20 December the airfield was declared unserviceable due to ice on the runways and night flying ceased. Following further lectures, everyone looked forward to the Christmas break.

The year 1947 will be remembered for its extreme winter conditions, in particular heavy snow. Kent was one of the worst-hit counties. West Malling was a 'white out' as the airfield was situated on high ground and blanketed

A No. 25 Sqn mechanic at work on Mosquito NF.36 RL125 'ZK-F' during 1946. This aircraft remained with the unit until disposed of on 29 June 1946. (G. Gilbert)

in heavy snow. Flying Officer Geoff Smythe, a navigator of No. 25 Sqn, recalls the conditions that prevailed in February:

> Unfortunately the onset of the storm coincided with a critical date in 25 Squadron's calendar. We had a Royal Task to perform, namely to escort their Majesties as they sailed down the English Channel in the battleship HMS Vanguard on their way to a State visit in South Africa. This was due to take place on Thursday. However when Monday of that week dawned, our world was covered with some six inches of snow. Instantly West Malling went into panic stations to clear the runway, and all airmen toiled with the shovel and brush (there being no mechanical aids in those days).
>
> A grateful higher hierarchy issued tots of rum throughout the day. At the end of Monday, as darkness fell, the taxiways were clear, and 6,000ft of black tarmac was there for all to see. We retired, aching but well satisfied to our beds. Some of us had noticed that strong wind got up. The next morning we were greeted by one of the weirdest sights ever. The world had been transformed again. The whiteness of the previous day had all but vanished. The wind had blown the powdery snow away. The roads were clear. The airfield was back to nearly its normal green. But the snow had not gone far. It had drifted into every gully and corner it could find. It found a convenient 'gully' between the 6,000ft long heaps of snow on either side of the runway. The net result was a mound of snow some 4ft deep at its mid-point and occupying the whole runway from end to end. The annoying thing was that, had we done nothing at all on the previous day, the runway would have been completely clear. As it was we were faced with an even greater task than before! We were able to clear enough runway to enable aircraft to take off. This was achieved late in the day when all aircraft were dispatched to RAF Tangmere where conditions were (momentarily) better. The Royal Task was performed from there.

At the time of No. 25 Sqn's arrival at West Malling, the airfield's reconstruction was still under way and several of the wartime blister hangars were in a poor state of repair. There was evidence of canvas that had previously been part of the roof. There was also evidence of occupation by hop pickers, and tents had been erected on the airfield, not in the surrounding countryside. It was

No. 25 Sqn mechanics and fitters pose for a photo in front of one of the squadron's Vampire NF.10s. The colour scheme on the nose was part of a private venture by the CO to ensure everyone knew that he was flying. Apparently the wing commander (flying) caught sight of it and it was restored to its original scheme within a week. (G. Gilbert)

a headache for the station warrant officer, who was tasked to remove the unwelcome residents from the airfield.

An inspection by the AOC, Air Vice-Marshal MacDonald was due, so it was agreed to keep him away from the occupied area. On arrival, the AOC and his entourage was met by Squadron Leader Singleton, and the group was ushered around barrack blocks, the parachute section, workshops and the MT section, followed by an inspection of the squadron. Unfortunately, it was noticed that the staff car was heading in the wrong direction and it stopped close to one of the more damaged blister hangars. Mosquitoes were lined up ready for the inspection but the AOC's attention was drawn to the hangar, and he remarked to Singleton: 'Good morning Singleton. That's an interesting building you have got there. Did you find it useful? In reply, Singleton said; 'I am sorry to say I don't know, it belongs to 85 Squadron!' During the afternoon, Mosquitoes provided an impressive fly past, comprising twelve aircraft each from both Nos. 85 and 25 Sqn.

The AOC was clearly impressed as twenty-four Mosquitoes roared overhead, but the station commander at the time, Squadron Leader R. Goucher

DFC, remarked; 'Of course, sir, most of the radar is unserviceable.' During afternoon tea the AOC discussed the matter with COs of both squadrons and the problem was soon resolved.

After the war there was a steady flow of contraband between Lubeck, Germany, and most of the RAF's home bases. For the outward journey, goods such as cigarettes and coffee were secreted away in boxes, labelled 'High Voltage'. These were exchanged for cameras and watches, which were flown back. Fortunately, customs officials never found out how the trade was done.

Night fighter training and air tests continued to occupy No. 25 Sqn, but they were plagued with radar problems at high altitude. The jet age somewhat overshadowed the night fighter Mosquitoes at this time as they found it difficult to intercept such aircraft as the Lincoln due to the increasing use of both radio and radar. The continuing snow and ice was causing delays in training and at one point in January 1947 the snow was at least 12in deep. However, snow ploughs were employed to clear the perimeter track leading to the hangars, and aircraft were taxied into them for de-icing and servicing.

On 14 January 1947 a bronze eagle and large metal white horse arrived from Detling, where No. 500 Sqn had been based during the war, which were the property of the squadron pre-war.

A thaw began in February, but No. 25 Sqn's aircraft remained at Tangmere and many crews went on a ten-day leave, although they were on recall should the weather improve so they could collect their aircraft. On 19 April, five crews were detached to Lubeck and were not due to return to West Malling until 3 July. The squadron operated from Acklington and Lubeck throughout 1947, and it was not until May 1948 that these exercises ceased.

Recruiting for the RAuxAF squadrons, including No. 500 Sqn, commenced on 8 November, and the *Kent Messenger* newspaper gave the unit some impressive publicity. In fact, it was headline news. A large proportion of potential applicants were ex-aircrew enquiring about joining. Some suitable applicants were interviewed by the adjutant, although recruiting ground crew was a problem. Flight training continued in the Mosquito T.Mk.III, flown by Flight Lieutenant Leggett, and Airspeed Oxford V4102, from Kirkbride. On 3 December, Flight Lieutenant Leggett, collected another Oxford from Dumfries and returned in it to West Malling, a distance of 358 miles, in one hour fifty minutes at an average speed of 195.3mph.

On 13 December an old comrades of No. 500 Sqn reunion was held at the Star Hotel, Maidstone. Anthony Eden, the squadron's honorary air commodore and future prime minister, and Air Marshal Barton, chairman of the Kent Territorial Association, were both present, together with 134 ex-members of No. 500 Sqn. Following Christmas, all Mosquitoes had a series of modifications completed within a twenty-four-hour period, and another Airspeed Oxford was test flown by the assistant adjutant. For the next two weeks, further interviews of respective personnel were arranged at the Town Headquarters, Maidstone. Officers and airmen attended lectures and a film on planned maintenance and local flying practice in Oxford aircraft.

It was still snowing hard on 27 January 1947 and any flying was out of the question. Many aircrew were again employed clearing the snow from the aircraft and squadron dispersals. By 13 March, a blizzard raged all day and there were snow drifts up to 7ft deep. The camp was isolated and all work ceased owing to the difficulty of getting about the airfield, although later in the month some air-to-ground firing practice went ahead as scheduled. The firing range at Dengie Flats was often used for such operations.

At the end of April a visit to Chatham Dockyard was arranged and the visitors were shown over HMS *Apollo*, a Royal Naval cruiser. In May 1947, No. 500 Sqn carried out normal flying practice at West Malling, while the flying programme also included bomber affiliation exercises, searchlight co-operation exercises over Norfolk and meteorological flights. The met flights, a new commitment, were shared between Nos. 25, 29 and 85 Sqn and carried out daily. For these operations, the Mosquitoes flew at 30,000ft.

Night flying was restricted to two nights per week, in addition to two bomber affiliations and one GCI flight and local flying. On 16 June, No. 29 Sqn was detached to No. 2 Armament Practice Station (APS) for a six-week course and five aircraft took off for Acklington, where they remained until 24 July. Two crews remained at West Malling and continued meteorological flights for the next two weeks. On 20 September, four aircraft of No. 29 Sqn took part in practice flights for RAF West Malling open day.

Following the hectic days of July and August 1944, when No. 85 Sqn was based at West Malling, flying the Mosquito Mk.XVII, the squadron returned to the airfield on 16 April, arriving from Tangmere with its Mosquito NF.36s. Before leaving, six aircraft took off in formation for West Malling led by Flight Lieutenant Durrant and carried out a fly past over Tangmere. On arrival at West Malling they had a look around the new squadron HQ, which was somewhat cramped. The following day was spent installing equipment in the new buildings. The CO and adjutant had offices of their own but the two flight commanders, the engineer officer, his assistant, the non-regular listed officer (NRL), the operations planning officer and the navigation officer were all in the same room, Flight Lieutenant Jacomb-Hood, DFC, was posted to No. 25 Sqn.

On 19 April, Warrant Officer White and Sergeant Collins went to Tangmere to collect Mosquito NF.36 'YV-A'. After checking the aircraft, Collins had taxied out but found that one brake was defective and was unable to avoid a parked Avro Anson. The Mosquito rolled into it, causing considerable damage, but Collins was uninjured. The squadron carried out normal flying practice during May, mainly night flying tests and cross-country flights by day and GCI practice on bomber affiliation, searchlight co-operation and cross-country flights by night. A Wellington T.XVIII of No. 228 OCU (Operational Conversion Unit) based at RAF Leeming used as a flying classroom for AI Airborne Interception training arrived during the early part of May and the squadron navigators were able to get in useful AI practice and to check their standard of operating.

On 17 May, the squadron moved to Lubeck for a fortnight. Night flying exercises and practice ground control interceptions and cross-country flights were carried out. In June the squadron spent part of the month at No. 2 APS at Acklington and intensive firing programmes were carried out. However, the highlight of the month was a cricket match between Nos. 29 and 85 Sqn at Acklington. No. 29 Sqn hit 72 runs but No. 85 Sqn won after scoring 100 for three wickets declared.

Despite the fact that on 5 September West Malling was almost devoid of squadron personnel due to a long weekend, No. 11 Grp suddenly demanded twelve aircraft on readiness to take part in Operation Smuggler, an air interception exercise. In spite of the complete absence of NCOs on No. 85 Sqn and very few other tradesmen, Nos. 29, 25 and 85 Sqn, with No. 500 Sqn, produced the necessary aircraft and crews. No. 85 Sqn could only provide one serviceable aircraft and was armed up within twenty minutes of the order being given. A standing patrol was kept up from dusk to dawn, and many aircraft were intercepted, which turned out to be civil aircraft on their scheduled flights or other Mosquitoes. Pilots were instructed to intercept suspicious aircraft, to follow them back to their base and land there if possible. However, nothing turned up. The squadron was put on standby, providing three aircraft every night at one hour readiness as a sequel to Smuggler. The squadron also formed the last vic in the West Malling contingent of the year's Battle of Britain fly past in September and also participated in an evening fly past over the West Country.

On 20 September, West Malling airfield was thrown open to the public and No. 85 Sqn participated in formation to help entertain the crowds.

Flight Lieutenant Durrant had broken his spine in a crash-landing in Mosquito NF.36 RL203 on 19 September. Despite the serious injury, he was making good progress and he had many visitors while in hospital. He remained in hospital for a few weeks, and had the plaster removed after three months. He had narrowly escaped death.

No. 14 Sqn took part in a mobile radar command post (MRCP) demonstration in the autumn for the School of Land/Air Warfare. Deployed to West Malling on 29 September, the squadron was billeted in accommodation that had just been vacated by German prisoners of war. There was no ground engineering equipment at West Malling, so parties were sent out to beg what they could from other RAF bases. Bomb trolleys were borrowed from Tangmere, Middle Wallop provided practice bombs, while 500lb live bombs were sourced from a maintenance unit in Norfolk. The MRCP practices started on 2 October and No.14 Sqn was scheduled to give the demonstration on 10 October. Unfortunately cloud covered the target, but the weather was deemed fit enough for it to go ahead.

Mosquito B.XVIs took off from West Malling with 500lb bombs in case the weather cleared completely and 250lb practice bombs in case it had not. Despite clouds, they were already committed to dropping the practice bombs, which they did with an impressive bombing error of only 70yd. No. 14 Sqn moved again on 17 October 1947 to RAF Wahn on the banks of the Rhine, where it re-equipped with Mosquito B.35s.

A tragic flying accident occurred on 4 October involving Flight Lieutenant J.E. Herrington, who was killed. His navigator, Pilot Officer Coombs, was critically injured, with burns on his face and arms, a fractured thigh and a suspected blood clot. Flight Lieutenant J.E. Herrington was buried at West Malling church with full military honours. In November, Flying Officer Collins with Pilot Officer Doe as his navigator, both of No. 85 Sqn, set off for Malta, flying to Tangmere first. Unfortunately, after taking off their aircraft collided with birds and the flight was abandoned.

Flying practice continued during the remainder of the year. However, the number of hours flown by No. 85 Sqn was low, mainly due to poor weather. A message was received from the AOC No. 11 Grp congratulating the squadron, along with Nos. 29 and 25 Sqn, on the large number of successful single-engine landings made during December 1947.

By 21 January, forty-eight aircrew, sixteen ground crew and six ground officers had been interviewed for No. 500 Sqn. In spite of the severe snow and ice, two auxiliary airmen made their way to West Malling and were medically examined and attested. They were then enlisted and were given the first two service numbers in the post-war RAuxAF. The weather had become so severe with snow falls and extremely dangerous conditions that further recruiting in Maidstone was cancelled and on 27 January the station commander ordered that the main runway and perimeter track had to be cleared of snow.

Flight Lieutenant Mersham, Headquarters, No. 61 Grp, arrived to discuss the location and installation of the Air Training Corps (ATC) Gliding School, at the time based at Detling. Many cadets had visited West Malling to gain flying experience in No. 500 Sqn's Oxford, AT587.

On 18 February, the weather was so bad that West Malling was closed down except for duty staff in staff HQ. That left two officers and twelve airmen on duty for care and maintenance of aircraft and to undertake routine duties. Oxford RR329 was damaged on 22 February when it was struck by a Mosquito being towed into the hangar. The towing party and Mosquito concerned belonged to No. 6029 Servicing Echelon (No. 29 Sqn's SE). Damage to the Oxford consisted of a tear in the nose of the fuselage. A work party was arranged by the squadron to clear ice and snow from around No. 500 Sqn's dispersal. Mosquitoes of both Nos. 25 and 29 Sqn had been diverted to Tangmere due to the bad weather and had

The RAF put on a display at the Rootes Garage in Maidstone during 1947. As well as being interesting for the public, it was a good platform to promote the RAF and hopefully inspire young adults to join the RAuxAF. (KAHRS)

been snowbound there. On 25 February ground and aircrew were ferried to Tangmere in order to retrieve aircraft of both squadrons. Safely collected, they returned to West Malling where, following immense effort, work parties had cleared dispersals and runways.

A party of air cadets from Tonbridge School No. 1601 Sqn ATC visited West Malling and were entertained by No. 500 Sqn with navigational and technical lectures. Had they arrived the following morning, the cadets would have seen the first of the new Mosquito NF.19s.

The adjutant addressed RAF Association members at Sevenoaks about the RAuxAF, while the chair was taken by Group Captain Farrington, DSO. During the same week, further recruitment continued. The interviews were conducted by the CO, RAF West Malling, at Astley House, Maidstone. March had been a busy month for No. 500 Sqn and it ended when a large group of air cadets arrived for camp, accommodated in the squadron barrack block. No. 500 Sqn flew all day on 30 March, and dual instruction was given to Flying Officer Saunders while cadets were flown in Oxfords. Wing Commander Heyes and members of No. 600 Sqn, RAuxAF, visited the squadron and were entertained to lunch. Throughout April, air cadets continued to be flown in the squadron's Oxfords and assisted in compass swinging of squadron aircraft. This was carried out on a concrete pad well away from any magnetic influence. The aircraft would be physically swung backwards and forwards to check the accuracy of the aircraft's on-board compass.

On 24 and 25 April, Mosquito NF.30 NT620 and TA352 were received by No. 500 Sqn and successfully air tested. Preparations were under way for an inspection by the AOC, No. 11 Grp planned for the beginning of June. On 7 June the AOC arrived by air and, accompanied by Wing Commander Pedley, the station commander, an inspection of ATC squadrons took place at 1550hrs and officers and airmen of No. 500 Sqn lined up before the squadron's aircraft.

The AOC spoke with officers and NCOs and airmen before inspecting Squadron HQ, followed by a meeting to discuss recruitment. At the end of the day, the AOC expressed how pleased he was with No. 500 Sqn's progress and the high standard conditions and efficiency at West Malling. A few days later a good report of the squadron's history, present function and recruiting plans were given on the front page of the *Kent Messenger*.

Throughout June a considerable amount of RAuxAF training was carried out. Several personnel, ground and flying, reported for instruction

The zig-zag pattern on the fuselage of these aircraft signifies they were all allocated to No. 500 (Kent's Own) Sqn, RAuxAF. Meteor F.8 WH426, second from left, remained with the squadron until 11 March 1959. (Robin A. Walker)

and photographers and reporters of the *Reserve Gazette* and *Daily Graphic* visited. By early July, No. 500 Sqn had three Oxfords and nine Mosquitoes on strength, and the squadron took part in an air-sea exercise in order to ensure the safety of a flight of Vampires crossing the Channel, which was carried out successfully. To assist with a recruiting drive, a stand with technical displays was erected for the annual Canterbury carnival. This was followed by a low-level fly past at 1230hrs on 26 July over Brighton during a recruiting drive in the town.

On 8 August, in fine weather, No. 500 Sqn paraded with the station for arrival of AOC, No. 11 Grp. Aircraft were inspected and a fly past was given by Nos. 25, 29 and 85 Sqn, while the AOC visited No. 500 Sqn's dispersal. Tangmere hosted No. 500 Sqn's annual camp and aircraft flew there in formation, landing at 1120hrs, followed by an Oxford piloted by Sergeant Crane. The main party consisting of fifty-four NCOs and airmen and the officer in charge arrived at Tangmere at 0930hrs.

Following a busy but enjoyable camp at Tangmere, the squadron returned to West Malling on 8 September No. 500 Sqn soon resettled, returning to normal duties. One of these was preparation for the annual Battle of Britain display, to be held on 20 September. On the evening prior to the start of Battle of Britain week, No. 500 Sqn took part in in a night exercise involving searchlight co-operation. This proved highly successful and provided the searchlight battery with excellent practice. Aerobatics and formation flying at the Battle of Britain display was performed by Flight Lieutenant Leggett and Flying Officers Dick and Trigg, accompanied by their navigators, Flight Lieutenant Rogers and Flying Officers Baker and Hammond. Following a commemorative service at the Agricultural Hall, Maidstone, on 21 September, the Mayor of Maidstone took the salute of a march past in Maidstone by No. 500 Sqn. The remainder of the squadron, who were not attending, were stood down for the afternoon.

No. 14 Sqn was assigned to take part in the Battle of Britain fly past over London in 1947 and flew practice flights from West Malling on 12 and 13 September. The weather was below limits on 15 September and the fly past was cancelled. Instead, the squadron put on a four-aircraft low-level bombing display at the West Malling open day on 16 September. The remainder of the month was taken up by Exercise Broadside, a large-scale Army exercise in Germany.

At 1430hrs on 11 October, a Mosquito flown by Flight Lieutenant Leggett and Flight Lieutenant Hanslip took off from West Malling to carry out an altitude test, attaining a height of 31,500ft and returning to base at 1530hrs.

Early in November, the squadron was stunned when Corporal Grant was killed in a road accident. His funeral took place on 7 November and was attended by a large part of No. 500 Sqn.

Also that month, Mosquito NF.30 aircraft were collected and flown back to join the squadron at West Malling. The delivery took place just in time for the occasion of the wedding of HRH Princess Elizabeth and HRH the Duke of Edinburgh, held on 20 November 1947. After pay parade the squadron was released from duty for the rest of the day in honour of the Royal Wedding, which was followed by a public dance at the Town Centre, Astley House, Maidstone.

By the end of December, it was time for No. 500 Sqn to assess its accomplishments during the year. The squadron strength now consisted of fifteen officers and eighteen airmen – comprising eight pilots (one NCO), six navigators, five ground officers and fourteen ground staff, nearly all recruited during the year. Total flying time was 500hrs, averaging sixty-two for pilots and thirty for navigators. Weekend attendance at West Malling had been fair, but many members fell short of the stipulated number of twelve hours, a figure considered the minimum required in building up the efficiency of the squadron, and developing it as a well-knit unit. However, considering that 1947 was the year of the rebirth of No. 500 (Kent's Own) Sqn, RAuxAF, it had achieved much in such a short time.

A few months later, during a demo at West Malling, No. 98 Sqn damaged three out of four Mosquito B.35s while making bomb drops – perhaps they were a bit low, or perhaps it was just a harder surface on the airfield, and debris struck the aircraft. They missed their target, just as four aircraft from No. 14 Sqn had done earlier.

They used 60lb bombs for the British Air Forces of Occupation (BAFO) air display at Gutersloh, Germany. carrying four bombs in each of four aircraft. The air display was originally planned for 15 June, but had to be postponed for a few days because of the weather. After flying past in squadron boxes of four, then in echelon and finally in line astern, the Mosquitoes of Nos. 98 and 14 Sqn cleared the area for displays by Vampires, Meteors and the Republic F-84E Thunderjets of the USAF's Sky Blazers display team.

The Mosquitoes then returned for the finale, a series of attacks on the enemy HQ. Flying Officer M.H. Levy reported that, 'all sixteen bombs were dropped in one salvo from the No. 14 Sqn formation and we obliterated the dummy factory which had been built on Gutersloh airfield. No. 98 Sqn came in last, and I'm not sure what was left for them to aim at.'

The air display season continued through the month and two days after the BAFO display the squadron was again detached to West Malling to take part in the RAF display at Farnborough. The sun shone on 7 and 8 July and 200,000 spectators attended, including the King and Queen, who enjoyed a magnificent show. Towards the end of the display a re-enactment of the famous Amiens prison aid of 1944 was staged. A mock-up of the prison had been built and the part of Group Captain Pickard's Mosquitoes, who led the raid, was played by twelve aircraft of Nos. 14 and 98 Sqn, with a force of Spitfires painted in German markings to represent the Luftwaffe. Flying Officer M.H. Levy flew as Number three in one of the No. 14 Sqn sections and recalled:

> For the sake of authenticity our attacks were made by echelons of three aircraft and this raised a certain problem. We were dropping practice bombs on the target, although explosive charges detonated from the ground were fitted in the target. Naturally we wanted our bombs to hit the target but its small size made this difficult for an attack in echelon. The target was an excellent representation of the original prison, but it was scaled down and was only about 100ft wide. As the wing span of a Mosquito was 54ft 2in, it will be realised that three aircraft could not be fitted into this width. We therefore flew

our echelons with the aircraft well stepped back with wingtips overlapping. Even so, as a Number 3, 1 could not get lined up on the target. I therefore decided to slide across and below the other two as we approached the target. As they were flying at about 50ft and the target was about 30ft high this got quite exciting, particularly as I was in the slipstream of the leading two aircraft! I tended to cross the target with rapid control movements to full travel in either direction.

After the summer air displays came more exhibitions of the squadron's bombing skills. From West Malling the squadron was able to support the School of Land/Air Warfare with the almost traditional MRCP bombing demonstration on West Down range. The last demonstration was given on 1 August, after which the squadron flew up to Linton-on-Ouse. From Linton it mounted low-level attacks as part of two fire-power demonstrations, one at Catterick on 8 July and another at Fylingdales the next day. By 10 July, the whole squadron had reassembled at Celle, Germany.

January 1948 opened with No. 500 Sqn continuing with routine work and flying, and the squadron was visited by Wing Commander Burnside, DSP, DFC, newly appointed to No. 61 Grp HQ. He presided over a meeting with No. 500 Sqn to discuss the future role of the squadron.

Flight Lieutenant Leggett had flown 660 hours in Mosquitoes and had a total of 2,214 hours on all types. On 18 January he and Flight Lieutenant E.R. Hanslip, the engineer officer of No. 500 Sqn, had taken off at about 1045hrs on a routine practice flight in Mosquito NF.30 NT619. Once airborne the aircraft appeared to be perfectly serviceable and a climb was commenced. Reaching 1,400ft, there was a sudden and complete loss of power from the starboard engine. According to Leggett: 'It felt as though someone had switched off both magnetos.' He attempted to feather the starboard propeller but this was unsuccessful and as height was being lost, a belly landing with full flap was carried out at Gravesend.

From the first point of impact to the final resting place was 28yd. The port propeller and reduction gear had been torn off and damage was consistent with a heavy belly landing. There was no evidence of structural failure while in flight. Both flaps were torn off during landing and the main planes were slightly damaged. The port tailplane had been cut in half by the detached propeller, while the starboard tailplane was damaged. As the undercarriage was retracted at the time of the accident it had suffered minimal damage and functioned when the aircraft was later lifted for removal. Fortunately, although somewhat shaken, both Leggett and Hanslip were not seriously injured. The engine, which had failed in flight, was returned to Rolls-Royce for a full strip examination, which revealed that the Dural drive gear for the fuel pump had failed. The fuel pump had been replaced two hours prior to the accident owing to shearing of the quill drive shaft, and the shock loading sustained by the previous failure undoubtedly led to the drive gear failure. The court of enquiry was led by Squadron Leader Mann, No. 61 Grp, and the conclusion was that the failure emphasised the importance of changing or complete inspection of the fuel pump drive whenever a fuel pump was changed due to seizure or shearing of the quill drive.

A further five sorties were flown on 18 January and twenty-two ATC cadets began a course of technical training under the supervision of the engineer officer with a view to them joining the squadron when fully trained. Several of the boys were later interviewed by Flight Lieutenant Kilduff, who had attended the course.

Squadron Leader Foxley-Norris, of the Reserve Command, visited the airfield regarding the changing of the squadron from night to day fighters. On 7 February an exhibition by No. 500 Sqn took place at Rootes Garage, Maidstone, and recruiting took place attended by C-in-C Fighter Command, while Flying Officer Barker represented the squadron at the opening ceremony.

Flying activities were interrupted by snow during February but some cine camera and AI practice flights were flown. ATC cadets from Tonbridge School visited the squadron at West Malling for further instructional training. The day 8 March was a busy one for No. 500 Sqn personnel, who had to attend two crashes at the airfield on the same day. Mosquito RL122 of No. 29 Sqn swung on take-off and the undercarriage collapsed, but the crew were uninjured.

Then, Mosquito RL147 of No. 85 Sqn crashed when both engines shut down in error after the wrong propeller was feathered during single engine training. The crash was proved afterwards to have been caused by a blocked fuel filter. The pilot, the only person on board, feathered the correct prop but it unfeathered itself again, an issue that was not unknown. As he was on his own, the pilot had to reach across the cockpit to feather it again but he was losing height quickly and the aircraft then hit the top of an elm tree, causing the other prop to feather, again proved by subsequent inspection showing damage to the feathering mechanism. Without power from either engine, the Mosquito was pretty much out of control and it ploughed into the orchard. The wings were ripped off before the fuselage hit the ground. The pilot was ejected through the top of the cockpit and landed some distance from the aircraft, still strapped into his seat. He suffered a badly broken leg, a broken arm and various minor injuries.

Two crews of No. 500 Sqn visited No. 501 Sqn at Filton and were lucky to be able to look over the massive Bristol Brabazon airliner. The following year, on 4 September 1949, the company's chief test pilot, A.J. Pegg, would take off in Brabazon 1 G-AGPW on its first flight. Originally planned for the London–Nice route, the Brabazon was plagued with technical problems, such as airscrew mounting cracks, and would never see production. The prototype was broken up in October 1953. One of the Mosquitoes flown to Filton suffered a severely cut tyre and had to remain at the airfield but it was collected following a wheel change and flown back to West Malling on 3 April.

Three Mosquitoes of No. 500 Sqn took part in an AA co-op exercise, attacking Aylesford Bridge, near West Malling, where Army units were deployed and more sorties were flown on the following night.

Six aircraft were detached to West Malling on 24 March for a low-level bombing demonstration. After several practices, the Mosquitoes carried out the demo, each aircraft dropping two 250lb bombs from 500ft with an eleven-second delay fuse, and the results were impressive. On 6 May, the squadron deployed to West Malling for the MRCP detachment, this time for No. 7 Special Senior Course.

At the beginning of May, the squadron had taken charge of a Harvard Mk.IIB FX432, and pilots of No. 500 Sqn were able to fly eleven sorties consisting of single-engine flying, formation flying and cross-country flying, while the assistant adjutant familiarised himself with the Harvard during the afternoon. Throughout May several pilots went solo on the Harvard and flying continued in both the Oxford and Mosquito. During May the weather was favourable and a full flying programme was carried out on every day of the month. Some twenty-six night sorties were flown, of which four were bomber affiliation, five were cross-country flights and the remainder were GCI.

A 'Snake' exercise was carried out with Nos. 25 and 29 Sqn as a prelude to more GCI exercises. The squadron was sent on attachment to Lubeck, a formation of six aircraft proceeding there on 28 May. Such exercises continued throughout the next few months and into the new year.

On 27 May, No. 500 Sqn took delivery of Spitfire F.22 PK654, and two days later another F.22, PK563, joined the squadron on loan from No. 615 Sqn. On 30 May, the Spitfire F.22 was first flown on an acceptance flight by the squadron adjutant. These Spitfires added to the squadron's fleet of aircraft.

On 7 June 1948, thirteen P-51Ds of J26, 16 Wing, Swedish Air Force, arrived at West Malling on a goodwill visit. (National Archive)

During October, five bomber affiliation flights were flown, the remainder of the exercises were flight interceptions, cross-country flights and ground flying exercises. Air-sea rescue flights were also carried out.

Affiliation exercises were flown with B-29 bombers of the USAF. These were successful, but as the bombers took no evasive action the interceptions were rather easy. Flight Lieutenant Alcock and Pilot Officer Stansfield flew in the B-29 and were impressed by the huge bomber, although both remarked that their Mosquito NFs had the American bombers 'taped'.

On 7 June the Swedish Air Force arrived at West Malling from Uppsala, Sweden, on a goodwill visit. The deployment of thirteen P-51D Mustangs and three Junkers Ju 86 aircraft was an impressive sight as they came in to land. That evening the Swedish guests were entertained by RAF and RAuxAF personnel.

In February 1945, Sweden had purchased fifty P-51Ds, designated J 26, which were delivered by American pilots in April and assigned to the F 16 wing at Uppsala as interceptors. In early 1946, the F 4 wing at Östersund was equipped with a second batch of ninety P-51Ds. A final batch of twenty-one Mustangs was purchased in 1948. In all, 161 J 26s served in the Swedish Air Force during the late 1940s. About twelve were

222

modified for photo reconnaissance and re-designated S 26. Some of these aircraft participated in the secret Swedish mapping of new Soviet military installations on the Baltic coast in 1946–47 (Operation Falun), an endeavour that entailed many intentional violations of Soviet airspace. However, the Mustang could out-dive any Soviet fighter of that era, so no S 26s were lost in these missions.

The J 26s were replaced by De Havilland Vampires around 1950. The S 26s were replaced by S 29C Tunnans in the early 1950s.

On 18 June two Spitfire F.22s lent by No. 615 (County of Surrey) Sqn for the purpose of the AOC's inspection were collected by Flight Lieutenant Bradwell and Flight Lieutenant Sowrey. Squadron Leader Mann and P.I. Stanley of Headquarters, No. 61 Grp, collected Oxfords AT587 and RR329 allotted to HQ, No. 61 Grp. During the morning of 20 June, eight Mosquitoes were airborne in practice formation for an afternoon fly past. After lunch, No. 500 Sqn paraded with an ATC squadron camped at West Malling for an inspection by the AOC.

The following day, four sorties were flown in good weather and Spitfire F.22 PK563 was returned to No. 615 Sqn at Biggin Hill. A Spitfire F.22, possibly PK654, of No. 615 Sqn was damaged following its return to that base on 18 June, and remained with No. 615 Sqn. Training flights continued into July involving Spitfire F.22, Harvard and Mosquito aircraft of No. 500 Sqn, which also included a Fighter Command exercise at Kenley in which Flying Officer Kay, with his navigator, Flight Lieutenant Farnfield, flew a Mosquito.

The same day, 11 July, Flying Officer J.J. Browne made his first solo flight in a Spitfire F.22, successfully taking off and landing. However, during another flight he managed to land wheels up! Apart from being shaken and a little embarrassed, he was not injured. There was, however, a court of inquiry convened by the station commander the following day, the outcome of which is not known but a lecture by the adjutant on accident prevention took place at Group Headquarters.

Four Mosquitoes of No. 500 Sqn performed a fly past over Maidstone Agricultural Show during the evening of 17 July, and at the end of July both Flight Lieutenant Kilduff and Flying Officer De Villiers flew Meteor F.4 aircraft. In all, four sorties were flown, including a cross-country flight to RAF Aldergrove, Northern Ireland.

When No. 500 Sqn had been re-formed in June 1946 as part of the RAuxAF revival it was given Mosquito NF.30s in keeping with the primary night fighter role of the other units at West Malling at the time. However, towards the end of 1948, Air Ministry policy was towards the conversion of all the auxiliary squadrons into day fighter units and later that year, No. 500 Sqn became the first auxiliary unit to receive Meteors, F.IIIs.

This gave the squadron an impetus and by 1949 it had worked up in its new role, achieving much publicity when its honorary air commodore, Sir Anthony Eden flew in the squadron's two-seat Meteor T.7 during a visit. In 1950, Meteor F.4s arrived and the following year the squadron was transferred from Reserve Command to Fighter Command. During the 1950s the squadron expanded in size and later was fully equipped with Meteor F.8s, then Fighter Command's standard day fighter, and took part in many exercises alongside its full-time counterparts. With increased proficiency came the opportunity to go abroad for its annual summer camp, held in Malta in 1953 and 1954 and Germany in 1955 and returning to Malta in 1956. However, when the Meteor began to be replaced by the Hunter in Fighter Command it was eventually decided that this was too high a performance aircraft to be flown by weekend pilots and as an economy measure all the auxiliaries were disbanded in the early months of 1957, No. 500 still being at West Malling.

So, in July 1948, No. 500 Sqn began conversion from the Mosquito NF.19 and NF.30 and the Spitfire F.22 to the new Meteor F.Mk.III. By 6 August, preparations were well under way for No. 500 Sqn to have its summer camp and by 14/15 August the squadron had settled in at Thorney Island, which was a great success with many training flights being completed.

No. 614 (County of Glamorgan) Sqn, RAuxAF, joined No. 500 Sqn at West Malling on 2 September for Operation Danger, flying Spitfire F.22s from its base at Llandow. No. 500 Sqn was unable to take part due to operational conversion onto Meteor F.Mk.IIIs, and No. 614 Sqn was deployed to an area of No. 500's dispersal area.

Four Mosquitoes of No. 500 Sqn were able to practise formation flying for the Battle of Britain display but during one such flight on 13 September Flight Lieutenant Ewart and Flying Officer Palmer were killed when their Mosquito, RL117 of No. 25 Sqn, collided with Mosquito T.Mk.III VT612 of No. 85 Sqn and spun into ground about a quarter of a mile from West Malling. Their aircraft's tailplane had been knocked off during the collision. Despite damage to VT612, it was repaired and flew until 12 June 1952 when, while serving with No. 231 OCU at Bassingbourn, the undercarriage collapsed on landing.

The Mosquitoes of No. 29 Sqn also practised their flying programme in preparation for a Battle of Britain fly past over London on 14 September, with a full-scale rehearsal taking place on 11 September. The fly past took place over London as planned, but the weather was terrible. One of No. 29 Sqn's Mosquitoes flew with a BBC reporter on board as a passenger and he recorded the event from the air.

On 18 September a farewell party was held in honour of their CO, Squadron Leader T.C. Wood, DFC, who was posted to No. 11 Grp. He had joined the squadron in December 1945 and was replaced by Squadron Leader D. Hawkins, DFC. On 24 October 1948, No. 605 (County of Warwick) Sqn landed from Honiley at 0845hrs with seven Vampires to practise a fly past due to take place over Hyde Park, which was cancelled due to poor visibility over London.

Later that day six Meteors of No. 500 Sqn escorted the Vampires on their way back to Honiley. The highlight of the week was a squadron ball held at the Tudor House, Maidstone, which was a great success with some 300 people attending. At the end of October, seven of No. 500 Sqn's new Meteor F.Mk.IIIs were airborne practising formation flying. It is worthy to note that, No. 500 Squadron was the first to be equipped with the F.Mk.III. They would later be re-equipped with the Meteor F.4 in July 1951 and the F.9 in November 1957, which they flew until the squadron's disbandment on 10 March 1957.

No. 29 Squadron had returned to Acklington on 5 January 1948, returning to West Malling on 26 February, and were detached to Lubeck on 14 May, returning again to West Malling on 27 May. By September the squadron was involved on aircraft interception training and Exercise Dagger, during which more than 100 hours' flying was completed. On 4 September the squadron lost one of the squadron's most efficient crews when Flight Lieutenant Copper and Flight Lieutenant McColl crashed during poor weather. Mosquito NF.36 RL192 was preparing to land when it dived into the ground a mile east of West Malling while returning from a Dagger sortie. Both men were killed instantly.

Due to shortage of serviceable Mosquitoes NF.36s, which were awaiting major servicing, several of No. 29 Sqn's T.Mk.IIIs, the trainer version of the aircraft, were loaned to No. 25 Sqn in February 1949.

The last two weeks of February were spent in moving the No. 29 Sqn dispersal to the other side of the airfield. This meant sleeping in Nissen sheds, which was not popular with aircrew as they had settled in their existing quarters and much work had been done on the surrounding garden area.

At the end of December 1948, information was received that No. 85 Sqn was to be encouraged to display squadron markings on its Mosquitoes and also to foster a spirit of 'pride of squadron'. A squadron tie was also designed, which was green with a narrow stripe of red and black squares. This design was also intended to be painted on squadron aircraft.

The squadron reaction was immediate and not a little caustic – somebody appeared to have forgotten the hexagon that had been displayed on aircraft of No. 85 Sqn since the days of Major Bishop, VC, in the First World War and that was incorporated on the squadron crest. A new design was submitted in which the hexagon was suitably prominent and, of course, the aircraft had the hexagon on the fin.

On New Year's Day 1949, a meteorological flight was carried out by Flight Lieutenant Stansfield and his navigator, Pilot Officer Bull. They had trouble with both engines on the way down but landed safely at West Malling. On 3 January, the squadron got away to a good start by flying four sorties in the afternoon and four at night.

One of the night efforts was abortive but the other three produced almost eight flying hours. The good start was not maintained, however, for the weather deteriorated and no night flying was possible for a week. Day flying was possible on occasions and the usual beacon tests, cine gun, air-to-ground firing were carried out. About the middle of the month the weather improved but the squadron was handicapped by aircraft shortages and some aircraft were also unserviceable. During a scheduled performance trial, a Mosquito NF.36 was armed and loaded to full wartime scale and flown to unprecedented heights to check the rate of climb, maximum speed at 30,000ft and maximum altitude. Pilot Officer Maxwell and Dee got up to 36,500ft. Flying Officer Collins and his navigator, Flying Officer Emsden, reached 36,000ft and Flying Officer Vasse and his navigator, Flying Officer Emberson, reached 37,000ft. The trials were successful and all considered the performance adequate. For ten days in March, No. 85 Sqn was detached to Leuchars, with six aircraft, nine crews and thirty ground staff.

On 8 February, Flight Lieutenant Don Mortimer and his navigator taxied out at West Malling in Mosquito NF.36 RL231 of No. 29 Sqn on a routine flight. However, as the aircraft gathered speed on take-off the port engine failed, the drill being to abandon the attempt. Mortimer managed to get the tail back down onto the runway so that the brakes could be applied, but the boundary fence was approaching rapidly and the practice was to pull up the undercarriage. The rotating propellers were a hazard, as they had been known to come through the cockpit sides, but their luck held as the aircraft crashed through the fence into a ploughed field and broke up. The crew were uninjured and climbed out through the top hatch, but the aircraft was a write-off. They had both had a narrow escape.

The remains of Mosquito NF.36 RL231, piloted by Sergeant Don Mortimer of No. 29 Sqn, who was one of a few post-war night fighter sergeant pilots. It crashed at West Malling on 8 February 1949 following engine failure.

One of the unusual duties performed by West Malling in 1949 was to send a detachment of airmen to help crew and maintain the seaplane tender ST *1500*, which was on station off Leysdown ranges, Sheerness. The air-sea rescue detachment was in attendance as a safety precaution as in the past there had been accidents during bombing and firing exercises on the ranges.

This vessel was built as ST *1500* in 1942 by the British Powerboat Company (BPB Co.), Hythe, to a design by George Selman, the chief designer of BPB Co. ST *1500* was the first of a commissioned batch. Her first placement was with No. 62 MU in Dumbarton on the Clyde. In March 1942, ST *1500* was taken over by Coastal Command at RAF Catfoss for the use of the Marine Section Bridlington as one of two seaplane tenders operating from the town. When two more arrived, ST *1500* was dedicated to air-sea rescue and a Lewis gun was fitted in her cockpit. In November 1942, she was transferred to Chivenor in Somerset, operating out of Ilfracombe. Her prime task was target towing. In late 1944, ST *1500* was seconded to the Catalina base at Killadeas in Northern Ireland. She was then moved to the Marine Aircraft Experimental Establishment at Felixstowe on 9 October 1945. In 1948, she was based at RAF Immingham Docks and in 1949 she returned to Felixstowe.

In 1953, there were terrible floods on the east coast and ST *1500* was involved in ferrying essential supplies on the Medway from Sheerness to

Sun Pier, Chatham, and provided a passenger service. She was also used for a short period at Woolwich, transferring the explosive officers who checked and supervised the loading of explosive on ships about 2 miles off Southend pier. On 11 June 1956, Range Safety Launch (RSL) ST *1500* was moved from 1103 MCU Felixstowe to No. 238 MU, Calshot, for repair. On 30 December 1957, her intended next movement was to HQ Far East Air Force (FEAF) for command reserve. She was repainted in tropical white, but remained in storage at Calshot until her disposal on 17 December 1958. She was bought by Milford Haven Marine Services and renamed *Pembroke Petrel*. By 1963, it had become uneconomic to provide the service to the Milford Haven oil terminals by boat and *Pembroke Petrel* was sold to the owner of a caravan park near Tenby. She was used until 1976 for running trips around the bay and was then gifted to the Tenby sea cadets. In 1983 she was disposed of and in 1993 bought and moved to Brightlingsea, then to Marchwood Military Port, Southampton. The current owners acquired the vessel in July 1995 and she is now based in Scotland.

The airmen's first job in February 1949 was to paint ST *1500*. The following day she left Sheerness for Leysdown ranges, but could only approach within 300yd of the pylon target, due to the depth of the water. The target was used for firing practice by RAF aircraft, and there was aircraft wreckage in the area, none of which was visible. A request had been made to seep the area to locate and remove any obstructions.

On 17 February, ST *1500* was moved to moorings at Queensborough, while dredging operations commenced. Following an inspection of the launch by Wing Commander Baker No. 19 Grp HQ, on 19 February, it proceeded out to sea on 22 February to test the radio communications with West Malling. To maintain communications with RAF Felixstowe, the wireless telegraph on board ST *1500* was tested, and the vessel went to sea again for compass swinging.

In July 1949, airmen from West Malling were also tasked with maintenance of another tender, ST *1530*, including, of course, painting the vessel. ASR detachment by personnel of RAF West Malling to Leysdown continued, and squadrons based at West Malling often used the Leysdown range for practice firing operations.

On 12 May, AOC No. 11 Grp visited the airfield on his annual inspection of No. 25 Sqn. It was again inspected on 31 May by the new C-in-C Fighter Command, Air Marshal Sir Basil Embry, CB, DSO, DFC, AFC. He spoke to all ranks and had an informal chat with the aircrew in the crew room.

Flying Officer R.J. Wilkie crashed and lost his life during a familiarisation flight on 7 June flying Mosquito NF.36 RL204. He had been practising single-engine circuits 4 miles west of the airfield. This was the last major crash of No. 25 Sqn at West Malling before the beginning of the new decade, in which the unit would join the jet age.

On 9 July, Group Captain H.N.G. Ramsbottom Isherwood, DFC, AFC, a New Zealander, took command of RAF West Malling from Group Captain J. Worral, DFC. The new CO had a distinguished career, including joining the staff of the Aeroplane and Armament Experimental Establishment as a test pilot.

West Malling was opened to the public on Saturday, 17 September. A section of Meteors 'toured' not only West Malling but Odiham, Biggin Hill and Booker, to mark the year's Battle of Britain celebrations. One aircraft was on static display, while four other aircrew made demonstration fly pasts at other RAF stations.

Following the open day, aircraft were serviced in preparation for Exercise Bulldog, which was to start in late September. The exercise was designed to test night fighter aircraft of No. 12 Grp. The activities of No. 25 Sqn during Exercise Bulldog were somewhat curtailed by adverse weather conditions that prevailed on the night of 23 September, two days before the start of the exercise, but the squadron managed to score nine enemy aircraft destroyed and Bulldog ended on 26 September.

No. 25 Sqn was again detached to Acklington for air-to-air and air-to-ground firing, returning to West Malling on 21 October. The squadron was pleased to retain the trophy for the highest average air-to-air score.

On 3 November, Mosquito NF.36 serial RL116 of No. 29 Sqn was airborne from West Malling to take part in yet another Exercise Bullseye, in which fighters co-operated with bombers, mostly Lancasters, in interception training. One of these aircraft, Lancaster TW908 of No. 148 Sqn based at Upwood, Cambridgeshire, was intercepted by RL116, but during the manoeuvres the Mosquito collided with its target. The wreckage crashed into the sea 8 miles south of Selsey Bill, Sussex. Of the crew of the Mosquito, Flying Officer A.L. Miller was recovered by HMS *Romola* but Flight Lieutenant E.C. Dalgety was not found. All crew members of the Lancaster were killed. They were pilot, Flying Officer Jack Oldham; navigator III, D. McUsbie McCall; flight engineer, L.H. Stevens; Signaller I, E.G. Clarke; Gunner II, S.A. Mason; Gunner II, C.J. Chapman; and Navigator II, W. Meldrum. For No. 25 Sqn, January 1950 began with seven night bomber affiliation sorties, and three other night interception sorties and nine day

Officers of No. 25 Sqn in 1952, when Squadron Leader D.C. Furse, DFC, was CO, seated centre front row. Furse was also CO of No. 85 Sqn in May 1946. The control tower behind them, to the centre-right, still stands today.

Meteor F.4 VT185 '4K', in which Wing Commander H.N.G. Ramsbottom-Isherwood DFC, AFC, lost his life on 24 April 1950. The aircraft crashed at Oak Green, Tonbridge. (Kent Messenger)

interception sorties, twelve cine camera exercises and five meteorological flights were carried out. Operations continued throughout 1950, still flying the now ageing Mosquito NF.36.

On the morning of 24 April, Group Captain H.N.G. Ramsbottom-Isherwood, the station CO, was returning from RAF Martlesham Heath in his Meteor F.4, VT185. After flying across the airfield at 200ft in snow, he decided to land at Manston. He did not reach the airfield but crashed and was killed about 10 miles away at Oak Green, Tonbridge. The crash was believed to have been caused by extreme ice accretion, but since so little of the Meteor was left this could not be corroborated. It was a devastating blow to all at West Malling as the CO was very popular with all ranks. He was buried at St Felix Church in his home town of Felixstowe, Suffolk, on 29 April.

Ramsbottom-Isher, DFC, AFC, a New Zealander, joined the New Zealand Rifles in 1924 and was commissioned as a second lieutenant. However, he later came to the UK to pursue his ambition of joining the RAF, which he did, becoming a pilot officer during July 1930. He was posted overseas to India and on return joined the Aeroplane & Armament Experimental Establishment as a test pilot with the Armament Testing Section (ATS).

By January 1941 he was a highly experienced pilot, serving with No. 9 Grp. Operation Benedict followed Germany's Operation Barbarossa the invasion of Russia, and was planned to defend the naval port of Murmansk and train Russians on Hurricanes during 1941–42. No. 151 Wing, comprising Nos. 81 and No. 504 Sqn, commanded by Group Captain Ramsbottom-Isherwood, was based at Vaenga, and during his leadership fifteen enemy aircraft were destroyed. He was later awarded the DFC and the Russians awarded him the Order of Lenin. He later commanded No. 342 Wing in Burma in 1943.

On his return to the UK in 1947, Ramsbottom-Isherwood took over command of RAF West Malling from Group Captain J. Worral, DFC, on 19 April 1948 until 9 July 1949. It is interesting to note that in 2009 his medals were bought at auction by a Russian for £46,000. His nephew tried to recover the collection, but the campaign to have them returned to New Zealand failed.

In July 1950 two No. 25 Sqn Mosquitoes carried out trial interceptions against two Meteor fighters to assess the suitability of Mk.10 air interception units, with large closing speeds between fighter and target. With maximum closing speeds of 730mph during a parallel head-on interception it was found that the Mosquito NF.36 lost no range.

The new decade brought co-operation flights between the RAF and European air forces, and on 26 August, three No. 25 Sqn aircraft were detailed to Villacoublay airfield near Paris and three to Twente in the Netherlands to take part in Exercise Cupola. They flew on patrol on the night of 26 August and returned to West Malling on 28 August. On 27 November, the squadron moved from its old dispersal to take up quarters in the one left by No. 29 Sqn when it left West Malling.

The Mosquito NF.36s of No. 29 Sqn were replaced with NF.30s in October 1950 and the unit moved to Tangmere on 25 November 1951, where, during July, it was re-equipped with the new Meteor NF.11, and a new era of flying began, described later. Exercise Emperor proved to be No. 14 Sqn's last Mosquito operation. The daylight raids in Exercises Foil, Bulldog and Cupola had all highlighted the Mosquito's vulnerability to jet fighters and BAFO's ground-attack units had already started to re-equip with the Vampire FB.5. Tension between West and East in central Europe after the blockade of Berlin and the outbreak of war in Korea in late 1950 drove the need to expand and re-equip the RAF. Exercise Emperor gave the Mosquito the chance to operate in the role it could still play successfully, as a night intruder. From 7 to 10 October, night attacks were flown against

No. 500 (Kent's Own) Sqn, RAuxAF, permanent staff at West Malling on 22 March 1948. The CO at the time, Flight Lieutenant Leggett, is seated seventh from right. The aircraft is a Mosquito NF.30; at the time the squadron also had a few Spitfire XIVs. (R. Moss)

RAF West Malling Review, dated April/May 1952, which was published for circulation at the airfield and useful for all ranks to indulge in humorous articles and news. (P. Kennett)

West Malling, Coltishall and Tangmere and some daylight raids were also flown against Biggin Hill, Middle Wallop and Odiham. BAFO's two Mosquito B.35 squadrons moved to Fassberg on 1 November while the FB.VI squadrons, 4 and 11, remained at Celle for conversion to the Vampire.

No. 500 (Kent's Own) Sqn Meteor F.4s. The nearest three aircraft are EE355, EE400 and EE289. The squadron registration at this time was 'RAA' followed by a single letter, such as 'RAA-F'. Two aircraft in the background are Harvards. (R. Moss)

Exercise Emperor was the largest immediate post-war joint operation involving units from both Fighter and Bomber Command and was held in 7–15 October 1950. In addition, at the weekend RAuxAF units took part. Some eleven squadrons took part, flying Meteors and Vampires, and USAF units also joined in with B-50 Superfortresses. The exercise cost the lives of some fourteen aircrew, including eight servicemen lost in a mid-air collision between two Wellingtons, LP846 and RP388, over Swinderby airfield. Another incident saw Wellington RP320 collide with a Belgian Air Force Mosquito, serial MB-18. Five of the Wellington's crew and two Belgians were listed as missing when they crashed into the sea 2 miles from Reculver, near Herne Bay. Wreckage from the Mosquito was recovered but the search for the crew was eventually abandoned. At the time No. 500 (Kent's Own) Sqn, RAuxAF, was based at Thorney Island, but still permanently at home at West Malling.

There followed a tragic mid-air collision when ten Meteors were flying in formation. Sergeant E.W.G. Chipperfield of No 500 Sqn, flying Meteor F.Mk.III EE290, collided with another F.Mk.III, EE283, which landed safely with no injuries to the pilot. Chipperfield attempted to crash-land on the mud flats within Chichester harbour at Emsworth, Hampshire, but the

Air Marshal Sir William Elliot (AOC, Fighter Command 1947–49) visits the airfield. His Spitfire, Mk.XIVe RW393, was painted white overall with a red flash on both sides of the fuselage, made up with red crosses and blue serial numbers. This aircraft was assigned to No. 602 (Glasgow) Sqn and is on display at the RAF Museum, Hendon. (Air Britain)

Meteor F.4s of No. 500 (Kent's Own) Sqn, RAuxAF. The closest aircraft is WT758, which later flew with No. 611 Sqn and was struck off charge on 23 May 1958. (Aeroplane)

Ground crew refueling Meteor F.Mk.III EE352 'RA-A' of No. 500 (Kent's Own) Sqn, RAuxAF. This aircraft had also served with Nos. 263, 74, 257 and 66 Sqn.

Meteor struck a submerged object, resulting in the break-up of the aircraft and the death of the pilot. Chipperfield was the son of Edward William and Eliza Chipperfield, of Belvedere, Kent. He was married to Vera Evelyn Lena Chipperfield of Belvedere.

'Chip', as he was known to his colleagues, had just reached his 30th birthday. He was employed with Siemens in 1936, working in the joint box department, first in the shops and then in the drawing office. In 1938 he joined the RAFVR, and at the outbreak of war he served in the Royal Artillery on aerial survey work, mainly over Norway. In 1943 he was recommended for a pilot's course and spent six months training in Canada and elsewhere, gaining his wings and being posted to Burma. He was mainly occupied with piloting Dakotas of Transport Command and later with the repatriation of British prisoners from jungle territory. Receiving his discharge in 1946, he went back to Siemens and joined the outside contracts department. He also became a 'weekend' pilot with No. 500 Sqn. Chip crew up in Belvedere with his parents. Since his early boyhood he had been keenly interested in the Scout Movement, having been a member of the 5th Erith Scout Group, and he was still a Rover Scout at the time of his death. His cheerful manner and steady disposition earned him the respect and esteem of all his friends and colleagues. The funeral service, with full RAF honours, took place on 21 October at All Saints Church, Belvedere, and afterwards at Croydon Crematorium.

Mosquito FB.Mk,VI RS679 'AU-P' of No. 4 Sqn, based at Celle, West Germany, between September 1945 and July 1950. It was perhaps calling into West Malling to refuel or during a Cold War exercise. (KAHRS)

During November 1950, a conference was held at West Malling airfield to discuss the international situation. The prime ministers of Canada, Australia. New Zealand, India, Pakistan and Ceylon and Southern Rhodesia attended. On the left is Blackburn Beverley WF320/G-AMUX, the first prototype, to the right an Avro Shackleton. (KAHRS)

In February 1951, seven pilots of No. 14 Sqn were detached to No. 93 Sqn at Celle to convert to the Vampire. The navigators started to be dispersed and the Mosquitoes were ferried back to the UK for disposal.

One of the navigators, W.D.R. Bond, remembers:

> I had just got engaged to a Sergeant WAAF who worked in SHQ, and was on leave with her, showing her off to my parents. The phone rang, and it was Ron Harding, a pilot, who had just come over on leave, and he was bragging about the beautiful shiny Vampire on the tarmac at Celle. My wife and I were not too happy about that, as apart from my having to leave the even more beautiful Mosquito, it meant that we would be split up when I was posted.

On 21 February, Squadron Leader R.A. Sutherland, DFC and Bar, assumed command of No. 14 Sqn and oversaw its start-up as a Vampire unit. The move was completed efficiently and the squadron was settled in after the move. On 22 December, the squadron closed down for the Christmas break. West Malling's stand down took place immediately afterwards and lasted until 9 January 1951.

Flight Lieutenant Don Mortimer joined No. 264 Sqn at RAF Coltishall in November 1950 as the Cold War was definitely warming up. The squadron had been flying the Mosquito NF.36 since March 1946. On one occasion he was scrambled at night to intercept an unidentified target flying off the French coast. He was vectored by the GCI on the Isle of Wight, and just as it passed out of range of RT contact, the target was picked up by AI. The Mosquito's first interception run was too fast, and despite throttling back in fine pitch with the radiator flaps open, it overshot underneath, Turning away, he returned to identify the intruder. There was just enough light to see the aircraft was an all-black Lancaster, without any identity or national markings.

Following the aircraft at 6,400m (21,000ft) as far as Dover, Mortimer regained RT contact. Alerting Coltishall to obtain instructions, as the Lancaster flew on, the Mosquito weaved from side to side, but there was no response from the aircraft. After a further ten minutes, Mortimer broke away and headed for West Malling, where on landing he was de-briefed after the strange encounter. The crew were later told that the Lancaster was being flown by a Russian crew on an intelligence-gathering flight from East Germany. The aircraft was a former RAF wartime aircraft that had flown over East Germany on a long mission and, unable to return to base, had carried on to Russia, where it had been left.

Chapter 7

Meteors, Vampires and Mosquitoes
The airfield in the 1950s

On the night of 18 January 1951, No. 25 Sqn took the part of bombers in an exercise with No. 12 Grp night fighters. In another exercise, it put up a formation of aircraft and they were attacked by aircraft of the RAuxAF, during which sixteen hours' formation flying were logged. It was announced in January that in the near future No. 25 Sqn was to be equipped with the new Vampire NF.10 night fighter.

It was to this end that pilots would be converted on the new jets, and Flight Lieutenant H.S. Leete was detached from the squadron to form the Flying

Mechanics of No. 25 Sqn hard at work on one on the unit's Vampire's NF.10s, which could be WM670 'B' or WP234 'B'. (G. Gilbert)

This Spitfire F.22 could be PK389, which flew with both Nos. 600 and No. 615 Sqn, RAuxAF. It is known however, that No. 500 Sqn operated some Spitfire F.22s of No. 615 Sqn, based at Biggin Hill. The two airmen are captioned as 'Dixie' and Leading Aircraftman Sargeantson; the photo was taken in 1953. (G. Gilbert)

Wing Training Flight, which had a Meteor T.7 and several Vampire FB.5s. In addition, four of the squadron's pilots were sent to day fighter squadrons for a month to gain experience in flying jets. Flight Lieutenant Winton and Flight Lieutenant Cogill went to Odiham, and Master Pilot Steinke and Sergeant Gardner were sent to North Weald. Their moves left the squadron short of crew and in consequence they gave two of their aircraft to No. 85 Sqn.

In early 1951 relationships between Egypt and Western European countries and the USA were not good. An order by Egypt to buy the new Vampire NF.10 was cancelled by the British Government, which was bad news for De Havilland at Hatfield, which had developed the new jet. The Air Ministry refused to allow the export of American AI Mark X radar, thus these twelve aircraft were handed over to Fighter Command, with a further eighty-three of the mark ordered. The decision was not popular with No. 25 Sqn, which in July was the first unit to receive the type, as the Vampire's performance was considered inferior to that of the night fighter Meteors. Critics of the Vampire were assured its acquisition was a temporary situation and the RAF would be re-equipped with the faster Venom, a similar aircraft, although No. 25 Sqn never received this type.

On 6 February, two Mosquito NF.36s carried out night interceptions on Meteors, which was followed by an exercise with the Royal Auxiliary Air Force on 18 February, and F-84 Thunderjets provided fighter cover. Seventeen ground-firing exercises were also carried out at Leysdown on the Isle of Sheppey.

The same month, three pilots of No. 25 Sqn, namely Flight Lieutenant Cox, Flight Lieutenant Young and Flying Officer Wright, were converted to Vampires by Flight Lieutenant Innes after two or three trips in the Meteor T.7. Since first going solo they had each got more than eleven hours in on the Vampire FB.5. They were followed by Sergeant Wilkes and Flight Sergeant Rawanski. No. 85 Sqn suffered another loss on 20 March when Mosquito NF.36 RK991 spun into the sea from 20,000ft during a night exercise 48 miles east of Harwich. Both Flying Officer J. Mackenzie, pilot, and Flight Lieutenant J.S. Christie, DFC, bailed out over the sea. Air-sea rescue later found both bodies. Christie was later buried at West Malling with several other crew from this period.

The eliminating heat of the Cooper Challenge Trophy was held on 20 May. One of the pilots taking part was Wing Commander K.T. Lofts, DFC and Bar, a distinguished pilot who had survived the Battle of Britain after joining the RAF in 1938 with No. 615 Sqn, RAuxAF. The heat was held at West Malling and involved very fast low-level flight in a triangular course from Brenchley, Cranbrook, Loose and West Malling over the Weald of Kent. Wing Commander Lofts was competing in Vampire F.3 VG700 of No. 604 Sqn based at North Weald.

By 1540hrs, VG700 was 500yd behind the two other aircraft, which made a wide turn. The Vampire made an acute 360 degree turn banked at 90 degrees at high speed. The aircraft was at 200ft when the turn was made and it suddenly went up to approximately 2,000ft in a left-hand spiral, then commenced a dive and a slight recovery. After this it spun to the right and dived into the ground. The Vampire struck the ground with the port wing first at an angle of approximately 30 degrees. It burst into flames, killing the pilot instantly.

The first object found proved to be the fuselage top nose cowling, which was nearly a mile away from the main wreckage. The perspex sliding hood had broken up and pieces were found half a mile away. The rest of the Vampire was concentrated in an area 32yd long and 20yd wide in Swiss Park, Cranbrook. At the inquest held on 21 May, the coroner,

Hugh Murton-Neale, concluded that Wing Commander Lofts died of multiple injuries. Local police from Cranbrook were on the scene of the accident within two minutes of it happening, also the local fire brigade. Wreckage was guarded by the RAF from West Malling. No. 49 MU dug out the wreckage and removed the aircraft to Colerne, Wiltshire, at the request of the court of inquiry.

Ted Sergison, who devoted much of his spare time to aviation research, remembered the accident:

> Although I was a young boy at the time, I can still remember this incident. I was living in Pinnock Lane, Staplehurst, and our house overlooked the area of Cranbrook, just a few miles away. My father was busy in his garden and my mother was talking to the lady next door, when a jet aircraft flew very low and near our houses. Flying towards Cranbrook, it climbed and then spun from the sky, leaving a lot of black smoke as it slowly went down. There was a distant rumble followed by more smoke but this time not so black, as it rose above the tree-line at Rockshill, a hill between Staplehurst and Cranbrook, a very wooded area where a No. 501 Squadron Hurricane had crashed during the war. I remember how upset my mother and neighbour were. Later that day I saw a blue ambulance drive through Staplehurst coming from the direction of Cranbrook. My dad said it had been there to pick up the unfortunate pilot.

Ironically, Lofts had taken off from West Malling, the same airfield where he had crash-landed during the Battle of Britain in 1940. The Cooper Challenge Trophy was eventually won by Flying Officer De Villiers of No. 500 Sqn, although it was a hollow victory marred by the fatality.

ATC cadets arrived on the same day and a few were able to fly. No. 85 Sqn's Tiger Moth, DF211, was one aircraft available and Flight Lieutenant Corre, DFC, flew one such cadet. Not long after leaving West Malling, the aircraft was seen to dive into the ground near Offham. Flight Lieutenant Corre was killed and the cadet injured.

West Malling was briefly used for temperature and humidity (THUM) flights. The task of collecting regular, detailed meteorological information to support weather forecasting had been performed daily by RAF aircraft since 1924, initially carried out by fighter aircraft flying from Duxford, and then Mildenhall. Later, a second flight was started, flying from Aldergrove.

During the war years the number of units devoted to this task multiplied, until in 1945 about thirty flights were made every day in the European theatre alone, involving a mix of short and long-range flights. For the usual short-range THUM flights, obsolete fighter aircraft were usually used – the meteorological flights were the last to fly the Gloster Gauntlet biplane fighter. Even in 1945 the Hurricanes and Spitfires had by no means ousted the last of the Gladiators, indeed the Shuttleworth flying Gladiator, L8032 (now K7985), was assembled from several met flight aircraft that were under overhaul at Gloster's factory at the end of the war. Post-war, the THUM task dwindled once more to a single daily flight that was flown by Mosquitoes from the night fighter squadrons based at West Malling. The last West Malling THUM flight was flown by a Mosquito NF.36 on 30 April 1951.

The task was then contracted to Short Bros and Harland, creating a dedicated Meteorological Temperature and Humidity Flight (usually abbreviated to THUM), which was formed at RAF Hooton Park in April 1951 and after trial flights it commenced operation on 1 May. Its role was to relieve operational squadrons of the task, making daily flights to obtain detailed meteorological information to assist Met Office forecasters. The THUM Flight was not at Hooton Park long, moving on 13 July to Woodvale along with other Shorts-operated units (University of Liverpool Air Squadron and No. 19 Reserve Flying School). The type of aircraft used was the Spitfire PR.19, which was selected for several reasons; first of all it had the required range and rate of climb, secondly a pressurised cockpit for high-altitude flying and thirdly it was optimised for photo-reconnaissance, it was extremely stable and could therefore 'fly itself' while the pilot was concentrating on this thermometers and barometers. The procedure, flown six days a week (not Sundays) whatever the weather, consisted of flying to a point 3 miles north of Worcester, and then, within a 10-mile radius of that point, measuring the air temperature on wet and dry bulb thermometers at different heights, starting at 540, 1,040 and 1,540ft above mean sea level, then at an air pressure of 900 millibars and climbing in steps of 50mb up to the 300mb level (about 30,000ft). The whole climb took around forty-five minutes, with the top of the climb to be reached at 0900 GMT. In addition, reports were made on inversions, isothermals, haze, visibility, types and amount of cloud, ice formations, contrails, turbulence and the prevailing weather.

On return to base, the readings were sent to Speke, Liverpool, where the information was checked and details were sent over the teleprinter network to the Central Forecasting Office at Dunstable. During 1953, the THUM aircraft began to include a stop at Speke in their daily routine, handing the results over directly to the Speke Met Office, so saving a needless delay in delivering the reports.

Spitfires were fitted with a balanced bridge psychrometer and an aneroid barometer, along with initially an eight-channel VHF radio. Meteorological duties, which were carried out under all weather conditions, called for the utmost skill and determination. They entailed an intense cockpit workload for the pilot during the forty-five minute climb. In all, more than 2,000 Spitfire meteorological climbs were carried out from Woodvale. One of the small pool of pilots, Flight Commander John Formby, logged 840 sorties, a total of 1,438 hours, on THUM Spitfire flights, quite likely setting records in the process.

Unfortunately two of the flight's pilots were lost while flying Spitfires. Gordon Hargreaves died on May 1952 when he returned early from a routine flight in PM549 with radio trouble and stalled on the approach. 'Tommy' Heyes was lost on 4 March 1954 in PM628 during a forced landing close to the village of Church Pulverbach, south of Shrewsbury. Other pilots who served with the flight included, Mr Allum, Mr Wood, Peter Brooke, Ginger Irving and Eric Richards. The flight was initially led briefly by T. Carter, then Mr Ackers, before being taken over just after the move to RAF Woodvale by Gordon Hargreaves until his death in May 1952, and then by 'Tommy' Heyes until his death in March 1954, followed by John Formby until disbandment 1 May 1959.

In the 1958 New Year's Honours List, Formby was awarded the MBE for his services to meteorology while commanding the THUM Flight. As the months and years rolled by, the old Spitfires became more and more difficult to keep airborne. On occasion, spare parts had to be sourced from places as far distant as Malaya, so the search for replacement aircraft started. In early 1956, a Spitfire F.24 was tried (at this time large quantities of Mk.24s and spares for them were stored at RAF High Ercall), but this mark lacked the necessary natural stability. In May 1956, a Mosquito TT.35 arrived for trials and although it was not entirely suitable for the job as it could not climb as fast as the Spitfire, it was eventually accepted. The last Spitfire PR.19 sortie was operated by PS853 on 10 June 1957. This was the last operational flight by an RAF Spitfire anywhere in the world, some twenty-one years after the prototype had flown.

The three remaining Spitfires proved reluctant to depart. A major SAFA air display was held at Woodvale on 12 June to mark their departure and

Meteor F.8 WL159 of No. 85 Squadron. Just visible is a Queen Mary aircraft transporter, behind that a 'T' type hangar. (Robin A Walker)

introduce the new Mosquitoes. PS915 refused to start, PM631 did one circuit then landed with R/T trouble, while PS853 took off, suffered engine trouble and smashed its propeller during the forced landing on the airfield. It hit a rabbit hole at slow speed, suffering only superficial damage.

All three successfully left the following day for what became the Battle of Britain Flight at Biggin Hill, subsequently moving to Duxford, Coltishall and now at Coningsby. Two of the Spitfires still perform regularly with the Battle of Britain Memorial Flight, while the third is airworthy with Rolls-Royce (although currently under repair following a mishap in 2012). This some fifty-six years after leaving the THUM Flight!

From early June 1957, the Mosquito TT.35 carried on the daily routine, still calling at Speke to drop off the recordings. An early loss was Mosquito TK604 when Eric Richards suffered an engine failure and could not lower the undercarriage on 29 October. The aircraft made a belly landing at Woodvale, slewing off the runway but fortunately not injuring the pilot.

The search for an alternative type continued as the Mosquitoes' age was also beginning to affect serviceability. Before 1957 was out a Meteor F.8 was delivered. It did several dummy runs and remained on the unit strength until the end, but even with ferry tanks it did not have the necessary range. Early in 1959, Meteor F.8s were allocated to replace the 'Mossies', while enquiries were made to find out if the flights could be shortened to make them more suited to the 'Meatbox' (a nickname given to the Meteor, as many crashed.) These enquiries revealed that the job could now be done by radar-tracked balloons, so the contract was not renewed.

The very last THUM flight was flown by Mosquito TT.35 TJ138 on 1 May 1959, thus completing the last of some 2,800 sorties flown by the flight in just over eight years, of which likely some 2,000 called at Speke. The readings taken by the flight greatly helped advance the 'science' of understanding weather systems and enabling more accurate short-term forecasting; this long before the satellites and computers that are such an essential part of weather forecasting today. The Mosquitoes were initially passed to No. 5 CAACU, co-located at Woodvale, for a month, before moving to No. 27 MU at Shawbury for scrapping.

No. 25 Sqn's first Vampire NF.10 to be delivered was WP238, flown in by the station CO, Group Captain George Daley, DSO. The example was used to convert aircrew from the Mosquito NF.36. Led by Squadron Leader D.C. Furse, DFC, the squadron had undertaken jet conversion earlier in the year when Flight Lieutenant H.S. Leete's had formed a Flying Wing Training

One of No. 85 Sqn's new Gloster Javelin FAW.8s on display at West Malling during an open day in the early 1960s. This aircraft remained with the unit until sold for scrap on 11 March 1965. (E.T. Sergison)

Gloster Javelin FAW.8 XJ116 of No. 85 Sqn during maintenance and static tests during 1964. This aircraft flew with the unit until moving to No. 9 School of Technical Training (SOTT) at Newton on 21 February 1964. (MAP)

Flight had used a handful of single-seat Vampires to provide familiarisation training:

> As the QFI for 25 Squadron, and in fact the only QFI in West Malling Night Fighter Wing (25, 29 and 85 Squadron), I was instructed in January 1951 to form a jet conversion flight, having earlier, in 1949, gained jet experience at the Empire Flying School, Hullavington. I was provided with a Meteor 7 and three Vampire 5s (VV528, VV678 and VV685). I started giving dual instruction to the 25 Squadron pilots in the Meteor on 6 February 1951, and I flew the Vampires myself as often as I could. The 25 Squadron pilots completed their jet conversion in May, and I returned to flying Mosquitoes.

Following the arrival of WP238, Flight Lieutenant Denis Leete flew the Vampire after the technical wing had completed acceptance checks, on 12 July. Vampires started arriving quickly and by mid-August No. 25 Sqn had re-equipped, becoming operational on 31 August.

Squadron Leader Ray Follis, DFC, was a navigator/radio leader with No. 25 Sqn at West Malling, and also flew as navigator for the CO, Squadron Leader Denis Furse. He had previously flown Mosquito NF.36s with No. 141 Sqn at Coltishall and with the Mosquito Training Squadron at No. 228 OCU, Leeming, where he was senior navigator/radio instructor. In mid-1951 Follis joined No. 25 Sqn during its conversion from Mosquitoes to Vampires, and recalls his role of a navigator/radio operator:

> The success of any night fighter crew depended on the rapport between them, and the speed of their reactions. It required the instant interception by the Navigator/Radio of what was happening on his radar screen, and the immediate translation of this into his commentary and instructions to his pilot. Similarly, it was equally important for the pilot to respond immediately to instructions given and sometimes to anticipate his navigator's next words. Our practice interceptions were mostly on other Vampires or piston-engined aircraft, and our awareness of the superiority of the other jets over us was best illustrated by a Canberra overtaking us with its air-brakes extended! Later confirmation that the Canberra had approached from behind in a dive and that its air-brakes were not all that effective did little to dispel our realisation that the Vampire NF10, together with its obsolete AI Mk.10 radar, was only a stop-gap fighter.

Following a tour with the RAF in the Middle East, then flying Spitfires and Vampires at Odiham, Squadron Leader Tony Bowie flew Vampire NF.10s with No. 25 Sqn at West Malling from 1951 until 1953:

> The Vampire NF.10 was a nice aircraft to fly and possessed a very reliable Goblin engine. It had, however several disadvantages as a night fighter: there was only one radio set and generator fitted, the forward view from the cockpit was restricted, and, most seriously, it lacked ejector seats. Eventually we were given miniature 'Gee', which was a great help whilst flying at night. Our greatest heart stoppers were low-level practice interceptions at night over the sea. The Vampire was not fitted with a radio altimeter, and slowing down to 105 knots waiting to meet the Lancaster's slipstream was quite exciting. However, for real stimulation, Exercise 'Lightstrike' helped to raise one's

adrenalin level. This was an air-to-sea exercise, undertaken at night, simulating gun attacks against fast patrol boats. We made dive attacks on the targets by the light of parachute flares dropped from MR Lancasters, to extend the length of the sortie and leave about 30 degrees of flap down to improve the handling at low speed. Again we had no radio altimeter, and I assumed that I was flying at minimum height when the Radio Operator screamed in my ear for me to pull up!

Two pilots of No. 25 Sqn returned from Odiham having flown twenty hours on the Vampire, including some night flying. At the end of July, the squadron moved from its old dispersal and took over new buildings in front of the squadron hangar. The move began on 31 July and was completed quickly.

After half a dozen practice daytime interception flights, the first night flying programme was introduced on 16 August. Flight Lieutenant Roy Winton, a flight commander, was detailed to do a night flying test in Vampire NF.10 WP237 under dusk conditions, and this was to be followed by night flying practice. At a point about 1,400yd from the start of the take-off run the engine noise was heard to die away. Without ever becoming properly airborne, the aircraft continued, at almost full speed, off the end of the runway, leapt over a banked up area of broken ground, and dived into a field, breaking up and bursting into flames. Both Winton and his navigator, Sergeant Thomas Petrie, died instantly and the rescue services could do nothing. Initially it was suspected the wing drop tank had started to jettison, and the pilot had tried to abort take-off, but both tanks were found some distance behind the wreckage. However, they could have been torn off as the aircraft reached rough ground. Winton had 2,260 hours flying time on various aircraft, including sixty-seven on jets, and his experience in the Vampire NF.10 amounted to two hours forty minutes. An eye witness to the accident was Gordon Cheeseman, who gave a detailed account of what he saw:

I am a Blacksmith employed by Associate Portland Cement Manufacturers at Snodland. On 16 August 1951, at about 2000hrs, I was standing against the fence bordering the airfield in the lane leading from the Mereworth main road, my own guess would be that I was about 200yds from the main runway. I had a friend with me, Ron Rose, we were watching aircraft take-off. An aircraft came in sight, approximately 500yds before the end of the runway, the engine appeared to be going at 'full bore'. After a further 250yds the aircraft still appeared to be in contact with ground. As the aircraft passed me the engine note died again and a mass of white vapour issued from the back of the aircraft. The vapour was thick but lasted only a second or two, and the aircraft disappeared from sight with the engine still running at reduced power. There was no screeching of brakes and the aircraft kept a dead straight course. I did not hear any bangs or any other indication of the aircraft breaking up, and the noise from the engine was such that I could not hear any damage being done. Ammunition stated to explode about half a minute after flames showed above the trees.

Following a week in which night flying by No. 25 Sqn's Vampires was suspended, operations commenced once more. It had been decided that the number of night flights would be limited and that a diversionary airfield be available such as Manston, which was well known for its long runway. Pilots were also issued with a white or green instrument rating card, which limited the pilots who could fly in poor visibility.

During September 1951, the squadron took part in several exercises and flew several formation flights in preparation for Battle of Britain week and open day on 15 September. Another Vampire NF.10, WP816, arrived on the squadron from Kemble and was allotted to 'A' Flight, bringing the total of NF.10s on strength to seven. During November, a large number of successful aircraft interceptions were carried out. Crews had mastered the art of medium-speed interceptions and continued with more high-speed flight exercises.

The squadron also took part in a Bullseye Exercise, registering sixteen kills on RAF Washingtons and Avro Lincolns, and a total of sixteen successful air-to-ground sorties were completed during November. A shortage of spares became a problem and parts from seven other Vampires were used to keep the squadron flying, however it managed to achieve thirty-five hours on the type during November. Minor damage was sustained by the squadron's Meteor T.7 trainer when Flight Sergeant Silvester landed at Shawbury on 3 February 1952. The damage was confined to the fuselage and resulted from striking a hedge on the approach.

On 21 February, the Air Ministry officially sanctioned a general press release on the jet night fighter squadrons, and West Malling was chosen as the best place for the demonstration of aircraft since both Vampire NF.10s

Meteor F.8 WH513 of No. 500 (Kent's Own) Sqn, RAuxAF, overshot the runway in poor weather and crash-landed at Leybourne on 7 February 1952.

and Meteor NF.11s were available for inspection and display. About sixty representatives from the national press and the Air Ministry publications department arrived at the airfield. They were allowed to take photos of Vampires and Meteors from a Ministry of supply Lancaster in the air and on the ground. This was followed by a low-level aerobatic display by two Vampires led by Flight Lieutenant K.G.M. James.

No. 25 Sqn was selected to take part in joint exercises with Lancaster maritime reconnaissance aircraft in simulated attacks on coastal launches, often in the Thames Estuary. These exercises were known as Lightstrike. The Lancaster would seek out a suitable vessel using its ASV radar, and Vampires would be standing by on the runway at West Malling until they were contacted by the Lancaster, giving the Vampires details of the ship's location. The Lancaster would be in the vicinity of the chosen target, dropping a flare to help the fighters set up a timed attack. The Lancaster would then drop a flare near the target and the Vampires would attack the illuminated target without being blinded by the light of the flare. A plot was kept by the Lancaster so the pilots of No. 25 Sqn could examine their attacks.

During one such exercise, Lightstrike 6, on 21 May 1952, the squadron lost one of its most popular pilots. Flight Lieutenant John King was to fly as a passenger on a Lancaster to see for himself how attack patterns were set up from the air. Early that morning, Lancaster Mk.III RE200 'CJ- B', of No. 203 Sqn based at St Eval, had taken off from West Malling, heading for the exercise area. Control at West Malling received a call from the Lancaster saying it was returning to the airfield as one of the flares in the bomb bay had ignited and that the crew were unable to extinguish or jettison the flare. Vampires were at readiness to take off at the end of the runway when the Lancaster was seen flying to the north at low altitude making for West Malling. Eye witnesses saw the glow visible in the lower part of the fuselage. The Lancaster sped low along the runway and as it flew past onlookers it disappeared over the wooded area, the glow from navigation lights no longer visible. Then came an almighty crash. It was sometime before the crash vehicles could get close enough to the aircraft, which although in one piece, had broken its back. The rear fuselage was extensively damaged, and King had been killed along with three other passengers. The crew had taken up their crash positions, but the passengers had not been able to as they had their backs to the aircraft's main spar, facing aft. On crashing, the Lancaster swung round 180 degrees, having collided with a tree, and carried on for about 100yd, tail first. Passengers were facing the debris at the rear of the fuselage, which was thrown towards them. About an acre of young apple trees and gooseberry bushes was devastated as the aircraft overshot a farmer's land at Mereworth.

The farmer, A, Kemp, told a reporter; 'My wife heard the plane at about 0100hrs and heard a bit of a bump. Then it was quiet. Soon after we heard shouting, both from the direction of the aerodrome and from the plantation about 400 yards from the farm buildings.' The pilot, who suffered a broken leg, managed to get out of the wreckage and fire Very lights to attract attention. Wreckage from the bomber, which was returning from a night exercise, was strewn across Latter's Farm. The farmer revealed it was the fifth time a plane had crashed in the area. The Lancaster undershot or overshot but either way it went through the perimeter fence, which was the boundary between Latter's Farm, Mereworth and the airfield. The hedge still exists but now divides farmland from the Kingshill housing estate, which comes right up to the perimeter. The end of the runway was approximately 150yd from the boundary.

The three passengers killed with King were Leading Aircraftman J.A. Bacon, Flight Sergeant W. McKune and Leading Aircraftman R.H. Pearson. All were serving with Nos. 25 and 85 Sqn. King had been a navigator in the Middle East and had been shot down on the thirteenth sortie of his first tour with No. 104 Sqn. He and his crew evaded capture and were rescued immediately by ground forces. After his return to England, he began a second tour of bomber operations flying Halifaxes. On the thirteenth sortie of this tour, he was shot down and made a prisoner of war. King was one of 'X' Organisation in Stalag Luft III and was involved in planning and implementing the escape of seventy-six officers, of whom fifty were later murdered by the Gestapo. He was not however one of the 'ticket holders' who made the Great Escape in March 1944. He left the RAF in 1945 to become a teacher but re-joined in 1949. He was married with two daughters.

One of the seven crew injured suffered head and leg injuries and was hospitalised for the best part of two years before finally losing a leg. He underwent thirty-one operations during that time. He said the plane broke in two, leaving him on the ground and fairly uninjured. However, the front of the plane carried on, hit an apple tree, spun around and came back, running him over. The open bomb doors may have run over him; one over his leg, one over his head. He was left under the wreckage unconscious and was not found until some time later. Apparently, while trapped and unconscious, some children heard him the next morning. He was unconscious for five days and, according to a telegram, was taken off the seriously ill list on 3 June.

During 1950 and 1962 Shorts Ltd operated ferry flights and an Admiralty Flight from its airfield at Rochester. The Admiralty Flight was formed on 16 November and had taken over from No. 780 Sqn. Its task was familiarisation flying for out of practice naval officers. The flight also operated as the Naval Instrument and Refresher Flying School. It was equipped with Harvard Mk.IIBs, Firefly T.Mk2s and Airspeed Oxfords, one of which was PH143. On 12 June 1952, in good weather conditions, PH143 took off on a routine training flight. Meanwhile, Vampire WM673 was also airborne, having taken off from West Malling. Not long after, the Vampire collided with the Oxford and both aircraft crashed in the vicinity of Gallants Farm, East Farleigh, not far from West Malling airfield.

The instructor flying the Oxford was Flying Officer Reid-Johnstone RAFVR, an experienced pilot with more than 2,000 flying hours to his credit, 125 of which was on the Oxford. Lieutenant Nicholson RN was his pupil, with 1,390 hours' flying experience, and sixteen hours' flying time on Oxfords. The instructor was briefed to carry out a normal instrument training flight, to include take-off and climb. Reid-Johnstone took off from Rochester at 1030hrs with a different pupil and returned at 1133hrs. The first pupil got out and Nicholson took his place in the aircraft. Both pilot and

The RAF Radar Defence Museum at Neatishead, Norfolk, has this interesting exhibit on display. This plaque was presented to pilots of No. 25 Sqn for the best results during firing practice from 1949 until 1953. (A.E. Wright)

pupil were wearing the observer-type parachute harness, one parachute being stowed in the parachute stowage at the aft of the aircraft, the second on the wireless operator's desk on the starboard side of the Oxford. They took off at 1141hrs and commenced training.

Meanwhile, Sergeant G.E.C. Fry of No. 25 Sqn at West Malling, who had been stationed at the airfield for just a year, was instructed by Flight Lieutenant E.C. James, AFC, DFM, on 12 June 1952 to carry out homings and descents to the airfield from different directions, the aim being to pass over the airfield at 2,000ft to hone navigator Sergeant E.F. Halls' skill at using 'Gee', a radio navigation system. Their flight in NF.10 WM673 had been correctly authorised and they took off at 1100hrs, reaching a height of 6,000ft in the neighbourhood of Southend. The Vampire then carried out one 'Gee' homing and descent, crossing West Malling airfield at 2,000ft. The navigator directed the pilot to climb in a south-easterly direction, arriving over Dungeness at 5,500ft. This brought the Vampire to 270 degrees, too far to port for West Malling, and the course was corrected to 290 degrees. Shortly after a course correction, the pilot commenced a let down to land at West Malling. Reducing the height to 4,000ft and speed to 230 knots, there was a loud impact and a bang, and the Vampire's crew saw a silver object pass below and ahead of them. Attempting to open the throttle, Fry found the engine did not respond, and instructed Halls to stand by to bail out, rolling the Vampire on its back to jettison the canopy. Finding he had lost elevator control, and with the nose dropping, he abandoned the attempt to bail out. He rolled the Vampire to the right and pulled Halls, who was half in and half out of the aircraft, back to his seat. The pilot decided to carry out a belly landing at West Malling straight ahead. The aircraft was very nose heavy and Fry held the control column back to keep it up. As they approached the airfield, they struck a tree and carried out a belly landing on the grass.

A witness stated the Oxford was flying in a southerly direction at between 2,000 and 3,000ft flying straight and level and on a steady course and collided with the Vampire on this converging course. Immediately, the Oxford went into a spiral dive to starboard and hit the ground at a steep angle, killing the two on board, who suffered multiple injuries. Both engines were still running as the aircraft crashed. The Vampire suffered serious damage to the leading edge of the port main plane. Wooden debris from the Oxford's main spar was found embedded in the Vampire's wing. The Accident Investigation Unit found that the Vampire's wing struck and cut off the outer portion of the Oxford's starboard wing. The enquiry found that neither crew had seen the other aircraft before it was too late and that the Vampire pilot's view was obstructed by the coaming on the starboard side in front of the navigator. This was aggravated by the poor vision through the starboard forward quarter panel owing to curvature of the perspex. In the Oxford the view of the instructor, who sat on the starboard side, was impaired to port by the head and body of the pupil. It was recorded that no blame for this tragic collision could be put on any of the crew members.

No spectacle could revive memories of the summer of 1940 better than a Spitfire flying gracefully in the bright blue skies above West Mailing on Saturday afternoon, 15 September, Battle of Britain Day, to the delight of the large crowd that had assembled from neighbouring Kent towns and villages. West Malling's regular squadrons of Vampire NF.10s and Meteor

NFs, had flown over the airfield in tight formation and had then left to visit other stations in the southern area. On return, West Malling received visitors from RAF Bassingbourn in the form of three Canberras, one with wing-tip fuel tanks. Bomber Command's representation was completed by formation fly pasts of Lincolns and Washingtons.

The abilities of No. 500 (County of Kent) Sqn, RAuxAF, were exemplified by a noisy and exciting low-level attack by Meteor F.8s on targets in the south-east corner of the airfield, but the outstanding items were the two formation aerobatics teams. Squadron Leader. D. de Villiers, CO of No. 500 Sqn and chief test pilot of DH Propellers, having given an excellent exhibition of aerobatics in a Meteor F.8, later took off with Flight Lieutenants Frank Sumner and Graham Moreau to thrill the crowd with a masterly display. Their line astern loop changing to vic formation was, in particular, brilliantly executed.

The precision and excellent placing of manoeuvres was matched by three of the station's Vampire NF.10s flown by Flight Lieutenants R. Bowrie, C.C.W. Smith and A. Wright. They were the first night fighters to undertake formation aerobatics. During the afternoon the exhibition inside a hangar attracted many visitors, while the assorted aircraft in the static display were a source of constant delight to the many small boys loose on the airfield. At the close of the programme, Flying Officer G.B. Bell took up a Meteor NF.11 to show off its agility and urgent climb.

On 18 December 1952, the squadron lost two more of its crewmen when Vampire NF.10 WM669 crashed in the sea 6 miles off Dungeness during a low-level practice. Both pilot Flight Lieutenant C.C.W. Smith and Flying Officer James McNicol Adams, the navigator/radio operator, were killed.

An article appeared in the April edition of *RAF Flying Review* advertising the fact that West Malling was Britain's first night fighter base, heralding the age of jet fighters:

> Red and green Very lights soar upwards into the gathering dusk . . . the signal to scramble. The jet orifice of a 3,350lb. thrust Goblin belches flame as a Vampire starts up. Flight Lieutenant Hugh James, with 5,000hr, a former Transport Command pilot who used to fly with the VIP Squadron, and whose greatest claim to fame was that he once ordered, Mr Attlee to 'put that so and so pipe out' during a flight, turns from the parking area on to the mile-long runway. Other aircraft follow close behind. In a minute and twenty seconds from the

'Go' signal he is airborne, undercarriage up and climbing like a rocket. The scene, enacted recently at the RAF West Malling, near Maidstone, heralded the start of a practice interception by crews of the RAF's first jet night fighters. Playing the part of 'enemy' jet bombers was the station's Meteor NF.11 Squadron, commanded by Squadron Leader. D. Hawkins, AFC, who flew night fighters with No. 219 Beaufighter Squadron in 1940. No. 25 Vampire Squadron, under Squadron Leader. C. Furse, DFC, another experienced wartime pilot, was given the task of locating and destroying the Meteors of No. 85 Squadron. As Flight Lieutenant James set course towards the Channel his navigator, Flight Lieutenant J.C. 'Chalky' White, radioed for instructions.

At the Ground Control Interception station, some miles from base, the Controller watches both forces on his radar screen. A loud-speaker in the flying control tower relays his instructions as he vectors the Vampire—'Quagmire 38'— towards the opposing Meteors. 'One o'clock warm,' says the Controller … then, a few seconds later, 'one o'clock hot.' The 500mph plus fighter streaks toward the opposing bombers. As range decreases, the navigator, locating the Meteors on his own radar AI screen suddenly replies: 'Contact'!

Then after a further pause, interception completed. Control Approach landing. Listen, as the GCA controller in his red-and-white chequered caravan at the edge of the runway talks him down: 'In line with the runway … three miles to go … heading 265 … on glide path … check wheels and flaps . . . left 30 … heading good … a little too high … adjust rate of descent.' And finally, out of the Kentish night, the Vampire comes whistling in over the perimeter. Such training has now become a regular routine at this famous day and night fighter station of World War II. Converting a few months ago from the now obsolete piston-engined Mosquito NF36s, pilots were first given jet experience on Meteor 7s dual trainers before taking up the NF10 or NF11.

Now, with many hours jet flying behind them, the crews of Britain's first all-weather squadrons think highly of their new aircraft. West Malling's Commanding Officer, Battle of Britain pilot G/Captain H.S. Darley DSO, had this to say: 'These latest machines are about 150 m.p.h. faster than the old Mosquito. They are very pleasant and easy to fly and I believe they will prove suitable stepping-stones to the still faster DH-110 and GA-5.' The crews of these first night jet squadrons maintain their operational efficiency at high peak by constant training— both in the air and on the ground, as one might expect, flying training lays special emphasis on air interceptions.

The aircraft usually work in pairs and after each exercise a 'post-mortem' is held to determine the success or otherwise of the operation. The Ground Controller provides a graphic record of the flight, which he has carefully charted by radar, and this provides the basis for analysis and future improvement. G.C.A. procedure is practised at the end of nearly every exercise, whether conditions demand it or not. Only by such constant practice can pilots reach the very high standard of instrument flying demanded, says the Officer in Charge of Flying, Wing Commander A. P. Dottridge, D.F.C. and bar—he won these awards while night-fighting with No. 53 Squadron in 1940 and later No. 219 Squadron in 1941. Our pilots must be comfortable on instruments by day or night, for they will be expected to fly operationally in almost any conditions.

This confidence can only be born out of long and rigorous training. In my experience, once they have acquired this high instrument efficiency, pilots prefer night-flying to day. Ground training at West Malling is treated with no less importance. Meteorology, Signals, Traffic Control Procedure, Dinghy Drills, Theory of Flight, Radar Operation and Maintenance— all these subjects and many others play a large part in crew instruction. Navigators, in particular, have a very intensive lecture programme, particularly in Air Interception and Signals. A Wing Navigation Officer, who usually flies with the Squadron Commander, is responsible for the continued efficiency of all the navigators of his unit. On such a Station, with flying going on almost right round the clock, servicing problems are many. Ground crews toil unceasingly to maintain serviceability. Some of the technicians have had long experience with both jet and piston-engined machines; others have barely more than a year's service. Perhaps the most outstanding member of the former category is Flight Sergeant

B. C. Grimsey, who joined as a boy entrant back in 1929 and has had over twenty years' active servicing experience. Asked what he thought of the National Service Airmen in his charge, he replied: 'You can hardly expect to produce really skilled tradesmen in a matter of months, but on the whole, they're a keen bunch and do a pretty good job.' That, from Flight Sergeant Grimsey, comes close to lavish praise.

Phase II of Exercise Momentum took place on the night of 19/20 August 1953. The West Malling night fighter squadrons were fully operational and being kept busy with all types of night raids. As was the case on every station participating in Momentum, West Malling was on an operational footing, with guards posted, aircraft dispersed and lights dimmed, as darkness approached, final preparations were made for a long night's operations. At 1930 hrs, crews received their briefing; the weather was none too hopeful, a front being expected to 'clamp' the airfield by the early hours of the morning; neither was there any indication of the type or strength of the threat which would have to be met. By 2030 hrs all crews were at ten minutes' notice to scramble and the ground control organizations ready. Trouble came almost immediately and two fighters scrambled as the sun sank below the horizon. The distinctive navigation light patterns of Vampires and Meteors could thereafter be seen moving up to the take-off point and then racing down the runway and climbing away to the clouds.

In the control tower, under dim fights, the airfield and CRDF controllers were at their desks, listening to several voices at once, and quickly giving the required reply to each; little could be seen but much heard, and the airfield was covered with varicoloured lighting systems. But the controllers knew each pilot and his individual characteristics; those in the air and on the ground understood each other's requirements. This understanding was also developed to a high degree between air crews and their GCI controllers, for night fighting is essentially an individualist occupation, and each crew had its particular preferences in manoeuvre and attack.

Night interceptions were always made by single aircraft, guided initially by GCI, and then relying on their own AI, and finally on visual identification, for their attack. Pilots carried out most of their flying on instruments and operated alone, as opposed to the day fighter, who had a wing man to provide tail cover. Night fighting required a pilot with considerable experience and often of a more advanced age, and it was interesting to hear at West Malling that pilots with transport and instructional experience were excellently suited for night fighting. The average age of the pilots was in the late twenties. A vital stage in an interception was the visual identification of the target.

Once the 'bogey' was identified as a 'bandit, the attack was made and, because of the nature of the game, the essential element of surprise is thereupon lost, the 'bandit' took evasive action, and disappeared rapidly into the night. At West Malling understanding of the human and mechanical or electronic subtleties involved in night fighting, and interesting discussions were unfortunately curtailed by the requirements of security, of which everyone was commendably conscious.

The night fighters are experts and enthusiasts, eternally in search of the best in equipment, and constantly developing and refining their techniques. During the night, some time was spent at the Meteor and Vampire dispersals; one Vampire crew, just returned from a sortie, reported an attack on a Canberra flying at 40,000ft at an impressively high Mach number. A Meteor NF.11 also coped comfortably with a B-29, which made a low-level attack on the airfield. As the night wore on, however, the expected front came slowly in, ahead of time, and pilots reported heavy icing; intakes and nose caps of the formidable NF.11s showed the familiar scars of rain and hail. The cloud ceiling fell lower and lower and a fine drizzle began, but as we left the friendly atmosphere of the station fighters were still going up to intercept and pilots expected an arduous night's work.

Flight Lieutenant Terry Johnson and his navigator, Flying Officer Geoffrey Smythe, of No. 25 Sqn were airborne in their Vampire on the morning of 3 November 1953. They had reached a height of 30,000ft and were flying over Kent, with the recorded time 1000hrs. They flew north and the weather that day was fine and bright with little cloud. Suddenly, Johnson spotted a bright light dead ahead the size of a full moon, and about a mile off: 'It was

Air Kruise, which flew from Lympne airfield, as did Silver City, had to operate temporarily from West Malling in late September 1953 due to poor weather. One such aircraft was G-AHJI, a Bristol Freighter Mk.21E. (MAP)

a bright circular object which was glowing with greater intensity around its periphery than at its centre.'

Johnson, now alerted to the object, or UFO as it could be called, had not seen it on the radar. Looking up, both crew saw it shoot across the sky: 'After about 10 seconds it moved to our right, to the east of our aircraft, at very high speed. It did not appear on Geoff's radar screen at any time as you would have expected a normal solid object to have done.'

The sighting was over in thirty seconds. They continued their reconnaissance flight and returned home to West Malling. Even in those days they were reluctant to report the incident as they were sure not to be believed and at least have their leg pulled. Pilots did not like reporting such observations for this reason. However, on landing the pilot and navigator were questioned by Squadron Leader Furze about their experience and he reported it to the station commander, Group Captain Hamley. Much to their surprise, Hamley was interested as he admitted he had also had a similar experience during the Second World War during a bombing mission over Berlin. Johnson said that at the time it was the first mention made of flying saucers.

However, this was followed a few days later by the news that the War Office had reported another incident that took place on the same day at 1430hrs, namely, an unidentified object had been tracked on ground radar based at Lee Green, Kent. The object was circular and motionless, and the radar echo appeared to show that it was approximately 200ft in diameter. After about ten minutes it moved out of radar range.

At 1445hrs a sighting was reported as being seen on radar at a nearby anti-aircraft workshop. The War Office said it had received three other reports of UFOs from 14 to 22 September. The crew were summoned by the Air Ministry to give a full report as the Duke of Edinburgh was interested in flying saucers. After forty-eight hours the War Office gave a press release on the incident. Later it said the object recorded at Lee Green was a meteorological balloon released at Crawley at 1400hrs and that the Vampire crew had also seen a balloon released earlier that day. This has always been denied by Johnson:

> If it had been a balloon then we would have approached it very quickly. The object moved off at high speed, something which weather balloons could not do. I have no idea what it really was but we were familiar with all aircraft of the day and it was certainly nothing we had ever seen.

Their argument was backed up by Sergeant Waller, one of the anti-aircraft workshop crew, who said that the object gave a distinct strong radar return and had to be metallic. He had also seen five objects flying in formation at impossible speeds. By 24 November, the Air Ministry had succeeded in explaining the sightings as balloons. Mr Issacs, Labour MP for Southwark, said: 'Will the minister agree that this story of UFOs was all *ballooney*?' We will never know but the crew of the Vampire remained convinced that their sighting was genuine.

In February 1954 concerns were raised regarding two families of squatters located at Canoncourt Gate, Wateringbury, close to the airfield at West Malling. Mr W. Watson had four boys, and Mr and Mrs. G. Donovan had a family. They had taken up residence in two RAF Nissen huts situated on the south side of the airfield. Both huts were in a very bad state structurally and were filthy inside, with no water or lighting available and no sanitation. Both huts had been scheduled for demolition. The Malling Rural District's clerk to the council, F. Miskin, advised the RAF that they could find accommodation for the families at East Malling Health Camp. The offer was accepted by the two families and once they had vacated the huts they were immediately demolished to deter any further squatters.

In June 1954, No. 85 Sqn was flying practice interceptions, and it was during one of these on 29 June that the squadron lost two more crewmen. Flying Officer J.F. Fisher, pilot, and his navigator, Flying Officer D.T. Cains, had taken off from West Malling at 0032hrs on their second sortie flying Meteor NF.12 WS600. Flight Lieutenant Hedley, flight commander, was flying another NF.12 as partner on the exercise. At 0118hrs at 17,000 and 18,000ft, Fisher reported that his port engine was 'out'. In a RT communication with Hedley, Fisher said that he was descending to 15,000ft to relight the engine. A few moments later, when under West Malling control, he advised that he had both engines 'out' and he was going to bail out, at a height of 10,000ft.

Squadron Leader B. Scandrett, AFC, CO of No. 85 Sqn, was in the control tower at West Malling when he heard Fisher transmit a distress call. Fisher said both engines had failed at 18,000ft while flying over Beachy Head, Eastbourne.

The Meteor crashed at 0126hrs at Cobbcourt, Berwick, Sussex. Webbing from the navigator's parachute was found attached to the fin and the pilot's body in his cockpit. Both bodies were found in the crater.

It was concluded in an inquiry that Fisher failed to select his auxiliary fuel tanks, with the result that the engines stopped as the rearward parts of the main fuel tank ran dry. Around 1.30 a.m., Estelle Miller, the housekeeper at Oakfields in Chalvington, was woken by one of her dogs barking outside. She looked out of her bedroom window and was astonished to see an aircraft on fire passing very low and making 'a grinding groaning noise' before crashing some half a mile away.

At the same time, William Puttock, a farm labourer of Yew Tree Cottage, Chalvington, was lying awake in his bedroom when he also heard the same type of 'groaning' noise. By this time, the aircraft had lost even more height. It was now almost level with his bedroom window and was giving off a pink glow. Meanwhile, Thomas Henry Dinnis, the owner of Mays Farm, Selmeston, was also aroused from his sleep by the groaning engines of the distressed aircraft, but by the time he got to his bedroom window all he could see was a mass of flames some 200yd away on his fields. The jet had obviously flown through the power cables located nearby on its doomed descent.

Mr Dinnis phoned 999 and quickly got dressed and rushed to the scene. He saw that the aircraft had crashed into the east bank of his wheat field next to a private road, some 800yd from the junction of the Berwick to Chalvington road. A mass of flames and heat greeted him on his arrival, making it impossible to get anywhere near the aircraft. By this time the nearby hedges were also alight from the aircraft fuel, and a partly opened parachute was found close by.

At first light, a helicopter from the Royal Naval Air Service was summoned by officers at RAF Wartling in order to search the immediate area, and the glass canopy of the Meteor was found at Bushy Lodge, West Firle, approximately 3 miles from the crash site. Further items of equipment from the aircraft were found in Selmeston and Chalvington, including the crew's flying helmets, a scarf, a map and the navigator's left shoe. The only part of the aircraft remaining of any size was the rear part of the fuselage and the tail fin, which had pieces of parachute harness caught in its leading edge. By 0050hrs an RAF corporal and six airmen from Tangmere had arrived to guard the crash site, and later the remains of the crew were removed to the mortuary at Hailsham.

An inquest was held on 1 July 1954, and it was confirmed by various witnesses that the aircraft had lost power over Beachy Head, had turned inland towards Selmeston and West Firle, and it had finally crashed between Cobb Court and Mays Farm, Selmeston. The coroner, Dr Somerville, returned a verdict of accidental death in both cases, commending Mr Dinnis for his invaluable help throughout the operation. It was recommended that the new lightweight Martin-Baker ejector seats be fitted in all Meteor NF.12s in the future.

In its main role, Meteor NF.14 'S', of No. 85 Sqn, returns from a night mission, guided in by an RAF airman. Just visible to the right is the control tower.

METEORS, VAMPIRES AND MOSQUITOES

One of the most popular boys' magazines, read by thousands of children during the 1950s, was surely *The Meccano Magazine.* This excellent publication covered not only the subject of Meccano but model railways, steam trains, shipping, articles of interest to keen modellers and those interested in transport and aviation. The magazine was published by John W.R. Taylor and, in his capacity as editor, he visited West Malling in early 1954 and wrote the following article, which appeared in the February 1954 edition:

> The Royal Air Force Station at West Malling in Kent was not opened until June 1940, but in just over 13 years it has built up a tradition of achievement and courage second to none. On the walls of the Officers Mess hang the badges of its squadrons, with an imposing record of decorations earned by their pilots and portraits of some of the great squadron commanders who flew from West Malling – men like Guy Gibson VC, DSO, DFC, heroic leader of the wartime dam-busters', who wrote that: 'Of all the airfields in Great Britain, here many say (including myself), we have the most pleasant. It is near London and also near the sea. The local people are kind and generous, probably because they saw the Battle of Britain rage above their heads, and know more than most what the Air Force has done for this country'. Guy Gibson goes onto explain that the Germans did their best to destroy West Malling in 1940 but it was put up again quickly amongst the trees, which made it difficult to see from the air – a hornet's nest cradled amongst green trees and green fields – a lively sight.
>
> Unfortunately I was able to see little of the beauty of Kentish countryside when I drove down from London recently to find out something about West Malling's present role in Britain's defences. The glare of my car headlights picked up only the hedges of country lanes, until the unique pub sign of 'The Startled Saint', showing Spitfires buzzing round the poor gentleman's halo, told me I was nearly at my destination. I could hear the roar of Vampire and Meteor night fighters taking off on practice interceptions as I drew up at the Station Guard House and presented my impressive-looking Air Ministry Pass. Fifteen minutes later I was trussed up like a Christmas turkey in the dark, cramped cockpit of Vampire

The cover of the February 1954 edition of *Meccano Magazine,* which featured an article about the night fighters based at West Malling.

NF10 night fighter 'E for Easy' resplendent in borrowed flying suit, complete with embroidered squadron crest, yellow Mae West lifebelt, helmet and oxygen mask. I had clipped together the four straps of my parachute and four more straps of the seat harness, and plugged in my radio-telephone (R/T). Despite which I discovered that, by releasing a small catch on the side of the cockpit, I could lean forward quite comfortably and have a good look at the complex radar screens and maze of other equipment which surrounded me. Soon the commander of West Malling's Vampire squadron, Squadron Leader. D.C. Furse, DFC, clambered into the pilot's seat to the left and slightly forward of my navigator's position. After strapping himself in and explaining to me the layout of the cockpit which is very similar to that of the Mosquito fighters he flew during the war, he slammed the hood shut and started the aircraft's Goblin turbojet by simply pushing one button on the instrument panel. There was a muffled explosion as the engine lit, and if I could have been in two places at once I should have seen a burst of flame from the tail of the jet-pipe. As it was, the instrument panel showed what was happening. R.P.M. and temperature indicators began to spin round like the second hand of a supersonic clock and the whistle of the turbine grew steadily more shrill until it settled down to a barely audible whine. The R/T crackled permission to taxi to the runway and we began to trundle round the perimeter track, with strings of amber and blue lights flashing under our port and starboard wing-tips respectively. There was little else to see. The Station buildings were dark on the skyline. Nearer was the double ribbon of the runway flare-path, more darkness, then the green wing-tip navigation light of our Vampire, outlining the square-cut wing and the big silver fuel tank beneath it. We waited while another Vampire landed – flown by one of the squadron's two Polish pilots. Then, a quick turn on to the runway, whose lights flashed past faster and faster as Sq. Ldr. Furse pushed forward the throttle. Slight pressure pushed me back against my seat; the air conditioning system whisked warm air past my face, and in an instant we were climbing and banking gently in a left-hand circuit, with the lights of Tonbridge twinkling like an immense diamond tiara to our right. Had we been on a proper interception sortie, we should at this stage have been passed from Local Control to a Ground Controlled Interception radar station. 'Climb to angels twenty-five (25,000 ft.) Vector one eight zero.' We should have been guided towards our target by an unseen, unknown 'somebody' inside a concrete building miles away on the ground – somebody who could see both us and our target as tiny blips of light on a radar screen, slowly drawing together. After a time we should have been brought close enough to the enemy bomber for our own A.I. (Airborne Interception) radar scanner, mounted inside the Vampire's fibreglass nose, to pick it up. The greenish screen in front of me would have indicated the bomber's range and bearing, as I guided the pilot in for the 'kill.' The finest radar in the world is, however, no substitute for a pair of good eyes, and at a distance of about 1 1/2 miles from the bomber the pilot would have started peering around for a first glimpse of tell-tale exhaust glow. A few seconds later, the bomber would probably have become visible as a dark silhouette that must be properly identified, for there were tragic cases of friendly aircraft being shot down by mistake in the last war. Once seen and identified, the bomber would have had little hope of escape from the Vampire closing in stealthily and invisibly from behind. Its silhouette would have become larger and larger in the gyro gun-sight. The fighter pilot's thumb would have closed on the gun button on his control column, and the night would suddenly have become brilliant with the flash of the Vampire's four 20mm. cannons. Such is the pattern of a night interception – a pattern calling for the closest possible co-operation between pilot, navigator and ground controller. There is no room for 'one-man bands' in night fighting, which demands steady, precise flying and tremendous patience and concentration. The more spectacular 'dash and dogfight' methods of the day-fighter boys have no part in it; and no more than a few seconds of accurate, deadly gunfire can normally be expected during each long, lonely patrol.

The fact that night fighting involves such complete understanding and high standard of training from its crew prevented us from making a practice interception during my sortie from West Malling, for I am no navigator or radar observer. But, sitting there in the darkness, gliding along so smoothly and quietly that it was almost impossible to believe the 300 knots on the airspeed indicator, it was easy to imagine the tense excitement of a night interception. All too soon the GCA controller was beginning to 'talk us down' to a landing. 'You are seven miles from the airfield, two degrees left of the centre-line, 500 ft. below glide path. Adjust your rate of descent.'

There was a slight bumpiness when Squadron Leader. Furse extended the air brakes. The airspeed indicator dropped back quickly. 'Five miles from airfield. Hold your course.'

More bumps as the undercarriage was lowered and the speed dropped to about 120 knots. 'Four miles ... three miles ... two miles ... one mile ...' still the calm voice of the controller came over the RT, only to be silenced as we glided down to a beautifully gentle landing. Soon I was back in Squadron Leader Furse's office, admiring two battered propeller blades covered with little metal swastikas, each representing a German

During an open day at West Malling in 1958, the public were invited to see the latest night fighters in RAF service. Here Meteor NF.12 WS613 of No. 25 Sqn is being inspected by young enthusiasts, while others eagerly await their turn to view the cockpit.

warplane shot down by members of his squadron in World War II. We were joined by a young pilot from West Malling's Meteor NF11 squadron, and it was apparent why the Station has achieved such a high standard of efficiency, because the friendly rivalry between the Meteor and Vampire crews has to be seen to be believed. Both are famous squadrons, and the hexagon badge carried by the Meteors of 85 Squadron has adorned the fighters of many famous airmen, including two 1914–18 War VCs – Billy Bishop and Micky Mannock – as well as John Cunningham in World War II, when its pilots destroyed 278 aircraft.

When I visited the crew rooms, I was not surprised to find a high proportion of pilots and navigators with wartime medal ribbons on their battledress, for the kind of temperament needed for night fighting is best found in older, more experienced airmen. But the young Meteor pilot who showed me proudly over his sleek, aggressive aircraft told me that when he first become operational a few months ago he was just 20 years old, and his navigator only 19! Nor should the ground crews be forgotten, for it is their devotion to duty and skill that keeps the Vampires and Meteors flying, and maintains the efficiency of the all-important radar and radio devices needed to ensure a successful interception. Many of these men are young. All seemed happy and proud of their squadron's record, although they often have to work long hours to keep aircraft in fighting trim, because so few youngsters today seem to realise the value of a free Service training in radar or aircraft engineering. I saw many other things at West Malling – things which renewed my confidence in the Royal Air Force as the world's greatest fighting Service, and in the ability of its airmen to protect these islands from attack by any force of fighters and bombers in the world. Under the leadership of its Station Commander, Group Captain P. H. Hamley, AFC, West Malling is undoubtedly an elite Station. It will be better still before long, for its Vampires and Meteors are scheduled to be replaced first by faster, more powerful Venoms and then by the RAF's superb new super-priority Javelin delta-wing, all-weather fighters – the finest aircraft of their type in the world.

Chapter 8

Heavy Losses

Night fighter operations in the late 1950s

During the late 1950s the RAF was expanding rapidly and wanted to recruit keen young men into the service, which could offer them an interesting career and the chance to fly or become aircrew and ground crew. Flight Lieutenant Paul Hobson served with No. 85 Sqn at West Malling and flew in the squadron's Meteor night fighters as a navigator and radio operator:

I joined the squadron at West Malling in January 1955, remaining with them until November 1958 when the squadron disbanded, the Meteor NF being withdrawn from service. No. 89 Squadron, flying the new Javelin, was renumbered 85 Squadron, much to their disgust. I was recruited into National Service at the end of 1951, but transferred to regular service, as National Servicemen were no longer being trained as aircrew.

I went through the training machine via No. 3 ITS at RAF Cranwell, No. 3 ANS Bishops Court in County Down, basic navigator/radio training at 238 OCU RAF Colerne, advanced navigator/radio, conversion to jets and crewing up at 228 OCU RAF Leeming, then posting to No. 85 Squadron. After leaving 85 Squadron I did a grand tour of Aden and Oman including stints as CO, RAF Masirah, Oman, and RAF Ryian, East Aden Protectorate.

On return to the UK I re-joined 85 Squadron flying Javelin Mk.8s at RAF West Raynham and when 85 Squadron again disbanded, finished my twelve years with No. 41 Squadron at RAF Wattisham. I flew around 50 different Meteor NF at OCUs and with 85 Squadron. Pilots would do night flying at AFS and

Flight Lieutenant Paul Hobson, a navigator with No. 85 Sqn, joined the unit in January 1955 and stayed until it disbanded in 1958. The aircraft is a Meteor NF.14, which he flew, often with Flying Officer Tulip, according to his log book from the period. (P. Hobson)

Meteor T.7 WL470 of RAF Malling's station flight/No. 85 Sqn during maintenance at West Malling. On 14 March 1962 it belly-landed at West Malling and was damaged beyond repair.

more at the jet OCU, whereas crew and their navigators would learn the ins and outs of the night fighter role. At West Malling we flew on a number of 'ad-hoc' exercises in addition to the large annual exercises. For example 'Bomex' would describe an incident when a night fighter under GCI control would be usually diverted to carry out an interception on a passing RAF aircraft, usually a Canberra, and later perhaps one of the 'V' Bombers, Valiant, Vulcan or Victor. ADEX was a small scale air defence exercise which could involve other fighter aircraft as well as bomber force. Piston-engined aircraft formed the Station Flight at RAF West Malling and there was an Avro Anson serial VV881 and a DH Chipmunk serial WP787, used for communications, though I do remember taking the Anson up to RAF Leuchars to collect a large salmon to be consumed at the summer ball; pilots had to keep in practice, and it gave the navigator a chance to brush up map reading skills. While at West Malling I only flew the Meteor and I am glad I never flew the Vampire, the Meteor was jokingly referred to as 'a gentleman's aerial carriage'. It was easy to fly, though take off at maximum weight and suffering engine problems could be a critical situation.

Happy Days! Aircrew of No. 85 Sqn pose for a group photo. Behind them stands a Meteor NF.14, and beyond that the squadron's hangar. The CO, Wing Commander L.G. Martin, is standing in the centre of the group. (P. Hobson)

Aircrew of No. 85 Sqn walking back for briefing following a daytime flight. The nearest Meteor NF.14, WS744, later served with the Air Navigation School. Another, WS723, flew with Nos. 153 and 25 Sqn, and later No. 220 OCU until struck off charge in April 1962.

Like all RAF Fighters, endurance was limited, and even with 2 x 100 gallon under-wing tanks and a 175 gallon belly tank, ninety minutes was about the maximum, there being no in-flight refuelling at that time. Each of the squadrons at West Malling took it in turn to do 'QRA' (Quick Reaction Alert), which involved a week's detachment to RAF Waterbeach and later RAF Wattisham. This involved aircraft being positioned on the ARP at the end of the runway, in contact with a GCI unit by landline with crew strapped in, live ammunition, who would be scrambled to intercept and identify unknown aircraft entering UK airspace. There was a QRA aircraft available somewhere in the UK twenty-four hours a day, 365 days a year. While on QRA a limited flying programme would continue, interspersed with stints sitting in the cockpit.

AI checks were carried out by visiting Bristol Brigand T4 basic radar trainers, in which we flew, such as RH797 based with 238 OCU at RAF Leeming or RAF Colerne. Their role was to check all navigators on their skills. An instructor would

Air interception checks were carried out by Brigand T.4 radar trainers, which were flown by No. 85 Sqn aircrew. One such aircraft was RH797, assigned to No. 238 OCU at Leeming or Colerne.

watch you doing your best, and were not slow to criticise. Operation Rat Trap was another exercise we took part in. We simulated a bomber stream, to be intercepted by various NATO forces along our route. Exercise Vigilant was a major exercise for air defence squadrons. Not much attention was given to the claims of Hunter and Mystere fighters, and if my pilot Johnny Tulip got a glimpse in his gunsight that was a claim. We saw a Westland Wyvern, a naval aircraft, which was almost certainly not involved in the exercise, but we shot it down anyway! These flights were connected to the move for 85 Squadron to RAF Church Fenton when West Malling closed for development to accommodate the new Gloster Javelins.

Married quarters were allotted according to rank, length of service and, for new arrivals, availability of a quarter. Many married men lived out in private housing, known in RAF speak as 'hirings'. At the time the majority of aircrew at West Malling were new or newish crews who had recently completed their training and were mostly in their early twenties and unmarried, as was I. We bachelors lived in the officers' mess, though due to numbers you might have to share a room in the mess building, or a tiny single room in a pre-fab block with only the

Meteor T.7 WA733 was allocated No. 85 Sqn in the early 1960s, seen here when it overshot the runway. Later this aircraft went to the Air Fighting Development Squadron, based at Binbrook. (P. Hobson)

An impressive display of Meteor NF.14s of No. 85 Sqn following their return to West Malling on 5 June 1956 following a display, when Air Vice Marshal V.S. Bowling, CBE, AOC No. 11 Grp, visited the airfield for his annual inspection. This shot is taken looking towards the top end of the airfield.

most basic amenities. By this time there were very few NCO aircrew, mostly older men, virtually all married and living in the married quarters.

I remember on one occasion when we paid host to the Cambridge University Air Squadron, who had a summer camp at West Malling in July 1957. They were going to do a fly past for a visiting VIP and I arranged to fly in one of their DH Chipmunks. Came the day and it turned out to be a mass formation of fifteen Chipmunks with my aircraft in the middle of the seething mass. When I rather nervously asked my pilot, one of the instructors, how much formation practice the UAS pilots had, he cheerfully replied, 'None, they'll tag along somehow!' A rather anxious 20 minutes followed, but happily all returned safely to West Malling.

With us at West Malling were Nos. 153, 25 and 500 (Kent's Own) Squadron, RAuxAF, which was disbanded on 10 March 1957 at West Malling and it was decided to have a 'disbandment party'. It was decided to blow up a derelict Austin A28 as part of the celebrations. One of the 500 Squadron pilots ran a quarry

Meteor NF.14 WS776 of No. 25 Sqn refueling at West Malling for night operations. This aircraft also served with Nos. 85 and 92 Sqn, and No. 228 OCU. Today it is on display at Bournemouth Aviation Museum.

A classic line-up of aircraft at West Malling. The nearest is Meteor NF.11 WD620 of No. 85 Sqn. Behind is a row of Vampire NF.10s of No. 25 Sqn, WP233, WP245, WP239 and WP240.

in the Downs north of Maidstone and had access to gelignite. On the appointed day the car was pushed into the sports field at the back of the officer's mess, a quantity of gelignite was inserted into the petrol tank and wired up to an electric plunger to explode it from a distance. At the stroke of midnight the owner was invited to do the honours. Unfortunately the quantity of explosive had been rather overdone and the result was a very impressive explosion.

No. 500 Squadron had certainly gone out with a bang! However, there were consequences. Within minutes police cars and fire engines started to arrive at the scene enquiring about the damage and casualties and what precisely had been blown up. After some lengthy discussion, the police and fire services duly departed, with, it is understood, 'thank you' gifts comprising a large portion of the mess stocks of good whisky. For some weeks after the event unfortunate defaulters could be seen patrolling the sports field collecting hundreds of pieces of a 1928 Austin. At the urgent request of the station commander, our hero was required to move the remains but declined on the grounds that the vehicle had already been scrapped and only changed his mind when the much put upon pilot handed over a much-prized £5 note.

Another incident that springs to mind. When the film Dunkirk was being made the owner of a German half-track on his way home from filming parked outside the Kings Head, Wateringbury for refreshments for himself and his friends.

On leaving the pub they were dismayed to find their half-track still resplendent in camouflage, black crosses and other German markings was no longer there! Imagine the surprise of the station commander to be knocked up in the early hours by an indignant owner, demanding to know why his half-track was parked outside the station commander's residence! Nothing could be proved but rumour had it that a party of 85 Squadron aircrew had been noted leaving the Kings Head long before closing time – a most unusual happening. The truth, I feel will never be known! Can't imagine the furore if these events happened today!

VIPs being escorted to the 'J' hangar during one of many inspections in the 1950s. The aircraft is Vampire 'FG-D' of No. 72 Sqn. In the background is a Mosquito NF.30 of No. 29 Sqn.

The CO of West Malling, Wing Commander F.N. Brinsden, welcomes Admiral Sir R. Durrant-Slater KCB to West Malling during 1955. Note the sign to the right and the RAF vehicle in the background, parked across the road at the main gate. (KAHRS)

On 28 February 1955, No. 153 Sqn all-weather squadron was re-formed at West Malling. The squadron had been disbanded at Scampton on 28 September 1945. It was equipped with the Meteor NF.12 and later re-equipped with Meteor NF.14s. The squadron remained at West Malling until 2 July 1958, when it was renumbered No. 25 Sqn.

No. 153 Sqn's first flight at West Malling took place in March 1955, a daylight reconnaissance flight flown by Squadron Leader Wicht, DSO, DFC, the CO, and his navigator, Flying Officer Pemberton. The first night operation took place the same month and was flown by Flight Lieutenant Bogue and Flying Officer J. Ledward. In April the squadron began day flying training, but poor weather limited night flying and there was further disruption due to a shortage of equipment. Despite the difficulties of starting a new squadron with the normal 'teething troubles', No. 153 Sqn was lucky enough to have the backing of West Malling's facilities, which enabled it to get off to a reasonable start.

At the beginning of summer 1955 the squadron suffered a tragic loss when Meteor NF.12 WS662 crashed, killing its crew. Two civilians were also

Meteor aircraft on parade during the AOCs inspection during 1955. The aircraft closest to the camera is a Meteor T.7. (KAHRS)

killed and damage caused to farm buildings. The accident occurred during take-off on 30 June. The Meteor taxied on to runway 25 and commenced take-off but failed to become properly airborne. It was one of a formation that was taking off in pairs and WS662 was No. 2 of the third pair and low on take-off. The weather that day was good with excellent visibility. The take-off was uphill, the end of the runway being about 60ft higher than the take-off point. The leader became airborne at about 100yd from the end of the runway, holding very low, and the Meteor in question was not at this time properly airborne, the wheels still brushing the runway. The aircraft continued over the escarpment of the overshoot area and crashed into an orchard of apple trees, disintegrating. The crew, Flight Lieutenant K.M. Charles and Flying Officer P.M. Rolfe, were both killed instantly and are buried at St Mary's Church, West Malling.

At the beginning of July, Sir Anthony Eden, now the Prime Minister and Honorary Air Commodore of No. 500 (Kent's Own) Sqn, arrived from Bovingdon in a DH Devon and was greeted on arrival by the Station CO, Group Captain P.H. Hamley. After inspecting the parade, Sir Anthony gave a brief address in which he thanked all members for the time and effort they devoted to making the unit efficient and recalled the high spots in

Sir Anthony Eden, Prime Minister and Honorary Air Commodore of No. 500 (Kent's Own) Sqn, RAuxAF, inspects pilots and airmen in early July 1955. On his left is Squadron Leader L.D.M. Clause, AFC. In the background are Meteor F.8s, with which the squadron had been re-equipped in November 1951, replacing its Meteor F.4s. (Flight Magazine)

the squadron's history. He then presented the Esher Trophy, awarded to a RAuxAF squadron each year for proficiency, to No. 500 Sqn CO Squadron Leader L.D.M. Clause, AFC. Following tea, Meteor F.8s of No. 500 Sqn took off and flew over the saluting base in arrowhead formation. Flying Officer R.W. Napier gave an excellent display of aerobatics. On the return of the Meteors to the airfield, the Prime Minister inspected the pilots and ground crews, shaking hands with each man. During the period of the Suez crisis, this visit was much appreciated by the whole squadron and everyone at West Malling.

Chapter 9

Care and Maintenance

The last RAF squadron leaves

Flying Officers F. Webb and D.R. Arundell were both killed on 1 January 1956 when their Meteor NF.14, WS727, of No. 153 Sqn, crashed. The accident occurred towards the completion of a cine photographic sortie in which the accompanying aircraft, Meteor NF.12 WS685 of No. 153 Sqn, flown by Flying Officers E.F. Munday and R.V. Percival, was to make a quarter attack. After being airborne for twenty minutes, the aircraft were

Meteor NF.12 WS727 of No. 153 Sqn, based at West Malling, dived into a wooded area at Hunton Hill. Both crew members, Flying Officers D.R. Arundell and F. Webb, were killed and were buried at St Mary's Church, West Malling. RAF personnel and local fire officers attended the crash scene.

observed flying in line astern at about 1,000ft and at 300 knots in the vicinity of West Malling. Without warning, WS685 started a turn to port, which developed into a steep climbing turn. WS727, formating, followed and took cine photographs. When both aircraft were at about 4,000ft, the leader commenced a roll to port at about 200 knots. WS685 followed until almost inverted, and then rolled out into a climbing turn as he considered the manoeuvre dangerous at that altitude. The leading aircraft, WS727, lost height and was last seen in a steep dive at about 2,000ft. Shortly afterwards, it struck the ground, killing the crew, while WS685 returned to base safely. It was concluded that an accident happened due to loss of flying control at a height insufficient for recovery. Other factors were the low speed when during the rolling manoeuvre, and a high all-up weight of the Meteor. A book, *The Day Wadhurst Changed*, by Michael Harte, which was published in 2006, tells the story of the accident and its impact on the village of Wadhurst, near Crowborough, Sussex.

No. 228 OCU was based at Luffenham in 1956 and Meteor NF.12 WS661 took off from there on Friday, 20 January on a local flying exercise. At about 1510hrs, only thirty-nine minutes into the flight, the aircraft crashed on Wadhurst. West Malling, being the nearest airfield, dispatched a crash detail to the site. Flying Officer L.C.M. Stoate, the pilot, and his navigator, Flying

Many ATC cadets visited West Malling. One such was Tony Smith, who recorded each flight he made in detail. During a visit on 15 March 1956, he took the opportunity to fly in Anson C.21 VV244 of No. 61 Grp HQ Flight, based at Blackbushe. (Robin A. Walker)

Officer A.W. Paterson, were killed, and a civilian lost his life. Buildings were damaged and demolished. Corporal Garberry and four other airmen arrived from West Malling to help with the aftermath of the crash, aided by the police and emergency services. The CO at West Malling, Group Captain G.V. Pryer, spent considerable time at Wadhurst talking to local people and others at the scene. On 21 January, a court of inquiry was convened by Air Officer Commanding in Chief Fighter Command, Air Commodore D.G. Lewis, DFC, and held at the airfield. Paterson was buried at his home town of Prestwick and Stoate was buried at Wadhurst Parish Church on 25 January, with a funeral party from West Malling in attendance.

Another tragedy occurred on 16 April when Meteor NF.12 WS694 crashed on take-off from runway 25. The Meteor was seen to climb about 400ft and the pilot, Flying Officer R.A. Hollingworth, was heard to make an R/T call that he was changing channels but no further transmissions were heard. The aircraft crashed about 1¾ miles south of the end of runway 25. Flying Officers R.A. Hollingworth and J.C. Langham, of No. 153 Sqn, died in the crash and are buried at West Malling church. The evidence indicated that the accident was due to loss of control shortly after take-off at night. There was no defect or failure found except that the port engine lost power at a critical stage during the take-off.

On 12 December, Westland Whirlwind HAR.2 XJ756 crashed into Whitehorse Wood, 4 miles north-north-west of the airfield. The helicopter was serving with No. 22 Sqn. The pilot had taken off from Felixstowe to fly to

Mystere IICs of Escadron De Chasse 2/10 'Seine' of the French Air Force shortly after their arrival at West Malling. This unit was based at Creil during 1956–57 and took part in joint operations with the RAF.

Thorney Island, accompanied by his navigator. On impact the helicopter caught fire, killing both crew. The weather was bad with low cloud over the trees and there was high turbulence with gusting wind.

In 1956, at the height of the Cold War, Leslie Woodhead was 18 years of age when he was called up for National Service, like many of his age. For many it was a time when boyhood was left behind, joining the ranks of the RAF, Navy or Army. Surviving the basic training in the RAF, Leslie was sent to the Joint School of Linguistics, at a bleak location on the east of Scotland. Receiving his posting, he arrived at West Malling and was immediately confronted by life on a post-war RAF base.

He and other new recruits soon got to know the tedium of National Service life. For several days the budding RAF airmen were subjected to parades and inspections, often encouraged by the delicate voice of the sergeant, 'Fall in, hairy arse,' being one of his favourite phrases. He was assigned to a Russian linguistics course, but no one at West Malling had heard of any Russian course, and were not sure what to do with Woodhead. For several weeks he was moved around the camp, moving and emptying dustbins on rubbish trucks and shifting furniture. He was also assigned to guard duty, armed not with a rifle but with a pickaxe handle, and struggled to remain awake. It was the year of the Suez crisis and there was a distinct feeling that there could be military action. Woodhead's home was Halifax and he occasionally managed to take leave, by walking, bus journeys and local and main-line trains, although on one occasion he gave up and stayed in London, enjoying the night life of Soho, bookshops, museums and jazz clubs in Chinatown. On one occasion he just managed to catch the last train back to West Malling, to another week of domestic chores. Then, in early 1956, he was informed that the required paperwork had arrived and he was sent to RAF Ruislip, only to be told on arrival that he should be in Scotland! Thus ended Woodhead's short assignment to West Malling.

During this period at West Malling work had begun on laying a concrete threshold on runway 25. Concreting was completed on 2 February 1957 and the asphalt would be laid on 9 February. Work on the area was scheduled to finish on 23 February. This was welcome news for aircrew as there were often complaints about the amount of loose stones in the area, which was a hazard to all aircraft movements. There was also several improvements being made to the air traffic control systems in the control tower, and rather ancient plumbing in the cloak room was also being upgraded. A new building for the Radio Servicing Flight was also being constructed, and due for completion on 7 March, despite a delay in the delivery of heating equipment.

Fairy Gannet AS.1 XA391 of No. 820 Sqn, HMS *Bulwark*, Fleet Air Arm, during Operation Make Way, the joint RAF/Navy exercise that took place in March 1957. (Fleet Air Arm Museum)

USAF aircrew were posted to West Malling in February, and the CO of No. 85 Sqn, Squadron Leader Gardner, arranged for the airmen to be billeted in former officers' married quarters, which was much appreciated by the Americans. However, some of No. 85 Sqn's crew were somewhat put out as they were having problems with mice in their own quarters, and an expert was called in to set traps for the uninvited quests. On 22 February, No. 25 Sqn, on detachment to Wattisham, moved back to West Malling. All the Meteor NF.14s returned under the command of Wing Commander D.A. Trotman, AFC, and the first take-off from Wattisham was at 1300hrs. All aircrew who were not flying returned by road and rail, as did the ground crews.

A joint exercise took place at West Malling between the RAF and the Fleet Air Arm on 5–14 March. The Naval contingent consisted of eight officers, six petty officers and twenty-five ratings, who took part in Operation Make Way. No. 820 Naval Air Squadron sent three Gannet AS.1s from RNAS Eglinton, County Londonderry, to West Malling on 1 March, followed by another aircraft on 3 March. They were expected to remain for two weeks and returned to their squadron on 15 March. However, in their absence, the unit had moved from Eglinton to RNAS Ford.

Canberra PR.7 WT528 *Aries V* of the RAF Flying College, Manby, which established a new record between Tokyo and West Malling on 25 May 1957. (AW12880)

In 1957, the Battle of Britain Memorial flight began its historic life with two Mk.XIV Spitfires and a Hurricane Mk.II. When three ex-THUM flight Spitfires arrived at Biggin Hill on 11 July, two of these aircraft, PS853 and PM631, began their new life as part of this flight, while PS915, unlike its two companions, was retired from active flying. On 8 August it was flown

The gate guardian at RAF West Malling from 31 August 1957 was Spitfire Mk.XIX PS915, which flies today with the Battle of Britain Memorial Flight. (D.G. Collyer)

Spitfire Mk. XIX PS915 was proudly displayed at West Malling from 31 August 1957 until 1960. (Kent Messenger)

by Group Captain P.D. Thompson from Biggin Hill to West Malling, where it became the airfield's gate guardian. Prior to its new role, the aircraft was given a complete overhaul by an RAF support flight, following which it was moved to its position at the main gate. It remained as West Malling's gate guardian until 20 January 1961, when it was sent No. 60 MU at Leuchars. Today it is with the Battle of Britain Memorial Flight and can be seen flying at many annual airshows and events.

RAF open days and flying displays were always well attended at West Malling, and on 6 August 1960 an 'at home' day took place. Even in those days no fly past was allowed to be carried out at West Malling below 500ft. No. 111 Sqn's Black Arrows, the celebrated Hawker Hunter aerobatic team, performed on the day with their usual impressive display.

The initial flying display took place at 1350hrs when a Canberra took off, while other aircraft taking part included Meteors, a Vulcan and Chipmunks of the University Air Squadron. Joining them that day were USAF F-100s, F-101s and a B-66. During the afternoon there were displays by Vampire T.11s, an Oxford and a Hunter F.6. At 1533hrs, the crowd was delighted

A truly magnificent line-up of RAF fighters at West Malling. Spitfires, Hurricane, Hunters and Javelin aircraft are being prepared for the 'at home' day on 6 August 1960. (KAHRS)

Apart from the aircraft flying on 6 August 1960, there were static displays and these included a Bloodhound ground-to-air missile, which formed part of the country's defences during the Cold War period. (KAHRS)

to see a display by a gyrocopter, which was followed by a Hurricane and Spitfire and concluded when a Shackleton took off with a Jet Provost. On static display were a Javelin FAW.8, recently re-equipping No. 85 Sqn, a US Navy Neptune, a Meteor F.8, Hunter, Vampire, Canberra, Shackleton and even a USAF T-33, most of these having flown during the day.

A nostalgic scene – the main entrance to RAF West Malling post-1960. Spitfire Mk.XIX PS915 has already departed to RAF Leuchars, Scotland. It once stood to the right of the gate.

Meteor F.8 WL159 of No. 85 Sqn during the early 1960s. This aircraft also served with Nos. 263 and 1 Sqn and was eventually struck off charge at West Malling on 8 November 1962. It is seen here at an RAF open day.

No. 1 Air Experience Flight was formed at West Malling on 12 September 1959 and it was to remain until 10 September 1960, when it moved to White Waltham. The Air Experience Flight scheme was inaugurated on 8 September 1958 to provide flying experience to ATC cadets on Chipmunks. The scheme was administered by No. 25 Grp until 1 July 1968, when it was transferred to No. 22 Grp. From 1 April 1996 the flights were each parented by a university air squadron, whose Bulldog and later Grob Tutor aircraft it shared.

During the early 1960s, exact date not known, Martin-Baker produced several mobile ejection seat training rigs for the RAF and mounted each of them on a Queen Mary, a long load trailer chassis. There is no specific information regarding this enterprise, as some Martin-Baker archive material was destroyed in a fire, but it is known that one such rig was based at West Malling. These rigs normally visited RAF flying training units, and pilots destined for the English Electric Lightning would already have used the test rig in training. The rigs normally incorporated a generic seat because the object of the exercise was to give aircrew the experience of pulling the face blind and firing themselves 20–30ft up the inclined track. They were not meant to represent a specific aircraft type.

An RAF officer poses for a photo seated in the Martin-Baker trainer used to test Mk.2 4BSB ejector seats at West Malling. This type was fitted into the Lightning T.4/5 trainers in the 1960s. (The Aviation Historian)

It is possible that West Malling may have had a Lightning cockpit to teach the procedures for operating the aircraft, which was vital because early on there was no Lightning T.4 trainer. This cockpit incorporated a fully representative Mk.4BS seat to enable authentic strapping in, sitting height adjustment and go-forward control operation as on an aircraft.

The first seat was tested by Bernard Lynch, an engineer fitter at Martin-Baker, on 24 July 1945, who ejected from a Gloster Meteor travelling at 320mph at 8,000ft over Chalgrove, Oxfordshire. At the time very little was known about how much the human body could withstand, but without a doubt Martin-Baker ejector seat training was essential and their seats, used by some ninety-three air forces, have saved 7,546 lives since 1946.

The RAF presence at West Malling gradually wound down in the late 1950s.

No. 500 (Kent's Own) Sqn with its Meteor F.8s was disbanded on 10 March 1957 as part of the axing of the RAuxAF fighter squadrons in a cost-cutting measure.

No. 153 Sqn, which had re-formed at West Malling in 1955 with Meteor NF.12s and NF.14s, remained at the airfield until 17 September 1957, when it was reassigned to Waterbeach. It was soon disbanded but re-formed on 2 July 1958 as No. 25 Sqn.

Also, on the move on from West Malling was No. 25 Sqn, It moved its Meteor NF.12s and NF.14s to Tangmere on 30 September 1957, and the unit was disbanded there on 1 July 1958.

On 18 September 1957, No. 85 Sqn moved to RAF Church Fenton, where it remained until it was disbanded on 30 November 1958, only to be re-formed at Stradishall on the same date. Having previously flown Meteor NF.11, 12 and 14 aircraft, it was now to be equipped with the latest RAF fighter, the Javelin FAW.2 and FAW.6, and was based at West Malling from 5 June 1959. It later took charge of two Javelin FAW.8s, armed with four Firestreak missiles and with uprated engines with reheat.

No. 85 Sqn finally vacated West Malling for West Raynham in September 1960, and it was a sad day when the delta-wing Javelins took off from the airfield for the last time.

A factor in the departure of the RAF was that the airfield was somewhat limited in its capability as it was hemmed in by the approaches to the airports at Gatwick and Heathrow.

With the final departure of No. 85 Sqn on 6 September 1960, and the remainder of its personnel and equipment leaving on 9 September, West Malling fell silent as an RAF airfield.

Chapter 10

The Final Years

The US Navy, gliding and Metair

The administration of West Malling was handed over to the US Navy on 17 October 1960. Following the end of the Second World War, the US Navy realised it needed to establish a communications squadron in Europe to service various activities. On 3 October, 1946 Utility Transport Squadron Four (VRU-4) was commissioned at Hendon, close to the Commander-in-Chief US Naval Forces Eastern Atlantic and Mediterranean, whose offices were located in central London. The squadron was equipped with two Beech JRB Expeditors and three Douglas R4D Skytrains.

With Hendon under threat of closure it was understandable that the US Navy would look for another airfield not too far from London, and having been advised that West Malling was available, the US authorities approached the Ministry of Defence. Proposals were sanctioned and almost immediately the withdrawal from Hendon began.

In May 1960 an advance party of the US Navy commanded by Commander T.A. Holl, arrived to begin preparations for the handover. The Americans officially took up residence on 1 June, when the number of RAF personnel remaining at West Malling was reduced to the RAF Liaison Party establishment.

The American Stars and Stripes and the RAF ensign were raised simultaneously at West Malling on Monday, 23 October as the administrative control of the RAF base was handed over to officers of the United States Navy Facility. During a brief ceremony in front of the HQ building, Wing Commander F.N. Brinsden told the assembled officers and airmen of the USN and RAF that he was gratified by the goodwill, co-operation and patience shown by all concerned with the changeover. He went on to say:

> Today I became the agent for the landlord and you, Commander
> Yonkers, became the chief tenant of this station. I know it's

294

Transport Command Comet C.2 XK697 *Cygnus* of No. 216 Sqn, RAF Lyneham, landed at West Malling on 14 June 1960 with AOC Air Vice Marshal A. Foord-Kelcey, No. 11 Grp, for a two-day visit. (E.T. Sergison)

> irksome to be hindered in your plans for settling in by the old tenant who is hanging about, but it has been a bitter pill for us to swallow to have to disband our station and hand it over to someone else.

The wing commander noted that, despite conditions that could lead to 'frayed and ill feelings', the changeover had been free from friction and mutual strength and respect had grown on either side. He went on to say: 'I wish all of you stationed at West Malling a happy and prosperous stay in England.' Commander George P. Yonkers, commanding officer of the American forces, said that he would rather be considered: 'a privileged

Another aircraft seen at West Malling, once the US Navy arrived, was C-131F 141021. Note the US Navy seaman standing by the steps. (E.T. Sergison)

P2V-7 135570/LH11 of VP-21 generated a lot of interest when it arrived at West Malling in 1960 and was in service with the US Naval Facility at the airfield. (E.T. Sergison)

guest who has a key to the front door than the master of the house, I am honoured to be taking over an RAF station with such a tradition.' Following addresses by the two commanders, Captain J.M. Catch USN, inspected the USN squadron, accompanied by Group Captain R.J. Gosnell, RAF. Commander. Yonkers said that additional US personnel would be arriving at West Malling and that he expected to employ several more civilian workers, if possible from the surrounding area. A small complement of the RAF was to remain at the airfield to act as a liaison group, and West Malling would always have an RAF commander, who would be the liaison officer with the Americans, which he did until January 1961.

The Naval Facility hosted Fleet Air Support Squadron 200, the purpose of which was to support US Naval units in Western Europe. The aircraft flown comprised a Convair R4Y known as an 'admiral's barge'. It was so named because this particular aircraft was the personal mount of the Commander-in-Chief US Navy Europe, and the unit fulfilled a role rather like the British Queen's Flight. For general freight and communications duties the Facility had the faithful R4D, which were the workhorses of the squadron, and several SNB-5 Expediters (Beech 18s) for trainee and refresher flying, mostly by chair-borne staff from London. It also had Grumman Albatross amphibians on the inventory for services with the US Naval attaché in Scandinavia. Regular weekly flights into West Malling were

The US Naval Facility's 'Stars and Stripes' is raised over West Malling during the official handover parade in 1960. (KAHRS)

A Douglas R4D-8, 12437, a descendent of the Dakota, was used as a transport aircraft for the United States Naval Facility that arrived at RAF West Malling in 1960. (E.T. Sergison)

carried out by C-130 Hercules from the support squadron VR-24, based at Rota in Spain. These were to bring in Mediterranean freight and passengers and to carry the regular US mail run. The facility also had many visiting aircraft from exercising squadrons, mainly anti-submarine P2V Neptunes and P-3A Orions, plus many carrier-borne aircraft from US aircraft carriers visiting British Naval bases.

By the beginning of 1961 the squadron title, along with its tail code 'FT', had disappeared from use altogether and the aircraft were from then onwards assigned to Naval Facility West Malling. While at West Malling, C-47J 50785 spent most of its time at Orly for use by the US Naval attaché at the US embassy in Paris. C-131F 141021, which had been based at Blackbushe in January 1959, replacing 140993, arrived in 1958, also operating from Northolt. It continued to be used as the 'admiral's barge', supporting the US Navy HQ in London.

In early 1964, the unit was relocated to Mildenhall and, with the exception of the C-131F, all aircraft went to the new base.

Oxford University Air Squadron (UAS) was formed at Oxford in 1925. It had a varied background and by 12 January 1959 was based at Bicester, Oxfordshire. It offered basic flying training and adventure training to graduates and undergraduates, encouraging them to join the RAF. By 1960 the UAS was under the command of Wing Commander A.J. 'Fred' Douch, the chief flying instructor being Squadron Leader D.H. Bennett,

The late Ted Sergison was given photographs of several of the US Navy Facility aircraft. This aircraft is C-130 Hercules 149790 'JM'. (E.T. Sergison)

An aircraft of the US Naval Facility Station Flight, Beech C-45 Expeditor 67227, attending an air display at an unknown British airfield. (E.T. Sergison)

who was nicknamed 'CFI Sid'. Qualified flying instructors (QFI) held their annual summer camp that year at West Malling. Among the officers attending were Flying Officer Phil Wilkinson (later Air Commodore), and Flight Lieutenants Dick Bates and Bill Beadle. West Malling was at that time commanded by Air Vice Marshal Sir Christopher Foxley-Norris, who had taken over from Wing Commander F.N. Brinsden on 4 August 1959 and stayed until 1 July 1960.

It was not Phil Wilkinson's first visit to West Malling, for in 1953 he was in the RAF section of his school's Combined Cadet Force, on summer camp at RAF Wellesbourne Mountford, Warwickshire:

> I was airborne in Air Speed Oxford NJ296 from the School of Photography. I recall seeing Warwick Castle from a near inverted position, fighter manoeuvring having stayed firmly in my Polish pilot's skill set. Earlier that year I'd taken another Oxford ride, this time from RAF West Malling, close to school and presumably a day out for air experience. I have got that logged as Oxford HM975, but I haven't got the serial number of the Chipmunk I went up in that day, which I recall as if it were yesterday – I was so excited I forgot to write the details down.

He had joined the UAS in September 1959, when the Chipmunk trainer had re-equipped the RAF as its main trainer aircraft. Wilkinson remembers one particular event that took place at West Malling:

> It was during summer camp that we felt we had to help the US Naval Facility to celebrate Independence Day on 4 July 1960. So, a bunch of midnight climbers paid no heed to normal security and painted a tribute to the young nation's 184th birthday on the roof of the 'J' hangar. I am not sure anyone ever admitted to the rooftop painting but it was not looked on kindly, given the implications for security even in those days.

However, this kind gesture was no doubt appreciated by the US Navy personnel stationed thousands of miles from home, who could only wonder who had managed to climb on to the roof undetected.

Air Commodore Wilkinson's RAF career started with National Service and continued with the University Air Squadron at Oxford, and then went on to total forty years in the RAF. This called for thousands of hours in

To welcome the US Naval Facility that moved to West Malling in 1960, staff of the university air squadron painted these words on the roof of the 'J' type hangar. (Air Commodore P.J. Wilkinson, CVO)

Chief flying instructors and NCOs of the Oxford University Air Squadron (UAS) during their summer camp at West Malling in July 1960. Flying Officer Phil Wilkinson is standing second right on the middle row. (Air Commodore P.J. Wilkinson, CVO)

the air – an activity he still tries to engage in as often as possible. His time on the ground was equally challenging, including exchange appointments with both the French and United States Air Forces, and assignment as commander of the RAF station in Berlin at the time of the fall of the Wall. His final period of duty was based in Moscow in 1993 as Defence and Air Attaché, during the turbulence of Russia's emergence from the Soviet era. He spent a lot of time travelling across the former Soviet Union, including journeys to Murmansk and Archangel, where he accompanied RAF and other British veterans as they revisited the scenes of their operations in the Second World War. He served with many flying and fighter control units, including No. 14 Sqn in November 1963.

In 1953, Alan Huggett began his RAF service as a boy entrant at RAF Halton, and became an armourer. He was posted to No. 85 Sqn at West Malling during 1957 and served in the original armoury building. Later the unit moved into new premises on the airfield. When Huggett left the RAF he joined the Meteorological Office, having passed the relevant examinations required. To his amazement he was again posted to West Malling, this time as a civilian, and remembered:

> It was a lovely posting and a pleasure to be back on the old airfield. When I joined in December 1964 we were operating

Chipmunks of Oxford University Air Squadron formate over Kent on 22 July 1960. The nearest, T.10 WD359, served with various training flights until 17 October 1973, when it was sold and re-registered G-BBMN. It is airworthy today. (Air Commodore P.J. Wilkinson CVO)

Chipmunk T.10s at the summer camp in 1960. The nearest, WK633, flew with several training flights and is today is registered G-BXEC and kept at Redhill, Surrey. (Air Commodore P.J. Wilkinson, CVO)

Chipmunk T.10 WD344 of No. 1 Air Experience Flight flew from White Waltham, Manston and West Malling between September 1959 and 10 September 1960. (KAHRS)

a 24/7 system, including over Christmas (the weather doesn't stop). We had a good relationship with the Short Bros pilots, some ex Navy pilots, some former RAF multi-engine pilots. The ex Navy pilots transported Fleet Air Arm aircraft around the UK using a Sea Prince twin-engined aircraft as their taxi. The ex RAF types were really employed as test pilots flying a DC3 Dakota and a Vickers Varsity on electronic device testing for Marconi Rochester.

Short Bros also carried out major servicing of the RAF Chipmunk primary trainers. The aircraft were test flown after servicing by a former WW2 Lancaster pilot whose name, if I remember, was Pete Harrison. Another of the ex RAF pilots flew Mosquitoes in WW2, his surname was Richardson, if I remember. I believe he took part in the famous low-level raid on the French prison. The Met Office was located in the Control Tower on the ground floor facing across the airfield. The instruments were in a fenced off area 20 yds or so in front of the tower. Only one of us was on duty overnight and at weekends. Night duty was very peaceful. The airfield was pitch black, except for the couple of dim visibility measurement lights. It wasn't ideal for anyone who was nervous or believed in ghosts. The airfield had many stories of ghostly apparitions! When it was windy the external door used to rattle.

The airfield was in 'Care and Maintenance' under the command of a Flight Lieutenant with a couple of RAF Policemen located in the Guard Room for security. After a couple of years all RAF personnel were withdrawn. RAF Air Cadets 618 Gliding School were located at the airfield, so being ex RAF I joined them for free Gliding at weekends. They also wanted local weather forecasts, especially winds. In the mid 60's the Beatles made the film 'Magical Mystery Tour' at West Malling, using my old squadron's hangar and dispersal area. Paul McCartney and John Lennon would come into the Met Office most mornings for a met briefing and a cup of coffee. The female employees of Shorts were always hanging around. I wish I had kept the group's autographs now. I gave them to my young brother-in-law, who promptly lost them!

The meteorological office was opened in the control tower in July 1964, and some of the equipment needed came from Uxbridge. Shortage of staff was a problem at the time, and Huggett and his colleagues worked a considerable amount of voluntary overtime. It was due to their hard work that the station was able to become operational so quickly.

West Malling became a twenty-four-hour weather observing station on 16 September 1964. The station comprised a large main office,

Varsity T.Mk.1 WL169 was issued to Short Brothers and used for development of low-light television (LLTV) equipment. (S. Glover)

Another view of WL169 as it takes off on a test flight from West Malling. Note the extended nose, which housed the LLTV equipment. (S. Glover)

teleprinter room, administration office, stores and a rest room. The manager lived in a small room off the main office and two assistants lived at home and two in a flat locally; it was found that few people wanted lodgers and hotels were expensive. Alan Huggett was living with his parents at the time but qualified for a council house, as did two other staff living locally with family.

Also in the mid-1960s, Short Brothers was renting the top floor of the tower, beginning on 17 August 1964, and operated sixteen daily flights by service aircraft under Shorts control. Short Brothers had been based at Rochester for a number of years and moved to the airfield with two Percival Sea Princes, WF132 and WP312, and a Vickers Varsity, WL681. These aircraft were operated by Shorts on a service contract with the Air Ministry for research work, and in addition the company also serviced several Chipmunk aircraft used by air experience flights in the south-east, such as Manston and White Waltham. A student and his instructor would deliver the aircraft; for example, on 19 April 1971 WZ873 arrived for maintenance and WD345 was flown back to White Waltham.

Short Brothers occupied the largest of the four hangars and reopened the control tower, which had remained closed since the US Navy had left. The airfield began to see aircraft movements, although nothing to the scale to which it was accustomed. Varsity T.Mk.1 WL169 was issued to Short Brothers in August 1973 was and operated from West Malling for low-light television trials, and also flew the first high-resolution thermal imaging system.

Vickers Varsity T.Mk.1 WL169 was issued to Short Brothers' Varsity and Chipmunk servicing facility at West Malling in August 1973. Today this aircraft is on display at the Imperial War Museum at Cosford.

The servicing unit used the airfield for a number of years, but with the gradual scaling down of the RAF about this period, Shorts eventually lost the service contract in 1978 and West Malling was left with just gliders.

By January 1971, the met unit, apart from serving RAF West Malling, also served No. 618 VGS, Short Brothers and Harland, Ministry of Public Works; Government Buildings at Tunbridge Wells; Rochester Airport and Maidstone Borough Council. However, on 1 June 1971 the unit was closed.

Investigations at the airfield into runway surface texture were carried out, intended to give improved braking surfaces. Eight trial areas were laid along the north edge of runway 07/25. Each area was 300ft long × 12ft wide. The areas were placed end to end to give a continuous trial. A strip was put down on the low side of the runway cross-fall, and a paved drainage channel of similar course construction, 8ft wide, separated it from the grass verge. All the trial areas were laid in July 1959. Skidding tests were carried out approximately five months after laying. The contractor employed for this exercise was Chittenden & Simmons Ltd, which had many years' experience. In 1906 the business was converted into a limited company, with head offices in Maidstone, and carried out large contracts for tarmacadam and bituminous road surfaces for Kent County Council, London County Council and other public bodies. Testing was carried out by the Road Research Laboratory using a small braking force trailer. Measurements of the braking force were made on each side of the eight trial areas, and on the rolled asphalt surfacing, by locking the wheel of the small trailer. A first inspection was carried out on 28 June 1960, when there was no evidence of movement over rolled asphalt base-course, or of loose aggregate on the surface or in the margins of the runway.

In 1942, when air cadet gliding was formally established, one of the first schools formed was No. 141 Gliding School at RAF Kidbrooke in south London. On December 1945, it moved to Gravesend, from where in June 1946 it went to RAF Detling and then to West Malling, between September 1949 and September 1950.

On return to Detling it was disbanded, and later merged into No. 146 Gliding School and No. 168 Gliding School, in 1956 both becoming No. 615 VGS at Kenley. In 1962, No. 677 GS in Northern Ireland was closed for security reasons and the school equipment was used to form a new school, No. 618 VGS, at Manston on 1 March 1963. It was staffed by some instructors of No. 166 GS, which disbanded in December 1955 at Hawkinge, and commanded by Flight Lieutenant J.C. 'Jimmy' Farrell, who became wing commander and OC of Kent Wing ATC. No. 618 VGS launched its first glider on 24 March 1963. The first year was devoted to the training of staff and winch drivers on the fleet of a Sedbergh, two Kirby Cadet 3s, three Land Rovers and two 'Eagle' twin-drum winches. Cadet Martin became the first student on a course to solo with No. 618 VGS on 22 March 1964. More students were sent on their first solos during that year and the first summer course was run, in which sixteen cadets soloed in a week.

The Kent Gliding Club was formed in 1930 and after the Second World War it moved around various airfields in Kent, including a spell at West Malling, before finding a permanent site at Challock.

With the US Naval Facility leaving West Malling in late 1963, the airfield was placed on a care and maintenance status. No. 618 VGS moved from Manston into West Malling in March 1965 and made its HQ in the old dispersal spider complex near runway 07. Aircraft and equipment were stored in one of the T2 hangars there until 1992.

In 1967, the fleet was increased to five Cadet Mk.IIIs and two Sedberghs. In 1969, Squadron Leader Gerry Fuller became the 'Boss'. During his eight years as OC, 618 VGS lived up to its new motto of 'We Fly Harder'. Progress was rapid and many cadets flew at weekends, on field days and during six weeks of continuous courses. These courses had twenty-two students in two intakes, and most learned to fly solo in the week. Around 200 cadets a year went solo on the Mark III during this era. On average,

No. 618 VGS, apart from operating various gliders also used this Grasshopper T.X1 WZ819, which was winched into the air with a cadet as pilot, to instruct the pupil in basic glider skills. (D.G. Collyer)

the school flew 12,000 launches a year. In 1977. Squadron Leader Ben Newman took command of 618. He had previously been OC No. 623 GS at Tangmere, which had disbanded when the RAF station closed. In 1979, No. 618 VGS expanded with seven Cadet Mk IIIs, three Sedberghs, three twin-drum winches and five Land Rovers.

There were also annual detachments to the air cadet soaring site at Halesland, near Cheddar. Staff attending the courses were able to fly over the picturesque Mendip hills and the 618 VGS songbook is full of ballads made up in the pubs of Somerset. The usual detachment was a week each year and included ten instructors and flight staff cadets. The idea was to improve the skills of the instructors at a site away from base. Halesland was on a ridge and some soaring and cross-county flying was possible. Back in Kent, at Biggin Hill during the Battle of Britain Air displays each September, No. 618 VGS detached a Sedbergh towed by a Chipmunk from No. 1 AEF at Manston. The Sedbergh then performed an aerobatic display.

In late 1982, No. 618 VGS was chosen to become the first school to re-equip with new glass fibre sailplanes. The Schleicher ASK 21, designated Vanguard TX1, was selected and ten initial airframes delivered. During June 1983, instructors underwent conversion training at the Air Cadet

Kent Gliding Club at West Malling during the late 1960s. It first flew at the airfield during 1963. The glider on the right is a Slingsby Cadet, in the centre an Olympia 2b. (D.G. Collyer)

DH.82A Tiger Moth G-ANMZ, *The Canon*, flown by the gliding school, preparing to leave West Malling airfield shortly before closure for Challock. It crashed there on 22 May 1969. (D.G. Collyer)

One of the few blister hangars still standing as late as the 1980s housed Westland Lysanders Mk.IIIs of No. 26 (Army Cooperation) Sqn from 18 June until 3 September 1940. The squadron returned to West Malling in 1942 flying Mustang Mk.Is.

In the late 1980s this Nissen hut could be found on the far side of the airfield, and many of these are still scattered around the UK on former RAF airfield sites today.

Central Gliding School (ACCGS) at RAF Syerston. Each instructor received a week's training at ACCGS. The first three Vanguards arrived at West Malling on 18 June, when final familiarisation on site took place. In September 1983, the last Cadet Mk.III flew at West Malling before being sold off. On 4 August 1983, Cadet Hazell became the first air cadet to be taught all through on the Vanguard, and went solo after only twenty-nine launches.

While No. 618 VGS was at West Malling, The Beatles, who released their album *Magical Mystery Tour* in 1967, produced a film of the same title. They filmed some sequences in Kent and in particular at West Malling airfield and Knole Park. Filming took place over a few days and is perhaps best remembered for the scene when the blast pens were used as backdrop.

Some sequences were filmed inside one of the hangars and several locals were recruited as extras, while Ringo Starr filmed a scene in the newsagent at 90 High Street. The film was shown by the BBC on 26 December 1967. Paul McCartney was later filmed with his new group Wings at another famous Kent airfield, Lympne, close by. A blue plaque was unveiled in West Malling in 2015 to commemorate the Beatles' filming.

War damage was evident on some of the airfield's buildings during the 1980s. This building repair work could clearly be seen.

The officers' mess Type 'B', as seen in the 1980s, is still standing intact today, well away from the airfield by the A228 Malling Road. This was a typical sight on many permanent RAF airfields in the UK, with many now sadly demolished.

The blast pens, which offered some noise reduction when Meteor and Vampire engines were being tested by ground crew. They achieved some notoriety during the filming of The Beatles' film, *Magical Mystery Tour.*

Chapter 11

Gradual Decline

Airlines, film work and closure

In 1971, the sale of the airfield by the Ministry of Defence to Kent County Council was to be the nail in the coffin regarding development for any long-term aviation use. Flying continued in the form of gliding, and there was much interest as there were several aircraft on the airfield used in the filming of the *Battle of Britain* film. One of these was Mosquito B.35 RS712 and this also starred in the film *633 Squadron,* eventually going to the EAA Museum at Oshkosh in America in 1987.

The original sergeants' mess, used in the 1980s by Kent County Council as an administration block, also survived the development of the airfield site.

The buildings and workshops, located north-west of 'T' type hangar used by No. 85 Sqn, were later demolished; the area is now covered by houses.

The guard room included a master at arms office, prison cells, warrant officer's office and sleeping accommodation. It was situated not far from the main entrance.

The Bofors light anti-aircraft gun tower, standing among fruit trees to the north of the main airfield site, close to the roundabout on the A228.

In 1983 No. 618 VGS shared the airfield with Metair Aircraft Equipment Ltd, from Dartford, later part of Hunting Plc. By November 1985, No. 618 had increased its Vanguards to eight and become the sole user of this type. Squadron Leader Newman was awarded the MBE for services to air cadet gliding in 1982. He led the school through the first years of the GRP era and this culminated, in 1998, in the award of the Sir Arthur Marshall Trophy for the best winch-launched gliding school. Newman retired at the end of March 1988, to be succeeded by Squadron Leader Ian Aitken. He moved up from the post of chief flying instructor, which he held from 1984. No. 618 VGS lost its Vanguards in February 1988, when the first of eight Vikings arrived at West Malling. Around this time, development on the site began to turn the airfield into a business park.

The first sign was building on the north of the field, which deprived No. 618 VGS of its grass north–south runway. To try to find an alternative site for No. 618 VGS, Squadron Leader Ben Newman and his team had begun a search for other green field sites in Kent. They were successful in finding a very large area at Grange Farm, on the North Downs near Boxley Village. This site was across the road from the old RAF gliding home of Detling. Squadron Leader Ian Aitken, with help from HQ Air

During the occupation by Metair in the late 1980s the control tower was used as an administration block and flying control. It looked much the same during RAF occupation and fortunately survived. Today it is a Costa Coffee house!

The control tower during development of West Malling in the 1990s. Its future was uncertain at the time after work began in 1989.

Cadets, managed to put a convincing case for the conversion of this field from crops to a grass gliding area complete with individual storage for each Viking and conversion of some listed farm cottages to provide HQ and accommodation. The local parish council was very supporting but Kent County council planning officials were distinctly hostile to the plans. Despite this, the problem of finding sufficient funding by the RAF put paid to these innovative plans.

The popular detachments to Halesland had ceased when the GRP fleet had entered service and Headquarters Air Cadets (HQAC) decided to find an alternative location for instructors and advanced students to improve their skills. The location chosen was Portmoak Airfield in Fife. The ridge and wave lift available made it a very suitable location for advanced training. Ever eager to be at the forefront, in 1992, No. 618 VGS provided the staff and students for the very first course run by a VGS to train advanced cadets on this site.

By that year the development work had increased to such an extent that a based company, Metair, was persuaded to move to Biggin Hill. It left the large hangar and the control tower vacant, and when the No. 618 VGS HQ was demolished in December 1992 the school moved into the tower and put its aircraft and equipment into the large 'J' hangar. Sadly, it was relatively

317

During the filming of *We'll Meet Again,* the television series of the 1980s, replica profiles of B-17 Flying Fortresses were constructed, which viewed from a distance were effective props. They were later abandoned on the airfield for some time. Seen here shortly before the arrival of Metair.

Fortunately several of the wartime buildings were renovated and remain today intact and in use. On closer inspection, on one such building the outline of camouflage is still clearly visible.

During 1946 No. 540 (Photo Reconnaissance) Sqn took this photograph of West Malling as part of an extensive survey of Great Britain. The unit was based at Benson and was operating a Mosquito.

short-lived as No. 618 VGS was given notice to leave West Malling by the end of September 1994. The last continuous course took place in August 1994. During that week, ten cadets went solo. On the last day of the course a reunion cricket match was held on the airfield, with a pitch mowed specially for the purpose. The match consisted of the old boys playing the current instructors. As usual, the old boys won. This was followed by a party and barbecue. All the commanding officers of the school since its inception were present. The last flight of a service aircraft took place on 25 September 1994, with Flight Lieutenant Allan Melmore and Flight Staff Cadet John Wotton making a short circuit of the airfield in Viking TX.1 ZE558.

The last glider launch took place three days later when a privately owned Slingsby Cadet MK. III was flown by the former supply officer, Flight Lieutenant (retired) Derek Smith and his wife Joan. From No. 618's formation until it left West Malling more than 3,000 cadets flew their first glider solo and gained their wings with No. 618 VGS. Due to the very good relationships with the British Gliding association (BGA), and in no small part to the work of Squadron Leader Robin Miller of ACCGS, HQAC struck an accord with Kent Gliding Club. The club had once been resident at West Malling, before No. 618 VGS was formed, and in 1963 it had purchased a small field at Challock near Ashford. As an experiment in operating a service gliding school alongside a civil club, an agreement was made for No. 618 VGS to operate there.

The same day as the last launch at West Malling, 28 September, most of the school's equipment was moved to Challock. As there was only a small blister hangar at Challock, only two Vikings were moved. Challock operations began on 1 October 1994 with site familiarisation. Challock has

An interesting view of buildings and workshops in 1984 looking over the airfield from the roof of the semi-buried control room.

no hardstandings around the field, and when the winter weather changed for the worse, the winch began to sink into the surface. At one point, the equipment was unusable for a month.

The first cadets attended in November and some of the best flying took place on the ridge, where, many sorties lasted longer than half an hour. The operating difficulties increased and it became clear that a full operation to train cadets with the circuit crowded with club gliders was impossible. With great sadness, as the winter of 1995 approached, No. 618 VGS suspended operations. It was never to resume flying at Challock, and in March 1996, No. 618 VGS ceased operations altogether and the staff were dispersed to other gliding schools.

The origins of Metair Aircraft Ltd can be traced back to Metallic Components (Bexley) Ltd at West Street, Erith, Kent, in 1980, where it specialised in aircraft interiors, including all types of hard trim installation for fixed-wing aircraft and helicopters, air conditioning installation, passenger and aircrew seating, galleys, toilets, baggage containers, floor panels, cabin lighting, hardware and fittings. However, the noise and dust clouds created by their equipment was not popular in the area. In 1983 the company was able to move to West Malling, as it had won a contract with Saab Aircraft to design and fit the interiors of its new twin-prop airliner, the SF340.

Another Saab SF340 is nearing completion in the 'J' type hangar used by Metair Aircraft Equipment Ltd. The customer was American Eagle, which operated fifty-three of these twin-engine turboprop passenger aircraft.

The Britten-Norman Islander had many variants. This airborne early warning (AEW) Defender BN-2T, G-TEMI, was fitted with Thorn EMI Skymaster radar, with a limited range of 100nm and a limited performance. No orders were taken and the project was dropped.

Metair worked on several different types, one of these being Jetstream 31 G-BKUY. Originally manufactured by Handley Page Ltd, it is seen here in British Aerospace livery.

G-44A Widgeon N444M/1411. Following a crash at Sevenoaks reservoir in 1981, it was given a complete overhaul and flown to West Malling on 19 October 1985 for repaint. Metair later restored the interior, when this photo was taken. This aircraft returned to the USA in 1987, where it flies today.

The company also customised each aircraft with the appropriate external livery of the operator, for example Crossair and Delta. A new location with large hangars and offices was essential and West Malling, with its intact buildings, was ideal. The offices in the control tower were taken over by senior staff. The large T2 hangar, opposite the control tower, became workshops and a paint shop was installed. The drawing office staff moved into the offices alongside and attached to the hangar. It was not an easy task converting and accommodating the Second World War buildings for new technology, as more than twenty years had passed since the RAF vacated the airfield. In fact, the roof still had visible damage from when the Luftwaffe attacked the airfield; fortunately the bomb that hit the roof bounced off and caused little damage apart from a dent.

At the time West Malling was completely intact, and even the blast pens situated at the lower end of the airfield had survived. Metair was one of only six companies, five being in the United States, that met the new and ever changing flammability test standards required. It had its own Ohio State University chamber, which enabled regular testing of new materials to be installed in the SF340s.

Hawker Siddeley 125 700B G-BHSU first flew in 1980 and was refurbished by Metair during the late 1980s. At the time it was owned by Shell Aviation.

Stored at West Malling in one of the 'J' hangars was Auster J.1 Autocrat G-AGYK. Built in 1946, this aircraft is still flying today.

The first SF340, registration SE-F22, destined for an unknown customer and carrying the Saab logo on the fuselage, was handed back to the Swedish company during a special ceremony on 9 June 1988. Some thirty-one different schemes were eventually fitted into 125 production aircraft. Each aircraft interior was unique as the customer specified the colour scheme for the interior materials and the galley, including the seating. Each aircraft arrived from Linkoping, Sweden, with a completely bare interior and unpainted exterior. The turnaround time was approximately fourteen days. One of the final checks before final handover was a flight to check the sound insulation. Staff could volunteer for this free flight, which involved a person seated at various locations in the aircraft, including sitting on the toilet, to check sound levels. As can be imagined, the waiting list was long and the author, who was employed as a draughtsman, eventually got a chance to fly in an SF340. By 1988 all aircraft were series 'A' but from No. 166 the series 'B' began to arrive.

As well as the SF340 contract, Metair worked on private and other manufacturer's aircraft. A Grumman Widgeon had a new interior fitted, and some technical installations were undertaken on small helicopters. One of the more unusual aircraft fitted was the Gulfstream IV, of which there were three: N43GA, N435GA and N17603. The customer of these was kept quiet, but one was destined for the Middle East and fitted with sumptuous

On 9 June 1990, Metair officially handed over a Saab SF340, the world's first commercial airliner to meet strict new phase-two international fire regulations which came into force in August 1990. Lord Brabazon, Parliamentary Under-Secretary of State for Transport and Minister of Aviation and Shipping, attended the event, and many Metair staff and guests were present.

Today, the control tower has been restored and is occupied by a Costa Coffee shop, at least it has been saved.

The entrance to the officers' mess, which can be visited if requested prior to a visit to the site, known today as Kings Hill Estate and Business Park. Many young pilots and crews passed through its doors.

materials and extremely expensive toilet and galley facilities. It was so hush-hush a small office was prepared for the customer's security guards!

Rumours began to circulate that Metair was to be taken over by Hunting Group and later Field Aviation Group, which took place in 1988–89. There were, of course, concerns that apart from jobs being lost, the company would lose its identity but the takeover seemed to run smoothly. However, Kent County Council along with the Rouse Kent company, wanted to develop the airfield for housing, a golf course and as a business park. Despite meetings and protests, this went ahead and Metair, now under the wing of Hunting Aviation Group, had to vacate the airfield. It moved to Biggin Hill to take over the T2 hangar originally used by No. 600 (City of London) Sqn, RAuxAF.

Sadly, like so many successful British aerospace companies, Metair no longer exists, but its contribution to British and international civil aviation and the history of West Malling will not be forgotten.

The RAF air displays at West Malling were popular in the late 1940s and 1950–60s, and who would have thought that West Malling would host such events again.

The warbirds air show on 27 September 1995. Far left is Dove G-ARDE, the pleasure flight aircraft is a DH.83C Fox Moth, and also visible is Fournier RF.4D G-AVLW. Blast pens can be seen in the background.

Fairey Flycatcher S1287 '5', a replica of this famous biplane, was first registered as G-BEYB on 17 July 1977. In July 1996 it moved to the Fleet Air Arm Museum and is now in the Reserve Collection. It is seen here at the 1984 Great Warbirds Air Show.

However, in 1981, following the success of the TV series *We'll Meet Again*, in which the main star was B-17G Flying Fortress G-BEDF, Ted White, who operated Euroworld Ltd, came up with the idea of the Great Warbirds Display. The first airshow took place in 1982 and it was a resounding success, with many classic aircraft flying throughout the show. For ten years these shows attracted thousands of spectators, including veterans, until the last took place on the weekend of 25/26 August 1991. With the impending closure of the airfield this was a sad event, especially for those who worked at Metair.

Mosquito T.Mk.III G-ASKH RR299 'HH-T', owned by BAE, appeared at the Great Warbirds Air Show on 1 July 1984. Tragically, it crashed during a display at Manchester Barton on 21 July 1996, killing Kevin Moorhouse and Steve Watson.

Fokker Triplane DR.1 G-BEFR, a Redfern replica constructed in 1976, seen at West Malling in 1984. Robin Bowes, pilot and owner, was killed when the aircraft crashed at Stourhead Gardens, Mere, Wiltshire, on 20 July 1995. Behind stands Pitts Special G-BBOH of the Marlboro display team.

On the Friday prior to the shows staff could indulge themselves in nostalgia, as some of the aircraft arrived for the event. It was also possible to have a look around the machines, chat to aircrew, pilots and technical staff, and take photos. Often Metair staff could be seen at lunchtime, pushing aircraft into hangars. Such opportunities sadly do not occur these days. During the show the flight line was close to the activities and the aircraft flew low overhead, performing their manoeuvres and delighting old and young. Those who worked for Metair were indeed privileged.

Hunter T.7 XL565 gave an impressive display at West Malling in July 1984. Today it can be found at Bruntingthorpe, Leicestershire, and owned by Geoffrey Pool, but it is only taxiable.

Doves on the flight line at the Great Warbirds Airshow on 25 August 1986. Left to right: G-ASMG, G-ALFM and G-ARDE.

In 1989 West Malling celebrated its history by commemorating the fiftieth anniversary of the inauguration of the airfield as an RAF station. On 1 June, the event began with a marchpast by No. 29 Sqn and The Queen's Colour Squadron RAF and Central Band through West Malling. At the airfield, a static display of aircraft awaited visitors, it was a low-key event and visitors were able to walk around the airfield and its historic buildings. Some were veterans who had served there, and those who attended knew it was the final opportunity to enjoy the site and sounds of this historic Kent airfield.

Today, despite the massive housing development, there remain many complete buildings once used by the RAF, and, of course, there is the magnificent memorial to those who served, which was finally unveiled on Sunday, 9 July 2002. Following the ceremony, a fly past was given by Carolyn Grace in Spitfire Mk.IX ML907 and the Tiger Club, then based at Headcorn. But despite all this, all the hangars and runways have gone. Some roads are named after aircraft and pilots, while several paving slabs display plaques celebrating aircraft and events. The control tower still stands and is a coffee house, and it does have echoes of its past history. At least this historic building was spared demolition, just! However, it could be said that the control tower would have been an ideal location for a museum, dedicated to all those who served at West Malling airfield, an airfield that not only contributed so much in its daytime role but as night fighter base during the Second World War and the Cold War.

Today the RAF officers' mess, now known as the Gibson Building, looks much the same as it appeared during the war and after. The plaque was added in recent times in memory of Group Captain Guy Gibson VC, DSO, DFC.

On Sunday, 9 June 2002, a memorial was unveiled at Kings Hill/West Malling. The sculpture was created by Kate Denton and is without a doubt a magnificent tribute to all who served at the airfield from its early days as a flying club until it finally closed.

The running pilot is flanked by four slabs. These two are engraved with a brief description of the event when, in 1943, several German Fw 190s landed by mistake. The other refers to Lysanders of No. 26 Sqn and No. 85 Sqn Javelins.

The other two slabs refer to twenty-eight years of RAF occupation of West Malling airfield, and also pays tribute to all RAF personnel and civilians who served there.

Visiting aircraft seen at RAF West Malling

Various aircraft visited West Malling. Hunter F.6 XG159 is identified as belonging to No. 56 Sqn by the chequered squadron markings below the cockpit. This photo was taken at the airfield during 1960.

A more unusual visitor to West Malling is Supermarine Swift FR.5 WK305 of No. 79 Sqn, which arrived during August 1959. This aircraft spent its last days being used for fire training at Leconfield.

P-255, an F-84F of No. 315 Sqn, Netherlands Air Force, visited West Malling in 1969. It had also been seen at Chivenor.

Meteor NF.14 WS725 of No. 25 Sqn on display at West Malling during 1956. It remained with the squadron until it was struck off charge on 16 April 1962. (E.T. Sergison)

During the 1950s the Prentice T.1 was used as a trainer and was considered to be an improvement on the Tiger Moth as it had a closed cockpit. Prentice VS322 'FB-DQ' was with No. 24 OTU. (MAP)

Auster TW461 'PF-D' of No. 227 OCU at West Malling during 1949. (E.T Sergison)

Anson T.1 VV881 was one of several aircraft assigned to West Malling's station flight for communication purposes, remaining at the airfield until May 1960. (MAP)

Shackleton MR.3 WR976/F of No. 206 Sqn, which appeared at the West Malling air display in 1960. This aircraft crashed into the sea off St Mawgan on 19 November 1967. (MAP)

Hunter F.6 XG159/P of No. 56 Sqn on display at West Malling in 1960. The chequered pattern on the nose section was unique to this distinguished squadron. (E.T. Sergison)

Jet Provost T.1 XD675 of No. 2 Flying Training School and Central Flying School was a visitor to West Malling in 1960. (E.T. Sergison)

Canberra B.6 WT303 of No. 12 Sqn at the air display in 1960. This aircraft eventually went overseas to India in 1969. (MAP)

Lincoln B.Mk.2 RA693 of the Bomber Command Bombing School. It was struck off charge on 17 December 1959. (MAP)

Provost T.1 XF685 of No. 20 Elementary Training Pilots School in 1960. This type was used extensively by the RAF and other air forces. (KAHRS)

This T-33A, 57-0547 of the 20th Tactical Fighter Wing at RAF Wethersfield, flew during the air display at West Malling during 1960. This aircraft also served with the 81st Tactical Fighter Wing at Bentwaters. (MAP)

339

The air shows of the 1980s attracted thousands of visitors. Dove G-ARDE was christened *Sir Geoffrey de Havilland*, in BOAC (British Overseas Airways) livery. This aircraft now hangs from the ceiling of the Al Mahatta Museum, Emirate of Sharjah.

Mosquito TT.35 RB580 'HT-L' (true identity RS712) in its markings for the films *633 Squadron* and *Mosquito Squadron*. It was stored by Short Brothers at West Malling in the 1970s. Six years later, during November 1975, Neil Williams, the well-known aviator, flew it to Scotland via West Malling, for the Strathallan Collection.

The Mosquito streaks past West Malling's main hangar, to the delight of spectators. RS712 was registered as G-ASKB and is now on display at the EAA Aviation Museum, Oshkosh, USA.

Appendix 1

V1s destroyed by squadrons based at RAF West Malling 1944

16 June – No. 91 Sqn (Spitfire MK.XIV)

Flight Lieutenant H.B. Moffet RCAF	RM617/DL-G	1035-1110	Kenley

17 June – No. 91 Sqn (Spitfire Mk.XIV)

Flying Officer G.C. McKay RCAF	RB174/DL-T	0520	Redhill area
Flying Officer P.A. Shade	RB180/DL-E	1550	Hastings
Flying Officer A.R. Cruickshank RCAF	NH654/DL-	Shared	

16/17 June – No. 96 Sqn (Mosquito Mk.XIII)

Flight Lieutenant D.L. Ward	HK415/ZJ-R	2302-0208	over Channel
Squadron Leader A. Parker-Rees	MM947/ZJ-?	2230	off Dover

17/18 June – No. 96 Sqn (Mosquito Mk.XIII)

Name	Aircraft	Time	Location
Flight Lieutenant W.J. Gough	MM499/ZJ-V	2241-0145	off Calais
Flying Officer R.F. Ball	HK372/ZJ-?	2250-0235	off Hastings

18 June – No. 91 Sqn (Spitfire Mk.XIV)

Name	Aircraft	Time	Location
Capitaine J.M. Maridor (FF)	RB161/DL-I	1200	West Malling area
Squadron Leader N.A. Kynaston	RB185/DL-	1420	London outskirts
Squadron Leader P. McC. Bond	RB161/DL-I	1510	Croydon/West Malling
Flying Officer A.R. Elcock	RB177/DL-I	1645-1750	West Malling
Flight Lieutenant A. Smith RNZAF	RB173/DL-	2015	West Malling area
Flying Officer R.A. McPhie RCAF	RB182/DL-V	Shared	
Squadron Leader P. McC. Bond	RB161/DL-I	Shared	
Flight Lieutenant R.S. Nash	RB169/DL-Q	2030	West Malling area
Flight Lieutenant A. Smith RNZAF	RB173/DL	Shared	
Flying Officer R.A. McPhie RCAF	RB182/DL-V	Shared	
Flight Lieutenant R.S. Nash	RB169/DL-Q	2040	Gravesend–London
Flight Lieutenant A. Smith RNZAF	RB173/DL-		
Flying Officer R.A. McPhie RCAF	RB182/DL-V	2210	Croydon area
Flight Lieutenant R.S. Nash	RB169/DL-Q	2315	Beachy Head
	RB169/DL-Q	2315-2350	Shared
Squadron Leader N.A. Kynaston	RB185/DL-	2320	off Dungeness

18/19 June – No. 96 Sqn (Mosquito Mk.XIII)

Flying Officer J. Goode	HK406	2230 and 2340	near Hastings
	HK406	2340	

19 June – No. 91 Sqn (Spitfire Mk.XIV)

Lieutenant H.F. de Bordas FF	NH654/DL-	1930	Beachy Head
Flight Lieutenant J.W.P. Draper RCAF	RM617/DL-G	1940	Tunbridge Wells
Lieutenant H.B. Moffet RCAF	NH701/DL-A	2155	Battle
Lieutenant H.F. de Bordas FF	RB181/DL-	2230	Uckfield
Flying Officer J.A. Faulkner RCAF	RM617/DL-G		
Flight Sergeant G. Kay	RB188/DL-K	2310 Shared	off Beachy Head

20 June – No. 91 Sqn (Spitfire Mk.XIV)

Flight Sergeant J.A. Brown	NH707/DL-	2240	Reigate area
Flying Officer C.I.M. Ettles	RB161/DL-I	2240	Bexhill area
Flying Officer C.I.M. Ettles	shared kill with Flight Lieutenant McCaw, No. 486 Sqn		

21 June – No. 91 Sqn (Spitfire Mk.XIV)

Flying Officer E. Topham	NH707/DL-	0640	West Malling area
Squadron Leader P. McC. Bond	RB161/DL-I	0720	Channel

30 June – No. 610 Sqn (Spitfire Mk.XIV)

Squadron Leader R.A. Newbery	RB159/DW-D	1145-1245	Channel
Pilot Officer R.C. Hussey	DW-?	2050-2155	Channel
Squadron Leader R.A. Newbery	RB159/DW-D	2130-2215	Channel
Flight Lieutenant D.W. Johnston	USAAF DW-?	2230-2310	Channel

21 June – No. 41 Sqn (Spitfire Mk.XII)

Pilot Officer N.P. Gibbs	MB875/EB-G	0745-0845	Hastings–Beachy Head

21 June – No. 322 (Dutch) Sqn (Spitfire Mk.XIV)

Flight Sergeant R.L. van Beers	VL-?	Dawn	Not known

22 June – No. 41 Sqn (Spitfire Mk.XII)

Flight Lieutenant C.R. Birbeck	MB841	0647	off Pevensey
Flying Officer R.E. Anderson RAAF	MB837/EP-B		
Flight Sergeant C.S. Robertson RAAF	MB875/EB-G	1125-1222	Pevensey area

22 June – No.322 (Dutch) Sqn (Spitfire Mk.XIV)

Flight Lieutenant J.L. Plesman	VL-?	0440	exploded in mid-air
Flying Officer C.R.R. Manders	VL-?	0555	
Flying Officer R.F. van Daalen Wetters	VL-L	1906	

345

22 June – No. 610 Sqn (Spitfire Mk.XIV)

Name	Aircraft	Time	Area
Flight Lieutenant J.B. Shepherd	DW-	0520-0625	Channel
Flying Officer G.M. McKinlay	RB142/DW-?		
Squadron Leader R.A. Newbery	RB159/DW-D	0540-0610	Channel
	RB159/DW-D	0700-0810	Channel
Warrant Officer R. Roberts	DW-?	1000-1130	

22 June – No. 91 Sqn (Spitfire Mk.XIV)

Name	Aircraft	Time	Area
Flying Officer K.R. Collier RAAF	RB188/DL-K	0540	Epsom area
Capitaine J.M. Maridor FF	RB180/DL-E	0750 Shared	Bexhill area
	RB180/DL-E	0800 Shared	Tunbridge Wells area
Flying Officer C.I.M. Ettles RCAF	NH698/DL-F	1900	Gatwick area

23 June – No. 41 Sqn (Spitfire Mk.XII)

Name	Aircraft	Time	Area
Flight Lieutenant T.A.H. Slack	EB-?	0450	Hastings area
Pilot Officer J.C.J. Payne	EB-?	0840	Rye area
Flying Officer M.A.L. Balaase (Belgian)	MB830/EB-	0830	Hastings area
Flight Lieutenant T. Spencer	MB856/EB-X	2302	Hastings area

23 June – No. 91 Sqn (Spitfire Mk.XIV)

Name	Aircraft	Time	Area
Flight Lieutenant R.H. Dibnah RCAF	RB173/DL-	0655	Tonbridge area
Flight Sergeant T.B. Burnett	RB174/DL-T	0655	Sevenoaks area

V1S DESTROYED BY SQUADRONS

Flying Officer G.H. Huntley	RB181/DL-	0710 Shared	Tunbridge Wells area
Flight Sergeant G. Kay	RB165/DL-	1630	West Malling area
Wing Commander R.W. Oxspring	NH714/RWO	1700 Shared	Redhill–Edenbridge
Squadron Leader N.A. Kynaston	RB185/DL-	1725	Hastings area
	RB185/DL-	1740	
Flight Lieutenant H.D. Johnson	RB188/DL-K	1745 Shared	Eastbourne area
Flight Sergeant G. Kay	RB165/DL-	1840 Shared	Uckfield area
Flying Officer J.A. Faulkner RCAF	RM617/DL-G	2125 Shared	East Grinstead area
Flying Officer K.R. Collier RAAF	NM698/DL-	2240	East Grinstead area

23 June – No. 322 (Dutch) Sqn (Spitfire Mk.XIV)

Flying Officer J. van Arkel	VL-V	2145	Tonbridge area
Flying Officer M.L. van Bergen	VL-N		
Maj. K.C. Juhlmann SAAF	NH586/VL-G	2230	

23 June – No. 610 Sqn (Spitfire Mk.XIV)

Squadron Leader R.A. Newbery	RB159/DW-D	0440-0520	Channel
Flying Officer S.A. Jones	DW-?		
Pilot Officer B.R. Scamen RCAF	DW-?	1535-1640	Channel
Warrant Officer R. Roberts	DW-?	2005-2110	Channel

24 June – No. 41 Sqn (Spitfire Mk.XII)

Pilot Officer N.F. Gibbs	MB875/EB-G	0615	Hastings area
Flight Sergeant R.L. Short	EN620/EB-F	dusk	Channel
Flight Lieutenant T. Spencer	EN224/EB-L	dusk	Hastings area

24 June – No. 610 Sqn (Spitfire Mk.XIV)

Squadron Leader R.A. Newbery	RB159/DW-D	0525-0640	Channel
Squadron Leader R.A. Newbery	RB159/DW-D	0525-0640 (shared Channel)	
Flying Officer P.M. Bangerter	DW-?	(shared)	

24 June – No. 91 Sqn (Spitfire Mk.XIV)

Flight Lieutenant J.W.P. Draper RCAF	NH165/DL-	0650	Hastings area
Flight Lieutenant H.D. Johnson	RB188/DL-K	0650	Hawkinge area

25 June – No. 41 Sqn (Spitfire Mk.XII)

Warrant Officer P.T. Coleman	MB841/EB-C	1850-2000	Bexhill area

25 June – No. 91 Sqn (Spitfire Mk.XIV)

Flight Lieutenant R.S. Nash	RB169/DL-Q	0425	Maidstone area
Lieutenant H.F. de Bordas FF	NH654/DL-	2310	Tenterden area

V1S DESTROYED BY SQUADRONS

27 June – No. 322 (Dutch) Sqn (Spitfire Mk.XIV)

Pilot	Code	Time	Location
Flight Sergeant R.L. van Beers	VL-H	0920	Beachy Head area
Flight Sergeant C. Kooij	VL-Q	1215	Frittenden area
Flight Sergeant J.H. Harms	VL-J	1353	Grid R23
Flight Lieutenant J.L. Plesman	VL-J	1400	Dungeness area
Flying Officer M.L. van Bergen	VL-N	1825	Malling area
Flying Officer J. van Arkel	VL-T		Edenbridge area

28 June – No. 322 (Dutch) Sqn (Spitfire Mk.XIV)

Pilot	Code	Time	Location
Flying Officer L.D. Wolters	VL-N	1310 (shared)	Wadhurst area
Warrant Officer J.A. Maier	VL-Q	1540	off Hastings
Flying Officer G.F.J. Jongbloed	VL-C	2230	West Malling area
Flight Sergeant F. van Valkenburg	NH649/VL-F	2240	off Beachy Head

29 June – No. 322 (Dutch) Sqn (Spitfire Mk.XIV)

Pilot	Code	Time	Location
Flying Officer F.W.L.S. Speetjens	VL-J	0635	Luckhurst area
Flying Officer G.F.J. Jongbloed	VL-K	0712	Tenterden area
Flight Sergeant M.J. Janseen	VL-D	0850	Staplehurst area
Flying Officer R.F. Burgwal	NH649/VL-F	1215	Grid R2951
	NH649/VL-F	1233	High Halden area

Flying Officer M.A. Muller	VL-T	1710	Staplehurst area
Flight Lieutenant J.L. Plesman	VL-W	1930	off Hastings
Flying Officer L.D. Wolters	VL-N	2047	Battle area
Flying Officer F.J.H. van Eijk	NH699/VL-R	2120	West Malling area
Flight Sergeant W. de Vries	VL-Q	2210	exploded in mid-air

30 June – No. 322 (Dutch) Sqn (Spitfire Mk.XIV)

Flying Officer L.M. Meijers	VL-J	0920	Newchurch area
Flying Officer J. van Arkel	VL-D	1010	Ashford area
Flying Officer R.F. Burgwal	VL-E	1950	Grid R1837
	VL-E	2135	Grid R1930
Flying Officer J. Jonker	VL-K	2200	Grid R1147

1 July – No. 322 (Dutch) Sqn (Spitfire Mk.XIV)

Warrant Officer J.A. Maier	VL-T	1735	

3 July – No. 316 (Warsaw) Polish Sqn (Mustang Mk.III)

Flight Sergeant A. Murkowski (Polish)	FB352/SZ-C	1910	exploded in mid0air

3 July – No. 322 (Dutch) Sqn (Spitfire Mk.XIV)

Flight Sergeant H.C. Cramm	NH699/VL-R	1700	off Dungeness

V1S DESTROYED BY SQUADRONS

Flying Officer J. Jonker	RB160/VL-A	1813	off Dungeness
Flying Officer F.J.H. van Eijk	VL-U	2300	West Malling area
Pilot Officer A.A. Homburg	VL-Y	2300	

4 July – No. 316 (Warsaw) Polish Sqn (Mustang Mk.III)

Warrant Officer A. Murkowski	FB374/SZ-A	1115	Lydd–Rye
Flight Sergeant A. Pietrzak	FB161/SZ-I	1145	off Boulogne

4 July – No. 322 (Dutch) Sqn (Spitfire Mk.XIV)

Flying Officer J. Jonker	VL-D	1857	Grid Q9328
Flying Officer R.F. Burgwal	NH649/VL-F	2030	Grid Q9959
Flying Officer F.W.L.S. Speetjens	RB160/VL-A	2248	Redhill area

5 July – No. 316 (Warsaw) Polish Sqn (Mustang Mk.III)

Flying Officer T. Karnkowski	FB352/SZ-C	1328	Ham Street area
Flight Sergeant S. Sztuka	FB378/SZ-X	1445	Rye area
Flight Lieutenant S. Litak	FB376/SZ-Q	1445	Staplehurst area
Warrant Officer C. Bartlomiejczyk	FB359/SZ-V	1645	Ashford area
	FB359/SZ-V	1650	Mereworth area
Flying Officer T. Karnkowski	FB384/SZ-Z	1803	Sutton Valence

5 July – No. 322 (Dutch) Sqn (Spitfire Mk.XIV)

Flight Sergeant M.J. Janssen	VL-D	1230	Fairfield area
	VL-D	1320	Grid R4377
Flight Lieutenant L.C.M. van Eendenburg	RB184/VL-B	1229	Grid Q78
	RB184/VL-B	1327	Appledore area

6 July – No. 316 (Warsaw) Polish Sqn (Mustang Mk.III)

Flight Sergeant S. Sztuka	FB378/SZ-X	0640	Wrotham area

6 July – No. 322 (Dutch) Sqn (Spitfire Mk.XIV)

Flight Sergeant Hendrik Cramm – claimed V1
destroyed but this was disallowed

7 July – No. 316 (Warsaw) Polish Sqn (Mustang Mk.III)

Warrant Officer F. Marek	FB391/SZ-E	0510	Battle area
Warrant Officer W. Grobelny	FB396/SZ-F	0615	off Beachy Head
Warrant Officer T. Szymanski	FB377/SZ-R	1519	Appledore
Sgt J. Mielnicki	FB386/SZ-N	1540	Bexhill area
Flight Lieutenant L. Majewski	FB351/SZ-B	1625	Alfriston area
	FB351/SZ-B (shared)	1630	Polegate area
Sgt J. Mielnicki	FB386/SZ-N	1955	Tonbridge area
Flight Sergeant A. Pietrzak	FB161/SZ-I	1958	off Bexhill

7 July – No. 91 Sqn (Spitfire Mk.XIV)

Flight Lieutenant R.S. Nash	RB169/DL-Q	0540	Dartford area
Flight Lieutenant A.R. Cruickshank RCAF	RB165/DL-L	1335	Pluckley Station
Flight Lieutenant A.R. Elcock	RM615/DL-H	1515	Rochester area
Flying Officer W.C. Marshall	NH720/DL-H	1523	Tunbridge Wells area
	NH720/DL-H	1730	Ham Street area
Squadron Leader N.A. Kynaston	RB185/DL-	2005	Detling area
Flight Lieutenant A.R. Cruickshank RCAF	RB165/DL-L	2035	Wormshill area
Flight Lieutenant H.D. Johnson	RB183/DL-M	2100	Appledore area
Flying Officer H.M. Neil	RB174/DL-T	2100	West Malling area
Squadron Leader N.A. Kynaston	RB185/DL-	2135	Ashford area
Flying Officer P.A. Shade	RM620/DL-E	2335	Rye area
Flying Officer W.C. Marshall	NH720/DL-T	2336	Dungeness area

8 July – No. 91 Sqn (Spitfire Mk.XVI)

Flying Officer R.A. McPhie RCAF	RB182/DL-V	2300	exploded in mid-air
Flying Officer R. McPhie RNZAF	NH705/DL-P	Shared	

8 July – No. 316 (Warsaw) Polish Sqn (Mustang Mk.III)

Flight Lieutenant A. Cholajda	FB384/SZ-Z	2132	Ticehurst area
	FB384/SZ-Z	2135	Rotherfield

Flying Officer T. Karnkowski	FB359/SZ-V (shared)	2150	Beckley area
	FB359/SZ-V	2155	Robertsbridge
Flight Lieutenant T. Szymankiewicz	FB391/SZ-E	2200	Beckley area
Flight Sergeant A. Murkowski	FB351/SZ-B	2205	off Dungeness

8 July – No. 322 (Dutch) Sqn (Spitfire MK.XIV)

Flight Sergeant H.C. Cramm	VL-T	0430	Dungeness area
Flying Officer R.F. Burgwal	NH586/VL-G	2127	Grid R4757
	NH586/VL-G	2134	
	NH586/VL-G	2142	
	NH586/VL-G	2153	
	NH586/VL-G	(shared)	
Flying Officer J. Jonker	VL-K	2206	exploded in mid-air
Flight Lieutenant L.C.M. van Eendenburg	RB184/VL-B	2316	West Malling area

9 July – No. 316 (Warsaw) Polish Sqn (Mustang Mk.III)

Flying Officer T. Karnkowski	FB351/SZ-B	0519	off Dungeness
Flight Lieutenant T. Szymankiewicz	FB391/SZ-E	0524	off Dungeness
Warrant Officer J. Feruga	FB378/SZ-X	2140	off Boulogne
Flight Lieutenant S. Litak	FB351/SZ-B	2230	Goudhurst area
Flight Lieutenant T. Szymankiewicz	FB396/SZ-F	2255	off Dungeness

9 July – No. 322 (Dutch) Sqn (Spitfire Mk.XIV)

Name	Aircraft	Time	Location
Flight Sergeant H.C. Cramm	NH699/VL-R	2245	
	NH699/VL-R	2248	

9 July – No. 91 Sqn (Spitfire Mk.XIV)

Name	Aircraft	Time	Location
Flight Lieutenant R.S. Nash	RB169/DL-Q	1205	Paddock Wood
Lieutenant H.F. de Bordas (FF)	NH720/DL-H	2020	Exploded
Flying Officer K.R. Collier RAAF	RB183/DL-M	2130	Swanley Junction
Flight Lieutenant J.W.P. Draper RCAF	RM620/DL-E	2158	Goudhurst area
Flying Officer W.C. Marshall	NH701/DL-A	2206	Exploded Lydd
Flying Officer K.R. Collier RAAF	RB183/DL-M	2220	Chatham area

10 July – No. 322 (Dutch) Sqn (Spitfire Mk.XIV)

Name	Aircraft	Time	Location
Flight Lieutenant J.L. Plesman	VL-	020	
Flight Sergeant L.C.M. van Eendenburg	RB184/VL-B	1440	

10/11 July – No. 409 (Nighthawk) RCAF Sqn (Mosquito Mk.XIII)

Name	Aircraft	Time	Location
Flight Lieutenant K.G. Rayment	HK514/PS-?	0155-0525	Portsmouth area

355

10 July – No. 91 Sqn (Spitfire Mk.XIV)

Lieutenant H.F. de Bordas FF	RB181/DL-W	0141	unknown
Flying Officer G. Balcombe	NH705/DL-P	1440	off Beachy Head
Squadron Leader N.A. Kynaston	NH714/RWO	1450	Tunbridge Wells
Flight Sergeant T.B. Burnett	RB181/DL-W	1630	Sevenoaks area
Flying Officer E. Topham	NH698/DL-Y	1920	Wittersham area
Flying Officer M.J. Costello RNZAF	RB161/DL-I	1922	Maidstone area
Squadron Leader N.A. Kynaston	RB185/DL-	2049	Hailsham area

10/11 July – No. 91 Sqn (Spitfire Mk.XIV)

Squadron Leader P. McC. Bond	RM162/DL-	0925	Sevenoaks area
Flying Officer J. Monihan	RM620/DL-E	Shared	
Squadron Leader N.A. Kynaston	RB185/DL-	1547	exploded in mid-air
Lieutenant H.F. de Bordas FF	NH720/DL-H	1748	Ashford area
Squadron Leader N.A. Kynaston	RB185/DL-	1940	Ashford area
Flight Lieutenant A.R. Cruickshank	RB182/DL-V	2056	exploded in mid-air

11 July – No. 322 (Dutch) Sqn (Spitfire Mk.XIV)

Flying Officer L.M. Meijers	VL-H	0917	Grid R2564
Flying Officer M.A. Muller	VL-T	1430	Bexhill area
Flying Officer C.R.R. Manders	VL-V	2055	Grid R3545

Pilot	Aircraft	Time	Location
Flying Officer F.J.H. van Eijk	VL-U	2058	exploded in mid-air
Warrant Officer J.A. Maier	NH686/VL-M	2103	Grid 3543
12 July – No. 322 (Dutch) Sqn (Spitfire Mk.XIV)			
Flying Officer C.R.R. Manders	VL-V	0855	Maidstone area
Flight Sergeant M.J. Janseen	VL-E	1515	Grid R3968
	VL-E	1730	River Medway
Flying Officer J. Vlug	RB160/VL-A	1749	Sissinghurst area
Flying Officer J. Jongbloed	NH586/VL-G	2110	Cranbrook area
Warrant Officer J.A. Maier	RM678/VL-Q	2110 (shared)	Dungeness area
12 July – No. 91 Sqn (Spitfire Mk.XIV)			
Flying Officer J.A. Faulkner RCAF	RB173/DL-	0715	off Dungeness
Flight Lieutenant J.W.P. Draper RCAF	RM621/DL-	0830	Beachy Head area
13 July – No. 91 Sqn (Spitfire Mk.XIV)			
Flight Lieutenant R.S. Nash	RB169/DL-Q	1004	exploded in mid-air
Squadron Leader N.A. Kynaston	RB185/DL-	1500	exploded in mid-air
Lieutenant H. De Bordas FF	NH720/DL-H	Shared	
13 July – No. 322 (Dutch) Sqn (Spitfire Mk.XIV)			
Flight Sergeant M.J. Janseen	RB160/VL-A	1005	No details

Flight Sergeant J.H. Harms	RB141/VL-L	1030	No details
14 July – No. 322 (Dutch) Sqn (Spitfire Mk.XIV)			
Flight Sergeant R. van Beers	VL-H	1516	Grid R3967
Flight Sergeant M.J. Janseen	VL-C	1805	Tonbridge area
Flight Lieutenant Plesman	VL-W	1826	Robertsbridge area
	VL-W	1830	exploded in mid-air
14 July – No. 91 Sqn (Spitfire Mk.XIV)			
Squadron Leader N.A. Kynaston	RB161/DL-I	1842	West Malling area
15 July – No. 91 Sqn (Spitfire Mk.XIV)			
Flight Lieutenant H.B. Moffet RCAF	NH701/DL-A	1728	Wrotham area
16 July – No. 91 Sqn (Spitfire Mk.XIV)			
Flying Officer P.A. Shade	RM654/DL-F	1230	off Dymchurch
16 July – No. 322 (Dutch) Sqn (Spitfire Mk.XIV)			
Flying Officer J. Jongbloed	NH586/VL-G	1035	Grid R2472
Flying Officer J. van Arkel	VL-V	1055	Grid R1565

18 July – No. 322 (Dutch) Sqn (Spitfire Mk.XIV)

Flight Lieutenant L.C.M. Eendenburg	RB160/VL-A	1740	Grid R0761
Flying Officer J. Vlug	VL-K	1937	Grid R4165
	VL-K	2206	Grid R2959

18 July – No. 91 Sqn (Spitfire Mk.XIV)

Flying Officer R.A. McPhie RCAF	NH705/DL-P	1700-1800	

19 July – No. 322 (Dutch) Sqn (Spitfire Mk.XIV)

Flight Lieutenant L.C.M. van Eendenburg	RB184/VL-B	0959	Paddock wood
Flying Officer G.F.J. Jongbloed	VL-E	1045	Grid R3159
Flying Officer J. Vlug	VL-D		
Flying Officer R.F. Burgwal	NH649/VL-F	1133	Wittersham area
Flight Lieutenant J.L. Plesman	VL-W	1320	Hawkhurst area
Flying Officer G.F.J. Jongbloed	VL-E	1320	GR1535
Flying Officer P.A. Cramerus	VL-U	1825	

18/19 July – No. 91 Sqn (Spitfire Mk.XIV)

Squadron Leader N.A. Kynaston	RM654/DL-F	1130	Maidstone area
	RM654/DL-F	1530	Maidstone area
Lieutenant H.F. de Bordas FF	RB165/DL-L	1827	East Grinstead area

20 July – No. 91 Sqn (Spitfire Mk.XIV)

Flying Officer K.R. Collier RAAF	RM686/DL-G	0620	Lamberhurst area
Flight Lieutenant J.W.P. Draper RCAF	RM686/DL-G	0823	Tonbridge area
Flying Officer K.R. Collier RAAF	TM685/DL-M	0940	West Malling area
Flight Lieutenant A.R. Cruickshank RCAF	NH703/DL-	0948	East Grinstead area
Warrant Officer F.A. Lewis RCAF	NH686/DL-G	1020	Etchingham area

20 July – No. 322 (Dutch) Sqn (Spitfire Mk.XIV)

Flight Lieutenant J.L. Plesman	VL-W	0727	Ashford area
Flying Officer M.L. van Bergen	VL-U	0820	Appledore area

21 July – No. 91 Sqn (Spitfire Mk.XIV) Detached to Deanland ALG

Flight Lieutenant A.R. Cruickshank RCAF	RM649/DL-	1857	Uckfield area
Flying Officer A.R. Elcock	RM685/DL-M	2004	Tunbridge Wells area

22 July – No. 322 (Dutch) Sqn (Spitfire Mk.XIV) Detached to Deanland ALG

Flying Officer G.F.J. Jongbloed	VL-E	2057	Grid R0551
Flying Officer R.F. Burgwal	VL-C	2101	Tunbridge Wells
	VL-C	2112	Grid R0747

23 July – No. 322 (Dutch) Sqn (Spitfire Mk.XIV) Detached to Deanland ALG

Flying Officer G.F.J. Jongbloed	VL-E	0937	Grid R5663
Flying Officer C.R.R. Manders	VL-Y	1520	Grid R0939

23/24 July – No. 85 Sqn (Mosquito Mk.XVII)

Flying Officer J. Chipperfield	VY-W	0018	off Thames Estuary
Wing Commander de C.A. Woodhouse	VY-F	No details	

24 July – No. 322 (Dutch) Sqn (Spitfire Mk.XIV) Detached to Deanland ALG

Flying Officer R.F. Burgwal	VL-K	1653	Rye area
Flying Officer J. Jonker	VL-D	No details	

24/25 July – No. 157 Sqn (Mosquito Mk.XIX)

Flight Lieutenant J.D. Mathews	MM671/RS-C	2305	Tonbridge area
	2310		Tonbridge area

25/26 July – No. 85 Sqn (Mosquito Mk.XVII)

Captain T. Weisteen (Norwegian)	MM636/VY-A	0415	West Malling area
	MM636/VY-A	0455	West Malling area
Flight Lieutenant R.T. Goucher	TA400/VY-J	0430	Dungeness area

25/26 July – No. 157 Sqn (Mosquito Mk.XIX)			
Flight Lieutenant J.W. Caddie	MM681/RS-?Lost on patrol, North Foreland		Hawkhurst area
26/27 July – No. 85 Sqn (Mosquito Mk.XVII)			
Flying Officer E.R. Hedgecoe	HK120/VY-P	0003	
27/28 July – No. 85 Sqn (Mosquito Mk.XVII)			
Flight Lieutenant R.H. Farrell	HK119/VY-S	2220-0105	No details
28 July – No. 322 (Dutch) Sqn (Spitfire Mk.XIV) Detached to Deanland ALG			
Flight Sergeant M.J. Janseen	VL-D	2220	Grid R2575
Maj. K.C. Kuhlman SAAF	NH586/VL-G	2245	Lamberhurst area
28/29 July – No. 157 Sqn (Mosquito Mk.XIX)			
Flight Lieutenant E.J. Stevens	MM674/RS-T	0225	West Malling area
29 July – No. 322 (Dutch) Sqn (Spitfire Mk.XIV) Detached to Deanland ALG			
Flying Officer M.L. van Bergen	VL-T	1935	Tenterden area
Flying Officer L.D. Wolters	VL-N	2147 (shared)	Tunbridge Wells area

2 August – No. 322 (Dutch) Sqn (Spitfire Mk.XIV)

Flight Sergeant R.L. van Beers	VL-C	1254 (shared)	Tunbridge Wells area
	VL-C	1300	Tunbridge Wells area

3/4 August – No. 85 Sqn (Mosquito Mk.XVII/XIX)

Flight Lieutenant R.H. Farrell	HK119/VY-S	0200	exploded in mid-air
Pilot Officer L.J. York	TA400/VY-J	0258	off North Foreland
	TA400/VY-J	0310	off Deal
Flight Lieutenant P.A. Searle	VY-Q	0332	West Malling area

3/4 August – No. 157 Sqn (Mosquito Mk.XIX)

Pilot Officer W.S. Vale RAAF	MM671/RS-C	0124	West Malling area

4 August – No. 322 (Dutch) Sqn (Spitfire Mk.XIV)

Flight Lieutenant J. van Arkel	VL-W	2010	Grid R9539
Flight Lieutenant J.F. Plesman	VL-Z	2015-2035	Hailsham area

4/5 August – No. 85 Sqn (Mosquito Mk.XIV)

Flying Officer A.J. Owen	TA400/VY-J	0430	Tenterden area
Lieutenant E.P. Fossum (Norwegian)	MM648/VY-G	0445	Herne Bay area

3/4 August – No. 322 (Dutch) Sqn (Spitfire Mk.XIV)

Name	Code	Time	Location
Flying Officer J. Jonker	VL-K	1635	Grid R0637
Flying Officer R.F. Burgwal	RB184/VL-B	1624	Hastings area
	RB184/VL-B	1640	Uckfield area

5/6 August – No. 157 Sqn (Mosquito Mk.XIV)

Name	Code	Time	Location
Flying Officer C.N. Woodcock	MM652/RS-S	0326	Tunbridge Wells area

6 August – No. 322 (Dutch) Sqn (Spitfire Mk.XIV)

Name	Code	Time	Location
Flight Lieutenant J.F. Plesman	VL-P	2309	Channel

7 August – No.322 (Dutch) Sqn (Spitfire Mk.XIV)

Name	Code	Time	Location
Flying Officer R.F. Burgwal	VL-L	2306	No details

7/8 August – No. 157 Sqn (Mosquito Mk.XIX)

Name	Code	Time	Location
Flight Lieutenant J.O. Mathews	TA401/RS-D	0507	West Malling area
	TA401/RS-D	0513	exploded in mid-air
Squadron Leader J.H.M. Chisholm	MM676/RS-W	0555	over land

9/10 August – No. 157 Sqn (Mosquito Mk.XIX)

Name	Code	Time	Location
Flight Lieutenant E.J. Stevens	MM674/RS-T	0424	West Malling area

10 August – No. 322 (Dutch) Sqn (Spitfire Mk.XIV)

Flight Lieutenant J.L. Plesman	VL-W	0438	No details

10/11 August – No. 157 Sqn (Mosquito Mk.XIX)

Squadron Leader J.H.M. Chisholm	MM674/RS-T	0047	off Beachy Head

11/12 August – No. 85 Sqn (Mosquito Mk.XVII)

Warrant Officer W. Alderton	HK299/VY-C	0302	Maidstone area

10/11 August – No. 157 Sqn (Mosquito Mk.XIX)

Warrant Officer B. Miller	TA400/VY-J	0030-0330	No details
Warrant Officer S. Astley	MM674/RS-T	0125	near Maidstone

12/13 August – No. 85 Sqn (Mosquito Mk.XVII)

Wing Commander H. de C.A. Woodhouse	MM632/VY-E	0440 (FTR)	Channel
Squadron Leader B.A. Burbridge	HK349/VY-R	0610	off Maidstone
Flight Lieutenant P.A. Searle	HK120/VY-P	0631	Channel

14/15 August – No. 85 Sqn (Mosquito Mk.XIX)

Pilot Officer L.J. York	MM648/VY-G	0030-0320	Channel
Flight Lieutenant T.W. Redfern	TA400/VY-J	0400-0610	Channel

14/15 August – No. 157 Sqn (Mosquito Mk.XIX)

Flight Lieutenant R.D. Doleman RAAF	MM678/RS-A	0230	West Malling area

14/15 August – No. 274 Sqn (Tempest Mk.V)

Flight Lieutenant O.E. Willis	EJ628/JJ-?	1845	Sittingbourne area

15/16 August – No. 85 Sqn (Mosquito Mk.XIX)

Captain T. Weisteen (Norwegian)	VY-B	0716	off Folkestone

16 August – No. 274 Sqn (Tempest Mk.V)

Flight Lieutenant O.E. Willis	EJ640/JJ-?	0705	Sittingbourne area
Flight Lieutenant J.A. Malloy RCAF	EJ640/JJ-?	1615	
Flight Lieutenant L.P. Griffiths RNZAF	EJ647/JJ-?	1905	Faversham/Sittingbourne
Flying Officer J.W. Lyne	EJ634/JJ-?	1950 (shared)	Hastings
	EJ634/JJ-?	1955 (shared)	Hastings
	EJ634/JJ-?	2005	Ashford area
Flight Lieutenant J.A. Malloy RCAF	EJ633/JJ-?	2050	Grid R3488

17 August – No. 274 Sqn (Tempest Mk.V)

Wing Commander J.F. Fraser	EJ628/JJ-G	morning	West Malling area

19/20 August – No. 85 Sqn (Mosquito Mk.XIX)			
Squadron Leader B.A. Burbridge	VY-B	2150-0035	off Dungeness
23/24 August – No. 157 Sqn (Mosquito Mk.XIX)			
Flight Lieutenant P. Merrall	MM652/RS-S	0135-0410	Channel
Squadron Leader J.H.M. Chisholm	MM674/RS-T	0345-0650	Channel

Appendix 2

RAF West Malling – Station Flight

It was the responsibility of the commanding officer of every RAF base to control aircraft of the station flight. Details of these units' formation and disbandment were poorly recorded. The aircraft's code letters for those attached to the flight at West Malling was 4K, being allocated during September/October 1945. The following is a list of aircraft on charge at the airfield during 1944–56.

Percival Proctor Mk.III HM429
Tiger Moth R5172 (became G-AOIS in 1954)
Miles Master Mk.III W8838
North American Harvard Mk.IIB FX432
DH Mosquito T.3 serial?
DH Mosquito NF.36 VA893
Auster AOP.6 VF637
DH Vampire T.11 XD383
Airspeed Oxford VT185 (Dived into ground in snowstorm, Oak Green, Kent, 24 April 1950)
DHC Chipmunk T.10 WD308
Gloster Meteor F.4 VT185
Gloster Meteor T.7 WL470
Gloster Meteor F.8 serial?
Gloster Meteor NF.14 VZ407
Avro Anson Mk.XI
Avro Anson T.21 VV881

Appendix 3

Select presentation aircraft based at RAF West Malling during the Second World War

Alberville Spitfire Mk.Vb EP491

Arrived from Kingsnorth ALG on 15 July 1943, with No. 130 Sqn until 15 August 1943.

Baltic Exchange III Spitfire Mk.Vb W3249

With No, 92 Sqn at Biggin Hill on 17 July 1941. Returning from sweep, ran out of fuel and force-landed at West Malling. Sergeant C.H. Howard uninjured.

Belgium Spitfire Mk.Vb W3368

Moved from No. 122 (Bombay) Sqn to No. 234 Sqn (Madras Presidency) at West Malling on 15 August 1943.

Black Velvet Spitfire Mk.IIa P8380

Alloted to No. 74 Sqn, Gravesend, on 30 June 1941 and flown by Pilot Officer R.J.E. Boulding from West Malling 9/10 May 1941.

The Darlington Spitfire Mk.Vb W3320

Moved from No. 118 Sqn at RAF Peterhead on 25 September 1943 to No. 64 Sqn at West Malling. Squadron code SH-L.

The Foxhunter Spitfire Mk.Vb P7493

From No. 9 MU, Cosford, passed to No. 66 Sqn on 24 October 1940 at West Malling. Squadron code LZ-F.

Mau Molo Ruri Hurricane Mk.IIB Z3263

No. 402 Sqn in 1942. This aircraft was gifted by the native chiefs of various tribes in Kenya and later went to No. 253 Sqn and finally to Russia.

Muzaffararh I Spitfire Mk.Vb AD571

Moved from No. 65 Sqn to No. 130 Sqn, West Malling, on 5 August 1943. Squadron code PJ-I.

Nyasaland IX Spitfire Mk.Vb W3900

Pilot Officer L.A. Stewart, No. 412 Sqn RCAF, landed on Somerfield tracking at West Malling. Tail wheel collapsed, repaired on site by No. 86 MU Sundridge (Salvage) Kent.

Palembang Spitfire Mk.Vb P8366

Joined No. 19 Sqn on 31 July 1941 from No. 8 MU, on detachment from RAF Fowlmere.

Shetlander Spitfire Mk.Vb BM264

Joined No. 133 (Eagle) Sqn on 12 April 1942 from RAF Kirton-in-Lindsey, with a detachment at West Malling. Shot down by Fw 190s over Ostend, killing Flight Sergeant W. York. His body was washed ashore and he is buried in Plot 'O', Grave 56, Folkestone Cemetery.

Sialkot Ia Spitfire Mk.IIa P9397

Joined No. 133 (Eagle) Sqn on 2 January 1942 at RAF Kirkton-in-Lindsey, with detachment at West Malling.

Spirit of Taranaki Spitfire Mk.IIa P7975

Joined No. 145 Sqn on 27 February 1941 from Tangmere, transferred to No. 485 (New Zealand) Sqn on 1 June 1941 detached from Leconfield. On 23 June, as part of West Malling wing, was shot down into sea by Bf 109, pilot. Pilot Officer R.J. Bullen RNZAF, lost.

Spithead Billy Spitfire Mk.Vb AR323

With No. 64 Sqn at West Malling from 28 March 1943. It was flown by Pilot Officer Armstrong, last operation being 14 September 1943. Also flown by Pilot Officer E.R. 'Bobby' Burnard.

Zaria Province Spitfire Mk.Vb BM543

Joined No. 234 Sqn on 15 August 1943 at West Malling. Moved to RAF Hutton Grunswick on 15 October 1943

Appendix 4

RAF West Malling – Mosquito air-to-air victories 1943–44

16/17 May 1943

XII	VY-A	85 Sqn	Fw 190A-4/U-8	nr Dover	Squadron Leader W.P. Green, Flight Sergeant Grimstone
XII	VY-G	85 Sqn	Fw 190A-4/U-8	nr Hastings	Flight Lieutenant G.L. Howitt, Flying Officer G. Irving
XII	VY-L	85 Sqn	Fw 190A-4/U-8	nr Dover Straits	Flying Officer B.J. Thwaites, Pilot Officer W.P. Clemo, DFM
					Probably destroyed
XII	VY-D	85 Sqn	Fw 190A-4/U-8	nr Dover Straits	
				off Gravesend	Flying Officer J.D. Shaw, Pilot Officer A.C. Lowton

18/19 May

XII	VY-Z	85 Sqn	Fw 190A-5	Kent	Flying Officer J.P.M. Lintott, Sergeant G.G. Gilling-Lax

Date			Squadron	Aircraft	Location	Crew
21/22 May						
XII	VY-V	85 Sqn		Fw 190A-5	25m NW Hardelot	Squadron Leader E. Crew, DFC, Flying Officer F. French
29/30 May						
XII	VY-S	85 Sqn		Ju 88S-1	Isfield nr Lewes	Flying Officer J.P.M. Lintott, Sergeant G.G. Gilling-Lax
5 June						
XII	unidentified	29 Sqn		Ju 88A-14	off Ostend	unidentified
11 June						
		256 Sqn		Do 217	South of Ford	Flying Officer Burnett
II	unidentified	85 Sqn		Ju 88	Bay of Biscay	Flight Lieutenant J. Singleton, Flying Officer W.G. Haslam
13/14 June						
XVII	VY-R	85 Sqn		Fw 190A-5	Wrotham	Wing Commander J. Cunningham, Flight Lieutenant C.F. Rawnsley
17/18 June						
XII	unidentified	85 Sqn		Fw 190	unidentified	Lieutenant Rad, RNWAF

Date	Squadron	Code	Aircraft	Location	Crew
21/22 June	XII VY-E	85 Sqn	Fw 190	River Medway	Flight Lieutenant W. McGuire, Flying Officer W.D. Jones
9/July	XII VY-Z	85 Sqn	Fw 190	nr Detling	Flying Officer J.P.M. Lintott, Sergeant G.G. Gilling-Lax
13/14 July	XII VY-T	85 Sqn	Me 410A-1	off Felixstowe	Flight Lieutenant E.N. Bunting, Flying Officer F. French
15/16 July	XII VY-G	85 Sqn	Me 410 A-1	off Dunkirk	Flight Lieutenant B.J. Thwaites, Pilot Officer W.P. Clemo, DFM
26/27 July	XII VY-A	85 Sqn	Ju 88	E of Ramsgate	Squadron Leader W.P. Green, Flight Sergeant A.R. Grimstone
22/23 August	XII VY-V	85 Sqn	Me 410A-1	Chelmondiston	Squadron Leader G.E. Howitt, Pilot Officer J.C.O. Medworth

XII	VY-R	85 Sqn	Fw 190	near Dunkirk	Wing Commander J. Cunningham, Flight Lieutenant C.F. Rawnsley
23/24 August					
XII	DZ302 VY-R	85 Sqn	Fw 190	off Dunkirk	Captain J. Rad, RNVR, Captain L. Lovestad, RNVR
24/25 August					
XII	VY-G	85 Sqn	Me 410A-1	unidentified	Squadron Leader G.E. Howitt, DFC, Flight Lieutenant C. Irving, DFC
6/7 September					
II	VF-V	85 Sqn	Fw 190A-5	3m E of Clacton	Wing Commander C.J. Cunningham, Flight Lieutenant C.F. Rawnsley
8/9 September					
XV	DZ302 VF-R	85 Sqn	Fw 190A	Aldeburgh	Flight Lieutenant B.J. Thwaites, Pilot Officer W.P. Clemo
XII	VF-L	85 Sqn	2 Fw 190A-5 1/ SKG10	off N. Foreland	

Date	Unit	Code	Squadron	Aircraft	Location	Crew
15/16 September	XII	VF-T	85 Sqn	Ju 88A-14	Tenterden	Flying Officer E.N. Bunting, Flying Officer F. French
22 September	XI	VY-F	85 Sqn	Me 410	off Orfordness	Flight Lieutenant G. Houghton, Flight Lieutenant Patston
2/3 October	XII		85 Sqn	2 Do 217K	off Humber Estuary	Captain T. Weisteen, RNAF, Flying Officer F. French
7/8 October	XII	'E'	85 Sqn	Me 410A-1	15m off Hastings	Flight Lieutenant W. Maquire, Captain L. Lovestad
7/8 October	XII	VY-D	85 Sqn	Me 410A-1	off Foulness	Flight Lieutenant B.J. Thwaites, DFC, Pilot Officer W.P. Clemo, DFM
8/9 October	XII	VY-Q	85 Sqn	Ju 88S-1	off Foulness	Flying Officer S.V. Holloway, Warrant Officer Stanton

Date	Unit	Sqn	Aircraft	Location	Crew
8/9 October		85 Sqn	Ju 88S-1	10m S Dover	Flying Officer E.N. Bunting, Flying Officer F. French
15/16 October	XII VY-K	85 Sqn	Ju 188E-1	Birchington	Flying Officer H.B. Thomas, Warrant Officer C.B. Hamilton
15/16 October	XII VY-E	85 Sqn	Ju 188E-1	Hemley, Suffolk	Flight Lieutenant W. Maguire, Flying Officer W.D. Jones
	XII VY-E	85 Sqn	Ju 188E-1	South of Clacton	Flight Lieutenant W. Maguire, Flying Officer W.D. Jones
17/18 October	XII VY-V	85 Sqn	Me 410A-1	Hornchurch/Little Warley	Flight Lieutenant E.N. Bunting, Flying Officer F. French
30/31 October	XII YV-G	85 Sqn	Ju 88S-1	30m SE of Rye	Flying Officer R.L.T. Robb, Flying Officer R.C.J. Bray

30/31 October

| XII | VY-J | 85 Sqn | Ju 88S-1 | 20m S of Shoreham | Flying Officer H.B. Thomas, Warrant Officer C.B. Hamilton |

2/3 November

| XII | VY-K | 85 Sqn | Fw 190 | S of Canvey Island | Flying Officer E.R. Hedgecoe, DSO, DSC, Pilot Officer J.R. Whitham, DFM |

5/6 November

| II | HJ917 | 410 Sqn | Me 410 | 10m S of Dungeness | Flying Officer C.F. Green, Pilot Officer E.G. White |

6/7 November

| XII | VY-W | 85 Sqn | Fw 190A | $\frac{2}{3}$m S of Hastings | Squadron Leader Selway, Pilot Officer N.E. Bamford |

8/9 November

| XII | VY-E | 85 Sqn | Me 410A-1 | near Eastbourne | Squadron Leader W.H. Maquire, Flying Officer W.D. Jones |

2/3 January 1944

| II | HK372 | 96 Sqn | Fw 190A | Rye, Sussex | Flying Officer N.S. Head, Flying Officer A.C. Andrews |

Date		Squadron	Aircraft	Location	Crew
2/3 January					
XIII	HK374	85 Sqn	Me 410	Sandwich	Wing Commander J. Cunningham, Flight Lieutenant C.F. Rawnsley
4/5 January					
III		96 Sqn	Ju 188-1	3m S of Hastings	Wing Commander E.D. Crew, Warrant Officer W.R. Croysdill
4/5 January					
XII		85 Sqn	Ju 88	off Dieppe	Flying Officer E.R. Hedgecoe, Pilot Officer J.R. Whitham, DFM
15/16 January					
III		96 Sqn	Fw 190	Dungeness	Squadron Leader A. Parker-Rees, Flying Officer Bennett
21/22 January					
XI	VY-N	85 Sqn	Ju 88	off Rye	Flight Lieutenant Dixon, Warrant Officer Jarvis
21/22 January					
XI	unknown	85 Sqn	He 177A-3	6m SE of Hastings	Flying Officer C.F. Nowell, Flight Sergeant F. Randall

Date	Mark	Serial	Squadron	Type	Location	Crew
21/22 January	III	HK414	96 Sqn	Ju 88	Paddock Wood Station	Sub Lieutenant J.A. Lawley-Wakelin, Sub Lieutenant H. Williams
21/22 January	III	HK425	96 Sqn	Ju 88	Tonbridge	unidentified crew
21/22 January	III	HK372	96 Sqn	2 Ju 88 (Probable)	S of Bexhill	Flight Lieutenant N.S. Head, Flying Officer A.C. Andrews
28/29 January	XIII	HK397	96 Sqn	Ju 88	near Biddenden	Flying Officer S.A. Hibbert, Flying Officer G.D. Moody
3/4 February	XIII	VY-P	85 Sqn	Do 217	20m E the Naze	Flying Officer H.B. Thomas, Warrant Officer C.B. Hamilton.
13/14 February	XIII	HK426	96 Sqn	Ju 188	nr Whitstable	Wing Commander E.D. Crew, Warrant Officer W.R. Croysdill

Date	Mark	Serial	Squadron	Enemy aircraft	Location	Crew
19/20 February	III	HK396	96 Sqn	Me 410	S of Dungeness	Flight Sergeant T. Bryan, Flight Sergeant Frillis
20/21 February	XVII	VY-Y	85 Sqn	Ju 188 (Probable)	Lydd	Squadron Leader B.J. Thwaites, DFC, Pilot Officer W.P. Clemo, DFM
22/23 February	III	HK370	96 Sqn	Me 410	W Uckfield	Squadron Leader G.L. Caldwell, Flying Officer Rawling
22/23 February	XVII	VY-Y	85 Sqn	Me 410	off Dungeness	Flight Lieutenant B. Burbridge, Flight Lieutenant F.S. Skelton
22/23 February	XVII	unidentified 85 Sqn	Me 410	35m S of Dungeness	Flying Officer E.R. Hedgecoe, DFC, Pilot Officer J.R. Whitham, DFM	
23/24 February	III	HK370	96 Sqn	Me 410	at sea	

Date / Aircraft	Squadron	Enemy	Location	Crew
23/24 February				
XVII VY-O	85 Sqn	Ju 88 (Probable)	Beachy Head	Wing Commander J. Cunningham, DSO, DFC, Flight Lieutenant C.F. Rawnsley, DFC, DFM
24/25 February				
III HK370	96 Sqn	Me 410	off Beachy Head	Flight Lieutenant D.L. Ward, Flight Lieutenant E.D. Eyles
24/25 February				
III HK415	96 Sqn	He 177 (Probable)	Sussex	Squadron Leader A. Parker-Rees, Flight Lieutenant Bennett
29 February/1 March				
III HK469	96 Sqn	Fw 190	off Dieppe	Unidentified crew
29 February/1 March				
XVII VY-S	85 Sqn	He 177	English Channel	Unidentified crew
1/2 March				
III HK499	96 Sqn	Me 410	50m SE Beachy Head	Flight Lieutenant W.J. Gough, Flight Lieutenant Matson

14/15 March					
III	HK406	96 Sqn	Ju 188A-4	Hildenborough	Flight Lieutenant N.S. Head, Flying Officer A.C. Andrews
III	HK406	96 Sqn	Ju 188A-4	English Channel	Flight Lieutenant N.S. Head, Flying Officer A.C. Andrews
22/23 March					
XIII	MM451	96 Sqn	Fw 190	SE Pevensey	Flight Lieutenant N.S. Head, Flying Officer A.C. Andrews
23/24 March					
XII	VY-R	85 Sqn	Fw 190	off Hastings	Squadron Leader B.J. Thwaites, Flying Officer W.P. Clemo
24/25 March					
XII	VY-O	85 Sqn	Ju 188	off Hastings	Flying Officer E.R. Hedgecoe, DFC, Flying Officer N.L. Bamford
24/25 March					
XVII	VY-M	85 Sqn	Do 217 + Ju 88	Straits	Flight Lieutenant B. Burbridge, Flight Lieutenant F.L. Skelton

Date	Mark	Serial	Squadron	Aircraft	Location	Crew
27/28 March	III	HK425	96 Sqn	Fw 190A	English Channel	Flight Lieutenant Morgan, Flight Lieutenant Kennedy
13/14 April	XIII	MM497	96 Sqn	Ju 88	nr Le Touquet	Pilot Officer Allen, DFM
13/14 April	XIII	HK497	96 Sqn	Ju 88	off Dungeness	Squadron Leader A. Parker-Rees, Flight Lieutenant Bennett
13/14 April	XIII	HK415	96 Sqn	Me 410	at sea	Squadron Leader A. Parker-Rees, Flight Lieutenant Bennett
18/19 April	XIII	MM499	96 Sqn	Me 410-1	Brighton	Wing Commander E.D. Crew, Warrant Officer W.R. Croysdill
18/19 April	XIII	MM495	96 Sqn	Ju 88A-4	Crashed nr Margate	Wing Commander W.P. Green, Flight Sergeant A.R. Grimstone

18/19 April					
XIII	HK405	96 Sqn	Ju 88A-4	Crashed nr Cranbrook	Pilot Officer Allen, Flight Sergeant Patterson
18/19 April					
XVII	HK349 'R'	85 Sqn	Ju 88	Sandgate	Flight Lieutenant B. Burbridge, Flight Lieutenant F.S. Skelton
25/26 April					
XVII	'B'	85 Sqn	Me 410	S Selsey Bill	Flight Lieutenant B. Burbridge, Flight Lieutenant F.S. Skelton.
5/6 June					
XIII		409 Sqn	Ju 88 (Probable)	S Coast	Flying Officer Pearce, Flying Officer Moore
6/7 June					
XIII	Unidentified	29 Sqn	Ju52/3m and unidentified aircraft	Coulommiers	Flight Lieutenant Allison, Flying Officer Stanton
7/8 June					
III	Unidentified	29 Sqn	Ju 188	S of Paris	Flight Lieutenant Barry, Squadron Leader Porter

Date	Mark	Serial	Squadron	Enemy	Location	Crew
7/8 June	XIII	Unidentified	29 Sqn	Unidentified	Dreux	Flying Officer F.E. Pringle, Pilot Officer W. Eaton
8/9 June	XIII	Unidentified	29 Sqn	Ju 88	Unidentified	Flying Officer Wigglesworth, Sergeant Blomfield
9/10 June	XIII	Unidentified	29 Sqn	Ju 188	Unidentified	Lieutenant Price
9/10 June	XIII	MM640	409 Sqn	Ju 188	40m SE Le Havre	Squadron Leader R.S. Jephson, Flying Officer C.D. Sibbett
10/11 June	XIII	MM453	409 Sqn	Ju 188	Unidentified	Flying Officer Fullerton, Flying Officer Castellan
10/11 June	XIII		409 Sqn	2 × Ju 188		Flying Officer Preece, Flying Officer Beaumont
10/11 June						

XIII	MM547	409 Sqn	Fw 190	Unidentified	Flight Sergeant S.H.J. Elliott, Flight Lieutenant R.A. Miller
10/11 June					
XIII	Unidentified		2 × Ju 188	Unidentified	Flying Sergeant R.E. Lelong, Flying Officer Beamont
10/11 June					
XIII	MM555	409 Sqn	Ju 188	over France	Flying Officer K. Livingstone
10/11 June					
XIII	MM523	409 Sqn	Do 217E	over France	Flying Officer A.W. Sterrenberg
13/14 June					
XIII	MM56G 'F'	409 Sqn	He 177	10m E Le Havre	Wing Commander J.W. Reid, Flight Lieutenant J.W. Peacock

Appendix 5

RAF airmen buried at St Mary's Church, West Malling

Aircraftman 1st Class Corporal L.B. Harris RAF – 18 June 1940
Aircraftman 2nd Corporal R.H. Lucas RAF – 3 March 1942
Aircraftman L.B. Harris RAF – 18 August 1942
Flight Lieutenant J.E. Herrington RAF – 4 October 1947
Flight Lieutenant R.J. Wilkie RAF – 7 June 1949
A.B. Bazen RAF – 5 April 1950
Flight Lieutenant R. Campbell-Peat RAF – 17 November 1951
Flight Lieutenant J.S. Christie, DFC, RAF – 20 March 1951
Flight Sergeant W. McKune RAF – 22 May 1952
Flying Officer P.M. Rolfe RAF – 30 June 1955
Flight Lieutenant K.M.
 RAF – 30 June 1955
Aircraftsman F.C. Goodwin RAF – 24 February 1955
Flying Officer R.A. Hollingworth RAF – 16 April 1956
Flying Officer J.C. Langham RAF – 16 April 1956
Flying Officer F. Webb RAF – 9 January 1956
Flying Officer D.R. Arundell RAF – 9 January 1956
Flying Officer B. Carse RAF – 28 June 1956
Aircraftsman H. Birch RAF – 3 August 1956
Squadron Leader A.E. Hall, DFC, RAF – 4 February 1956
Flying Officer A. Levett RAF – 4 February 1956

Appendix 6

RAF squadrons and units based at RAF West Malling

11 Group Jun 1940–1944, Closed Aug 1964

51 Wing HQ 6–10 Jun 1940

148 Airfield/Wing HQ 1–12 May 1944, 12 May–19 Jun 1944

3 Sqn 14 May–11 Jun 1943

14 Sqn 29 Sep–17 Oct 1947, 13 May–4 Jun 1948

19 Sqn Feb–16 Aug 1941

25 Sqn 5 Sep 1946–19 Apr 1947, 3 May–16 Jun 1947, 25 Jul 1947–5 Jan 1948, 27 Feb–30 Apr 1948, 14 May 1948–30 Sep 1957

26 Sqn 8 Jun–3 Sep 1940, 19–31 May 1942, 26– 31 Jul 1942

29 Sqn 27 Apr 1941–13 May 1943, 1 May–19 Jun 1944, 29 Oct 1945–12 Jan 1946, 27 Jan–11 Feb 1946, 21 Mar–6 Apr 1946, 18 Oct 1946–26 Feb 1947, 31 Mar–3 May 1947, 16 May–16 Jun 1947, 24 Jul 1947–5 Jan 1948, 26 Feb–14 May 1948, 27 May 1948–25 Nov 1950

32 Sqn 5 May–14 Jun 1942, 7 Jul–14 Aug 1942, 20 Aug–10 Sep 1942

41 Sqn 19–28 June 1944

64 Sqn 6–25 Sep 1943

65 Sqn Detached Jun 1941

66 Sqn 30 Oct–7 Nov 1940

80 Sqn 5 Jul–29 Aug 1944

85 Sqn 13 May 1943–1 May 1944, 21 Jul–29 Aug 1944, 16 Apr–16 Jun 1947, 30 Jun 1947–5 Jan 1948, 26 Feb–28 May 1948, 11 Jun 1948–18 Sep 1957, 5 Jun 1959–6 Sep 1960

91 Sqn 23 Apr–21 Jul 1944, 3–10 Jun 1946

124 Sqn 20 Sep 1943–5 Jan 1944, 18 Jan–18 Mar 1944

130 Sqn 5 Aug–18 Sep 1943

133 Sqn Feb–3 May 1942

141 Sqn 11 July–25 Jul 1940

153 Sqn 28 Feb 1955–17 Sep 1957
157 Sqn 21 Jul–29 Aug 1944
234 Sqn 5 Aug–16 Sep 1943
247 Sqn 1 June–12 Jun 1946, 7–16 Sep 1946
255 Sqn 20 Sep 1941–2 Mar 1942
264 Sqn 14 Apr 1941–1 May 1942
274 Sqn 5 Jul–17 Aug 1944
287 Sqn 10 Sep 1945–15 Jun 1946
316 Sqn (Warsaw) 4–11 Jul 1944
322 Sqn (RNAF) 20 Jun–21 Jul 1944
350 Sqn (Belgium) 7–19 Sep 1943
409 Sqn (RCAF) 14 May–19 Jun 1944
410 Sqn (RCAF) 20 Oct–8 Nov 1943
411 Sqn (RCAF) 16 Aug–20 Aug 1942
421 Flt 31 Oct–6 Nov 1940
485 Sqn (RNZAF) 16–22 Aug 1942
486 Sqn (RNZAF) 10–29 Oct 1942
500 Sqn (RAuxAF) 10 May 1946–10 Mar 1957
531 Sqn 8 Sep–2 Oct 1942, 9 Oct 1942–25 Jan 1943
567 Sqn 26 Apr–15 Jun 1946
609 Sqn 19 Aug–20 Aug 1942
610 Sqn (RAuxAF) 16–21 Aug 1942, 19–27 Jun 1944
616 Sqn (RAuxAF) 3–7 Jul 1942, 18 Mar–24 Apr 1944
1452 Flt 7 Jul 1941–8 Sep 1942

RAF and Miscellaneous Units

1 Air Experience Flt 12 Sep 1959–10 Sep 1960
4 Refuelling and Rearming Party 1 Aug 1941–9 Feb 1942
30 Air Disarmament Unit 2 Oct 1944–17 Jan 1945
101 Mobile Air Reporting Unit 2 Feb 1943, became No. 1 MARU
130 Emergency Labour Squadron Unknown
139 Emergency Labour Squadron Unknown
141 Gliding School 30 Jun 1949–1950/51
307 Mobile Signals Unit 4 Nov 1943–5 Apr 1944
309 Supply & Transport Column 10 Oct 1943–28 Feb 1944
504 (AAF) Servicing Echelon 4 Aug–18 Sep 1943
618 Volunteer Gliding School 9 Jan 1965–Mar 1995

731 Defence Squadron 29 Jul 1944–1 Nov 1944

1003 Servicing Wing 19 Jun 1944–30 Jun 1944

1018 Servicing Wing 4 May 1944–21 Jun 1944

1028 Servicing Wing 18 Jan 1945, Redesignated 1023 SW 8 Mar 1945

1030 Servicing Wing Redesignated 1025 SW at West Malling 8 Mar 1945

1528 Beam Approach Training Flt 21 Apr 1942–7 Dec 1942

2707 Squadron, RAF Regiment 5 Oct 1944–21 May 1945

2710 Sqn RAF Regiment 20 Sep 1942–1 Jul 1943, 12 Jul 1943–1 Oct 1943

2735 Squadron RAF Regiment 30 Jul 1944–2 Oct 1944

2768 Sqn RAF Regiment 29 Jun 1942–27 Jun 1945

2769 Sqn RAF Regiment 9 Jan 1945–9 Sep 1945

2797 Sqn RAF Regiment 4 Oct 1944–3 Jan 1945

2852 Sqn RAF Regiment 29 Jul 1944–30 Aug 1944

3002 Servicing Echelon 15 May–11 Jun 1943

3003 Servicing Echelon 5 May–18 Jun 1942, 7 Jul–7 Sep 1942

3011 Servicing Echelon 20 Sep 1943–1944

3012 Servicing Echelon 7–19 Sep 1943

3013 Servicing Echelon 1 March 1943–1 Oct 1944

3038 Servicing Echelon 4 Aug–20 Sep 1943

3041 Servicing Echelon 6–25 Sep 1943

3057 Servicing Echelon 1 Mar 1943–1 Oct 1944

3062 Servicing Echelon 1 Mar 1943–1 Oct 1944

3066 Servicing Echelon 1 Mar 194 –1 Oct 1944

3067 Servicing Echelon 1 Mar 1943–1 Oct 1944

3203 Servicing Commando 'B' Flight 9–19 Feb 1942

3208 Servicing Commando 3–9 May 1943

4085 Anti-Aircraft Flight RAF Regiment 17 Mar 1943–26 Apr 1943

4186 Anti-Aircraft Flight RAF Regiment May 1943–Apr 1944

5011 Airfield Construction Unit 31 Mar 1945–15 Dec 1945

5133/34 Bomb Disposal Unit 5 May 1944–1 Aug 1946

6025 Servicing Echelon 5 Sep 1946–17 May 1948

6029 Servicing Echelon 29 Oct 1945–17 May 1948, Cadre 25 Sep 1946

6041 Servicing Echelon 19–28 Jun 1944

6080 Servicing Echelon 5 Jul–29 Aug 1944

6085 Servicing Echelon 22 Mar–1 May 1944, 17 Apr 1947–17 May 1948

6091 Servicing Echelon 3–10 Jun 1946

6096 Servicing Echelon 22 Mar–20 Jun 1944

6205 Bomb Disposal Flight 5 May 1944–1 Aug 1946

6222 Bomb Disposal Flight 5 May 1944–1 Aug 1946

6316 (Polish) Servicing Echelon 1–10 Jul 1944
6409 (RCAF) Servicing Echelon 14 May–19 Jun 1944
6610 Servicing Echelon 19–27 Jun 1944
6616 Servicing Echelon 22 Mar–24 Apr 1944
Air Sea Rescue Detachment 1 Feb 1949–28 Feb 1950
Central School of Aircraft Recognition 11 Mar 1957–20 Mar 1959
Mobile Operations Room Unit 21 Oct 1942–24 Jan 1944
United States Navy Facilities Flt 1965–1967

Appendix 7

RAF West Malling 1940–60
Station Commanders

Wing Commander R.W.K. Stevens	1 July 1940
Wing Commander T.B. Prickman	28 July 1940
Flying Officer F.A. Lewis	18 August 1940
Flight Lieutenant V. Mercer Smith	25 August 1940
Wing Commander A.M. Wilkinson, DSO	14 March 1941
Wing Commander S.C. Widdows, DFC	14 June 1941
Wing Commander V.J. Wheeler, MC, DFC	25 June 1942
Wing Commander C.M. Wight-Boycott, DSO	30 December 1942
Wing Commander P.W. Townsend, DSO, DFC	25 January 1943
Wing Commander T.N. Hayes, DSO, DFC	18 June 1943
Wing Commander J.A. O'Neil, DFC	1 February 1944
Squadron Leader G.T. Block	24 November 1944
Squadron Leader H. Baxter, MM	9 March 1945
Wing Commander A. Ingle, DFC, AFC	3 October 1945
Wing Commander M.G.F. Pedley DSO, QBE, AFC	1 November 1946
Wing Commander D.S. Wilson-Macdonald, DSO, DFC	26 January 1948
Wing Commander H.S. Darley, DSO	2 February 1948
Group Captain J. Worral, DFC	19 April 1948
Group Captain H.N.G. Ramsbottom Isherwood DFC, AFC	9 July 1949

Group Captain H.S. Darley, DSO	12 June 1950
Group Captain E.W. Whitley, DSO, DFC	18 July 1952
Group Captain P.R. Walker, DSO, DFC	8 September 1952
Group Captain P.H. Hamley, AFC	7 August 1953
Group Captain G.V. Fryer, OBE, AFC	28 November 1955
Group Captain E.G.L. Millington, DFC	1 November 1956
Squadron Leader J. Davis, AFC	2 March 1959
Wing Commander F.N. Brinsden	24 February 1959
Group Captain C. Foxley-Norris, DSO	4 August 1959
Wing Commander F.N. Brinsden	1 July 1960–1 January 1961

Appendix 8

Surviving aircraft known to have flown from or been based at West Malling

Spitfire Mk.XIX PS915	RAF Memorial Flight, Biggin Hill, June 1957. West Malling, 31 August 1957 until 1960. Leuchars, 1966–67, gate guard. Henlow, 1967. *Battle of Britain* film, 1968. Leuchars, 1969–75 gate guard. Coningsby, 1975–80. Brawdy, 1975–84. Moved to Battle of Britain Memorial Flight, June 1984. Restored and flies today with BBMF.
Meteor T.7 VZ638	No. 500 Sqn, 1952–53. No. 25 Squadron, 1953. Gatwick Aviation Museum, 2016, displayed externally.
Meteor F.8 VZ467	No. 500 Sqn, Temora, NSW, Australia, since March 2014.
Meteor NF.14 WS726	No. 25 Sqn, 1954–57. No. 1855 ATC Sqn, Royton, since 1967.
Meteor NF.14 WS739	No. 25 Sqn. On display at Newark Aviation Museum.
Meteor NF.14 WS744	No. 85 Sqn, 1954–56. Malta Aviation Museum, 2006.
Meteor NF.14 WS776	No. 25 Sqn, 1954–58. Bournemouth Aviation Museum, 2005.
Javelin FAW.8 XH992	No. 85 Sqn, 1960. Newark Aviation Museum.
Sopwith Dove G-EBKY	Owner C.H. Lowe-Wylde, on display at Shuttleworth Trust.

Spitfire Mk.Vb BL614	No. 64 Sqn, 1943. MAP Medway. 1995. Displayed RAF Museum, Hendon.
Spitfire MK.XVIe RW393	No. 602 (Glasgow) Sqn. No. 603 (Edinburgh) Sqn. Personal aircraft of the AOC Fighter Command, Air Marshal Sir William Elliot (AOC Fighter Command 1947–54. Turnhouse gate guard, 1976. Eventually delivered to RAF Museum, Hendon, 2015, for permanent display.
Anec II G-EBJO	A.H. Wheeler, West Malling, 1930s. At Shuttleworth Trust, Old Warden.
Chipmunk T.10 WD359 G-BBMN	Served with 11 RFS, CUAS, PFS, AOTS and OUAS training flights until demobbed in 1970s. This aircraft has had one civilian owner and is currently for sale and kept at North Weald airfield, Essex.
Chipmunk T.10 WK633 G-BEXC	Served at Cottesmore, Mildenhall, Cerney, Leuchars, Hull and various training flights. Today can be seen at Redhill, Surrey.
Varsity T.Mk.1 WL169	Issued to Short Brothers Varsity and Chipmunk servicing facility at West Malling in August 1973 and operated from West Malling by Shorts. On display at RAF Museum Cosford.

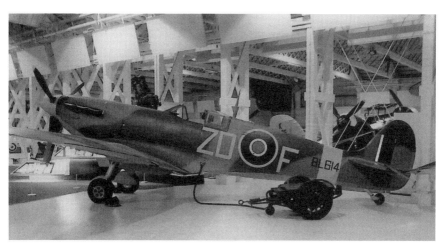

Spitfire Mk.Vb BL614 served with No. 64 Sqn at West Malling, where it was involved in bomber escort and coastal anti-shipping strafing attacks. Today this aircraft is on display at the RAF Museum at Hendon.

Appendix 9

Aircraft delivered to RAF West Malling by the Air Transport Auxiliary (ATA)

Pilot Lettice Curtis during 1942–44

31-5-42	Beaufighter Mk.IF R2195	St Athan–West Malling, FIU*.
28-9-43	Typhoon Mk.IB JP800	Aston Down–West Malling, No. 181 Sqn.
11-5-44	Mosquito Mk.XIII MM548	Hullavington–West Malling, No. 29 Sqn.
17-7-44	Spitfire Mk.XIV RM680	Colerne–West Malling, No. 41 Sqn.
27-8-44	Tempest MK.V EJ692	Aston Down–West Malling, No. 80 Sqn.

*FIU Fighter Interception Unit

Lettice Curtis learnt to fly at Yapton, later RAF Ford, Sussex, in 1938. She joined the Air Transport Auxiliary (ATA) in the summer of 1940, remaining until it was disbanded in November 1945. Lettice flew many types of aircraft and was the first of a dozen or so women to qualify to fly heavy bombers. Post-war, she was a flight test observer with A&AEE at Boscombe Down, and later worked for Fairey Aviation. She moved to the Ministry of Aviation in the 1960s, and became flight operations inspectorate for the Civil Aviation Authority. She retired in 1979 from Sperry's at Bracknell when British Aerospace took over the company.

Bibliography

Birtles, Philip, *Mosquito – A Pictorial history of the DH98*, Janes Publishing, 1998.

Bishop, Edward, *Mosquito – The Wooden Wonder*, Airlife Publishing Ltd, 2002.

Boot, Henry & Ray Sturtivant, *Gifts of War*, Air-Britain (Historians) Ltd, 2005.

Bowman, Martin, *Mosquito Panik!*, Pen & Sword, 2004.

Braham, J.R.D. Bob, Wing Commander, DFC, DSO, AFC, CD, *Scramble*, William Kimber, 1961.

Bratley, Anthony, Squadron, Leader, DFC, *Smoke Trails in the Sky,* William Kimber, 1984.

Brew, Steve, *Blood Sweat and Courage*, 41 Squadron RAF 1939–1942, Fonthill Media, 2014.

Brew, Steve, *Blood Sweat and Valour*, 41 Squadron RAF 1942–1944, Fonthill Media, 2012.

Brooks, Robin J., *From Moths to Merlins*, West Malling Airfield, Meresborough Books, 1987.

Brooks, Robin J., *Kent's Own 500 Squadron (County of Kent) RAuxAF,* Meresborough, 1982.

Brown, Hamish, *Wine, Women and Song – A Spitfire Pilot's Story,* Fonthill Media, 2012.

Caygill, Peter, *In All Things First*: *No. 1 Squadron at War 1939-1945*, Pen & Sword Aviation, 2009.

Chipperfield, Jimmy, *My Wild Life*, Putnam & Sons, 1976.

Cole, Christopher & E.F. Cheesman, *The Air Defence of Great Britain 1914–1918*, Putnam, 1984.

Corbin, Jimmy, *Last of the Ten Fighter Boys,* Sutton Publishing, 2007.

Cossey, Bob, *Tigers – The Story of No. 74 Squadron* RAF, Arms & Armour Press 1992.

Docherty, Tom, *Swift to Battle – No. 72 Fighter Squadron RAF in action*, Pen & Sword, 2009.

Franks, Norman, *Sky Tiger – The Story of Sailor Malan*, William Kimber, 1980.

Freeman, Roger A., *The Mighty Eighth War Diary,* Arms and Armour, 1990.

Gull, Brian & Bruce Lander, *Diver! Diver! Diver!*, Grub Street, 2008.

Franks, Norman, *The Greatest Air Battle – Dieppe 19 August 1942*, Grub Street, 1992.

Franks, Norman, *Sky Tiger – The story of Sailor Malan*, William Kimber, 1980.

Halpenny, Bruce, Pennymore, *Action Stations 8: Military Airfields of Greater London,* Patrick Stephens Ltd, 1984.

Hall, Peter, *No. 91 'Nigeria' Squadron*, Osprey Aviation, 2001.

Hall, Peter, *By Day and By Night*, RAF West Malling 1940–1960, Kent Libraries, 1987.

Hunt, Leslie, *Twenty One Squadrons*, The History of the RAuxAF 1925–1957, Garnstone Press, 1972.

Long, Jack, T.C, *Three's Company,* Illustrated History of No. 3 Fighter Squadron, Pen & Sword, 2005.

Mason, Francis K., *Hawks Rising, The Story of 25 Squadron RAF*, Air Britain, 2001.

Morris, Richard, *Guy Gibson,* Viking, 1994.

Napier, Michael, *Blue Diamonds-The Exploits of 14 Squadron RAF 1945–2015*, Pen & Sword, 2015.

Watkins, David, *The History of RAF Aerobatic Teams from 1920*, Pen & Sword, 2010.

Winston, G., *The Battle of Britain Then and Now* (Edition 4) After the Battle, 1987.

Rawlings, John, *Fighter Squadrons of the RAF and Their Aircraft,* Macdonald, 1969.

Rawnsley, C.F. & Wright, R, *Night Fighter,* Collins, *1957.*

Spurdle, Bob, *The Blue Arena*, William Kimber, 1986.

Sturtivant, Ray, Hamlin, John & Halley, James, *RAF Flying Training & Support Units,* Air-Britain (Historians) Ltd, 1997.

Index

INDEX

411

Luftwaffe Personnel

General Index

INDEX

Luftwaffe Units

INDEX

436

INDEX

INDEX